The Pimping of Prostitution

"The first step in recognizing a big injustice is often an end to blaming the victim - say, to stop assuming that most poor people are lazy, or that battered women could just leave, or that our prisons are so racially imbalanced because the imbalance is deserved. To find out the truth behind all those "Pretty Woman" myths about the global sex trade read this well documented book by Julie Bindel."
—Gloria Steinem, *feminist, journalist and social and political activist*

"This book is comprehensive, authoritative, personally revealing, and a clear headed rage against a tide of modern double think. It will help feminism untangle itself from all the knots of faux progressiveness about prostitution, which is repackaging sexual abuse as empowerment. Bindel is a fearless, uncompromising voice who deserves to be universally heard."
—Janice Turner, *Times Newspaper columnist*

"A profoundly impressive piece of reporting and polemic into a commercial industry. You may love Bindel's work, you may profoundly disagree with it. But it will never leave you indifferent, and it will always make you question, which is why there should be more of it."
—Rose George, *Author and journalist*

"No one in Britain knows more than Julie Bindel about prostitution - the politics, the debates, the myths, the scale, and the damage to individuals and to the culture that sustains it. Every word in this long-awaited book is worth reading. It combines scholarship, activism, personal narratives and political analysis. It is a mighty challenge to the pessimism of 'the oldest profession' and above all it offers hope of a society free of sexism and sexual exploitation."
—Bea Campbell, *writer, activist, and author of The End of Equality*

"An excoriating response to those who say prostitution is inevitable, that it is work like any other, and that prostituted women need labour rights and state regulation, not abolition. Bindel exposes gender inequality at its most brutal and violent in this intelligent, well-researched and well-written critique. Agree or disagree, I've no doubt it will become a core text for the study of patriarchy and its consequences."
—Karon Monaghan QC, *leading human rights and equality law practitioner*

Julie Bindel

The Pimping of Prostitution

Abolishing the Sex Work Myth

Julie Bindel
London, UK

ISBN 978-1-137-55889-3   ISBN 978-1-137-55890-9   (eBook)
DOI 10.1057/978-1-137-55890-9

The print edition is not for sale in Australia and New Zealand. Customers from Australia and New Zealand please order the print book from: Spinifex Press.
ISBN of the Australian and New Zealand edition: 9781925581232

Library of Congress Control Number: 2017939330

Cover illustration: Sam Johnson

Printed on acid-free paper

This Palgrave Macmillan imprint is published by Springer Nature
The registered company is Macmillan Publishers Ltd.
The registered company address is: The Campus, 4 Crinan Street, London, N1 9XW, United Kingdom

This book is dedicated to the late Denise Marshall, as a small gesture of gratitude for everything she did to end men's violence towards women and girls throughout her too-short life. Denise was the finest feminist and friend who saved lives and changed hearts and minds. I am sure that her legacy will be to inspire new generations of feminists to be the best they can.

Preface

I have been an active feminist campaigner against male violence towards women since 1979. For the past two decades of that time, I have focused much of my energy on fighting for the abolition of the global sex trade, alongside other feminists, many of them survivors of the sex trade themselves.

For me, prostitution is a human rights violation against women and girls. Not everyone shares this understanding. We are now at a crossroads, with a number of countries around the world under pressure to either remove all laws pertaining to the sex trade (including those governing pimping and brothel owning), or to criminalise the purchase of sex (known as the Nordic model). However, the polarised debate on the sex trade, being played out within academia, media, feminist circles and human rights organisations has reached a critical point.

No other human rights violation towards women and girls is so grossly misunderstood. While domestic violence has often been, and sometimes still is, assumed to be the fault of the victim ('She was nagging him', 'She failed to understand his moods'), there has been a significant improvement in the way that those experiencing it are supported and the perpetrators called to task thanks to feminist campaigning and interventions.

Rapists are often seen as men who 'couldn't help themselves', or who were coerced into committing such crimes by the behaviour and dress sense of the victims. But increasingly, again as a result of feminism, rape is viewed as an expression of misogyny rather than one of uncontrollable sexual desire.

Not so prostitution. In recent years, despite the increasing numbers of women with direct experience of being prostituted coming out as 'survivors' of the sex trade, the dominant discourse is one of prostitution being about 'choice' and 'agency' for the women involved. The human rights abuse involved in the sex trade, according to the liberals, libertarians and many of those who profit from selling sex, is when men are deterred from purchasing sex, and not when they rent the orifices of a woman for sexual release. The women selling sex, according to this logic, are the victims of pearl-clutching moralists who wish to take away their right to earn a living.

Indeed, supporting women to exit prostitution has been described as 'an affront to human dignity' in one academic paper,[1] authored by four academics, three of whom have been campaigning for total decriminalisation of the sex trade for a number of years. The war that rages between feminists such as myself who seek to abolish the sex trade, and those who see prostitution as a valid choice, is fuelled by the widely held belief that feminist abolitionists wish to 'rescue' 'fallen women' and 'demonise' the men who pay for sex.

The redoubtable feminist writer Andrea Dworkin once described herself as a 'radical feminist: not the fun kind'. I use this phrase to distinguish myself from those neoliberal 'choice' feminists who have absorbed the argument about 'sex work' being empowering. These fun feminists ensure that they never upset men, and appear to be happier tearing down tried and tested theories of patriarchy and male power being the driver for the sex trade than they are asking how prostitution can be sexual liberation for the prostituted. I and other abolitionists are accused by

---

[1]Cusic, L., Brooks-Gordon, B., Campbell, R., Edgar, F. (2011.) *'Exiting' drug use and sex work: Career paths, interventions and government strategy targets.* Retrieved 15 June 2017, from http://www.tandfonline.com/doi/abs/10.3109/09687631003776901?src=recsys&journalCode=idep20.

the fun feminists of being 'whorephobic', since they claim we hate the women in the sex trade instead of the pimps, buyers and brothel keepers.

I became an active feminist partly in response to the police investigation and media coverage of a serial killer who operated in the North of England during the 1970s. Peter Sutcliffe, named 'the Yorkshire Ripper' by the tabloid press, turned out to be an ordinary, married man living in a suburb of Bradford. The Sutcliffe case brought attitudes about women in general, and prostituted women in particular, out into the open, which in turn led me to join forces with some of the most passionate and committed anti male violence activists in the country.

The public was led to believe, thanks to the police leading the case and the media reporting of the murders, that Sutcliffe hated prostitutes, when in fact only a minority of his victims were involved in the sex trade. The mythology that built up around the killer meant that police excluded a number of cases of women found murdered in England because they did not fit the profile. It also served to perpetuate the notion that women in prostitution somehow deserved their fate, and that rape and murder were merely occupational hazards.

During the 1970s and into 1980, Sutcliffe killed at least 13 women and left seven others for dead. The body of his first murder victim— 28-year-old Wilma McCann—was discovered in 1975 and, from the beginning, the West Yorkshire Police were guilty of dragging their feet and bungling the investigation. Complacent police officers overlooked vital clues, and inadequate technology was used to collate the thousands of interviews and intelligence reports they gathered. Amid all this, Sutcliffe just kept killing—with hammers, screwdrivers and knives— and police were no further forward by the time the body of his fifth murder victim, Jayne MacDonald, was discovered in June 1977.

MacDonald's killing was described by police and press as a 'tragic mistake'. The previous victims had all been labelled as prostitutes and therefore, in the eyes of many, complicit in their own demise. But MacDonald was 16 and described by police as 'respectable and innocent'. Victims were duly divided into deserving and undeserving women.

Officers made a plea to the women of West Yorkshire to look out for strange behaviour in their sons and husbands. But they failed to listen to one of Sutcliffe's surviving victims: a 14-year-old girl who had had a good look at the man who chatted to her about the weather before striking her about the head several times with a hammer. When the girl reported the attack, she saw the photo-fits compiled by other survivors and told police it was the same man. They dismissed her because she was not in prostitution, and it was assumed the Ripper was only interested in prostituted women. On 30 June 1977, an open letter from the *Yorkshire Evening Post* to Sutcliffe said: 'Your motive, it's believed, is a dreadful hate for prostitutes—a hate that drives you to slash and bludgeon your victims'.

When MacDonald was murdered, I was 15 and already thinking about feminism. I had been outed at school as a lesbian, and the misogyny I experienced from boys taught me that girls were judged as either slags or lezzers, and that boys were the ones doing the naming and shaming. Sexism within popular culture was neither subtle nor occasional in the 1970s, and I learned that sexual violence was endemic in reality and widely viewed as entertainment.

In 1979 I moved from my home in Darlington, in the North East of England, to Leeds where I met a group of radical feminists who were campaigning against male violence towards women and girls. At that time, the main focus of the group was to challenge the appalling attitude of police and journalists towards the victims and potential victims—and all women were potential victims—of this serial killer.

One night in November 1980, I was followed while on my way home from a lock-in at the pub near the YWCA hostel where I was living. The man who followed me was of medium height with a dark, full beard, wiry hair and black, piercing eyes. I was 18 and new to Leeds. I ran into another pub to shake him off. Friends persuaded me to report it to the police and I completed a Photofit, but it was obvious they were not taking me seriously. The next day the body of the final victim, Jacqueline Hill, was found less than half a mile from where I was followed. When Sutcliffe was arrested and his photograph published, my Photofit was almost exactly like him.

Sutcliffe's victims were named as deserving victims, sluts, slags and whores. I heard it from men on buses and on the streets. In the open letter of 1977, the murderer was asked how he felt knowing that he had killed an innocent, respectable victim rather than a prostitute. Surely he felt remorse about mistakenly killing Jayne McDonald?

During Sutcliffe's reign, I remember the jokes ordinary men in the North of England used to make about this serial killer before he was caught. 'There's only one Yorkshire Ripper', football fans would chant. 'Ripper 12, police nil', was one particular jibe during Leeds United football matches where the police were penalising unruly fans. 'Give us a kiss, love, I'm not the Ripper' was a regular crack heard in nightclubs around the country. In the 1980s, a group of anarchists named themselves The Peter Sutcliffe Fan Club because they saw him as the ultimate rebel.

In 1990 I was one of the founders of the organisation Justice for Women, a feminist campaign group that mainly challenged the convictions of women who had killed an abusive male partner. In 1992 I received a letter from a woman called Emma Humphreys. Emma had killed her violent pimp, Trevor Armitage, when she was 16 years old and had been in prison since 1985, having been convicted of his murder. In her letter, Emma described the violence and brutality she had endured at the hands of punters and explained that the night she killed Armitage he had threatened to rape her.

As a child, Emma had witnessed her mother being beaten by her stepfather, who also sexually abused Emma. When she was 12, Emma ran away. She slept rough and was abused into prostitution on the streets. When she met Armitage, a sex buyer on the streets of Nottingham, Emma was drinking heavily and self-harming. One night, when Armitage had threatened to rape Emma yet again, she stabbed him. Too traumatised to take to the witness box and represented by lawyers with no understanding of the effects of sexual violence, Emma was convicted and sent to prison, which was effectively a life sentence for under-18s.

Emma wrote to me seven years into her sentence, and for three years I, and many others, campaigned for her release. On 7 July 1995, Emma had her conviction overturned and was released from the Court of Appeal. The following day, most national newspapers carried front-page stories on Emma's campaign, showing a smiling young woman leaving the court surrounded by hundreds of cheering supporters.

Prior to getting to know Emma and the details of her nightmare in prostitution, I had heard of and been involved in debates and discussion about the sex trade, but Emma's story moved me to the point that I began to prioritise campaigning against the sex trade within my feminist activism, writing and research.

In 1996 I was one of the organisers of an international conference in Brighton, UK, on violence and abuse of women, the brainchild of feminist academics and well-known campaigners against male violence Professors Jalna Hanmer and Catherine Itzin. At the conference I met speakers from all over the world who were pioneers in the fight against the international sex trade. Some of these women were survivors of the sex trade. Each had the same goal: to abolish the system of prostitution. However, Austrian pro-prostitution lobbyists at the event tried to disrupt one of the sessions, claiming we were ignoring the voices of 'sex workers'.

At the conference were feminist anti-sex-trade campaigners such as Andrea Dworkin, Janice Raymond and Norma Hotaling, founder of Standing against Global Exploitation (SAGE): a San Francisco-based centre offering services to help women out of prostitution. Hotaling had also founded the world's first John School in 1995, a re-education programme for men attempting to buy sex on the street.

Fiona Broadfoot, a survivor of prostitution whom I had met during the organising of the Brighton conference, chaired a workshop on the violence of prostitution. With her was Irene Ivison, author of *Fiona's Story*, a book Ivison had written about her daughter Fiona, who was murdered in 1993 at the age of 17 by a punter, having been exploited into prostitution by her older 'boyfriend'. Ivison had not known that Fiona had been prostituted for three weeks before her death, although she had spent the previous three years battling with police and social services to try to stop the abusive relationship in which her daughter had been involved since the age of 14.

The following year, in December 1997, I co-organised a conference entitled 'Prostitution: Violence against Women and Children'. A small group of pimps brought along prostituted women and tried to disrupt proceedings. They were thrown out. Emma Humpreys had been released from prison two years earlier and spoke at the conference about her experiences. Also speaking was Angel, a volunteer at SAGE who co-ran the San Francisco John School with Hotaling.

As the conference began, two men approached the registration desk and began peeling off money from large wads of £50 notes. In a deliberate and cynical pantomime, the men were dressed in stereotypical US 'pimp' attire: long fur coats and fedora hats. With them were two women, dressed in stereotypical 'prostitution' clothing.

Humphreys movingly described her own experiences of prostitution and called for sex buyers to be criminalised. She died a few months later in the summer of 1998, three years after her victorious release from prison. A few weeks before she died, Humphreys was raped by a man who dragged her into her flat as she was fumbling for her keys. For her, it was the last straw. Deciding to report it to the police, Humphreys spent the next few weeks taking too much medication and drinking in an attempt to calm her nerves about making a statement. One morning, having been unable to contact her by phone, I let myself into her flat and found her dead in bed. The inquest into her death ruled that she had died by 'misadventure', but I knew it was the pain of living with the legacy of prostitution that had killed her.

At the time that Humphreys died I was in the final stages, alongside Jalna Hanmer, Fiona Broadfoot, Irene Ivison and others, of setting up the first UK-based John School in West Yorkshire. The conference and the John School signified the beginning of the abolitionist movement in the UK and I was at its forefront. I linked up with a small number of survivors of the sex trade and we set out to challenge the bigger, louder pro-prostitution lobby. However, by now the 'sex workers' rights' movement had entered academia.

In 1998 a conference was held at East London University entitled 'Sex Work Reassessed: A National Conference', including a workshop called 'Cause for Concern'. At the workshop were various speakers including Jo Doezema, a 'sex workers' rights' activist and academic, and a nameless man who spoke as a sex buyer. They spoke against any intervention with 'clients', and argued that the John School would cause harm to women in the sex trade because educating men about the realities of prostitution would further stigmatise the women. Then I announced who I was and pointed out that the police had agreed to the demands of the John School founders to stop arresting the women, at least for the duration of the pilot. Doezema said she did not believe me.

Taking its name from the workshop and made up of more than 20 agencies across England that provide support for women in prostitution, Cause for Concern was founded in order to convince policymakers and criminal justice agencies to oppose the kerb crawler scheme. Around 500 women linked to the agencies signed a petition against it. This all happened a month prior to the first John School being held but, nevertheless, our opponents seemed to know that we were holding sex buyers accountable.

The first meeting of Cause for Concern, held in Leeds, was chaired by the then director of the Bradford Working Women's Project (BWWP), at which Fiona Broadfoot had volunteered before leaving to set up her own support organisation: a telephone helpline called Street Exit that she ran from her home.

BWWP was notorious for being very pro-legalisation. I had invited the director to speak on a panel at the 1997 conference on prostitution, and during her presentation she made it clear that any police intervention would not be welcomed by her organisation. She specifically mentioned the legalised regime in the Netherlands as a good practice model.

Ivison, Broadfoot and I decided to ask if we could come along to the meeting of Cause for Concern to answer questions on the scheme, and hopefully put the members' minds at rest. Julia, who described herself as a street sex worker, used a large flip chart to list her weekly expenses and expenditure, arguing that she needed a job that would pay at least £600 a week to be able to give up selling sex. At that time, my salary as Assistant Director of a research unit at Leeds Metropolitan University paid less than half of the amount Julia said she needed.

The three of us had clearly failed to make an impression on the meeting and we left feeling dejected. Afterwards we heard that Broadfoot had been dismissed as 'not right in the head' because of a family tragedy that had prompted her to escape the sex trade. It was common knowledge in West Yorkshire that Fiona's cousin Maureen had been murdered by a sex buyer, George Naylor. Naylor had previously been jailed for 11 years in 1984 for killing Deborah Kershaw, also a prostituted woman, two months after the BBC's *Rough Justice* programme helped free him early from a 15-year sentence for raping a 60-year-old in her home in 1995.

Following the 12-month pilot of the John School, I embarked on a two-year project funded by the UK Government's Department for International Development to develop and deliver training for non-governmental organisations (NGOs), social workers and law enforcers in several Balkan countries on anti-trafficking initiatives.

It was the year 2000 and the UK had only recently woken up to the fact that women and girls were being transported from poor and conflict-ridden countries into brothels in Western Europe. I had been attending the annual Police Vice Conference of England and Wales since 1998, as one of the few civilians among at least 200 police officers specialising in crimes relating to the sex trade. Head of the Metropolitan Police Clubs and Vice Unit, Inspector Paul Holmes, would give a detailed presentation on the various surveillance jobs that had led to a number of dangerous traffickers being arrested.

I had also recently been invited to speak at an anti-trafficking conference in Albania, at the invitation of Vera Lesko, founder of Vlora Women's Hearth, an innovative project set up by Lesko in 1997. Lesko set up the Hearth because she became aware that the main economy in Vlora was from trafficking women and girls out of Albania. As a result of her work, Lesko had been physically attacked in public on several occasions and, following threats to her family, felt it necessary to send her daughter to live with relatives in Italy.

After the seminar, Lesko told me that she was sick of projects setting up safe houses for young women who had been rescued from traffickers 'and only teaching them to do macramé and what to do with half a kilo of minced beef. Those girls need a gun and a driving licence', she told me with a glint in her eye.

My project in the Balkans was my first introduction to the pro-prostitution politics of international human rights organisations based in unstable countries and regions. I had understood but disagreed with the arguments put forward by the 'sex workers' rights' lobby in the UK (for example, the English Collective of Prostitutes and Scot-Pep[2]), and at the

---

[2]Scot-pep.org.uk. *Promoting safety and rights, fighting for social justice and inclusion.* Retrieved 15 June 2017, from http://www.scot-pep.org.uk/.

Brighton conference had heard a number of presentations from international speakers on the false distinction between forced and chosen 'sex work' from organisations funded to combat human trafficking.

During the course of the project I spent time in Albania, Bosnia and Herzegovina, Croatia, Kosovo, Macedonia and Montenegro. My scoping trip to Sarajevo, Bosnia, included a trip to the offices of the UN Office of the High Commissioner for Human Rights, where I met the head, Madeleine Rees.

Rees is the human rights lawyer who campaigned alongside Kathryn Bolkovac, the whistleblower who exposed DynCorp, the private contractor providing US personnel for the UN mission in Bosnia, who were not only sexually exploiting trafficked women but were also on the traffickers' pay-roll. Rees told me, during a tense meeting in her baking-hot office, that our training was not needed in the Balkans, as there were local NGOs that knew the terrain better than internationals. However, when I pushed Rees, it became clear that she and her colleagues did not like the fact that the training included sessions on the harms of prostitution, and how to curb the demand. Although our training sessions did go ahead, the local anti-trafficking human rights organisations circulated petitions calling for our training to be boycotted, stating that the trainers were 'conflating prostitution, which is a choice, with trafficking, which is clearly a human rights violation'.

During the two years I spent travelling in the Balkans and encountering similar attitudes to Rees's, I decided to stop doing research on trafficking into the sex trade and focus on local and national sex trade and the women caught up in local prostitution. Trafficking is merely a process in which some women and children are prostituted. Prostitution itself is the problem.

Having decided to leave academia to pursue journalism, in 2003 I contacted the then features editor of *Guardian Weekend Magazine*, Katherine Viner, whom I knew from the occasions she had asked me to write the odd opinion piece for the paper. I told her I had read some fascinating and disturbing research by two British academics, Julia O'Connell Davidson and Jacqueline Sanchez Taylor, on female sex tourism in the Caribbean. I told Viner that the only coverage I had seen on this topic to date was either making monsters or idiots of the women, or dismissing it as a bit of a laugh.

I was delighted when Viner gave me a commission to travel to Jamaica and investigate female sex tourism from a feminist perspective, and I knew that with the 4500 word limit I could do it justice. However, I was met with a wall of resistance from some feminists prior to my trip, who told me they were worried that by drawing attention to the fact that 'women do it, too' and also pay for sex, it would provide a get-out clause for male sex buyers. This attitude shocked me. My intention was to investigate the exploitation of young, impoverished black males by white, relatively wealthy Western women. I assumed that if the women were paying for sex either directly or indirectly, there would be a pimp industry to support it. I was right.

In Jamaica, I found that wherever there were female sex tourists, there would be third-party exploiters ready to sell the 'beach boys' and broker the deals. I also found that while the women justified their treatment of the young men by using racialised and class-privileged mythology, female sex tourists are, in most respects, unlike the men who travel to poor countries to buy women and children, in that they rarely, if ever, inflict direct violence on the men. The men are not frightened of the female sex tourists, and there is far less stigmatisation faced by men who sell sex in this way compared to women in prostitution. My article, published in July 2003 as a cover story, made such an impact that it inspired the playwright Tanika Gupta's *Sugar Mummies* that was staged at the Royal Court Theatre in 2006.

One year later, as I was packing up my desk in the university, ready to enter the unknown and rather scary world of full-time freelance journalism, I had a visit from Denise Marshall, CEO of Eaves for Women, a feminist charity that provided services for women who had experienced male violence. Two years earlier, Marshall had set up the Poppy Project, the first service in the UK to support women trafficked into the UK sex trade. Poppy was an acronym for 'Pissing off Pimps and Punters, Yay!', but Marshall told the Home Office, which funded the service, that it was named after one of the first victims of trafficking referred to Eaves.

Marshall told me she needed me to come to Eaves on a part-time consultancy basis for six months to build up some research capacity within Eaves, and to write a response to 'Paying the Price', a government consultation document on how best to deal with prostitution in the UK. I stayed at Eaves rather longer than six months. When the charity went into administration in 2015, weeks after Marshall died of stomach cancer aged only 53, I had just submitted my final piece of research under its name.

Marshall was an innovator and a fierce abolitionist. Together we built up a successful research unit within Eaves and I led on a number of projects, all of which caused consternation among the pro-sex work service providers and academics.

In 2008 Eaves published 'Big Brothel: A Survey of the Off-Street Sex Trade in London'. It was the largest study on the indoor sex trade in the UK to date. We gathered information from 921 brothels in the capital, and to do so my co-author Helen Atkins and I recruited male volunteers to help with the research. They telephoned brothels posing as potential sex buyers, with a list of questions including 'What nationalities are on offer tonight?', 'Do the girls do anal?', 'How about oral without a condom?', and 'What age are they?' The idea was to find out as much as possible about how the brothel owners and managers marketed the women and what was being sold. Had we gone in wearing suits and carrying clipboards to ask research questions, it is likely we would have been told where to go.

The pro-prostitution academics in the UK and beyond went berserk on seeing the national publicity on our findings, and quickly put together a letter, signed by 27 academics, slating its methodology (unethical), aims and objectives (ideological) and conclusions (*Carry On Criminology*, according to Dr Belinda Brooks-Gordon).

The following year I was part of an international research team interviewing men who pay for sex, led by the psychologist and feminist academic Dr Melissa Farley. At that time, I was in the middle of frantically fending off a potential libel case. I had received a letter from notorious prostitution apologist Dr John Davies, then of Sussex University/University of the Witwatersrand who, through his lawyers, threatened me with litigation unless I paid £5000 to a 'women's charity of his choice'. I now suspect that the charity was Sompan Foundation through which he defrauded the British government of £5 million (some of which was used to pay prostitution apologists): a crime for which he was recently imprisoned for 12 years.

In 2009 I began a study on women exiting prostitution. During my time interviewing the men who create the demand and the women on the supply side, I realised just how persuasive the misinformation and mythology surrounding the sex trade is. Talking to the sex buyers, it became apparent that many of them delude themselves that the women they buy actually enjoy the sex of the transaction, and believe that most prostituted women actively and happily choose to earn money through the sex trade.

Since 2009 I have continued to investigate and write about the sex trade. This work continues to be my main priority as a feminist campaigner.

Over the years I have been accused of being a Christian moralist, a prude and a man-hating monster. I have also met and worked with the finest abolitionists and human rights campaigners in existence. One thing I can say for sure, from everything I have learned about the global sex trade, is that it is built on the exploitation of women by men, and that it could not exist without the institutionalised oppressions of gender, race and class. I wish to see an end to prostitution because it is both a cause and a consequence of women's subjugation at the hands of men and I am, after all, a feminist. It is surely right and proper that I do my bit to dismantle this monstrosity?

As Dworkin said: 'I have spent 20 years writing these books. Had I wanted to say men are beasts and scream, that takes 30 seconds'. I hope this book gives a fair account of the struggle by those harmed by the sex trade, who we will see make up the majority of those involved, and that the popular tropes about 'choice' and 'freedom' within the sex trade are challenged by the testimony of its survivors.

London, UK   Julie Bindel

Acknowledgements

Having found that she had some spare time on her hands, Lee Nurse asked me if I needed any help with my work. Over the two years it took me to research this book, Lee transcribed every interview, helped me organise my data, and was always there to assist in any way necessary. Because of Lee, I was able to do a huge amount of travel and research I otherwise would not have been able to contemplate.

To the Indigenous, African-American, and other women of colour who patiently explained to me how colonialism and racism intertwine with misogyny, and helped me better understand those particular dynamics of the sex trade.

Heartfelt thanks to the survivors who entrusted me with their stories, and for their courage and determination in exposing the truth about the sex trade.

To Rachel Moran for writing *Paid For*, and for bringing together survivor abolitionists from all over the world to fight to end the sex trade. Throughout this project, Rachel has been a constant source of inspiration.

Fiona Broadfoot is the founder of the modern-day survivor abolitionist movement in the UK. Meeting Fiona in 1996 was a pivotal moment for me, and for the other feminists whose lives she has touched.

Sara Maguire, for her positive attitude, and her air miles.

Patricia Holmes for making me laugh about things we probably should not laugh about. Ashley McGuire, a great friend who told me to 'never give up' and to ignore the sticks and stones coming my way. Sandra McNeill, one of the most committed and determined feminists I know, for taking me under her wing and introducing me to proper feminism when I arrived in Leeds aged 18.

Jinny Keatinge, Janice Raymond, Jalna Hanmer and Melissa Farley for offering editorial guidance. Sarah Ditum and Jane Duffus for wading through my typos and reorganising my more chaotic pages. Brigette Lechner for summarising a deeply disturbing document.

Roger Matthews, Helen Easton, Anna Zobnina and Maddy Coy for daring to be abolitionists in the hostile environment of academia.

Lynda Dearlove for providing good coffee and a place of refuge.

Thank you Andrew Minney from Australia an honourable copper and a good friend of feminism.

My gratitude to Michael Shively for guiding me through the complex scientific data on AIDS/HIV, and explaining ideological bias in the field.

Thank you so much to those who contributed to my byline.com crowdfunding campaign. I used this money to book flights to and accommodation in the places I needed to visit, and to pay local fixers to help me navigate my way around some tricky situations.

Angie Conroy in Cambodia, who organised my trip to Phnom Penh and provided invaluable support.

Lee Lakeman and her colleagues at the inspirational Vancouver Rape Relief, who made it possible for me to spend time in the city, and organised a set of brilliant interviews and events. I am beyond privileged to be part of a global feminist movement, which sustains me.

My agent Becky Thomas, who always has my back.

The Coalition against Trafficking in Women (CATW) gave invaluable support throughout this project, as has SPACE International.

Twiss Butler's contribution to the movement is invaluable, and her guidance and wisdom much appreciated.

I am grateful to those from the 'other side' of the debate who agreed to be interviewed by me, and trusted me to represent their views and words fairly.

To Harriet Wistrich, always.

The late Ernest Wistrich gave me his love and support throughout the 28 years we were in each other's lives. He was a good man.

To my dear, survivor abolitionist friends who died in combat—in particular Emma Humphreys, Andrea Dworkin and Norma Hotaling. Lest we forget that there are many who do not survive.

Contents

Introduction

During a powerful speech on the future of feminism in 1995, the writer Andrea Dworkin asked the audience to:

> remember the prostituted, the homeless, the battered, the raped, the tortured, the murdered, the raped-then-murdered, the murdered-then-raped; ... I want you to think about those who have been hurt for the fun, the entertainment, the so-called speech of others; those who have been hurt for profit, for the financial benefit of pimps and entrepreneurs. I want you to remember the perpetrator and I am going to ask you to remember the victims: not just tonight but tomorrow and the next day. I want you to find a way to include them—the perpetrators and the victims—in what you do, how you think, how you act, what you care about, what your life means to you.[3]

The debate on the sex trade has reached a new nadir. Globally, groups are being funded to lobby for decriminalisation of all forms of prostitution. Most, if not all, of the major funders describe themselves as

---

[3]Speech at the Massey College Fifth Walter Gordon Forum, Toronto, Ontario, in a symposium on 'The Future of Feminism,' 2 April 1995. First published by Massey College in the University of Toronto, 2 May 1995. Copyright ©1995, 1996 by Andrea Dworkin.

human rights-based organisations. So-called 'sex workers' rights activists' are marching in the streets, waving their red umbrellas (a symbol of the 'sex workers' rights' movement) and shouting about the rights of women, and men, to do what they wish with their bodies.

Feminist abolitionists, many of whom are sex trade survivors are attempting to counter this dominant discourse, and are pushing for the introduction of laws to criminalise those who pay for sex and to decriminalise those who sell it.

There is no issue as contentious between feminists, liberals and human rights defenders as the sex trade. Radical feminists tend to argue that prostitution is both a cause and consequence of male supremacy, and that if women and men were equal, prostitution would not exist; it also means that if women and men are ever to become equal, prostitution must not exist. But for liberals who believe in an essential freedom to buy and sell sex, or for human rights campaigners who see access to sex as a human right, abolition is simply not an option. While acceptance of the sex trade has become mainstream, the idea of ending it has become even harder to imagine.

The Laws on Prostitution

Currently, a number of countries around the world are in a state of flux in terms of legislation and policy around the sex trade. Several countries—including Ireland, Northern Ireland, France, Norway, Sweden and Iceland—have introduced a law criminalising those who purchase sex, while also decriminalising those who sell sex. There are calls from abolitionists, including many survivors of the sex trade, to introduce this model globally. On the other hand, the pro-prostitution lobbyists are calling for laws similar to those currently in place in New Zealand.

In July 2016, the UK Parliament's Home Affairs Committee published an interim report on prostitution, which looked favourably at decriminalisation of the sex trade. It also made clear that the committee members, chaired by Keith Vaz MP (who three months later was exposed by a tabloid newspaper as a sex buyer), were unlikely to recommend introducing a law to criminalise those who pay for sex. The Committee said the report was 'not yet persuaded that the abolitionist law is effective in reducing, rather than simply displacing, demand for prostitution, or in helping the police to tackle the crime and exploitation associated with the sex trade'.

The way that governments regulate the sex trade sends out a powerful message about how seriously we take the issue of sexual exploitation and violence against women more generally.

The Two Models

Legalisation/Decriminalisation

The pro-prostitution lobby adopted the term 'decriminalisation', and stopped using 'legalisation' during the early 2000s. This was around the time that New Zealand introduced the Prostitution Reform Act, which decriminalised its sex trade (2003) by a majority of one vote; and when it became official that the legalised regime in the Netherlands had been an unmitigated disaster (the same year).

An increasingly popular response to the question 'What should we do about prostitution?' is to decriminalise the entire market, and remove all specific laws relating to the sex trade. It is also argued that prostitution should be treated as any other job. Under this regime, third party profiteering from the sex trade should be freely allowed and this approach is advocated by the Joint United Nations Programme on HIV/AIDS, Open Society and Amnesty International.

The difference between the decriminalisation and legalisation of prostitution is that in a decriminalised context, prostitution is treated like any other business and subjected to same of the same regulations. Alternately, the legalisation of prostitution means that the State 'recognises prostitution as a lawful activity' but requires the licensing of brothel prostitution and may retain criminal laws against other forms of non-brothel prostitution, such as street prostitution.

What unites full decriminalisation and legalisation is that neither regime would result in either a reduction or an end to the sex trade, but sets in stone the notion that prostitution is an inevitability, and that there will always exist both a supply and demand. They also make pimping, brothel keeping and sex buying legal.

The Nordic Model

This law was first introduced in Sweden in 1999. It is a set of laws and policies that criminalises the demand for commercial sex, and decriminalises those selling sex. The Nordic model has two main goals: to curb the demand for prostitution and promote equality between women and men.

The Nordic Model has since been adopted by Norway, Iceland, Canada, South Korea, Ireland, Northern Ireland and France. Governments in Israel, Latvia and Lithuania are considering the law, and in 2014 the European Parliament and the Parliamentary Assembly of the Council of Europe passed recommendations that the law should be implemented as the best way to tackle European prostitution.

Myths about the sex trade include saying that prostitution is necessary, inevitable and harmless. I will show clear evidence that these beliefs, propagated by the 'sex workers' rights' movement, are based on misguided neoliberalism and fallacious mythology.

My Research

During my research I conducted around 250 interviews in 40 countries, cities and states. I talked to survivors of prostitution, current 'sex workers' rights' activists, pimps, sex buyers, brothel owners, AIDS activists, lesbian, gay, bisexual and transgender groups, police officers and feminists opposed to prostitution. I interviewed regular members of the public who knew very little, if anything, about the sex trade. All of these people had a strong opinion.

I went where my views put me firmly in the minority. At an academic conference on prostitution policy and laws in Vienna, Austria, entitled 'Troubling Prostitution', I was one of only four delegates out of 185 who appeared to be troubled by it at all. The other 181 held the view that all aspects of the sex trade should be decriminalised.

In Leeds, UK, I spend a freezing cold evening close to the 'managed area' on which Daria Pionko, a 21-year-old prostituted woman, was fatally wounded. As we go to press, a 24-year-old man believed to be her pimp is awaiting trial for her murder. I spoke to residents, police officers, other journalists and the women themselves. No-one tells me 'yes' when I ask if such zones will reduce the danger to those operating within them.

I visit legal, state-sanctioned brothels in the USA, Germany and the Netherlands. At the Porn Awards in Los Angeles I meet Siouxsie Q, founder of *The WhoreCast: Sharing the Stories, Art and Voices of American Sex Workers*, and the next morning, in a cafe in Hollywood, I talk to a man who is a former victim of sex trafficking.

In Vancouver, Canada, I am taken on a tour of the deprived Downtown East Side by Courtney, a young Indigenous women who works for a rape crisis centre. Hundreds of Native women and girls disappeared from this area, some of whom were murdered by serial killer Robert Pickton, who fed his victims' body parts to the pigs on his farm.

In Gujarat, India, I travel to a village built on prostitution and meet a man who is pimping his wife, sister, aunt and mother.

In Dubai, UAE, I discover that what is supposed to be a shelter for trafficked women is, in my view, a holding pen run by the government until the victims can be deported back to their home countries.

In Sweden, where women's bodies are not for sale, I share home-cured salmon with Carina, a 'sex workers' rights' activist who tells me she is so appalled at the views of feminist abolitionists that 'I could never even speak that word "feminist" from my mouth'.

In Istanbul, Turkey, I speak to men queuing outside one of the city's legal brothels, but am warned off by security who tell me that 'only men are allowed here'.

At the central police station in Bergen, Norway, is the very first Exiting Prostitution unit. I am shown around by police officer Jarle Bjorke who goes into schools and asks the students, 'Is it a human right to buy somebody else's body?' Norway criminalised the purchase of sex in 2009, and Bjorke tells me that understanding how this came about is simply a matter of the citizens 'knowing right from wrong'.

At Den Haag, the Dutch Parliament, I meet the abolitionists who are finally able to speak out against the sex trade in the Netherlands. I am told that hostility from so-called feminists towards anyone who criticised the sex trade prevented any debate on the topic.

During a trip to Cambodia, I hear from some of the prostituted women who live on a disused railway line in Phenom Peng with no water or sanitation. With them is a board member of Women's Network for Unity (WNU), a local NGO that is funded to present the women as 'sex workers' rights activists'.

In Northern Ireland, undoubtedly the most devout part of the UK, I hear the story of how the abolitionist law, introduced by the Democratic Unionist Party's Lord Morrow, was enacted by 81 votes to 10.

Boston, Massachusetts, is home to a vibrant abolitionist movement. I have brunch with fast-talking Donna Gavin, Sergeant Detective and Commander of the Boston Police Human Trafficking Unit, who tells me that the pimps targeting young, vulnerable women are becoming more brutal and sadistic than ever.

I tour the legal brothel site in Zurich, the business capital of Switzerland, and interview passers-by in sight of the drive-in brothel.

A group of feminist abolitionists in Seoul, South Korea, take me on a tour of the indoor red light district in Cheongnyangni, where I see men of all ages going in and coming out of window brothels. It is 5 p.m. Perhaps they were popping in for a quick one after work.

A tuk tuk driver in Phnom Peng drives me around the prostitution sites, where I talk to British sex tourists, the young women they are buying, and groups of prostituted women in the park, identifiable by black face masks.

In a suburb of Amsterdam I stay the night at the Happy House B&B and have dinner with Xaviera Hollander, who co-authored a book entitled *The Happy Hooker* based on her experiences as a prostituted woman turned pimp. During dinner, I asked Hollander, a passionate believer in legalisation, if she thought pimping could ever be eliminated from the sex trade. 'The average hooker, the most simple-minded hooker who sits behind the window and just plies her trade', says Hollander, 'is like a sheep and will follow the orders of her pimp'.

I discuss the links between 'queer politics' and prostitution in Paris, France, and problems with implementing the abolitionist law in Norway.

During my time with survivor abolitionists in New York City, Los Angeles, Minnesota, Boston, Munich, Sweden, Montreal, Vancouver, Cambodia and the UK, I chart a social justice movement and come to understand how we have come to misunderstand the global sex trade.

At the High Court in Northern Ireland, which also criminalised paying for sex in 2015, I listen to the arguments put forward by a QC in a judicial review of the law, brought by Laura Lee, a 'sex workers' rights' campaigner who campaigns for blanket decriminalisation of the sex trade.

The Chapters

Chapter 1 explores the origins and rise of the modern-day abolitionist movement. We meet the activists, politicians, police officers and the survivors of the sex trade who have come together in an attempt to dismantle the sex trade. I explore the emergence, from 1985 to the present day, of the movement.

In Chap. 2 we meet the 'sex workers' rights' lobby, and look at its origins and key figures. I outline its key arguments and tactics, and the aims and objections of the people—many of whom are involved in the sex trade—who campaign for full decriminalisation. I meet Xaviera Hollander, whose 1971 memoir popularised the notion that prostitution is fun.

Chapter 3 focuses on what I refer to as the 'sanitisation' of the sex trade, where language has lost all meaning thanks to the pro-prostitution lobby, so that pimps become 'managers', prostituted women become 'sex workers' and rape is an 'occupational hazard'.

In Chap. 4, the consequences of legalisation and decriminalisation of the sex trade come under scrutiny. During visits to Australia, Nevada in the USA, Germany, Switzerland and the Netherlands (all with legalised regimes) I explore the implications of legalisation for the women, the sex buyers, pimps, brothel owners, police and the public.

Sex buyers come under scrutiny in Chap. 5. Despite increased attention, the punters are still largely invisible in the media, academic research, law enforcement and campaigns against harm in the sex trade. I outline the views of both the 'sex workers' rights' lobby as well as the feminist abolitionists, and talk to the men who pay for sex and the women they buy.

Chapter 6 tackles the role of the liberals and human rights organisations pushing for full decriminalisation of the sex trade. I explore the reason that women have been left out of the human rights debate when it comes to male sexual access.

The HIV/AIDS industry and its support for the pro-decriminalisation lobby is examined in Chap. 7. Since the 1980s, service provision, policy, legislation and opinion have been shaped by the approach and funding of the HIV community. I will explain the links between a number of the key players in the 'sex workers' rights' lobby and the AIDS world, as well as the main funders behind it.

Chapter 8 is an examination of the way that some criminals involved in the global sex trade utilise and co-opt the language of the 'sex workers' rights' movement. Using examples from the Republic and North of Ireland, this chapter looks at ways in which pimps invade the movement against the laws to criminalise demand.

Chapter 9 considers the reason why the majority of academics within the UK, US and elsewhere have formed the view that the abolitionist view of the sex trade is counter to the campaign for the human rights of 'sex workers', and examines the influence of the academy on pro-prostitution policy.

In recent years, prostitution has been increasingly portrayed as a sexual identity, with the claim made that those involved in the sex trade are part of the 'queer community'. In Chap. 10 I examine the conflating of prostitution and LGBTQQI[4] rights and identity, and ask how and why it began and which side of the debate this conflation best serves.

Chapter 11 charts the survivors of the sex trade. The 50 women (and two men) interviewed are all campaigning for an end to prostitution, and many are expert trainers, service providers, writers and educators.

---

[4]The 'alphabet soup' has now extended to 'lesbian, gay, bisexual, transgender, queer, questioning and intersex'.

It should be clear to the reader that I do not pretend to come to this topic without a point of view. For the past 35 years I have campaigned to end male violence towards women and girls, and I see prostitution as one way that men exert their control over us. But I have learned a great deal in gathering the material and data for this book. It is right and proper that we continue to learn from each other, and shift and expand our views and beliefs.

I have conducted approximately 250 interviews during my research for this book, with a wide range of individuals, including representatives of certain professions and organisations. Every interviewee was informed prior to the interview that I would possibly be using direct quotations from them, as well as the information provided during the interview, in this book, and in any subsequent publicity surrounding the book both prior to and post-publication. At the beginning of each interview I requested permission to audio record the interviews, and was granted it by each and every one of the interviewees. I also asked if they were happy for me to use their real names, and identify the organisation which they represented if appropriate. In some instances I was asked to use a pseudonym, and I agreed that pseudonym with the individual.

All of the interviews have been transcribed and stored safely, as have the audio files. On two occasions I was asked by the interviewee if they could check the transcript prior to agreeing whether or not I could directly quote them (this was at least in part to do with the fact that English was not their first language and they want to check that their words have been translated appropriately). I agreed to these conditions. Every interviewee happily consented to be quoted in my book, including those who profoundly disagree with my views and position on prostitution and the sex trade.

1

The Abolitionist Movement

Andrea Dworkin once mused, 'Surely the freedom of women must mean more to us than the freedom of pimps'.[1] To many, prostituted women do not matter at all.

In this chapter I chart the growth of an exciting and vibrant abolitionist movement. It is a movement with many obstacles to overcome, and I outline the barriers and hostility its members face from the sex trade apologists. It will document the true face behind the international campaign to deregulate an abusive and dangerous industry. It asks why the liberal left is so supportive of the sex trade, when it is a trade built on inequality and the disenfranchisement of the world's poorest and most vulnerable women and children.

Through the voices of survivors and other feminist abolitionists from numerous countries and states, you will hear about the ordinary, everyday common practices and experiences of prostitution, and the reasons

---

[1]Speech at the Massey College Fifth Walter Gordon Forum, Toronto, Ontario, in a symposium on 'The Future of Feminism', 2 April 1995. First published by Massey College in the University of Toronto, 2 May 1995. Copyright ©1995, 1996 by Andrea Dworkin. Reprinted from Life and Death.

© The Author(s) 2017
J. Bindel, *The Pimping of Prostitution*,
DOI 10.1057/978-1-137-55890-9_1

why prostitution and the entire global sex trade must be abolished before women can live as equal citizens in this world.

The Beginnings

The abolitionist movement began in 1860 when Josephine Butler, a social reformer feminist activist, saw the plight of young, homeless girls and women being sold to men for sex. Butler was appalled. As a child she had learned about social injustice from her father, John Grey, who was a supporter of the abolition of slavery. Butler's main achievement was her successful campaign to repeal the Contagious Diseases Acts: a brutal piece of legislation that permitted police to round up women in military towns whom they believed to be involved in prostitution in order to test them for venereal diseases.

Some women were locked up in hospitals for three months until they were cured. Butler said that these acts 'removed every guarantee of personal security that the law has established',[2] and questioned why it was women who were tested when in fact it was women who were the victims of venereal disease, and it was men who were 'the cause of the vice and its dreadful consequences'.[3]

Butler was ahead of her time in that she firmly placed the blame for the abuse of the women in prostitution, and for the existence of the sex trade, on the shoulders of men: something that many feminists today are reluctant to do. Butler was clear that prostitution was male sexual slavery of women and she attacked the pimps and profiteers, as well as the State that allowed the sex trade to flourish yet also blamed the women for the spread of sexually transmitted infections.

Butler has been accused of anti-sex, Christian moralism, and written off as a 'rescuer' and patronising to working-class women. In reality, Butler is an important figure who advocated on behalf of prostituted

---

[2]Millar, A. (2015, April 28.) *Josephine Butler: The forgotten Feminist*. On Digital Victorians. Retrieved 15 June 2017, from http://mhm.hud.ac.uk/digitalvictorians/josephine-butler-the-forgotten-feminist/.

[3]Millar, A. (2015, April 28.) *Josephine Butler: The forgotten Feminist*. On Digital Victorians. Retrieved 15 June 2017, from http://mhm.hud.ac.uk/digitalvictorians/josephine-butler-the-forgotten-feminist/.

women whom much of society considered to be worthless and 'scum'. Not only did Butler take women into her home who were in the direst need, but she also challenged men's right to sexual access to prostituted women and children. Butler was clear that prostitution hinders women's human rights, and that men are to blame for the existence of prostitution.

During her life Butler achieved huge social and legal reforms at a time when women did not even have the right to vote. She travelled all over the USA and much of Europe, inspiring individuals, stimulating local organisations into action and addressing meetings, from small gatherings of women to public meetings attended by hundreds of working-class men.[4]

The abolitionists of today stand on Josephine Butler's shoulders and are, in turn, accused by the 'sex workers' rights' lobby and advocates of decriminalising pimping of being moralistic, anti-sex man-haters. The feminist abolitionist movement is made up of many survivors of prostitution and other forms of male violence, as well as women, and some men, who recognise the harm the sex trade causes to wider society.

What is clear is that the abolitionist movement is global and it is growing. Despite the lack of funding and support the movement receives compared to the 'sex workers' rights' lobby (which, as we will see in Chap. 7 is awash with AIDS/HIV prevention money), the abolitionist movement is gaining ground and finally being taken seriously by a number of policy and lawmakers around the world. As the evidence continues to mount on the disaster caused by legalisation and decriminalisation of the sex trade, so do the benefits and successes of the Nordic Model—legislation first introduced in Sweden in 1999 that criminalises paying for sex and decriminalises selling sex. Although, as I show in Chap. 9, academia is dominated by pro-prostitution scholars and doctoral students, a number of brave and robust academics across various countries and disciplines are daring to carry out and publish credible research on the negative consequences of prostitution and legalised prostitution systems.[5]

---

[4]Millar, A. (2015, April 28.) *Josephine Butler: The forgotten Feminist.* On Digital Victorians. Retrieved 15 June 2017, from http://mhm.hud.ac.uk/digitalvictorians/josephine-butler-the-forgotten-feminist/.

[5]Bindel, J. (2010, Jul 2.) *Legalising prostitution is not the answer.* In The Guardian. Retrieved 15 June 2017, from https://www.theguardian.com/commentisfree/2010/jul/02/prostitution-legalise-criminalise-swedish-law.

Links to the Movement to End Male Violence

The other side were claiming prostitution is not all about violence, and it can be very empowering for women and certainly a better job than working at McDonalds. So I said to them, 'Well at least when you work at McDonalds you're not the meat'. (Evelina Giobbe 2015)

Abolitionists argue that the only effective way to tackle any trade that is built on vulnerability, exploitation and desperation is to support those desperate enough to sell sexual access to themselves and ensure that those creating the demand pay the price. There is as little room for pimps to be reclassified as respectable businessmen—which they are under the New Zealand model where the sex trade is decriminalised—as there is for police officers to consider it a mere perk of the job to have sex while investigating activities in a brothel.

'I started talking about the similarities between the Left and Right', Evelina Giobbe, sex trade survivor and founder of Women Hurt in Systems of Prostitution Engaged in Revolt (WHISPER),[6] told me. 'They both want control over and access to women's bodies. The Right Wing does it through marriage and the Left Wing does it through prostitution and pornography. You can marry it, you can buy it—and we're it.'

There is a cost to those survivors who name prostitution as male violence towards women. Prostitution is not some unusual but generally harmless activity, such as collecting rare insects or mountain climbing, as much of the Left would have it. Rather it is both a cause and a consequence of women's oppression, situated firmly within the patriarchy. Women have long been punished for naming male violence and for insisting we examine and campaign against it as something institutionalised and normalised, instead of seeing it as the actions of individual, atypical men.

When women first named domestic violence as a tactic to shore up and maintain male supremacy over women and their children, they were duly punished. Those who do the same with child sexual abuse, rape, sexual assault and forced marriage are accused of lying,

---

[6]WHISPER became the organisation known as Breaking Free. Breakingfree.net. Retrieved 16 June 2017, from http://www.breakingfree.net/.

manipulation and man-hating. The upholders of male supremacy define sexual violence as pleasurable sex.

In 2005 I appeared on a popular daytime TV programme to debate the UK's appallingly low conviction rates for rape. Immediately after the broadcast I went to my local bank to deposit a cheque. A man asked if I was the woman he had just seen on TV. When I told him yes, he screwed up his face and told me I was 'too ugly to rape'. A young female bank clerk who overheard this sought to reassure me that the man was talking rubbish, as I was 'very pretty'—which goes to show how much we internalise the need for male approval. The stigma that is imposed on women accused of denying men sexual pleasure is debilitating and humiliating. But despite this, the women who can best testify to the truth about prostitution continue to speak out.

Nowhere is the conflation of sexual desire and sexual abuse more prevalent than in the debates on prostitution. Abolitionists are routinely accused by the pro-prostitution lobby of hating men, sex, orgasms and the female body. Abolitionist criticism of the sex trade has been rationalised by the pro lobby as a reaction to a failure to acquire 'a good fuck'. I have watched sex trade survivors give talks about prostitution to large audiences, and then receive intrusive questions about their sexual orientation, sexual history and sexual behaviour. The implications were obvious: were they frigid, sex-hating prudes? Because prostitution is rewritten as sex by the apologists, speaking out against the sex trade is cast as speaking out against sexual pleasure. Often they are accused of 'hating sex' due to their 'bad experiences' of prostitution, as though this is an unusual response to years of unwanted sex.

The History

'We are speaking out because we are sick of the myth of the *Pretty Woman* version of prostitution', Janette Westbrook, survivor activist and SPACE member told me in 2014. 'For too long the happy hooker stereotype has dominated.'

The contemporary survivor movement began in earnest 30 years before Westbrook and I met in New York. WHISPER, founded in 1985 in the USA, was a direct challenge to the notion that prostitution is either a free choice or labour.

'I am 65 years old. I was literally sold into prostitution—it's called trafficking now', says Giobbe. 'I was sold to a pimp as a 14-year-old kid that ran away from home. I was gone for two days. Kids who run away from home are not thinking their whole lives; they're just escaping a moment in time.

'A man was very nice to me and listened to my sad story. He said I have to meet a friend of mine, he took me to the man's house. I was really an innocent and the man who brought me there left. The other man said "You're mine, I bought you, you're going to be a prostitute". I looked at him incredulously and I said "no" and turned around to leave and he beat me half to death and that was the beginning.'

Had Giobbe not gone to a Women Against Pornography meeting in 1985, the modern abolitionist movement may have taken rather longer to garner support. The 'sex workers' rights' movement, as we will see in Chap. 2, was already in full swing.

'Oh my God, they were everywhere', says Giobbe. 'The big push was Margot St James and COYOTE (a pro-prostitution lobby group founded in the USA in 1973, standing for Call Off Your Old Tired Ethics[7]). They were the first and last word on prostitution, anywhere. Literally, their arguments, word for word—is exactly what you're hearing from Amnesty [AI] today.'

Giobbe describes the panel session at the conference that was made up of pro-sadism and masochism (S&M) and prostitution activists and Women Against Pornography members. 'The audience were like the bride's side of the family and the groom's side of the family', she says. 'There were the liberals, and there were all leathered out S&M girls and there were the feminists, like regular people. I was looking for a seat and I had a sharp haircut and the leather jacket, so they see me and think I'm one of them. These women are making room for me to sit down, so I go and sit down.

---

[7]Coyote. Retrieved 16 June 2017 http://www.coyotela.org/.

'Somebody was going on and on about the whole argument for decriminalisation, and [saying prostitution is] a job, and finally I raised my hand and the chair called on me to speak. I got up and just said, "That's a total lie. I was in prostitution and that's not true". Everybody who knew me looked at me and was stunned. No one had any idea that this woman from Queens, this housewife, had been in prostitution.'

WHISPER was born. 'That was sort of the beginning. Afterwards women came over to me during the conference and told me they had been prostituted. I was like, "Wow!" Suddenly I wasn't alone. I was collecting phone numbers from everybody who told me they had been prostituted. I said, "We should have a newsletter"' I made up the name WHISPER when I was on the bus.'

The hostility from the 'sex workers' rights' activists began immediately when WHISPER was founded. 'So every conference we went to, except the ones we planned, we would have to get on these panels with ['sex workers' rights' activists]. They would make fun of us', says Giobbe. 'Somebody called us WHIMPER once—actually it was pretty clever but I was pissed off. They said we didn't care about protecting women, that prostitution was a choice and we were infantilising them, that we wanted to keep it criminalised.'

The 'WHIMPER' slur is a topical one used against feminists who campaign to end male violence. We are accused of creating a 'victim mentality' and inventing or exaggerating the prevalence and effects of sexual abuse. Laura Agustin, 'sex workers' rights' activist and author of *Sex At The Margins*, claims that: 'Victims become passive receptacles and mute sufferers who must be saved, and helpers become saviours, a colonialist operation warned against in discussions of western feminism's treatment of third-world women and now common in discussions of migrant women who sell sex'.[8]

'When I was in prostitution I would always say, "I'm fine, I love what I do". I had to or I would have gone mad', says Giobbe. 'It is only when we get out, if we are lucky enough to get out alive, we can admit the hell, the horror of what was happening to us.'

---

[8]Agustín, L. (2008.) *Sex at the margins*. London: Zed Books. p. 39.

According to Giobbe, in the early days of the modern abolition-ist movement, activists would point to men's demand for prostitution as the root cause of the problem, but had no blueprint for a solution. 'We didn't have the knowledge that people have now with the Nordic model', says Giobbe. 'We didn't know how to put that together. How do you do that without decriminalisation? So we would say "women don't deserve to go to jail". This whole industry is driven by men's demand for unconditional sexual access to women based on their social, economic and gender power—in other words patriarchy.'

Giobbe found that women both inside and outside of the women's movement preferred to hear the arguments from the 'sex workers' rights' lobby rather than the feminist abolitionists. 'If you want to stop pros-titution and you want to stop the men who are driving it, the johns, then all you have to do is look across the breakfast table. Women don't want to do that. So I think women—regular women, not prostituted women—women with not a lot of knowledge, just step back. They have to believe that this is a choice, or they would have to believe that men are rapists.'

Soon after WHISPER was founded, several other groups began to emerge. In 1988 the Coalition Against Trafficking of Women[9] was set up. It was the first global feminist abolitionist organisation, and has affiliations in countries including the Philippines, Bangladesh, Indonesia, Thailand, Venezuela, Puerto Rico, Chile, Canada, Norway, France and Greece.

SAGE (Standing Against Global Exploitation), a resource, advocacy and counselling centre for women in prostitution, was founded in 1992 by Norma Hotaling, a survivor of child sexual abuse and street prostitu-tion. In 1989, after a short spell in prison during which she detoxed from heroin, Hotaling had begun to support other women suffering drug abuse and associated violence.

The abolitionist movement in the 1980s was indivisible from the feminist anti-male violence movement, with little or no interference from the religious right, or conservative moralists. Just as the wider

---

[9]Coalition Against Trafficking Of Women. Catwinternational.org. Retrieved 16 June 2017, from http://www.catwinternational.org/.

feminist movement sought to end male violence rather than contain or make it more palatable, the abolitionist movement sought the end of the sex trade. To achieve this, men had to be deterred from paying for sex and women assisted out of prostitution.

More Than Condoms and Needles

Since the 1980s, when money designated for HIV/AIDS prevention became channelled towards services for those involved in prostitution, harm minimisation was the predominant service provided. Clean needles, condoms and STI testing was usually all the women accessing such services could expect.

In 1996, Breaking Free[10] was founded in Minnesota, USA, by sex trade survivor Vednita Carter. Based in St Paul, the capital and second most populous district, Breaking Free provides support, counselling, exiting services, education, housing and a range of other services for women who are escaping, or who are at risk of prostitution.

Breaking Free is a good model of a service dealing with the range of issues facing women who are being, or had previously been, prostituted. A sizeable percentage of the client base is young African-American women, who are particularly at risk of sexual exploitation in North America. Carter, herself African-American, is also a member of SPACE International. As I write, Carter, now in her early 60s, has stepped aside as executive director of Breaking Free and is president of its board, giving talks and appearing at public events in order to speak about the sex trade and the abolitionist movement.

Carter, who I have met on a number of occasions at abolitionist and other feminist events, is clear that services need to be directed towards women at various stages of their exiting progress. 'I want women to know that they will not be turned away just because they're not ready that minute to exit. It can be a long, complicated process', she says. 'If we let those girls down, and if they feel judged in any way because they're not making that easy transition into another life, we will lose

---

[10]Breaking Free. Breakingfree.net. Retrieved 16 June 2017, from http://www.breakingfree.net/.

them. In particular, African-American girls need to know they have a place to go. They are so marginalised, and often seen as 'choosing' the life, because to many white folk that's the way they view these girls and their lack of opportunities.'

Rae Story is a survivor who exited in 2015, and is a feminist and social-ist activist. Story has been prostituted in a number of countries, includ-ing under legalised, decriminalised and regulated regimes. For her, one of the most important aspects of an abolitionist movement is the provision of specific support and exiting services for women in prostitution. Many abo-litionists are rightly concerned about the dominance of faith-based service provision in a number of countries. This is not to say that some of those services are not really well run, or that in any way they require women to either practise religion prior to leaving prostitution, or to adopt religion once they are involved in those services, but feminist-run exiting services are very specific in that those running them are often sex trade survivors themselves, and are required to be experts in the cause and consequences of male violence towards women. Therefore, the women themselves will never be blamed, judged or held responsible for what happened to them, and the responsibility will be put firmly on the men who perpetrate the abuse.

'We need temporary shelters, free counselling, support and advocacy with welfare and disability benefit for those of us suffering with mental health issues as a result of prostitution', says Story, 'as with women who are trying to exit domestic violence'.

When Story tried to leave the sex trade the first time around, she had to make a choice between prostitution and homelessness. 'I shouldn't have to make that choice', she says. 'Another friend was trying to get [benefits]. She got into prostitution because her mental health made it hard to find work. So [we need] support services specifically for prosti-tutes to help them make that transition.'

The Origins of the Law to Criminalise Punters

Although the second wave abolitionist movement (if we count Josephine Butler as leading us into the first one) was established some years before the introduction in Sweden of the law to criminalise demand, in 1999 this law broke new ground and helped to galvanise the movement. A number of feminists had been fighting for the introduction of this law for many years because they saw prostitution as simply another form of men's violence towards women. The unsolved murder of Catrine da Costa,[11] a street-prostituted young woman found decapitated near to the notorious street prostitution zone in Stockholm, gave a further push to the campaign to focus on sex buyers.

The arrest of two seemingly respectable men for da Costa's murder provoked the women of Sweden to organise against the sex trade. They marched through the city centres; circulated petitions; and appeared on television programmes protesting against the ill treatment of women, particularly vulnerable females such as da Costa. The case led to a change in the law on prostitution and the act of paying for sex has been criminalised since 1999.

According to the Swedish-based journalist and feminist activist Kajsa Ekis Ekman: 'I think the important thing was that if the goal of Sweden is to have equality between men and women, then prostitution is an obstacle to that goal. It wasn't [the intention to claim that the women were] all victims, with the government saying "we're going to save them". That's what's been distorted in the international press'.

I first met the Swedish feminist and lawyer Gunilla Ekberg in the late 1990s. Prior to this she had played a pivotal role in promoting the benefits of the Nordic model and is credited with being a key figure in the campaign to introduce Sweden's groundbreaking legislation in 1999, which decriminalised selling sex and criminalised the purchase and attempted purchase of sex. I met Ekberg in Malmo, Sweden, to ask her about how the law to criminalise the punters came to be. 'It is different in Scandinavia than other countries because there's been a Labour democrat rule since the 1930s until the 1980s so, if you wanted to change something, you had to interact with party politics', says Ekberg. 'Also [we have] an open democracy—everything is public. It's very easy to get

---

[11]Bindel, J. (2010, Nov 30.) *The real-life Swedish murder that inspired Stieg Larsson*. On Telegraph. co.uk. Retrieved 16 June 2017, from http://www.telegraph.co.uk/culture/books/8157585/The-real-life-Swedish-murder-that-inspired-Stieg-Larsson.html.

in contact with the government, you can meet them easily, it used to be you can call them and say can we meet?'

Margareta Winberg was the Deputy Prime Minister in Sweden from 2002–2003, and a Social Democrat Party member of Parliament from 1981–2003. She is currently Swedish Ambassador to Brazil. I asked her to tell me the story of how the law to criminalise sex buyers was passed by the Government.

According to Winberg, discussions within her party about criminalising demand had been going on since the beginning of the 1990s. Many of the politicians were split on the issue, and some research on the potential benefits of this law had taken place. Winberg was chair of the women's movement within the Social Democratic Party at that time, and presided over debates about whether or not the buyer and the seller should be criminalised, or whether the problem lay solely with the punter.

In 1993 the item was listed at the Social Democratic Party Congress (SDP) for discussion. Wynberg was the chair but thought that the item would not come up until much later in the evening. Having gone into her office to get a cup of coffee, she was surprised when a colleague came running in shouting: 'We have just criminalised the buyers!'

'There were no abstentions', says Winberg. 'After that we made a huge strategy on how to get it to pass as a law. We prepared lots of people, including men, because as you know men talk to men and men, at that time at least, men also talk to most of the women. They stood up and talked in favour of criminalisation. We had at that time … it must have been between 1995 and 1998. Eventually, we succeeded to convince the congress to criminalise the buyers.'

Sven Axel Mansson, now Professor of Social Work at Malmo University, was a radical social worker at the time the law was being debated in Swedish Parliament. Since becoming an academic, Mansson has conducted a number of research projects into the commercial sex trade, in particular focusing on men who buy sex. We met at a conference on demand in Den Haag, Holland. I asked him to give me his perspective on the history of the law. According to Mansson, at the time that the abolitionist law was being debated, there was no viable pro-prostitution lobby in operation in Sweden. Alongside that, the law was compatible with the socialist view that those most in need should be taken care of by those with more privilege, and was ideologically in sync with the feminist principles that located prostitution as men's violence against women.

'The SDP women developed a fantastic sexuality manifesto in 1984 that talked about prostitution as harmful, so that [attitude] funnelled into most of the parties', says Mansson. 'There was this anti-violence package that then was voted through the Parliament in 1998. That included different legislative measures and money and monitoring and focusing on the women's movement and the shelters and in the mix was the law. So it was indicated from then that the law is part of Violence Against Women.'

For Kajsa Ekis Ekman, the law criminalising demand was never about condemning or protecting individual men or women, but about the type of society that is desirable to live in: 'It wasn't about the individual prostituted woman and how she felt. That's how we avoided that debate. We had the debate prior to the law. We said, "It's not about you, it's about the whole of society. Do we want this in the whole of society?" That's how we did it'.

Janice Raymond, author of *Not A Choice, Not A Job: Exposing the Myths about Prostitution and the Global Sex Trade*[12] and long-time feminist activist, became co-director of the Coalition against Trafficking in Women (CATW) in 1994. She has been involved in the abolitionist movement since the late 1980s, having attended the founding conference of CATW in 1988, and making the connections between sexual and reproductive trafficking (surrogacy).

Raymond said: 'The Swedish law was a real milestone, a sea change in just shifting viewpoints in the media because then the media had to talk about the demand, and then when Norway passed it and Iceland passed it and then South Korea—which everyone just ignores—passed it also … those were again milestones so I think that my outlook at this point is really optimistic. I think we've come a long way, baby. I don't think we appreciate that enough or capitalise on it enough'.

---

[12]Raymond, 2013, *Not a Choice, Not a Job: Exposing the Myths about Prostitution and the Global Sex Trade*. http://www.nebraskapress.unl.edu/product/Not-a-Choice-Not-a-Job,676533.aspx.

Julia Tiberg is a member of PRIS (Prostitutes Revenge in Society),[13] an organisation in Sweden made up of women who have had experience of the sex trade. Most members are survivors, with some currently still involved. Its aims include developing exiting services, educating the general public about the harms of prostitution, and increasing penalties for sex buyers.

PRIS was founded in response to the pro-prostitution movement in Sweden, to add another voice. Talking to Tiberg via Skype, she says that much of the research produced by Swedish academics is critical of the law criminalising demand, and is uncritical of the sex trade. 'This research is supposedly based on the experiences of women who have left the sex trade', she says, 'but as far as we can see, they haven't spoken to one survivor. They merely interview their pro-prostitution friends.'

For Tiberg, the most useful direction the abolitionist movement could go in would be to form a European network for better communication. 'I would invite psychologists, survivors, feminists, police officers … in other words anyone working against prostitution and for abolition.'

An International Focus on Demand

Norma Hotaling, founder of SAGE, devised a programme that was to become known as the John's School; a programme aimed at educating sex buyers about the harms of prostitution, which came to be replicated across scores of cities in the USA and Canada. Charges against first offenders were dropped if they paid a fee and attended a one-day course, including sessions run by former prostitutes, on the realities of the sex trade. Most of the fees went to help women attend the SAGE programme.

I remember meeting Hotaling at the 1996 Brighton conference and the impact it had on me. Hotaling told me how, after a stint in prison during which she detoxed and decided to exit prostitution, she adopted a homeless dog. 'The unconditional love between me and that dog was the first time I ever felt safe', she said.

---

[13]Prostitutes' Revenge In Society. Xn--ntverketpris-gcb.se. Retrieved 16 June 2017, from http://www.xn--ntverketpris-gcb.se/start-english.html.

For many of the delegates at the Brighton conference, hearing Hotaling speak as a proud survivor and activist, who had been in the worst possible position in life and went on to create such an inspirational service for prostituted women, was a turning point. Prior to that conference, women in the UK and elsewhere in Europe were reluctant to tackle the contentious issue of prostitution head on. The 'sex workers' rights' movement was well underway, well funded and, unsurprisingly, supported by a number of high-profile liberal and leftist men and women.

Fiona Broadfoot, a British survivor of the sex trade, was also at the Brighton conference. In the months leading up to the event, I was employed as its press officer and given the role of coordinating workshops on pornography and prostitution. One day, as I sat in the office at Bradford University's Violence, Abuse and Gender Relations Unit, a heavily pregnant woman walked in and asked if I was Julie Bindel. She seemed nervous and was holding some A4 pages. When I confirmed that I was the person she was looking for, Broadfoot introduced herself, saying she had set up and ran a telephone support service for women wishing to leave prostitution called 'Street Exit'. Broadfoot handed me the paper she was holding and told me, 'It's my story', asking me to read it and get in touch with her. As she was leaving the office, Broadfoot said she wanted 'a chance to help other women like me'.

As I read Broadfoot's story, I realised how rare it was to meet someone like her in the women's movement. I had met other women who had survived the sex trade, but no-one who had been willing to speak out publicly about their experiences, or who was spending their time helping other women.

When Broadfoot was living at home with her parents aged 15, she was targeted and groomed into prostitution by the man she believed was her boyfriend and taken to work on the streets and in hotels. If Broadfoot refused, the pimp beat her: 'I was a child. I was terrified. I had no choice'.

During the 15 years she was prostituted, Broadfoot experienced horrific violence, abuse and humiliation at the hands of her pimp and punters. 'I was once driven 70 miles out of London by a punter who held me in a semi-derelict house and raped, beat and tortured me for an hour', she wrote. 'I got away from him by spraying perfume in his face and running naked into the street.'

Eventually, Broadfoot was rescued by two passers-by who gave her clothes and drove her back to London. 'My pimp told me to wash the blood away, stop crying and get back to work', Broadfoot wrote. 'He said getting back on the streets was like riding a horse after a fall, and that unless I get back up there I would never ride again.'

Broadfoot did as she was told. Eleven years later, in June 1995, Broadfoot saw a mugshot of her 17-year-old cousin Maureen Stepan flash up on her TV screen. Stepan, also prostituted and addicted to heroin, had been brutally murdered by a punter. Broadfoot left the sex trade, vowing to raise awareness among the general public about the realities of prostitution.

At the Brighton conference, which was the beginning of her public activism, Broadfoot spoke at a workshop with Andrea Dworkin and another woman called Irene Ivison.

Ivison, a middle-class peace activist who described herself to me as 'a bit like a mother out of an Enid Blyton tale', had met Broadfoot at a meeting in Bradford about prostitution. A few months before the Brighton conference, Ivison had set up the Coalition for the Removal of Pimping (CROP). Three years earlier, Ivison's daughter, also called Fiona, had been murdered at the age of 17 by a punter, having been pimped into prostitution by her older 'boyfriend'. Ivison had spent the previous three years battling with police and social services to try and stop the abusive relationship in which her daughter had been involved since the age of 14, but no-one intervened. It was only after her daughter's death that Ivison learned Fiona had been prostituted three weeks before her murder. In 1997, Ivison's book about her daughter, *Fiona's Story*,[14] was published. It won praise from professionals and activists in the area of child protection and criminal justice.

The 1996 Brighton conference gave birth to the UK-based survivor-led abolitionist movement in the UK. In 1997, Jalna Hanmer, the director of the Violence, Abuse and Gender Relations Unit, whose brainchild the Brighton conference was, asked me to work with her in

---

[14]Irene Ivison, 1997, *Fiona's Story: A Tragedy of Our Times.*

organising the first UK-based conference that named prostitution as violence against women and girls, at which several survivors attended and spoke, including Emma Humphreys.

The media went berserk with excitement, because tackling the punters provided a fresh angle on reporting prostitution-related stories and events. The BBC shadowed the organisers in the build-up to the first course, and in December 1998 it aired a 50-minute documentary on the scheme.[15] National newspapers such as *the Guardian, Independent* and *Observer* ran in-depth pieces on it, and it was regularly featured in local newspapers and radio programmes.

There was also an immediate and massive backlash to the scheme from the 'sex workers' rights' lobby as soon as word got out about our plans, which was a full year before the first course was held. I detail this backlash and its ramifications in Chap. 5, 'The Invisible Man'.

The Opposition

The English Collective of Prostitutes (ECP) was extremely active during the following years, while the abolitionist movement was less active and received no funding whatsoever. However, one feminist organisation provided the space and resources from which to conduct research, influence policy, and campaign against the efforts to decriminalise the entire sex trade and to rewrite prostitution as work. Eaves Housing for Women[16] began life as a homelessness action in the 1970s, and had provided housing for me when I moved to London in 1987. Denise Marshall became chief executive of Eaves in 2000 and was a staunch abolitionist. Within Eaves, Marshall set up the very first support and housing service for women trafficked into the UK.

In 2004 I made the decision to leave academia, and had just submitted my final piece of research on behalf of The Child and Woman Abuse Studies Unit at London Metropolitan University, which

---

[15]1998. *Modern Times: Paying For It.* UK, BBC2.

[16]Eaves, supporting vulnerable women who have experienced violence. Eavesforwomen.org.uk. Retrieved 16 June 2017, from http://www.eavesforwomen.org.uk/.

examined the links between lap dancing clubs and prostitution. Marshall contacted me and asked if I would agree to be employed on a part-time consultancy basis at Eaves for a period of no more than six months. The government had recently published a consultation document on the sex trade and Marshall wanted me to write the response on behalf of Eaves. I readily agreed: it was going to be difficult transition area between leaving a full-time position and breaking into freelance journalism full time. Marshall asked if I would help build up the research and policy side of Eaves. The main focus for Eaves until then had been running the services for trafficked women. The majority of the funding was for this, and for services such as housing legal support and counselling for women experiencing other forms of male violence.

I remained a consultant at Eaves for 11 years. During that time, I, along with others, conducted several pieces of research on various aspects of the sex trade. Marshall and I shared the same outlook: we did not want to focus only on the horrors of international pimping, or trafficking as it is more widely known, and believed it to be crucial to look at local sex markets to highlight the fact that the only difference between international and local pimping is that some women are pimped across borders, and others are not.

Sex trafficking is an embarrassment to the pro-prostitution lobby in the same way that lung cancer is to the tobacco industry. Despite claims to the opposite, feminist abolitionists do not 'rely' on scaremongering about the numbers of trafficking victims, or exaggerate the extent of the abuse and violence they endure.

Rachel Moran, a sex trade survivor from the Republic of Ireland, author of the best selling political memoir *Paid For: My Journey through Prostitution*,[17] and founder of SPACE International (Survivors of Prostitution Abuse Calling for Enlightenment)[18] is opposed to the idea of presenting all prostitution as sex trafficking: 'It's a wrongheaded political strategy. I'd never get on board with that. To begin with, it suggests that prostitution itself is not the problem. Prostitution is exactly the problem'.

---

[17]Moran, R. (2013.) *Paid For: My Journey Through Prostition*, London: WW Norton & Co.

[18]Space International. Spaceintl.org. Retrieved 16 June 2017, from http://www.spaceintl.org/.

From the moment I arrived at Eaves, both Marshall and I were on the receiving end of hostility from the pro-prostitution lobby. Every piece of research we published was publicly criticised by academics and service providers who did not like our focus on the dangers inherent to prostitution. However, Eaves became the engine room from which the London abolitionist movement would flourish. In 2005, I invited the writer and campaigner Andrea Dworkin to speak at an evening event at Eaves. The room was packed with as many women standing as there were sitting, all listening to Dworkin speak of the early campaigns against the normalisation of prostitution.

'It was only at that meeting, hearing Andrea speak, that I realised there wasn't actually an abolitionist movement in the UK as such', said Marshall to me in an interview a year after Dworkin's visit.[19] 'Yes there were events, research, protests and various things that were more endemic to the anti-violence against women's movement, [but] there was nothing coordinated. There was no umbrella movement. Like the anti-rape movement, we needed an abolitionist movement that had its own identity and direction.'

As with the campaigns against domestic violence, rape and child sexual abuse, survivors lead the way in setting up such organisations and movements. As a rule, feminist activists tend not to be 'do-gooders' as many liberals tend to be. The very women who experience the oppression of male sexual violence are the ones who then lead the fight to end it.

Sex Trade 101[20] was founded by Natasha Falle and Bridget Perrier in 2007. Both women are survivors of the sex trade and Bridget Perrier is Native Canadian. I meet Perrier in New York City at a SPACE International members meeting. Perrier is full of energy and verve, and passionately proud of her Indigenous culture. Having been abused into prostitution as a child, Perrier eventually was given support to leave and attend college. Having volunteered for a Native organisation that helped abused women, Perrier was nominated for The Woman of Distinction Turning Point award in 2006 by the local YWCA.

---

[19]Denise Marshall died in 2015 of stomach cancer.

[20]Sextrade101.com - Public Awareness and Education. Sextrade101.com. Retrieved 16 June 2017, from http://www.sextrade101.com/.

'This is when I knew I was an activist', says Perrier. 'I won the award. I was recognised for my good behaviour, finally. I knew that I still was different from those women even though I idolised a few of them. I'd written this speech and it took me months. I'm the only one in Toronto YWCA woman of distinction alumni that ever received a standing ovation in the middle of her speech. They would say "What did you do?" and they'd hear "Bridgett Perrier escaped from the clutches of prostitution". If they had only seen me when I was back in that place, they would never have given me the award'.

'In my speech I said that my award was for every prostituted woman who I knew that was murdered and I said their names, so the first minute was names from across Canada. The Mayor of Toronto was in tears, he didn't know what the hell to do. I could see the YWCA staff running back and forth and looking at their speech that they had. They couldn't turn on the music or do anything because the audience was captivated. That day I knew, they wouldn't remember Bridget Perrier the bad girl, they would remember Bridget Perrier the woman that beat the odds.'

Perrier met up with Natasha Falle at another meeting, and they made an instant connection. 'I ran into her at the organisation where she was running a diversion programme', says Perrier. 'It was like it was meant to be. Later, Natasha called me up and said, "I have an idea". She told me her vision for Sex Trade 101. We wanted only survivors in management positions.'

Removing the Mask from the SWR Movement

A number of survivors and other abolitionists have long suspected that those prominent in the media and the 'sex workers' rights' movement who claim to be involved in the sex trade are fudging the truth. The pro-prostitution lobby includes pimps, brothel owners and other third-party exploiters in their use of the term 'sex worker'—they do so because in their view facilitating exploitation is a viable job, and if in fact it were it would be technically correct for those profiting from prostituted women and men to label themselves as such.

It turns out the suspicions of survivors and others were right. It has been proven that pro-prostitution lobbyists blatantly lie about their role in the sex trade during debates and other events.

Janice Raymond, the feminist academic and leading abolitionst, recalls an article written by survivor, activist and scholar Jane Anthony, who published an article in *Ms Magazine* in 1992 entitled 'Prostitution As 'Choice',[21] in which she examined the membership of COYOTE.

'Jane was the first person to look at who actually was in prostitution in that organisation. She found a book written by Valerie Jeness,[22] a pro-sex work academic. It reveals that nobody in COYOTE had been in prostitution, including Priscilla Alexander and Margot St James, other than taking dinners from boyfriends in college.

'So Jane took a lot of that evidence that was in the Jeness book and wrote about it from the viewpoint of a survivor who really understood what was happening here and how these organisations that claimed to represent women and prostitution were actually professional, institutionalised, public relations groups for legalising prostitution.'

In her article, Anthony explains that that pro-prostitution ideology, often considered sexual liberalism, ignores the fact that women's choices are restricted by patriarchy, and therefore inadvertently trivialises prostitution. Anthony also calls into question those who see prostitution as a form of empowerment for women:

> COYOTE claims to be not only representative of prostitutes' voices, but constituent of them as well. Indeed, one of COYOTE's by-laws is that only active prostitutes can vote on organisational issues.[23]

> By the end of 1974, COYOTE boasted a membership of over 10,000 (Matzger 1975; Reinholz 1974), and by 1981 COYOTE leaders claimed to have 30,000 members, 3 percent of whom were active prostitutes. Consistent with these reports, both the mainstream and the so-called alternative media have presented the prostitutes' rights movement in a way that implies the presence of prostitutes in the various organizations.

---

[21]Anthony, J. (1992.) *Prostitution as 'choice'*. Ms. Magazine. 86–87.
[22]Jenness, V. (1993). *Making it work*. New York, NY: Aldine De Gruyter.
[23]Anthony, J. (1992.) *Prostitution as 'choice'*. Ms. Magazine. 86–87.

The media have referred to COYOTE as a 'self-proclaimed prostitutes' union', 'a national organisation of hookers', 'the biggest pros group in the US', 'the first prostitutes' guild', 'the first prostitutes' union', 'a hookers' union', 'a hookers' organisation', and a 'prostitutes' trade union'. Labels such as these strongly imply that COYOTE is an organisation of and for prostitutes.[24]

From Liberal to Abolitionist

Abolitionists face bullying, slander and even ostracisation from many so-called feminist and leftist organisations and friendship groups. Despite this, many are brave enough to defy the status quo and stand up for what they believe is right. For some, it means a public reversal of their position on the sex trade.

Meghan Murphy is a feminist activist and writer based in Vancouver, Canada. She began blogging under her site *Feminist Current*[25] in 2008, and went on to study for a BA and MA in Women's Studies in Vancouver. At first Murphy was drawn towards the pro-lobby debate, but meeting survivors who were active in the abolitionist movement soon changed that: 'The way that you learn to discuss these issues in university is with nuance and to not have an opinion and to look for empowerment as opposed to victimisation, they really push that. I didn't realise that was what they were doing at the time, but in retrospect', says Murphy. 'I remember doing my BA and thinking, "I'm going to find prostitutes who are empowered when I start my research", because that's what [the university] encourages you to do.'

Soon Murphy came face-to-face with the reality of the sex trade, after meeting survivors and other abolitionists who patiently explained how mythology around the issue is very persuasive. 'I started learning about the issues more and I knew about the debates', says Murphy.

For her blog *Feminist Current*, Murphy interviewed Trisha Baptie, a sex trade survivor from Vancouver, who, post-exit at the age of 28,

---

[24]COYOTE, Retrieved 28 Aug 2017, from http://www.coyotela.org/
[25]Feminist Current. Retrieved 16 June 2017, from http://www.feministcurrent.com/.

became a citizen journalist for *Orato*, an online newspaper to cover the murder trial of Robert Pickton, a serial killer of prostituted women.[26]

'I also met Cherry Smiley, an indigenous Canadian feminist abolitionist. Any doubts that I had around what I felt about prostitution were no longer there once I had talked to Trisha and Cherry', says Murphy. 'After learning about how Aboriginal women are over represented and how European men came over and put women in brothels, and understanding about the missing and murdered women,[27] to me there was no doubt in my mind that it was about inequality and racism and poverty and about misogyny. I couldn't understand why others didn't see things that way. If you're a progressive person and you care about human beings naturally you'll see that this is unacceptable.'

Sarah Ditum is a writer and feminist activist based in the UK. In 2012 she took part in a debate on the porn industry with Gail Dines,[28] entitled 'Is Porn Hijacking Our Sexuality?'[29]

As is clear from the following extract of her article, at the time of writing, Ditum obviously considered pornography to be potentially liberating for women: 'There were two key things I had to understand before I changed my mind about the sex trade', says Ditum. 'The first is that being in prostitution (or being a prostitute or sex worker, as I would have thought of it then) isn't a sexuality: there isn't a group called 'prostitutes' who will sell sex regardless of conditions and must be kept as safe as possible.'

Ditum came to understand that prostitution is always about the sex buyers' desires, never about the desires of the prostituted. 'There's a lot of cultural conditioning telling us that female sexuality is naturally submissive, and that women's authentic desires are to do what men want

---

[26]Baptie, T. (2007, Dec 6.) At the Pickton trial: A personal notebook. The Tyee. Retrieved 16 June 2017, from https://thetyee.ca/Life/2007/12/06/PicktonTrial/.

[27]https://www.theguardian.com/world/2005/aug/05/features11.g2.

[28]Ditum, S, (2012, 6 April.) *Pornwars! A New Left Project debate with Gail Dines*. Retrieved 16 June 2017, from https://sarahditum.com/2012/04/06/pornwars-a-new-left-project-debate-with-gail-dines/.

[29]Ditum, S. (2012, April 2.) *Is porn hijacking our sexuality?* (Part 1). Newleftproject.org. Retrieved 16 June 2017, from http://www.newleftproject.org/index.php/site/article_comments/porn_hijacking_our_sexuality.

them to', says Ditum. 'That's the nature of prostitution, and its defenders elide sexual exploitation and sexual pleasure. But tolerating what someone else pays to do to you isn't pleasure, obviously: it's abuse.'

Another feminist who has changed her approach to prostitution in recent years is the journalist Renate Van Der Zee, based in the Netherlands. I first met Van der Zee in 2012 on a research trip to Amsterdam. I was put in contact with her by a colleague who was aware that she had recently written a book on trafficking of women into the sex trade. At that time Van Der Zee was not an abolitionist; rather she made quite a stark distinction between trafficking and other forms of prostitution. How did her shift in perception happen?

'I've always been writing about freedom of women', Van der Zee says. 'I wrote a book about honour killing and articles about incest in a Moroccan family. Then I started thinking about what is the worst thing that can happen to a woman, and thought "being a sex slave and being a victim of human trafficking".'

After Van der Zee published her book on trafficking, she began to think that perhaps there was much more that she had not uncovered in the local sex trade near to where she lives in Dan Haag. 'I was thinking, "if this is what goes on in the sex trade, I need to take a broader look at prostitution per se". Then I started realising there is no such thing as free prostitution, it just doesn't exist', she says. 'That was such a new thing for me, a totally new thing for me. Then I decided to write a book about it. In 2013, *De Waarheid Achter de Wallen* (The Truth Behind the Red Light District) was published, which takes a fresh, critical look at what is happening in the sex trade.'

Until recently, very little attention has been paid to the punters in legalised regimes, such as Holland. Van der Zee decided to correct this by writing a book on the demand for prostitution[30] entitled *Mannen Die Seks Kopen* (Men who Buy Sex), which was published in 2015.

'There is a consensus now between policymakers and people from the shelters and even people who are pro-legalisation 'that legalisation hasn't worked out', says Van Der Zee. 'It hasn't made the situation better for prostitutes and it hasn't done anything in the field of stopping

---

[30]Zee, R. (2015.) *Mannen Die Seks Kopen*. Amsterdam: Uitgeverij SWP.

trafficking. Everybody agrees with that. The people who are pro-legalisation are saying what we need is to make legalisation perfect.'

I asked Van der Zee what she thinks, if anything, could be done to improve legalisation so that it is effective. 'Nothing', she replied. 'It is a flawed system.'

When we met in 2012, Van Der Zee considered legalisation to be the best option. Today she is an abolitionist and has so far organised two conferences in the Dutch Parliament that have enabled a discussion about the failures of legalisation, the possibility of introducing the Nordic model, and creating a sea change within a culture that has been brainwashed by promises from the Government, aided by pro-prostitution groups and pimps, that legalisation would remove the problems inherent to the sex trade.

'Five years ago it would have been unthinkable to have an abolitionist movement in this country, but today it is growing and on the way to thriving', says Van der Zee, smiling widely.

Abolitionist Feminists Living Under Legalisation/ Decriminalisation

The same can be said for Germany. In December 2014, Kommunikationszentrum für Frau Arbeits (KOFRA), the feminist abolitionist group based in Munich, organised the international congress 'Stop Sexbuying' for the abolition of prostitution. The position taken by the congress was that prostitution is an obstacle to equality and prostitution is violence against women. Three hundred delegates attended, many of whom were staunch abolitionists, and some who were unsure of their position but were only too aware of the well-deserved reputation that Germany has earned in recent years of being 'the brothel of Europe'.[31]

---

[31]Schon, M (2016, May 9.) *Legalization has turned Germany into the 'Bordello of Europe" and we should be ashamed.* Feminist Current. Retrieved 16 June 2017, from http://www.feministcurrent.com/2016/05/09/legalization-has-turned-germany-into-the-bordello-of-europe-we-should-be-ashamed/.

I had been unable to attend the Congress but a year later visited the feminist organisation that had organised it. I wanted to hear about the origins of the new abolitionist movement in Germany.

I travelled to Munich with Rachel Moran, who was launching the German edition of *Paid For* at the Women's Centre. For Moran, the Munich Congress was one of the most important events in the contemporary abolitionist movement. Moran recalls sitting on a panel with other speakers, one of whom described the brothels in Germany that advertise deals where the buyer pays a flat rate for a burger, beer and 'as many fucks as he can manage'. Another spoke of the case of a 19-year old, heavily pregnant woman who was hired for a gang-bang in a German brothel by six men, four of whom wore horror masks. One woman talked about women she knew who had been used by 60 men a day. 'I tore up my speech. It had become meaningless', says Moran. 'I was raging and only spoke for about three minutes. I was very close to the edge of losing my temper and finished by shouting, "You've GOT to stop this or your country will pay for it in the annals of history!"'

Moran added: 'You know, I've spoken in over 20 countries across the world and I've seen a lot of different reactions from audiences, and oftentimes there will be patterns in those reactions, but that is the one single time I've seen a quarter of the audience spontaneously burst into tears in the same moment. The German activists know the hell that's happening in their country and it is breaking their hearts'.

Women attended the conference from numerous neighbouring countries, including those with similar laws such as Austria and Switzerland. 'Women poured into that conference from all over Europe, but there were also a lot of German women', says Moran. 'This was the beginning of a new movement. The dam had burst and there was no going back from it.'

Huschke Mau is one of a growing number who believe that legalisation in Germany has been a disaster. She, along with a politician and a social worker, has founded Sisters e V,[32] a new anti-prostitution organisation which helps women to exit the sex trade.

---

[32]Die linke Freude an der Prostitution - Huschke Mau an die Bremer Linksjugend. On Sisters-ev. de. Retrieved 16 June 2017, from http://sisters-ev.de/2016/04/21/die-linke-freude-an-der-prostitution-huschke-mau/.

Mau, who spent 10 years in prostitution before finding a way out in 2012, said that she struggled to find the kind of support that Sisters offers. 'I was in an advice centre in my town, and I told them that I couldn't stand it anymore and that I wanted to get out. And they said, "What's your problem? It's an okay job, why don't you just stop going to the brothel?"'

Hydra Berlin,[33] a pro-prostitution advice group founded 35 years ago, argues that it already offers counselling for women in the sex trade. It considers Sisters to be a missionary service that 'rescues' women and sits in moral judgement of them.

Manuela Schon is one of the founding members of Abolition 2014, an organisation made up of survivors, leftist activists, members of the Green and Social Democrat parties, feminist activists and journalists. Its main activity is awareness raising, and it organises a series of public events and hosts speakers who are experts on the sex trade, geared in particular towards dispelling the myths surrounding it.

A feminist activist and sociologist who does counselling in her free time, Schon began to be involved in abolitionist politics through her voluntary work counselling unemployed people, in particular Roma families that had been shunned by the welfare state. 'I could see the racism and exploitation as well as economic coercion they were subjected to', says Schon.

Schon is also co-founder of Linke gegen Prostitution (members of the left party against prostitution), which she says is gaining support from members of local municipalities as well as parliamentarians. Schon has represented the organisation in Spain, Germany, Norway and other countries and tells me that the abolitionist movement is stronger now in Germany than it ever has been. Despite this progress, there is still some significant opposition within the country.

'My feminist group within the German left party wrote a paper that the party did not like so much', says Schon. 'We got into serious problems because the party is very much pro- "sex work" and almost all women from my group left the party in the end, leaving only me and one other.'

---

[33]Hydra Berlin. Retrieved 16 June 2017, from http://www.hydra-berlin.de/startseite/.

Helping Others See the Problem

Autumn Burris is a SPACE International representative, and spends much of her time educating police officers, social workers and anyone else who wishes to improve their knowledge and practice in dealing with prostituted women and the men who buy them. I had got to know Burris at the SPACE summit in New York in October 2014. We meet again in Los Angeles where I was attending the Porn Awards the following year, to explore the links between pornography and the wider sex trade, as well as the growing number of queer-identified women and men who were both producing and featuring in pornography. Burris has been doing this work since 1997, shortly after she exited the sex trade. I asked how she became involved in the abolitionist movement.

'I was speaking at the UN [United Nations] in December 2012 on a panel in preparation for CSW [Commission on the Status of Women]', says Burris. 'Everyone had a business card, everyone had a logo and they assumed I was a consultant [as a trainer in survivor issues]. A friend of mine had been telling me I should start to do my work on a professional basis—i.e. get paid for it. I said, "Oh no, no, I don't want to go into business, I don't want the responsibility". She got really angry with me and she said, "You work 16 hours a day, and on top of that you're paying to work". She said "I'm going to give you some seed money and you're going to get started whether you like it or not".'

For Burris, funding for survivors to carry out this work does not dissolve its radical edge, but rather enables women with direct experience of the sex trade to build alliances with those who can support the abolitionist movement from positions of influence.

'I think the survivor movement is continuing to shift in positive ways', says Burris. 'When we unite as survivors and when we have allies that are supportive, respectful, inclusive alongside us, we have power and momentum. Every action I take is based on the person who's still being exploited right now.'

From Prostitution, to Pimping, to Abolition

For the majority of women in the sex trade, there is no promotion in their so-called job. In fact, the usual trajectory is downhill, as the physical and mental health consequences take their toll. Some women end up running brothels in order to stop being prostitued. Kathleen Mitchell is one such woman.

Mitchell escaped prostitution in 1989. Born in 1943 into a strict Catholic household, she experienced child sexual abuse, the death of a sibling and, as a direct result of that tragedy, an angry, alcoholic mother. As a way to escape her unhappy life, Mitchell married a man she did not love and who was violent. In 1968, she left her husband for a man who promised to take care of her.

'He tells me that I didn't deserve to live like that, I deserve to be treated well and that he would never lie to me', says Mitchell when I meet her in a hotel in Minnesota, USA, where we are both attending an abolitionist conference. 'I hated him at first. I didn't like him because I had a friend who was my best friend all through school and [he got her] into prostitution. I knew he was a pimp when I met him, but then fell deeply in love with him [over a period of] three years. He was always good to me. He had other women, but he did not tell me that. For a long time I did not realise that his mother had been a prostitute.'

After three years of what Mitchell describes as 'brainwashing', she was 'turned out' by her boyfriend and remained in prostitution for 21 years. 'I never got into drugs, I never got into alcohol. What I got into was a lifestyle. The lifestyle of having all kinds of money, all kinds of jewellery, to having Cadillacs, to having mink coats, to having everything that any rich person would ever buy.

'I'm going to go back to the time I got raped. I came home—[the rapist] took all my money and I had to tell [my husband] that he took all my money, [and my husband] told me, "You gave my pussy away". So not only was I raped and had all my money taken, but [my husband] was mad at me and wasn't talking to me for two weeks.'

Mitchell could take no more so began pimping. 'Instead of turning any more tricks I went to the point of having escort services and massage parlours. There was one time I had 17 escort services and four massage parlours. I was running them and sending women out to do what I couldn't do anymore. Did I keep the money? No, [my husband] got every dime of it.

'We kept having our escort service busted. So then I got charged with illegal operation of a business, operating without a license and the promotion of prostitution through *Yellow Pages*. [My husband] ended up getting two years in jail, and I got three years probation because I coughed [up] to it.'

In 1989, having tried to go straight, Mitchell was convicted of running another brothel and spent six months in jail, during which time all of her possessions were stolen. 'While I was there I kept watching women go in and out—the revolving door of prostitution—in and out for the same thing. They had AA and other stuff for women in jail but they didn't have anything for my problem, which was the money and prostitution. So I started a programme in jail with the jail coordinator and we called it DIGNITY (Developing Individual Growth and New Independence Through Yourself).

'It started with two or three women but we ended up with 26–30 in a group. It was just amazing. I got to know all the police down there. They all supported me. They would leave me alone with whatever. I had a lot of support from the police department and the Sheriff's department. After I got out, I kept talking to women and did street outreach. I went to school and got my degree in counselling. When I got off probation I was the first women ever to be able go back to jail to work with the women. This programme kept going all the time I was there.'

I meet Daniel Cormier at the feminist organisation Vancouver Rape Relief (VRR) in 2015. Cormier was born and raised in Quebec and became estranged from her family as a result of their anti-lesbian bigotry towards her. Still in her teens, Cornier found herself street homeless. In her early 20s, she became involved in prostitution.

'Having already had a life that had taught me, through various experiences, that my body could be had by anyone who wanted it basically', says Cormier, 'I figured like many do that I might as well pay the rent.'

What kept Cormier locked in prostitution was poverty, and the lack of any support to exit. 'Not one single person ever said to me, "What's happening to you is not OK with me". I remember waiting for it almost like holding my breath, every time I met a new social worker or whatever. If one person had said, "How about we talk about other options?" I think I might have exited sooner.'

Eventually, Cormier decided to run her own escort agency as a way to 'leave' prostitution. 'Me and other women who were working in the agency decided to leave and start our own outfit. At the time my mentality was, "I can do this better. I can do this fairer, charging the minimum and not being an arsehole about it". We took care of each other. After a few months it didn't make sense to me and it was repeating the same behaviours. No matter how I spun it I couldn't feel good about it', says Cormier. 'So I stopped doing that. I'm telling you this because it kept me silent for a long time. I carried a lot of shame about that and still do a little bit.'

According to Rachel Moran, much was made by the pro-prostitution lobby of the fact that one of SPACE International's first Irish members, Justine Riley, had a brothel keeping conviction between October 1999 and March 2000. Riley spent a total of 17 years in prostitution, and had started operating brothels in a brief period in order to escape being bought and sold herself.

'She joined our group over a decade later, in 2012, two years after she had finally gotten out of prostitution', says Moran. 'Hers is a familiar story. What I find remarkable is that the people who try to smear our reputation as an organisation on the back of her conviction are the very same people who say that brothel keeping should be decriminalised. In their own view of the situation, Justine did nothing wrong, which is not a view shared by either Justine or ourselves. In an incredible example of double-speak, they are castigating her—and by extension us—for criminal behaviour that they say should not be criminalised at all!'

Policing and Criminal Sanctions

A common consensus among the pro-prostitution lobby is that feminist abolitionists are either dismissive of, or do not care about, criminal sanctions on women in prostitution, or police violence, abuse and corruption. This is a clear misrepresentation of the facts.

Audrey Morrissey is the Associate Director of My Life, My Choice,[34] a survivor-led organisation supporting prostituted young people in Boston, USA. 'The very first car that I got in was with a police officer, who showed me his badge and asked me to give him a blow job. That was my first encounter', says Morrissey. 'I hear this story everywhere I go in the world, so I always encourage the girls to go to the police station and ask for a female officer if they are in trouble.'

Bridget Perrier says: 'I never thought I would ever align myself with the police. Now we have to train law enforcement officers. They are on the frontline, so they need to understand that women are human beings and they are not bad'.

The Asian Women Coalition Ending Prostitution (AWCEP)[35] is based in Montreal, Canada. I met with the group during a visit in the Autumn of 2015, and asked how they work alongside law enforcement. The group's objective, says one member, is to force the local council and the police to fulfil their obligations to protect women and girls by enforcing the new laws.

'In different cities and at different times in Canada there have been calls to create red light districts or tolerant zones', she said. 'There've always been official and unofficial city management [programmes] regarding prostitution. Arresting only the women and girls and letting it be known that if the Johns cruise women [in] specific parts of town [the industrial area and strip clubs or Asian massage parlours] they won't have to worry about the police.'

Giobbe believes that for the movement to survive against the more powerful 'sex workers' rights' lobby, women need to take to the streets and reclaim the old radicalism that has been replaced with fun feminism. 'I look at what we did in the past. I remember giant Take Back the Night rallies that are now called Slutwalks, for God's sake. I could have died when I heard that.'

---

[34]Fighting Exploitation: My Life, My Choice. On Fighting Exploitation. Retrieved 16 June 2017, from http://www.fightingexploitation.org/.

[35]Asian Women Coalition Ending Prostitution. Retrieved 16 June 2017, from http://awcep.org/.

As I am leaving the sisterly warmth of VRR,[36] having met with and interviewed a number of survivors, Daniel Cornier tells me: 'My dream is to have [women] live in a world where they're not seen as a commodity. Period. Where every billboard doesn't tell them to show their breasts and their bones and their midriffs and then accuse them of doing the exact thing and then tell them it's their fault if they're objectified. I would love that so much. I've actually thought of moving to Sweden. But I think it's more important to stay put and fight for it here.'

Abolitionists have a goal: to bring about an end to the global sex trade, and to inhabit a world where no woman, man or child is prostituted—a world where sex is not bought, sold or brokered. As we will see in subsequent chapters, the abolitionist movement is emerging in New Zealand, and also within those states in Australia where the sex trade is legalised.

Why does this sound so crazy to so many people? In Chap. 2 we enter the world of the 'sex workers' rights' lobby, learn its history, goals and tactics. Who are the leaders in this movement? What motivates them to campaign to normalise and decriminalise the global oppression of women and girls?

---

[36]Vancouver Rape Relief & Women's Shelter. Retrieved 16 June 2017, from http://www.rapereliefshelter.bc.ca/.

2

The 'Sex Workers' Rights' Movement

With or without external supporters I have 3 million sex workers behind me. (Irina Maslova, leader of the 'sex worker movement' Silver Rose, Russia, 2015)

I don't foresee a situation where there will be no sex workers – in Kenya, in Africa, in the world – because there is demand for it. Sex is a human right, whether it's free or there's monetary considerations. (Penina Mwangi, Executive Director, Bar Hostess Empowerment and Support Programme, Kenya, 2015)

The contemporary 'sex worker's rights' movement is made up of a number of perspectives and positions, but the various strands have one core view in common: a passionate dislike of any legal or State intervention. This is a shift from the 1980s and 1990s, when the movement was united in supporting legalisation, such as the Dutch and German models. Today, most Sex Workers' Rights Activists (SWRAs) oppose legalisation, with the exception of a number of activists in Germany, the Netherlands, and Nevada in the USA. But even in those areas, where the off-street sex trade is fully legalised, the system is staunchly criticised by those who wish to see an end to any regulation at all. Therefore, New Zealand, which has fully decriminalised all aspects of the sex trade (see Chap. 1 for a description of the various legal regimes) has become the preferred model.

© The Author(s) 2017
J. Bindel, *The Pimping of Prostitution*,
DOI 10.1057/978-1-137-55890-9_2

Supporters of legalisation often cite the Netherlands as a shining example. For a number of years, beginning immediately after the sex trade was legalised there in 2000, delegations were brought from the Netherlands to elsewhere in Europe to sell the model. More recently, and especially since decriminalisation was introduced in New Zealand in 2003, the SWRAs are unlikely to admit that their side of the political fence ever supported legalisation and criticise the regime for being over-regulated.

Since its inception, the 'sex workers' rights' movement has been successful in identifying key issues and problems faced by women in prostitution, such as police violence and harassment, and social stigma. During its early days, as we will see in this chapter, the movement was led by socialist women who had a class, rather than gendered, analysis of prostitution, but who genuinely fought for better 'working' conditions and rights for the most disenfranchised women in the sex trade.

The History

The term 'sex work' was coined in the early 1980s by Carol Leigh and was popularised by a 1987 anthology of the same name.

As she describes in *The Prostitution Papers*,[1] the feminist icon Kate Millett was at a 1971 women's liberation movement conference at which some SWRAs became very angry with the feminists there. They became particularly enraged when a panel entitled 'Towards the Elimination of Prostitution' was organised including 'everyone but prostitutes'. Things rapidly degenerated into chaos. Prostitutes had gathered their still nebulous rage against their own lives and redirected it towards the movement of women who appeared to be summarily 'eliminating' prostitution: aka the means of their livelihood. The argument became so heated that a physical fight broke out.

In the mid-1970s, Helen Buckingham[2] promoted herself as the main spokesperson for women in the sex trade in Britain. Buckingham has

---

[1]Kate Millett, 1971, *The Prostitution Papers*.
[2]Real name, Bridget Allerdyce.

been described as a 'high-class call girl'[3] and claimed to have a number of regular, wealthy punters. In 1975 she was declared bankrupt by the Inland Revenue, which demanded tax from her earnings in prostitution. Buckingham argued that if she was required to pay tax, she must be allowed to work legally. Buckingham founded a group PUSSI (Prostitutes United for Social and Sexual Integration) which later changed to PLAN (Prostitution Laws are Nonsense) and allied herself to Selma James, founder of the International Wages for Housework Campaign, which demands money from the government for women's unwaged work in the home. Together they founded the English Collective of Prostitutes (ECP) in 1975.

In the early days, the ECP were abolitionists. The aims and objectives of James and her colleagues were clear: women should be paid for all labour, including housework and sex. 'For prostitutes, against prostitution', was its mantra. The ECP positioned itself as part of the working-class movement for more money and less work. They referred to the introduction of the kerb crawling law as 'the new suss law' ('suss' is the abbreviation for a stop and search law in England and Wales that permitted a police officer to stop, search and potentially arrest people on suspicion of having committed a crime).

Meanwhile, the prostitutes' rights movement in Europe was launched in Lyon, France, in 1975, when French prostitutes occupied a church in protest at the way in which they were treated by the police. They went on strike to protest against the savage police repression and corruption in Lyon, which had been experiencing a wave of brutal murders of prostitutes.

Margaret Valentino and Mavis Johnson of the ECP provide an introduction to the volume of life stories of French women involved in the strike, and an analysis setting out the ECP position. They explain that: 'Prostitution was one way women had been fighting to get paid for housework—by getting paid for all the sexual services all women are always expected to give for free'.[4] The cause of prostitution was 'poverty and women's refusal of poverty', and 'the end of women's poverty is

---

[3]http://journals.sagepub.com/doi/full/10.1177/2158244016679474

[4]Valentino & Johnson, 1980, *The dark net*, p. 25.

the end of prostitution'. The ECP approach was abolitionist rather than celebratory. Rather than arguing that 'sex work' is empowering or even enjoyable, the ECP saw it as exploitation, the same as they did for all labour under capitalism.

COYOTE (Call Off Your Old Tired Ethics) was founded in the USA out of WHO (Whores, Housewives and Others) in 1973 by Margo St James, who described herself as an ex-prostitute. St James was given money by the Point Foundation at Glide Memorial Church, San Francisco, and later received $1000 dollars from the Playboy Foundation. St James recruited 50 high-profile individuals to form the COYOTE advisory board, as well as prostituted women to campaign for decriminalisation. Interested parties, including students, sex buyers, politicians, media personnel, activists and representatives from other advocacy organisations were invited and encouraged to become members of COYOTE.

In 1976, COYOTE filed a lawsuit against Rhode Island. In the case of *COYOTE v. Roberts*, the argument was based on how much power the state should have to control the sexual activity of its citizens. The lawsuit also alleged discrimination on how the law was being applied. Data was submitted that demonstrated selective prosecution as the Providence Police were arresting female 'sex workers' far more often than their male customers. St James testified in the case. Although the case was eventually dismissed when the General Assembly changed the prostitution statute in 1980, COYOTE and St James are given credit for contributing to the decriminalisation of prostitution in Rhode Island.

St James attended a number of international conferences throughout the 1970s, promoting the view that prostitution is 'liberating' and should be decriminalised and viewed as 'work'.

Fundraising involved an annual hosting of the well-attended Hookers' Ball, which nabbed 20,000 attendees in 1978. Cherie Jimenez, an abolitionist campaigner and survivor of the sex trade, recalls the annual event. 'For several years I remember doing the so called Hookers' Ball', she told me. 'A costume party at a club in Cambridge that was also raising money for PUMA [Prostitute's Union of Massachusetts]. There was a bail fund for women, I do remember that. I still know some of these women, and we continue to argue our positions.'

Valerie Jennes writes in her book on COYOTE[5]: 'As one newspaper stated, "It was something between the 1906 earthquake and fire, and the opening of the opera"'.[6] *The Chicago Tribune* reported: 'For the press it was an orgy. They filmed, photographed and interviewed anyone who was generous with her eyeshadow'.[7] More locally, the *San Francisco Chronicle* described the events as 'wild masquerades that drew the kind of people who really knew how to party [and that became] legendary, even though they only lasted a few years'.[8] The tide was turning from politics to glamour.

Unsurprisingly, COYOTE soon began to be lauded by the liberal male elite. Jennes records that in the first year of COYOTE's existence, the *Seattle Post Intelligencer* reported: 'Margo is "in" socially this year. Well-to-do liberals invite her to things and seek her company'.

The movement had become less about workers' rights, and more about 'happy hookers'.

Former 'sex worker' Xaviera Hollander claims credit for coining the term 'happy hooker', although it is likely it was thought up by Robin Moore, who co-authored the bestselling book of the same name about Hollander's life. The book went on to be an international bestseller, was adapted into a 1975 film starring Lynn Redgrave, and has also been performed as a play and an opera.

Despite the influence of *The Happy Hooker* on popular culture, it is now clear that it was composed almost as a piece of fiction, with two ghostwriters orchestrating the account of Hollander's life in the sex trade. They could not even decide if this was about a pimp or a 'hooker'. '[Moore] actually hired Yvonne Dunleavy who was a famous journalist at the time. She was the one who wrote the book. They taped me, simply asking [me] questions about my life and had the chapters spewed out in three months,' Hollander told me. 'She wrote it, he edited it. He tried in vain to write a chapter, it was a piece of shit.'

---

[5]Jennes, 1974, *First Annual Hookers' Ball*.
[6]Cited in James, Withers, Haft & Theiss, 1977, p. 73.
[7]Keegan, 1974, *Book Title Here*, p. 1.
[8]Rubin, 1986, *Book Title Here*, n.p.

When I asked Hollander how long she had sold sex for before living off the earnings of other women, she answered: 'I was a physical hooker for about half a year to learn the trade. I went from an L shaped apartment to a five-bedroom penthouse apartment in rocket time'.

Prostitution is 'Work' or 'Labour'

In 1985, 15 years before the Dutch government lifted the ban on brothels and effectively legalised the sex trade, the 'sex workers' rights' organisation Red Thread (a government-funded 'union' for people in prostitution) organised a congress that led to the forming of the International Committee for Prostitutes' Rights. The draft of a World Charter for Prostitutes' Rights was drafted and finalised at a second international congress in 1986.

Its 'Statement on Prostitution and Feminism' declares that prostitution is 'legitimate work'.[9] The World Charter includes a defence of sex buyers, explaining that: 'The customer, like the prostitute, should not … be criminalised or condemned on a moral basis'.

The prostitution as 'work' approach was spearheaded by Australian groups such as Scarlet Alliance. This was clearly an appropriation of the liberationary arguments adopted by the gay rights movement and the HIV/AIDS crisis that transformed the 'sex workers' rights' movement into an international force. Large amounts of government funding were made available for HIV/AIDS prevention projects (as we shall see in Chap. 7), and this money was used to found organisations including TAMPEP (The International Foundation: European Network for HIV/STI Prevention and Health Promotion among Migrant Sex Workers),[10] the Network of Sex Work Projects and COYOTE.

---

[9]Name Pheterson, *Title of Book/Paper*, 1989a, p. 193.

[10]TAMPER: European network for HIV/STI Prevention and Health promotion among migrant sex workers. Retrieved 16 June 2017, from http://tampep.eu/.

Unionisation

The International Union of Sex Workers (IUSW) is a lobby group that campaigns for total decriminalisation of the sex trade.

'Sex work' activists recognise that 'downsides' exist in prostitution, such as violence, stigmatisation, poor pay and conditions of employment, and job and employment insecurity. However, these are believed to be a result of how society views 'sex work' and to also be present in other areas of non-sexual employment.

'Working in the sex trade is often a way for migrants to avoid the unrewarding and sometimes exploitative conditions they meet in the low-skilled jobs available to them, such as: waiting in restaurants and bars, cleaning, food packaging, etc.' said Nicolas (Nick) Mai, a UK-based academic and filmmaker whose research on migrant 'sex workers' in the UK, as we will see in Chap. 7, was used to convince a number of politicians that concerns about trafficking was largely a 'moral panic'.[11]

Pro-prostitution organisations argue that treating prostitution as 'sex work' would make addressing those incidents of 'forced' prostitution and trafficking easier. By acknowledging prostitution as a legitimate form of 'work', prostitutes would then have access to a range of resources to protect them (legislations, grievance processes, officially recognised unions).

There are a number of key tactics used by the 'sex workers' rights' activists to promote blanket decriminalisation of the sex trade and to lobby against the criminalisation of sex buyers. And today's movement blames feminist abolitionists for the danger and abuse faced by those in prostitution and names them 'whorephobic'.

But while third wave 'fun feminists' get their thongs in a twist about the very idea that this multibillion-dollar capitalist industry is not above criticism, the most vocal strand of the SWRA movement in the UK and

---

[11]ICRSE (2009, May 30.) *Update: ESRC releases first findings on 'Migrants in the UK sex industry'*. Retrieved 16 June 2017, from http://www.sexworkeurope.org/es/news/icrse-past-articles/update-esrc-releases-first-findings-migrants-uk-sex-industry.

in a number of other European countries is linked to the wider anti-capitalist movement.

Academic, anthropologist and political activist Chris Knight is one of the founders of the IUSW. I interviewed him in 2010 when I was researching an article on the so-called union. At the time, Knight was living in a tent on Parliament Square, London, UK, as part of an anti-war protest. He said: 'The whole point of setting the union up is to end prostitution. But there are different ways of going about that. Marx said all workers are prostitutes. If we want to end prostitution we have to end capitalism'.

Ana Lopes, an academic and another founder of the IUSW, said: 'The name International Union of Sex Workers occurred in a discussion with Chris Knight. It had been agreed in the first meeting that the group's main aim would be to establish sex work as legitimate work. Therefore it made sense to follow the footsteps of other workers and claim our place in the mainstream trade union movement. The word "international" came from our perception that the industry has gone global and therefore a successful mobilisation of workers should overcome national borders too'.

The IUSW is not an actual union, as I discovered both from whistle-blowers and extensive research. Offering discounts to its members in self-defence classes and lingerie products, the IUSW is a mouthpiece for pimps and punters. The IUSW was founded in 2000, 3 years before the British-based trades union the GMB[12] endorsed it and allowed a 'sex workers' branch' to be formed in 2003. The IUSW described itself as the campaigning wing of the sex workers' branch, but would allow outsiders to believe that the IUSW was the actual branch within the union.

Such organisations are politically motivated lobby groups campaigning for total decriminalisation of the sex trade, hence the number of pimps and punters involved. There appeared to be few people in the organisation who actually sold sex for a living.

Douglas Fox used to be a well-known face of the IUSW. He and his partner John Dockerty run Christony Companions, one of the biggest

---

[12]A general trade union in the United Kingdom, which has more than 631,000 members.

escort agencies in the North East of England. Fox used the GMB membership as a way to legitimise his business. In fact, the GMB logo was used as a kite mark on the Christony Companions website as a way to endorse his 'product': the women.

Many members of the IUSW were academics, some doing their research on 'sex work'.

According to Chris Knight: 'Ana Lopes achieved a first in 1998/1999 then a masters degree at UCL in 2000 and said "I really want to do something with my knowledge, in particular the sex strike stuff". When I next saw her she said, "I am a sex worker". We made a banner and she said that if you are trying to organise a sex strike we need to get into where the commercial sex is going on. We had a sex strike in Soho [a London district which houses a large off-street sex market]. We were on a "no sweat" demonstration and Ana approached a GMB rep and he said "Let's meet".'

The IUSW, in its heyday, was led by managers who supported the Conservative Party. In fact, they got money from the Conservative Party.

Cambodia: Fake Unions

One human rights activist working on trafficking prevention in Cambodia, who asked not to be named, told me that: 'A group with trafficking in their title that were pro-prostitution in the early 2000s—they came and helped form the Women's Network for Unity [WNU] and helped them form the language. It was an outside group that came in, they worked with a lot of the groups in the region and they helped them start. Because Cambodia has built a strong protest movement, we are one of the few garment factories in the region that has a workers' union, so they have set up a lot of their language to match the garment union workers' rights'.

In Cambodia, I had arranged to meet a group of women who were members of the sex workers' union in Phnom Penh, which had been founded by the WNU. The WNU, which has received funding by the

Open Society Foundation,[13] a philanthropic organisation committed to building democratic societies,[14] came out of the Womyn's Agenda for Change (WAC). Their activities in the first year of operation (2003–2004) included WNU and WAC hosting a visit by two representatives of the INSW. Two members of the WNU secretariat participated in a 'sex workers' rights' conference in Hong Kong on 1 May 2004 and two 'sex workers' were sponsored to participate in a UN conference on AIDS in Thailand. So the WAC (also funded by Open Society) had a clear pro-prostitution agenda from the very beginning.

Our meeting was scheduled for 8 a.m. and it had been decided that I would take with me a translator from another Cambodian women's non-governmental organisation (NGO). On arrival at the venue, we were surprised to find that one of the board members of WNU had also decided to attend. I had received an email from her a few days before I arrived in Cambodia, asking me to submit my questions in advance so that she could reassure the women that my research would be beneficial to them. I did so, including several questions about police corruption and brutality. I assumed, on seeing the board member, who was not herself in prostitution, that she was doing some kind of 'gatekeeping' on behalf of the women.

However, all became clear when the women arrived, having been 'working' all night. They were warm, open and desperate to tell their stories of the daily violence and abuse they endure from sex buyers, and how much they hated selling sex for a living. They talked over each other, ignoring my questions to start with and simply offloading about how terrible their lives were. The board member would interrupt them regularly and often spoke for them. I asked: 'What are the benefits of being in the Union?' and was answered not by the women, but by the board member. She spoke solidly for five min about the benefits for members: for example, if the women are beaten by the police, they are given legal training on their rights; if they are arrested, the WNU

---

[13]Open Society Foundations. Retrieved 16 June 2017, from https://www.opensocietyfoundations.org/.
[14]Open Society Foundations. Retrieved 16 June 2017, from https://www.opensocietyfoundations.org/.

will provide food during the time they cannot work; and if one of the women dies, they will help to buy the coffin. Knowing their rights 'empowered them', I was told.

The prostituted women sitting cross-legged on the floor near me looked anything but empowered. Two had babies with them, both born of sex buyers. Another was pregnant with a buyer's child. At least one was HIV positive. All had been raped on multiple occasions. Each one told me they could get out of prostitution if only they had $200 to buy formal identification papers, because this was the only way to secure legitimate employment such as in the service industry or a factory. When I asked if the WNU could help them do this there was silence.

In the meantime, WNU representatives claim they have 6500 Cambodian 'sex workers' on their books, all fighting for 'sex workers' rights'. None of the women, the translator told me, used the term 'sex work' to describe what they do, or 'sex worker' to describe who they are. This language was used by the WNU. One of WNU's aims is 'to challenge the rhetoric around sex work, particularly that concerned with the anti-trafficking movement and the "rehabilitation" of sex workers'. All of the women asked where they could get help to escape the hell they were in. And while they endure this, the WNU board members and paid staff travel the region, speaking at 'sex workers' rights' conferences, distorting the voices of the exploited women.

The women I met in Cambodia would really benefit from linking up with the survivor-led abolitionist movement. Every single word said by these women made clear to me how much they hated prostitution. They were openly begging for alternatives, only to be talked over by the coordinator. The coordinator told me that she had been at a regional conference with other 'sex workers' rights' activists. She told me that she had 50,000 'sex workers' in Cambodia signed up to this so-called union. The women I spoke to did not know that they were 'sex workers' rights' activists.

The experience of these women had been colonised. They were being used by this NGO to promote the idea that legalisation would somehow be of benefit to them. The horrific tales the women told me about the violence perpetrated upon them by sex buyers stay with me to this day. But all the coordinator could speak about was the abuse and exploitation the women suffered at the hands of the male police force. There is no doubt that the police treat women in prostitution appallingly in Cambodia, as they do elsewhere. There is also no doubt that decriminalising the women selling sex would help immeasurably. But the coordinator was not interested in the stories the women had to tell of the everyday abuse within prostitution, perpetrated by pimps and punters. It was blatantly obvious that this did not suit her narrative.

The women had been up all night, being used and abused for enough money to be able to afford food to feed their dependents. They clearly had no idea what a survivor movement would be like. They had no concept of political activism that would put their experiences at the forefront, and that would respect their lived reality. The difference between them continuing to be abused on the streets of Phnom Penh, or in the provinces, was not just the $200 that they would need for identity papers that would allow them to apply for jobs. The biggest barrier was the NGO that was supposed to be helping them. This NGO considered the concept of 'sex workers' rights' to be above and beyond the importance of the lives of the women themselves. I asked the board member if they were planning on raising the money to help the women out of prostitution. She told me: 'No'.

Feminism Is All About Women Having Personal 'Choice' and 'Agency'

As part of the My Body My Rights campaign, Amnesty International sought to develop a policy around the decriminalisation of sex work. The My Body My Rights campaign seeks to raise awareness of, and advocate for, sexual and reproductive rights. One of the guiding principles of this campaign is that people should be able to exercise autonomy over their bodies, reproductive capacities, and sexual choices. (Amnesty International Australia)

Those engaging in 'sex work' often use 'choice feminism' to defend prostitution: the notion that a woman choosing to do whatever she wants is performing an inherently feminist act. In accordance with this, the abolitionist argument is anti-feminist: it is an effort to constrain the 'free choices' of other women who are perfectly capable of making their own decisions. Julian Marlowe, a male pro-prostitution activist who was previously involved in escorting writes: '[T]o suggest that prostitutes who do not see themselves as victims just don't know any better is patronising and contradicts the very essence of feminism—the freedom to make one's own choices'.[15] Perhaps unsurprisingly, this argument is commonly used by women prostituting in relatively independent and low-risk areas of the sex trade.

Pimps Redefined as 'Sex Workers'

One argument which is played out on social media and in the press concerns who gets to speak for women in the sex trade or, as the pro-decriminalisation lobby puts it, 'sex workers' (a handy way to remove any notion that prostitution is based on the oppression of women).

In Norway I meet with Indian sex-trafficking abolitionist Ruchira Gupta, who has flown in from Delhi to speak at a conference on the sex trade. I ask Gupta about the pro-prostitution lobby in India. 'The term 'sex worker' was literally invented in front of our eyes. There was no poor woman or girl who thought that sex and work should go together. The pimps and brothel keepers who were on salaries began to call themselves sex workers and they became members of their own union. This is the only union in the world where the employers are members along with customers and the academics.'

Valerie Jennes's book *Making It Work: The Prostitute's Rights Movement in Perspective* (1993) inadvertently exposes COYOTE founder Margot St James as being strategically dishonest about the organisation consisting largely of women in prostitution when she explains that:

'COYOTE spokespeople have not taken serious or consistent action to debunk the notion that it is an organization of prostitutes. On the contrary, organizational leaders have been central in creating and

---

[15]Julian Marlowe in Nagle, 2013, *Whores And Other Feminists.*

promoting the image of COYOTE as an organization that is of and for prostitutes. As a 1988 edition of *COYOTE Howls* declared on the first page, 'most members of COYOTE are either prostitutes or ex-prostitutes, with a few non-prostitute allies'.[16]

Whilst SWRAs often accuse survivors of lying, they themselves are not averse to using the tactic of identifying as a 'sex worker' while refusing to disclose in what way they were involved in the sex trade. For example, the ECP could be using the hard left tactic of identifying as a 'worker' (in this case, at the coalface of the sex trade) as many privileged Oxbridge graduates did by taking jobs in factories back in the days of radical leftist politics.

Douglas Fox describes himself as a 'sex worker' but in fact is co-owner of one of the biggest escort agencies in the North East of England. By my definition, that makes him more pimp than prostitute. Fox is described on the *Guardian*'s *Comment is Free* website as '… an independent male sex worker. He is an activist for the International Union of Sex Workers and has appeared in a Channel 4 show called *The Escort Agency*. His agency has been operating for ten years. Most of its 20 escorts are now members of or in the process of becoming members of the IUSW/GMB London branch'.

I interviewed Fox, alongside the feminist writer and union activist Cath Elliott, in 2010 for an article about the IUSW. During our interview, Fox claimed he was a 'sex worker' and not a 'manager'. His partner John owned the agency, said Fox, and he simply helped out 'as any husband or wife would do'. I asked why he had never identified himself as such previously. Fox said: 'Well it's not selling women and it's not pimping, it's management. I think John's a sex worker as much as I'm a sex worker, but I had not come out as being a frontline sex worker, i.e. speaking with and seeing clients'.

In another example, Melissa Gira Grant, pro-prostitution activist and author of *Playing the Whore: The Work of Sex Work*,[17] refused to tell a Channel 4 news anchor about her involvement in the industry, despite

---

[16]Jenness, V. (1993.) *Making it work*. New York, NY: Aldine De Gruyter.
[17]Gira Grant, M. (2014.) *Playing the whore: The work of sex work*. London: Verso.

having written a book in which she described herself as a 'former sex worker' during a debate on the legitimacy of sex work as labour.[18] Gira Grant, it turned out, was a stripper and webcam girl.[19]

'Trafficking Would Be Bad if It Existed but It Is a Myth Anyway'

> Sex law is often a front for ideology that constrains rather than liberates women. What most appals me about the recent conflation of trafficking and sex work in law and policy is that some feminists support the confusion. These women would normally never dream of telling other women how to behave, because they have fought against imposed constraints in their own lives. (Melissa Dittmore, former inaugural Chair of the Advisory Board of the Sex Workers' Project)

This stance draws a clear distinction between 'sex work' (empowered, chosen, non-violent) and trafficking (disempowered, forced, violent). It is a key argument of the Global Alliance Against Traffic in Women (GAATW), which presents itself as an anti-trafficking organisation but uses its platform to campaign for drawing a sharp distinction between 'sex work' and human trafficking.

Its working paper, 'Exploring Links Between Trafficking and Gender', argues that 'commercial sex work is not inherently exploitative',[20] that 'policies created or actions performed in the name of anti-trafficking have at times resulted in gross human rights violations against sex workers, including economic exploitation and physical and sexual violence by law enforcement'.[21]

---

[18]Gira Grant, M. (2014.) *Playing the whore: The work of sex work*. London: Verso.

[19]Gira Grant, M. (2014.) *Playing the whore: The work of sex work*. London: Verso.

[20]Global Alliance Against Traffic in Women, (2010). *Exploring Links Between Trafficking and Gender*, p. 29.

[21]Global Alliance Against Traffic in Women, (2010). *Exploring Links Between Trafficking and Gender*, p. 29.

This paper also warns against an over-focus on sex trafficking and suggests avoiding using the term: 'A sole focus on trafficking for the purposes of prostitution can also divert attention and urgently needed resources from human rights violations in other sectors, e.g. labour exploitation'.[22].

This argument ignores: the blurred lines between sexual exploitation, trafficking and so-called 'chosen' 'sex work', and the evidence that those 'entering' prostitution do so with, at the very least, constrained choices.

In its submission to the All Party Parliamentary Group (APPG) on prostitution, 2016, the Sussex Centre for Gender Studies argued that: 'Defining prostitution as violence against women erases sex workers' rights to agency and autonomy. This places all decision-making about their lives in the hands of the state, reduces their power to act for themselves, and increases the likelihood they will be subject to violence (World Health Organisation 2013, Amnesty International 2015). Since the majority of workers in the sex trade are women, this perpetuates gender inequality (GAATW 2011)'.

The submission continues: 'If all sex work is violence, there is no way to distinguish between sex workers who are working voluntarily and those who are being exploited, and sexual encounters which are consensual and those which are not'.[23]

The submission includes a defence of sex buyers: 'Clients who believe that women are commodities and it is impossible to rape a sex worker may be more likely to be violent, exploitative and abusive than those who subscribe to ideas of sex workers' rights (e.g. that services should be negotiated and that sex workers have a right to be safe) (GAATW 2011). O'Connell Davidson (2003)/ found that men who saw prostitution as a sector of work were more likely to be concerned about trafficking, while those who were most likely to use the services of trafficked sex workers perceived women as commodities and felt that payment signified ownership rather than exchange'.

---

[22]Global Alliance Against Traffic in Women, (2010). *Exploring Links Between Trafficking and Gender.* 29–30

[23]http://data.parliament.uk/writtenevidence/committeeevidence.svc/evidencedocument/home-affairs-committee/prostitution/written/29135.pdf accessed 27th August 2017

Here, the author is suggesting that the abolitionist—as opposed to the 'sex workers' rights' approach—can be held responsible for punters becoming violent and abusive.

Men Who Attack and Murder Women in Prostitution Are 'Posing as Clients'

'Decriminalise now! Stigma kills' chanted the protesters outside the Swedish Embassy in 2013. Stigma does not kill women in prostitution. Men do.

In an article entitled 'The Bloody State Gave Him The Power: A Swedish Sex Worker's Murder',[24] Pye Jakobsson, in an interview with Caty Simon (whose blog *The Virtues of Vice* contains articles praising pimps and intravenous drug use), claimed that 'stigma' brought about by criminalising punters resulted in the murder of the 'sex workers' rights' activist Petite Jasmine.

Eva Marree Smith Kullander ('Petite Jasmine' was the name Kullander used in prostitution) was not, in fact, stabbed to death by stigma, but by her violent ex-partner during a contact visit with the children she had lost custody of several years earlier. Kullander's murderer was not a pimp or a punter but a domestic abuser. Kullander had not lost her children because, as the Rose Alliance[25] (a 'sex workers' rights' organisation based in Sweden) claimed, she refused to accept that prostitution was bad, but because she was reported to social services for misusing alcohol and drugs.[26]

Following her death, rallies in 36 countries and six continents[27] were held by 'sex worker's rights' organisations calling for full decriminalisation of the sex trade and an end to the laws criminalising demand.

---

[24]Simon, C. (2013, Jul 16.) *The bloody state gave him the power: A Swedish sex worker's murder.* On Tits And Ass. Retrieved 16 June 2017, from http://titsandsass.com/the-bloody-state-gave-him-the-power-a-swedish-sex-workers-murder/.

[25]Rose Alliance. Retrieved 16 June 2017, from http://www.rosealliance.se/en/about-ra/.

[26]There is no evidence that this claim is true.

[27]Gira Grant, M. (2013, Jul 22.) *Sex workers rise up after fatal stabbings.* On In These Times. Retrieved 16 June 2017, from http://inthesetimes.com/uprising/entry/15337/sex_workers_rise_up_after_fatal_stabbings.

In an article focussing on Kullander, Gira Grant mentions 'Dora Özer, a Turkish trans woman who was murdered by "a man posing as a client"'.[28] It is unclear why Grant assumes the murderer 'posed' as a sex buyer as opposed to actually *being* a sex buyer. This is a common tactic used by 'sex workers' rights' activists to minimise or deny the endemic violence inherent in the sex trade.

Writing in the *Huffington Post*, Kate L Gould claimed that Özer was also 'stabbed to death by stigma', although she said that Özer was 'murdered by a client' as opposed to a man masquerading as one. Gould argues that the cause of Özer's murder was the Government closing some of its 54 State-run brothels.[29]

Carol Leigh, the COYOTE spokesperson who coined the term 'sex work', made a video about the two murders,[30] and also claims that Özer's killer was 'posing' as a client. It makes me wonder why Ugly Mugs[31] (schemes that circulate information regarding violent and abusive punters to women in prostitution and advocacy services) exists if no actual punter is responsible for violence against prostituted women?

Since decriminalisation in New Zealand, as documented in an article by Penny White on *Feminist* Current,[32] several prostituted women have been murdered. In Germany, there are at least 55 women who have been murdered by punters during the past 14 years, and in the Netherlands that figure is 28. I have been unable to find any evidence of a single 'sex workers' rights' protest organised on behalf of these murdered women.

---

[28]Gira Grant, M. (2013, Jul 22.) *Sex workers rise up after fatal stabbings*. On In These Times. Retrieved 16 June 2017, from http://inthesetimes.com/uprising/entry/15337/sex_workers_rise_up_after_fatal_stabbings.

[29]Gould, K. (2013, Jul 18.) *Stabbed to death by stigma*. On Huffington Post, Retrieved 16 June 2017, from http://www.huffingtonpost.co.uk/kate-l-gould/sex-workers-sweden_b_3610665.html.

[30]Leigh, C.; Jakobsson, P. (2013). *Jasmine and Dora 4-Ever*. Retrieved 16 June 2017, from https://vimeo.com/87450331.

[31]National Ugly Mugs (NUM). Retrieved 16 June 2017, from https://uknswp.org/um/about/.

[32]White, P. (2015, Nov 3.) *Remembering the murdered women erased by the pro-sex work agenda*. On Feminist Current. Retrieved 16 June 2017, from http://www.feministcurrent.com/2015/11/03/remembering-the-murdered-women-erased-by-the-pro-sex-work-agenda/.

'Prostitution Is not About Gender Inequality or Patriarchy'

In their research into 'Statistics on Sex Work in the UK',[33] Nicola Smith and Sarah Kingston argue that:

> Perhaps the most dominant stereotype of commercial sexual exchange is that only women sell sex. This was not borne out by our analysis, which found that one in three (33%) people advertising as escorts self-identified as male. In addition, 4% of escorts self-identified as trans, of whom 70% self-identified as female, 27% as male and 3% as non-binary. Just under 63% of total escorts self-identified as female. Our findings support those of another recent, large-scale survey, the Student Sex Work Project, that sex work does not equate to 'women's work' – indeed, male students were found to be more likely than female students to engage in commercial sexual activity.[34]

The study was not about sex buyers. It was solely about one escort prostitution website's advertising. What is advertised is not necessarily what you get. That is true in all advertising, not just in the case of prostitution.

They continued:

> The site isn't specifically/primarily geared towards LGBT/Q escorts, although it does have a partner site that is. Another recent, large-scale study found that many more sex workers are male than is conventionally assumed is the Student Sex Work Project,[35] which found that male students were actually more likely to engage in sex work than were female students.

---

[33] http://data.parliament.uk/writtenevidence/committeeevidence.svc/evidencedocument/home-affairs-committee/prostitution/written/29161.pdf accessed 27th August 2017.

[34] Sagar, T.; Jones, D.; et al. (2015, March.) *The student sex work project: Research summary.* Swansea University. Retrieved 16 June 2017, from http://www.thestudentsexworkproject.co.uk/wp-content/uploads/2015/03/TSSWP-Research-Summary-English.pdf.

[35] Sagar, T.; Jones, D.; et al. (2015, March.) *The student sex work project: Research summary.* Swansea University. Retrieved 16 June 2017, from http://www.thestudentsexworkproject.co.uk/wp-content/uploads/2015/03/TSSWP-Research-Summary-English.pdf.

I emailed Nicola Smith, co-author of the report, a number of questions, all of which she politely responded to. For example, why did they choose to not name the website they relied on to gather their data? Smith responded by arguing that it was simply to protect the anonymity of those advertising on the site.

I asked why the authors concluded that prostitution should not be seen as an issue of women's gender inequality, when it was known that the majority in the sex trade are female? I further asked if they gathered any supportive evidence, other than relying on data from one website, that rising numbers of sex buyers are women? Smith responded by saying that: 'We do not claim that most clients are women but rather that a large proportion of people advertising as escorts on the website advertise to women, which we believe troubles assumptions that "most" clients are men'. But 'advertising to women' is not the same as 'women paying for sex'.

The report states: 'Calls for national policy to follow a "Swedish model" of criminalisation depend upon constructions of sex workers as victimised women and their clients as predatory men. Our research directly contradicts such assumptions, and instead points to a diversity of identities and practices in the contemporary sex trade'.[36]

The aim of 'de-gendering' the sex trade is to argue against those of us who point out women's structural oppression in relation to men, and to argue that it should never be included in legislation, policy or discourse about violence against women.

Discrediting Abolitionists

The denunciations of decriminalisation come from a strange alliance of feminists who regard all sex workers (including porn stars and strippers) as victims of oppression and Christians who see them as drenched in

---

[36]http://data.parliament.uk/writtenevidence/committeeevidence.svc/evidencedocument/home-affairs-committee/prostitution/written/29161.pdf accessed 27th August 2017

depravity. Both exploit the sense that some types of sex are shameful, dangerous and intolerable – an attitude that long fuelled the persecution of gays. (Steve Chapman, 2015) [37]

This argument positions abolitionists as prudes who are 'anti-sex'. A key tactic of activists who use this argument is to draw comparisons between abolitionists and religious moralists.

For example, in an article entitled 'If You're Against Sex Work, You're A Bigot',[38] 'sex worker' Conner Habib calls abolitionists 'anti-sex activists' and compares an argument made by an abolitionist about the bodily impact of prostitution (vaginal tearing, pregnancy, disease) with a Christian, anti-gay YouTuber on the damage caused to the rectum through anal sex: 'Same gesture, same hate, same simplifications'.

This argument ignores the fact that feminist abolitionists' reasons for opposing the legalisation of prostitution are not built on flimsy moralistic grounds but on solid research on violence and coercion in prostitution. It also ignores the strong links between LGBT and feminist activism.

In Chap. 10, we explore the attack on abolitionists/survivors in more detail.

The Attack on Abolitionists as Racists and Colonialists

In a charming little piece, written by white transgender activist Paris Lees, entitled 'Ban sex work? Fuck off white feminists', published in that well-known bastion of women's liberation *Vice* magazine,[39] the notion that it is desirable to end prostitution was ridiculed.

---

[37]Chapman, S. (2014, Aug 26.) *Outlawing prostitution is a crime*. In Chicago Tribune. Retrieved 16 June 2017, from http://www.chicagotribune.com/news/opinion/chapman/ct-prostitution-amnesty-international-cindy-mccain-sex-workers-trafficking-rape--20150826-column.html.

[38]Habib, C. (2014, Jun 24.) If you're against sex work, you're a bigot. In The Stranger. Retrieved 16 June 2017, from http://www.thestranger.com/features/feature/2015/06/24/22436683/if-youre-against-sex-work-youre-a-bigot

[39]Lees, P. (2015, Aug 10.) *Ban sex work? Fuck off, white feminism*. In Vice. Retrieved 16 June 2017, from http://www.vice.com/en_uk/read/ban-sex-work-fuck-off-white-feminism-paris-lees-807.

The slur 'white feminism' is now commonly used by pro-prostitution 'feminists' to discredit abolitionists. In fact it has recently become short-hand for describing radical feminists, particularly those who campaign to end male violence towards women and girls. The implication is that those who practise 'white feminism' are far more privileged than those who are in political opposition to them. In the past it was used by black and other minority ethnic feminists to critique feminists who failed to understand or recognise the privilege afforded to white people. It was never used against women of colour, and certainly never used by white women towards women of colour. By implication, Lees is denying the existence of survivor abolitionists and any woman of colour in the movement. This omission is particularly shocking, as well as insulting, bearing in mind the disproportionate number of women of colour who are prostituted.

Lees, who was raised male and, prior to his transition, was briefly involved in the sex trade, felt qualified to lecture abolitionists about how cruel it would be to 'ban sex work' while some women were 'relying on food banks'.

There appears to be something missing from this analysis. Not only are abolitionists assumed to be speaking for women in the sex trade, they are also assumed to be white. Or, a political category that Lees has devised where 'White' is capitalised, used as an adjective and employed to describe women of colour who dare to speak against the sex trade. Bearing in mind that the abolitionist movement is led by survivors, this seems not only patronising but also massively and embarrassingly ill informed.

'Take the open letter to Amnesty International [AI], signed by Lena Dunham, Meryl Streep and Emma Thompson last week', writes Lees in another article,[40] giving the impression that, because those three signatories are white, wealthy and successful, all signatories were. Nothing could be further from the truth. I asked Taina Bien-Aimé, Executive Director of the Coalition Against Trafficking in Women (CATW), her view of the accusation that the letter to AI was, as Crabapple suggested, signed by 'many fancy white ladies'. In response, Bien-Aimé, who is of Haitian

---

[40]Ward, V. (2015, Jul 29.) *Hollywood stars urge Amnesty International not to decriminalise sex trade.* In The Telegraph. Retrieved 16 June 2017, from http://www.telegraph.co.uk/news/celebritynews/11769766/Hollywood-stars-urge-Amnesty-International-not-to-decriminalise-sex-trade.html.

heritage and very familiar with the argument about 'White Feminism' in relation to the abolitionist movement, sent me a breakdown of the signatories to the letter: 'I counted about 50 (known) Caucasian women out of 400 plus', says Bien-Aimé. 'The vast majority of survivors who signed are of colour. Not a bad percentage for "White Feminism"'.

'Sex workers need a voice', Lees continues in the *Vice* article. 'There are a handful of current and former sex workers in the public eye – Brooke Magnanti, Stoya and Molly Smith for starters – but we're a teensy minority.' One small fact had clearly escaped Lees: all three aforementioned women are white. Magnanti is hardly representative of the women in prostitution: she describes herself as a former 'high-class call girl', has a doctorate, has written several books and has made a fortune from the television adaptation of her life in prostitution. Lees speaks from a media platform, and Smith is from a middle-class background and is involved in the campaign to legalise the sex trade.

Another white feminist who is offended by 'White Feminism' is Gira Grant, who wrote in an article (in which she blamed 'White Feminists' for Donald Trump being elected)[41] that 'Black feminists and womanists, queer feminists, Arab feminists, disabled feminists, trans feminists, and sex worker feminists, to name just a few, have long called for white feminism's funeral'.

I met Siouxsie Q, a 'sex worker', porn performer and journalist based in California at the Los Angeles Porn Awards in 2015. She also defines abolitionist politics as 'white feminism':

I think the problem with feminist abolitionists and sex work is that they are rooted in the white middle-class rescue industry. White Feminism has historically been something for the middle class to do, and white feminists have really tried to rescue different marginalised populations, dating back to the very beginnings of feminism, the first wave when it was linked to the slavery abolitionists. I'm not saying that's a bad thing – we do have to acknowledge that as white people we are trying to rescue poor unfortunate brown people. It's not quite what we know is good in the social justice – what you actually do is you go to marginalised groups and say 'Hey, what do you need? What do you want? How can I help with

---

[41]http://theweek.com/articles/668061/what-feminism-age-trump.

my privileged resources?' That's not what I see with feminist abolition sex work, folks.

Academic and pro-prostitution lobbyist Thaddeus Gregory Blanchette, anthropologist at Federal University of Rio de Janeiro, Brazil, also seems to think that only 'privileged' feminists are critical of the sex trade. In 2016, Blanchette wrote on his blog: 'I go in and out of brothels every week, registering working conditions, talking to the women, counting clients, passing out literature. All things none of these young, white, middle class women would ever dream of doing. And I am a pimp, simply for relating to whores. Of course, whores have it worse. I guess I can say I am now finally feeling a part of the stigma attached to them'.[42]

It is telling that white, highly educated men and women vilify those who campaign to end the sex trade, when the vast majority of prostituted women and girls are poor and otherwise disadvantaged. Vast numbers of Native women and women of colour populate the sex trade,[43] and the survivor/abolitionist movement reflects this.

Abolitionists Don't Listen to 'Sex Workers'

One of the most exploitative things anti-sex bigots do is select voices of former sex workers who've had terrible experiences and prop those voices up as representative of the entire population, even though they're not. (Conner Habib, 'sex worker' and journalist)

This argument completely ignores the fact that most studies show the vast majority of 'sex workers' experience high levels of rape, sexual assault, physical violence and harassment. It also ignores the fact that many of the most vulnerable people in prostitution—children, for example—cannot safety advocate for themselves, and therefore visible 'voices' of sex work can never represent the true picture.

---

[42]Blanchette, retrieved June 2nd 2017, https://www.blogger.com/profile/09359423010378429288
[43]Nelson Butler, C. (2015.) *The racial roots of human trafficking*. UCLA Law Review. Retrieved 16 June 2017, from http://www.uclalawreview.org/wp-content/uploads/2015/08/Butler-final_8.15.pdf.

Sex Work Is Helpful and Liberating to Women Who've Been Sexually Abused

Prostitution is described as 'cathartic' in that it is a way to deal with the negative effects of male violence rather than an extension of it. For example, Alison Bass in her book *Getting Screwed* argues that:

> Just as sex work can be an avenue for some women to take control in a situation where they had none, some sex workers and psychologists see it as a way to triumph over tragedy. That's certainly how Maddy Colette, the high-end escort from North Carolina, frames it. When Maddy was 17 and on a vacation trip to Costa Rica with her mother, she was violently raped and left for dead … At the age of 18, Maddy went to live in Spain, and that's where she began working as an escort.[44]

When interviewed by Bass, Maddy added: 'My Spanish clients were paying me thousands of Euros and it was very empowering. They gave me extravagant gifts, took me out to the opera. That feeling of being in control helped me heal'.[45]

Whilst sex trade survivors routinely describe the everyday reality of prostitution as 'violence', 'sex workers' rights' lobbyists claim that the only violence comes from the police and other state actors.

'The Nordic Model Puts 'Sex Workers' in More Danger'

Frankie Mullin is a journalist with a longstanding involvement in 'sex work', based in the UK. I asked Mullin, who writes about the 'failures' of the Nordic Model,[46] why she was so against criminalising demand.

---

[44]Bass, A. (2015.) *Getting screwed*. US: University Press of New England. p. 75.

[45]Bass, A. (2015.) *Getting screwed*. US: University Press of New England. p. 75.

[46]Mullin, F. (2014, Nov 7.) *British politicians need to do more to protect prostitutes*. In Vice. Retrieved 16 June 2017, from https://www.vice.com/en_ca/article/protest-sex-workers-frankie-mullin-942.

'Jumpy, paranoid men make dangerous clients,' says Mullin. 'Picture yourself trying to arrange a meeting with someone who refuses to give their name, or trying to discuss safety or condom-use on the street with a man who is terrified being arrested. You'll be forced to work in more isolated areas, possibly later at night. You'll have less time to negotiate before you climb into someone's car. Police will be watching you because that's how they'll catch the buyers.'

In the 18 years the Nordic Model has been operational in Sweden, not one prostituted person has been killed by a sex buyer. But the argument persists, with academics such as Jay Levy, whose book, *Criminalising the Purchase of Sex: Lessons from Sweden*[47] giving credence to such claims.

'How can women in Sweden be in more danger than they were before the law?' asks Simon Häggström, a police inspector from the Prostitution Unit of the Stockholm Police. 'When all she has to do is pick up the phone, even if [the punter] is rude to her, and we will arrest him because he is already committing a crime.'

Many of those high-profile pro-prostitution lobbyists who speak as 'sex workers' are what I would call 'tourists'. Melissa Gira-Grant for example, who is highly educated and earning her living as a journalist; Brooke Magnanti, who holds a PhD, has written several books, and worked as a scientist; and Douglas Fox, whose partner owns one of the largest escort agencies in Britain, are not representative of the sex trade.

The model of framing prostitution as labour, and decriminalising the entire market, would be the best model for the 'tourists' and is the sensible approach to take. But it would work simply because these women (and men) are atypical, privileged ideologues. They are the student revolutionary International Socialists[48] of the 1960s, taking a job in a factory to be close to 'the people'. This bourgeois model does not work for those who have been drawn into the sex trade by horror and abuse rather than by ideological choice. And such women make up the majority of those in prostitution.

[47]Levy, J. (2014.) *Criminalising the purchase of sex: Lessons from Sweden*. London: Routledge.
[48]International Socialists. On Wikipedia. Retrieved 16 June 2017, from https://en.wikipedia.org/wiki/International_Socialists.

Their arguments work because of the very women and men making the argument—the privileged minority. This is why the public are convinced by it, because it is coming from the mouths of those who appear to have done rather well out of prostitution. The next chapter will look at the way that the pro-prostitution lobby have become adept at disguising the harm and horrors of the international sex trade.

3

Sanitising the Sex Trade

In the past few decades, prostitution and the sex trade have been given a serious makeover. The title of this book, *The Pimping of Prostitution*, is meant to convey how sanitised commercial sexual exploitation has become. *The Urban Dictionary* definition of pimping is 'to make something "cool", "better" or "awesome"'.

In recent years, the sex trade has been rebranded to give the impression that it is not harmful, nor even prostitution. Academics and pro-prostitution activists have begun to use terms such as 'selling love', 'transactional sex' and 'compensated daters'. Those who support the sex trade use terminology that masks the reality of what it actually is: one person, almost always male, having sex with another person, almost always female, without mutual desire. The sex buyer knows that the woman he is buying does not want to have sex with him, otherwise he wouldn't have to pay her.

I have only ever heard survivors of the sex trade speak about the actual sex of prostitution. The pro-sex trade lobby dresses it up in euphemisms, using a narrative more appropriate for a description of labour rather than a sexual act performed upon a person.

© The Author(s) 2017
J. Bindel, *The Pimping of Prostitution*,
DOI 10.1057/978-1-137-55890-9_3

The pro-prostitution lobby rarely speaks about regular prostitution: where a buyer hands over cash to a woman in order to gain access to the inside of her body for one-sided pleasure. Nor did they speak about the actual sex. I have only ever heard survivors, or those still in prostitution but wishing to get out, talk about what the sex is like in reality.

Unlike the pro-prostitution lobby, whose members speak of 'safe sex', the other women I have interviewed recount the detail. They speak of the horrendous smell of the punters, and the pain of a dry, bruised vagina being penetrated by multiple men. The horror of having his semen or other bodily fluids anywhere near her face. His beard rubbing her cheek until she bleeds. They tell me about how their necks get sore from whipping their head away from his tongue as he tries to kiss her. About being unable to eat or drink or kiss her children, because of what she has had to do with her mouth. How her arm and elbow aches from desperately trying to get them to ejaculate so she does not have to be penetrated one more time.

After the 1996 Brighton conference, when I heard survivors speak about what actually happened to them in prostitution, and being extremely familiar with the abuse that Emma Humphreys had suffered during her years in the sex trade, I began to ask the so-called 'sex workers' rights' activists who spoke out to describe exactly what they did for a living. Without exception they objected to this question, despite the fact that they had insisted that this was just work like any other job. At one conference in London, I asked a speaker during the Q&A session exactly what aspect of prostitution she was involved in. I had heard from numerous people, including other pro-prostitution lobbyists, that she had worked as a receptionist in a brothel for six months some years ago, then become involved in the Red Umbrella Campaign (the red umbrella was adopted in 2005 by the International Committee on the Rights of Sex Workers in Europe [ICRSE] 'as a symbol of resistance to discrimination'),[1] before securing a significant amount of money from a charitable trust to provide 'services' for street-prostituted women in a British city.

---

[1]Under The Red Umbrella. *In International Committee on the rights of sex workers in Europe.* Retrieved 16 June 2017, from http://www.sexworkeurope.org/campaigns/red-umbrella-campaigns.

When the pro-prostitution lobbyist asked 'How dare you?' in response to my question, I replied that I didn't see why she couldn't speak about her activities, and that I was perfectly willing to tell her about the research I was involved in and describe my work. She declined my offer.

In her article, 'Webcamming: the sex work revolution that no one is willing to talk about',[2] author Rachel Stuart (who is researching a PhD entitled 'The discourses that pertain to webcamming as a form of sexual commerce, how webcam is experienced as a form of labour by female performers', at the University of Kent, UK) claimed that: 'Webcamming is an easy market to enter. All it takes is a computer, a decent webcam, access to a high speed internet connection and a webcam hosting site. The hours are flexible, the working environment is safe and the salary can be very rewarding'.

Not everyone agrees that webcamming is safe. Investigative journalist Jamie Bartlett conducted in-depth research into the underworld of the Internet for his book *The Dark Net*. Bartlett found that the women involved in webcamming can be at risk of violence and even be driven to take their own lives. '[C]amming can kill', writes Bartlett. 'Camwhores are usually teenagers who strip for the benefit of users of the horrible website 4chan. Many are "doxed" [identified] and their names passed to friends and parents. They are subjected to cyberbullying and anybody who protests is dismissed as a "moralfag". Some kill themselves as a result.'[3]

Bartlett describes how webcamming is becoming a hugely profitable business, thought to be worth $1 billion per annum, and comprising approximately one-fifth of the porn business. It is also becoming increasingly normalised, with around 15% of British adults under 40 having appeared naked on a webcam.

According to Stuart, webcamming is a good way to earn money and is largely beyond reproach. 'Webcam performers are often highly

---

[2]Stuart, R. (2016, Dec 19.) *Webcamming: The sex work revolution that no one is willing to talk about.* In The Conversation. Retrieved 16 June 2017, from https://theconversation.com/webcamming-the-sex-work-revolution-that-no-one-is-willing-to-talk-about-69834.
[3]Bartlett, J. (2014.) *The Dark Net: Inside the digital underworld*, London: Windmill. p. 303.

entrepreneurial, and they harness mainstream social networking sites such as Twitter, Facebook and Tumblr to build and maintain relationships with customers. It's difficult for radical feminists to claim that a shrewd businesswoman has been victimised by her involvement in this form of pornography.'

I spoke to one woman who was involved in webcamming for 12 months during her time as a mature student. 'Jane' had been introduced to the idea by a 'glamour' photographer, who told her that she could earn as much in an hour webcamming as she could in a week working in a bar.

'At first I thought I could cope', said Jane. 'After all, there was no direct contact with the client and I could make my own rules.' Soon, Jane realised that she was terrified the sex buyers would be able to track her down and she found herself unable to sleep. 'I realised I didn't have control over what I was doing,' she said. 'They demanded I did things that made me feel dirty, disgusted and ashamed. They would have me acting as a really young child, pretending to be their daughter and asking me to beg "daddy" to "fuck me".'

The 'Sex Work' Revolution

The sanitation project began with the introduction of the term 'sex work', now used by the majority of police officers, media outlets and human rights organisations. There are even those who use the term 'juvenile sex work' to describe sexually abused children. The sanitisation of language to describe the sex trade and activities associated with it has reached what I hope is a nadir. The term 'forced sex work' has become widely used among some international non-governmental organisations (including, for example, Action Aid), which strikes me as an oxymoron. If we are to take the intended meaning of 'sex work' (to engage in sex as labour), surely if the 'sex' part of sex work is forced, it is actually rape or slavery? Indeed, Action Aid's paper on the topic is entitled 'Position Paper on the Rights of Sex Workers', and is written by the International Women's Rights Team. The only 'rights' considered within this framework appear to be those of women to be prostituted.

A 1984 article[4] published in *The Associated Press*, a Californian newspaper, with the headline 'Cops' Survey Finds Hookers Well Paid And Enjoy Their Work', is a clear example of how confused and contradictory, as well as biased, much reporting is on the issue of prostitution. The article was based on the findings of a San Jose police officer with a Masters in Criminology, who had conducted a survey of 100 prostituted women around Silicon Valley. According to the researcher, Ronald Martinelli, these women 'earn $74,000 a year, enjoy their work and don't worry about getting caught'.

So far, so good. However, further findings highlighted in the article contradict this rosy picture. Of those surveyed, 88% admitted that prostitution is related to other crimes, including robbery, assault and murder. The majority of the women surveyed said they prefer sex buyers who were married because married men won't go to the police if they are robbed or assaulted. I can only assume (the report is not online, and my efforts to contact the author were fruitless) that this is because crimes against sex buyers are also rife.

According to Martinelli, only 2% of the women surveyed were pimped or otherwise coerced. Some 71% said that they liked their work, despite the fact that almost all of the women were children when they were first prostituted; 21% said they entered prostitution 'for excitement and to meet interesting people'.

One of the most telling statistics that came out of the survey was that 'only five percent said they entered prostitution to support a drug habit, although most said they have since turned to narcotics because of the easy availability and to help reduce the stress of their work'. A common argument that has long been used by the pro-prostitution lobby is that women enter street prostitution primarily to pay for drugs.[5] Those of us who understand the harm that is inherent to the sex trade have long argued that many women turn to drugs because of the horrors they have to deal with in prostitution.[6]

---

[4] *The Associated Press*, 1 November 1984, 'Cop's Survey Finds Hookers Well Paid And Enjoy Their Work', California.

[5] UK NWSP. (2008.) *Working with sex workers: Exiting.* Retrieved 16 June 2017, from http://www.uknswp.org/wp-content/uploads/GPG5.pdf.

[6] Matthews, R.; Easton, H.; Reynolds, L.; Bindel, J.; Young, L. (2014). *Exiting prostitution: A study in female desistance.* London: Palgrave.

So rosy were the claims by Martinelli that even 'sex workers' rights' activists took issue with some of the statements. Priscilla Alexander,[7] already a major figure in the pro-prostitution movement, and at the time that the article was published she was action coordinator for the National Organisation for Women in California,[8] said that the figure of $74,000 average earnings was hugely inflated and was actually closer to $15,000 and $20,000 per annum.

The Benevolent Pimp

During my interview with Thierry Schaffauser, former senior member of the International Union of Sex Workers (IUSW), I asked what his definition of a 'pimp' was. Along with a number of other pro-prostitution lobbyists, Schaffauser holds the view that the 'pimp' is a racist figment of the abolitionists' imagination.

'Outside the [pro-prostitution] movement I would be careful about using the word pimp' says Schaffauser. 'The pimping laws in many countries like UK and France are a very broad definition. I know sex workers who let other sex workers use their flat when they were on holiday and when they came back, the police arrested them.'

To argue that there is no such thing as a pimp means that there is no such thing as a pimped person. The same goes for trafficking. A number of academics and pro-prostitution Academics and pro-prostitution lobbyists argue that trafficking is actually migration for 'sex work', which means that there are no trafficked victims and no traffickers.

Take, for example, Laura Lee, who describes herself as a 'sex worker and dominatrix'. Giving evidence to the Northern Ireland Assembly in January 2014, when it was considering whether or not to bring in the law criminalising those who pay for sex, she said: 'In all my time working as a sex worker, I have never come across a woman whom I would deem to have been coerced or trafficked in any way'.

---

[7]Delacoste, F.; Alexander, P. (1987). *Sex work: Writings by women in the sex industry*. London: Cleis Press.
[8]California NOW. Retrieved 16 June 2017, from http://canow.org/.

From the early 2000s onwards, it became popular among pro-prostitution campaigners and lobbyists to focus on the drug-using street prostituted women, in order to argue that 'crack is the new pimp'.[9] This argument was quite handy for the lobby because it took the responsibility away from third-party profiteers and sex buyers, and didn't even put it in the hands of the drug dealers but rather the prostituted woman herself. Her addiction meant that she did 'sex work' in order to feed it. She was driven by neither a pimp nor men's demand for prostitution sex.

Sanitising Use of Language

The most effective way to sanitise any human rights abuse is to rename it. For example, as Janice Raymond points out in her book *Not A Choice*,[10] a pro-slavery strategist in the West Indies suggested: 'Instead of SLAVES, let the Negroes be called ASSISTANT PLANTERS and we shall not then hear such violent outcries against the slave trade by pious divines, tender-hearted poetesses and short-sighted politicians' 13th February 2014.

Language is a powerful weapon in the ideological battle over prostitution. The term 'sex worker' entered popular parlance following the publication of *Sex Work: Writings By Women In The Sex Industry*[11] in 1987. Today, in the UK and elsewhere, the term is used by police officers, policymakers, politicians and human rights organisations. Most media outlets also favour it over 'prostitution'. The evolution of 'sex workers' rights' language has had a profound effect on how the sex trade is viewed by the general public.

In 2015 I attended the first international conference organised by ProsPol ('Comparing European Prostitution Policies: Understanding Scales and Cultures of Governance'), held in Vienna, Austria.

---

[9]Thompson, T. (2013, Oct 12.) *Crack turns vice girls into slaves to sex*. In The Guardian. Retrieved 16 June 2017, from https://www.theguardian.com/society/2003/oct/12/drugsandalcohol.drugs.

[10]Raymond, J. (2014.) *Not a choice, not a job: Exposing the myths about prostitution and the global sex trade*. London: Potomac.

[11]Delacoste, F.; Alexander, P. (1987). *Sex Work: Writings by Women in the Sex Industry*. London: Cleis Press.

Delegates had been invited to submit papers under the conference banner 'Troubling prostitution: Exploring intersections of sex, intimacy and labour'. On the flight I had read the book of abstracts in detail, my eyes growing wider as I ploughed through headings such as 'Between Love and Work: negotiations of economic and intimate ties among sex workers and pimps', and 'The 'Trafficking' of Sex Work: migration, working conditions and exploitation'.

At the conference I attended a number of workshops and keynote speeches that were peppered with the type of euphemisms that serve to distort the reality of the sex trade, for example:

- 'Contract breach'—rape
- 'Business practices'—pimping
- 'Facilitate disabled people's sexual lives'—disabled men buying sex
- 'Occupational health risks'—violence, sexually transmitted diseases, rape
- 'Job amenities'—the ability to turn down undesirable clients
- 'Affective-erotic services performed by prostitutes'—sex acts
- 'Third parties'—pimps
- 'Sex work management'—running a brothel and/or women
- 'Grooming gangs'—pimps who target girls under the age of 18
- 'International marriage community'—mail-order brides.

'Coerce', 'victim', 'trafficking' and 'survivor' were put in scare quotes in the conference materials.

Millions of dollars were poured into anti trafficking initiatives but the problem did not abate. Feminists such as the Coalition against Trafficking of Women sought to raise awareness on the international stage about the vast numbers of women being exploited both within and across borders for the purposes of prostitution. It was at the beginning of the 2000s that the pro-prostitution campaigners and academics began to deny that trafficking was such a big problem after all.[12]

---

[12]Weitzer, R. (2005, Sept/Oct.) *The growing moral panic over prostitution and sex trafficking.* In The Criminologist: The Official Newsletter of the American Society of Criminology. Retrieved 16 June 2017, from http://www.bayswan.org/traffick/Weitzer_Criminologist.pdf.

John Davies, the convicted fraudster and suspected baby trafficker, was one of the first academics to dispense with the bother of prefacing his theories on trafficked women with 'of course trafficking is terrible, but it is not the same as prostitution' type of statement.[13] Davies simply described the women as trafficked, prescribing them 'agency' and 'choice'. I discuss Davies in more depth in Chap. 9.

Nicola Mai, a UK-based academic who studies prostitution-related issues, conducted research into the trafficking of Nigerian women into Italy and France,[14] and also prescribes these trafficked women 'agency' and 'choice'.

For example, the stories of the Nigerian women in his film *Travel*[15] tell us clearly that they have been trafficked, coerced, pimped and otherwise abused into the sex trade. However, according to Mai, this is far better than them remaining in Nigeria to face poverty and hardship. In other words, for these two academics and a number of others, in recent years even trafficking has been sanitised to the point where it is seen simply as a process that the women choose to go through, to avoid something worse at home.[16,17]

The Myths of Health and Safety

Pro-prostitution lobbyists deny the harm to women in prostitution, unless they are ascribing that harm to police officers or feminist abolitionists.

---

[13]Bindel, J. (2016, Oct 6.) *The shocking tale of John Davies, pro-prostitution academic and trafficking denier, recently jailed for fraud*. On Feminist Current. Retrieved 16 June 2017, from http://www.feministcurrent.com/2016/06/10/john-davies-pro-prostitution-academic-trafficking-denier-jailed/.

[14]Mai, N. (2016, Nov 30.) *'Too much suffering': Understanding the interplay between migration, bounded exploitation and trafficking through Nigerian sex workers' experiences*. In Sociological Research Online. Retrieved 16 June 2017, from http://www.socresonline.org.uk/21/4/13.html.

[15]Mai, N. (2016). *TRAVEL – The Trailer*. Retrieved 16 June 2017, from https://vimeo.com/139963138.

[16]Mai, N. (16 April 2016) The inaugural lecture of Prof Nicola Mai, Kingston University. Retrieved 16 June 2017, from http://www.kingston.ac.uk/events/item/1943/20-apr-2016-the-inaugural-lecture-of-prof-nicola-mai-sexual-humanitarianism-migration-sex-work-and-trafficking/.

[17]Institute of Ideas. (2010, Oct 31.) *Trafficking: New slave trade or moral panic?* Retrieved 16 June 2017, from https://archive.org/details/TraffickingNewSlaveTradeOrMoralPanic31stOctober2010.

Some of the clearest examples of the way in which risk to health and harm is sanitised by the pro-prostitution lobby is in *A Guide to Occupational Health and Safety in the New Zealand Sex Industry*, published in 2004 by the New Zealand Department of Labour. This document, despite being published in 2004, is still the most up-to-date version, and advertised on the New Zealand Prostitutes' Collective website in the section 'Business Matters: Information for Brothel Operators'. Health and safety guidelines were based on those previously prepared by the Scarlet Alliance, the Australian forum for 'sex workers' rights' organisations, and the Australian Federation of AIDS Organisations publicaation *A Guide to Best Practice: Occupational Health and Safety in the Australian Sex Industry*.[18]

The document addresses issues such as condom breakage, repetitive strain injury, violence from punters, and rape (described in the document as 'Unfortunately, incidents occur where workers are forced by clients to have sex without a condom against their will'), and 'mopping up semen': 'Use disposable paper and place it in sealable plastic bag(s) for safe disposal. Is not to be directly handled; hard surfaces to be sponged with cold water and soap or detergent. Ditto for carpets and rugs; bedding to be machine washed separately in warm water and detergent and then dried.'[19]

This document outlines a number of life-threatening 'occupational hazards' in a way that makes clear these are common occurrences. HIV/ AIDS, rape, sexual violence and other serious crimes are endemic to the sex trade. According to Prostitution Research and Education, 70–95% of women in prostitution experience physical assault during 'work', 60–75% are raped, and 95% experience sexual harassment that in other industries would result in legal action.[20]

---

[18]Scarlet Alliance. (2008, Nov 11.) *Occupational health & safety*. Retrieved 16 June 2017, from http://www.scarletalliance.org.au/issues/occ-health-safety/.

[19]New Zealand Department of Labour. (2004.) *A guide to occupational health and safety in the New Zealand sex industry*, p. 45.

[20]Farley, M.; Butler, E. (2012.) Prostitution and trafficking: Quick facts. Prostitution Research & Education. Retrieved 16 June 2017, from http://www.prostitutionresearch.com/Prostitution%20 Quick%20Facts%2012-21-12.pdf.

The Erasure of 'Prostitution' and the 'Sex Work' Euphemism

In recent years I have noticed that the word 'prostitution' is used far less than 'sex work' or other euphemistic terms. One way to get a sense of the changing attitudes towards the words 'sex work' and 'prostitution' is to examine their use in the media. For this purpose, I utilised a major archive of digitised newspapers (LexisNexis) and counted the number of uses per month of the word 'sex work' (or 'sex worker[s]') and 'prostitution' (or 'prostitute[s]') from 2005 to 2015 in the UK. This included not only the major broadsheets but also other smaller newspapers, Press Association reports and a variety of other sources listed in the UK Publications category.

While the word 'prostitution' was and remains the more common phrasing, the use of the word 'sex work' has been increasing. In 2005, the ratio of the use of the word 'sex work' to 'prostitution' was 1:20; that is, there were 20 uses of the word 'prostitution' for one use of the term 'sex work'. This moved slightly over the next few years, with the ratio rising to 1:9 in 2013. In recent years, the increase has seemed to come more rapidly with the ratio rising to around 1:6 in 2014 and 2015 (January–September).

The Girlfriend Experience

My first introduction to the persuasive myths about the sex trade was the 1990 film *Pretty Woman*.[21] A romantic comedy, the story goes like this: Julia Roberts, whose character is a street-prostituted woman, meets Richard Gere, who plays a rich businessman, and he takes her back to his opulent hotel. It turns out that the punter wishes to have a 'girlfriend experience' (GE) with the prostituted woman and there are various scenes of sipping champagne and eating strawberries. Gere parades Roberts around his similarly rich business contacts and their upper-class

---

[21]Marshall, G. (Director). (1990.) *Pretty Woman*. US. http://www.imdb.com/title/tt0100405/.

wives and it becomes clear that she is not one of them. But eventually they fall in love and live happily ever after.

The relationship between sex buyer and prostituted woman is seen as one of a knight in shining armour rescuing a down-at-heel but conventionally beautiful woman who, through no fault of her own, has ended up in dire circumstances on the street. By saving her, Gere cleanses Roberts of her 'whore' status. Similarly, he escaped being a predatory john or a sad character who can't get a real date.

In 1991 I was in Moscow, speaking to a group of 16–18-year-old girls in a high school. I was there as part of the British Council's programme to educate those vulnerable to being trafficked into prostitution. I asked them what they would like to do as a career, and more than 50% of them said that they would like to be a prostitute. Shocked, I asked why. The most common answer, apart from the fact that they could migrate from Russia to the West, was that they could meet a man like Richard Gere and have a happy ending.

Nowhere are class and other social dividers more stark that in an opulent setting (such as a five-star hotel room) where one person can easily afford the bill, and the other does not even have a bank account. Sex trade survivor Fiona Broadfoot tells me that on the street 'they [sex buyers] make you feel like shite when they have a posh hotel room that they can buy you in. You're the dirty whore and they have a load of money and power. At least on the street you are both looked at as scum, to one degree or another, by the residents and police'.

Di Martin exited prostitution in 1984 when GE was not marketed to punters as an actual distinct 'service'. 'The mechanics of [GE] existed in terms of being booked for two days, having to go out to dinner or the casino with them, and paraded at business events', says Martin. 'I even remember having to undergo a pre-interview at a restaurant in Chelsea to ensure my knowledge of current affairs was up to par! To me, these were the worst jobs because I had to find a way of not letting them have access to 'me' but also provide an engaging, charming persona that convinced him he was fascinating.

'It was exhausting. This is all a way of men showcasing what they've bought and also a way of them pretending that they haven't had to pay for it. Also they might be charming at dinner or at the casino but you still never knew what was going to happen at the end of the night, so [I had] prolonged anxiety.'

Anja was also prostituted in the legal brothels in Germany. 'I always tell the people how ugly it is, because they think it's easier when a john treats you friendly like a 'girlfriend' but it's much more cruel, because you have to be conscious all the time, no chance to dissociate because you always have to play a role, you always have to interact with the john. I hated it.'

Huschke Mau was prostituted in Germany, including in so-called 'mega brothels'. 'When you sell sex you have to pretend you are someone else, you need to practise disassociation. When they come and take your hand and kiss you and cuddle you and ask you things about your private life, it feels like you have no borders around yourself', says Mau.

'I expect to get what I pay for', a British sex tourist visiting the window brothel area of Amsterdam told me, 'and if it's a quick blow job, fine, but if I am paying for her to be my girlfriend, that's what she has to be. I want her "in the moment"'.

Courtney was involved in prostitution for ten years in the decriminalised and legalised regimes within New Zealand and Australia. 'The middle-class white male was the most frequent requester of "the girlfriend experience". Upon reflection, the idea of the girlfriend experience perplexes me. When I think about myself being a girlfriend, I expect my boyfriend to court me, take me to dinner, massage my shoulders and prove that he is eventually going to be a good husband and father', says Courtney. 'The reality within the sex trade is very far from that. It has been the source of much pain and distrust, countless times of fighting off men who believed they had the right to violate me above and beyond, all because of a scummy $50. I wonder what they think when they meditate on the idea of a girlfriend? Has it really been reduced to the access of a sexual interaction?'

The story the sex trade survivors tell are, unsurprisingly, vastly different from what we hear from the academics, pimps and sex buyers.

The term 'selling love' and the description of those selling the GE is also referred to as 'selling love' or 'professional girlfriend'. These terms are being increasingly used among the post-modernists and anthropologist academics, and I heard it several times during that long weekend at Prostpol in Vienna. I recalled a conversation with Rachel Moran, an Irish survivor of the sex trade and founder of SPACE International. Moran was trying to explain why sex could not be viewed as a commodity to be purchased for money, and asked me to name two other things that also could not be viewed as such. I suggested humour and love.

But according to a growing number of academics and 'sex workers' rights activists', 'love' rather than 'sex' is on the prostitution market place. During the Vienna conference, I heard several academics and PhD candidates use the phrase 'selling love'.

As Heidi Hoefinger claims in her book *Sex, Love and Money in Cambodia: Professional Girlfriends and Transactional Relationships*[22]: 'Although they might be stigmatised by the wider conservative Cambodian society, PGs use their own forms of discursive, emotional and sexual power in attempts to advance their mobility and secure a better future for themselves – as do many women who identify as sex workers.'

In a review of *The Girlfriend Experience*, a drama on cable TV channel Starz, which is based on the 2009 film by Stephen Soderbergh, Brian Moylan writes: 'The problem with Christine is that she's a bit of a cypher. She is closed off, cold and doesn't like to be around other people. I'm sorry, but if there is any job in the world that requires being a people person, it's sex work. We know Christine needs the money and is vaguely interested in being transgressive, but her emotional inner life is as unknowable as a stripper's real name.'[23]

This assumption is a direct contradiction of the testimony of prostituted women the world over. 'I cut off from myself', said Moran. 'It is how we cope with the invasion of our bodies and of our souls.'

---

[22]Hoefinger, H. (2014.) *Sex, love and money in Cambodia: Professional girlfriends and transactional relationships*. London: Routledge.

[23]Moylan, B. (2016, Jan 27.) *The Girlfriend Experience: Sex work drama needs a lighter touch*. In *The Guardian*. Retrieved 16 June 2017, from https://www.theguardian.com/tv-and-radio/2016/jan/27/the-girlfriend-experience-starz-sex-worker.

I interviewed 50 survivors during the course of researching this book and every single one said variations on the same theme: they dissociate, leave their bodies, go to another place in their heads. If prostituted women were present during every encounter with a sex buyer, even less of the women would survive, and I would imagine the morgues would be overflowing with johns. But of course, Moylan's take on the GE is that it is not really prostitution.

Georgina Perry, former CEO of the charity Open Doors in East London (an NHS-funded harm reduction agency), further perpetuates the notion that hanging out for a weekend is merely a leisure activity for which one is paid. 'Far from being a distant underworld, sold sex is relatively common. Research shows that around 10% of men in the UK, from all walks of life, have paid for sex – a percentage that would surely be much higher if it included people other than heterosexual men, and more ambiguously transactional intimacies.' The fact that Perry included what she considered to be 'transactional intimacies' as distinct from prostitution shows quite how embedded the notion of 'selling love' has become.

Trafficking Denial

A similar view of who the baddies are exists within the discourse of 'sex workers' rights'. We repeatedly hear how the trafficking of women from poor, war-torn countries is bad, but prostitution is different because the women choose it (and presumably, none of them is pimped or exploited). Pimps and brothel owners also use this cleansing excuse, such as Dennis Hof, author of *The Art of the Pimp: One Man's Search for Love, Sex and Money*, and owner of a string of legal brothels in Nevada in the USA.

During my week with Hof in 2012, in which I visited several of his brothels, I asked him why he considers legalisation safer and better than any form of criminalisation. Hof told me: 'The legal environment is like the world's greatest singles bar. There is no trafficking, no rape, no HIV, no illegal activity. It's safe here.' In 2016, Hof announced that he is working with state legislators to discuss ways in which he can start a campaign to end trafficking, and described it as his 'last goal in life'. 'I hate traffickers', Hof told me. 'They give our business a bad name.'

Sugar Daddies, not Punters

The website *Seeking Arrangement*[24] is one of the most popular sites used by those wishing to enter into such a deal. According to the website, there are 12 females to each male looking for a 'partnership'. 'Sugar Babies and Sugar Daddies have on-going relationships not transactions', reads the introductory blurb. 'More often than not, a sugar relationship will resemble that of a girlfriend–boyfriend relationship. There are real connections and real possibilities at romance, something that is not in the realm of possibility with an escort or prostitute.'

In Boston in 2015, I met a man whom I will call Philip. I contacted him via an online dating agency that specialised in linking older, wealthy men seeking 'dates' with young, attractive women. Philip agreed to speak to me on the proviso that I made it clear that he was 'not a john':

> I like sex, I like beautiful girls and I'm divorced. I am solvent. I think I'm an interesting guy, and there are young women out there who had bad dating experiences with young immature men who don't know how to treat them. Maybe these girls find it difficult to pay their rent or their college fees, but either way this is a mutual arrangement of benefit to both sides. It is as far from prostitution as you can get – we have dinner, we have sex if we both feel like it, I pay her bills. End of story. If I wanted prostitutes I would go to brothels or on the street. I don't, those women are different. This is a normal relationship.

Philip would be greatly reassured by the description of 'sugar' contracts on Seeking Arrangement:

---

[24]Seeking Arrangement: Sugar Daddy Dating. Retrieved 16 June 2017, from https://www.seekingarrangement.com.

Sugar is a lifestyle choice, not a profession. A sugar baby is a woman who wants to date financially secure men who can provide her with the lifestyle she desires. She's selective about who she dates; a prostitute isn't picky about who she takes on as a client. The risks involved with prostitution are countless, and include exposure to crime, abuse, sexually transmitted diseases and theft of service. Many prostitutes are also subject to physical and emotional abuse, especially when involved with a pimp. And in sugar, sex is never a requirement only an aspiration.

I meet Annabel, a conventionally attractive woman in her early 20s who is in her second year of studies at a university in the North of England. Annabel had been introduced to the world of 'sugar babies' by a friend who was in an 'arrangement' with a married man in his 60s.

'In reality, what I was expected to do was just sex work,' says Annabel. 'I met Doug and it was clear from the beginning that sex was expected, and that he was road testing me before he came up with any offer as to helping me out financially. I was in massive debt and saw no other way out. I ended up sleeping with a disgusting old man for money and it made me feel so bad about myself that I ended up dropping out of my studies.'

But according to Seeking Arrangement, the women brokered via its website are totally distinct from 'prostitutes', despite what either the women feel or the men expect: 'You may meet hundreds of prostitutes before finding anyone to fulfil your emotional needs. Prostitutes are hired to roleplay for the evening – they'll be whomever you want them to be, but they won't necessarily be themselves.'

Mail-Order Brides

The mail-order bride industry is built on prostitution. It is, for the women who are purchased in this manner, potentially a lifetime of 24-hours-a-day prostitution. It is an aspect of the sex trade that has been re-marketed to look as though it is nothing more than Internet dating.

In Kiev, Ukraine, I met the men who are looking to buy a bride, the agency owners and the women who had signed up to them in the hope of escaping poverty and other hardships.

I met Bridget in Kiev, who had already been through a divorce and been left with two young children. Her husband was a violent alcoholic. Bridget told me that she made a decision to sign up to the mail-order bride website because it was a better option than selling herself in a bar or on the street. Bridget married a man from Canada, whom she had only previously met twice. She barely speaks any English. 'I was nothing more than a full-time prostitute', says Bridget. 'I was expected to be on call, 24 hours of every day, and not only for sex. I had to wash his clothes, clean his toilet, clean the shirts onto which I bled when he was rough with me, and make his food and smile at him when he came in from work. In fact, I was his slave. I belonged to him. He got me cheap.'

Bridget's experience is far from uncommon. What is not that common, however, is for people to understand or to admit that the mail-order bride industry is part of the sex trade. Indeed, it is far more common to describe this industry as the marriage industry. The men I spoke to who were buying women to marry were offended by my use of the term 'mail-order bride industry'.

At one of the 'shop front' agencies, Kiev Connections, I talk to its manager Veronica about the industry and the women on her books. It is not long before a customer turns up hoping to meet his 'date' with whom he has been corresponding on Skype and email for three months. Robert from Delaware in USA is in his mid-60s, and has been looking for a Ukrainian bride for four years. He tells me that Ukrainian women tend not to be tainted with feminist ideology and 'have a little bit of better fit for what old-style America is about'.

I speak to Marta Gosovska, a former student in Ukraine who was paid by a marriage agency to translate letters between the men and the potential brides. 'The women were very young, very beautiful, badly educated', says Gosovska. 'Almost none of them spoke English, and used only nouns and simple verbs. The men were almost all over 40, in bad physical condition, overweight. I was 22 and horrified that someone would want to have a relationship with such a person.'

Gosovska tells me about a 70-year-old Canadian man who 'auditioned' 11 women at the same time in his hotel room in order to choose a bride. 'He was a desperate person wishing to find himself a housewife. Not a wife, not a partner but a housewife to look after his house and have sex whenever he wanted. Another man asked me which of the 12 women that he was interested in had children', says Gosovska. 'These men know the women with children are more vulnerable.'

I made contact with a former mail-order bride via a support project for migrant women in North America. Kamon (not her real name) married Dave, a former Marine from Chicago, but escaped soon after she was brought from Thailand to the USA. 'I was a dancer in a bar [in Bangkok] and the manager told me I would get lots of money from dating rich American men by joining his bride agency', Kamon told me over the telephone. 'I was in trouble with money, so when I met Dave and he told me he would take care of me I did not even think, I just agreed to go home with him.'

What happened next was, says Kamon, 'my worst nightmare'. Trapped in a small town, thousands of miles away from home and unable to speak much English, Kamon became depressed, which in turn 'made him hate me'. She continues: 'He wanted sex when he wanted it, food when he wanted. If I cried he would shout at me, and I had to do what he told me because he said he could have me deported back to Thailand. The man I met [in Thailand] disappeared as soon as he got home'.

The very existence of an industry designed to market and sell human beings is exploitation and degradation. This is the case regardless of any alleged 'consent' on the part of the woman being sold. 'It was torture', Kamon tells me. 'I thought it would be better than selling myself in bars, but I ended up being a full-time prostitute and slave. I weep for other women who think this is a good idea.'

Sex Surrogacy

Retraining former prostituted women as 'sex surrogates' gives the impression that the women are being professionally qualified to do a respectable job and that they have been exited.

An article in the *Daily Mail* pegged on the 2012 release of the film *The Sessions*, a real-life story about the late polio sufferer Mark O'Brien and his so-called 'sex surrogate' Cheryl Cohen Greene, was headlined 'We're not prostitutes: The sex surrogates helping real life 40-year-old virgins overcome crippling inexperience with one-on-one coaching'.[25]

'You need a partner to resolve most sexual problems and for single men that is obviously an issue', said Greene in the article. According to Greene, 10% of her clients are 'academics or career-focused virgins who failed to concentrate on their love lives'. An average course is 12–15 sessions, with penetration happening halfway through the course. 'I'm not a prostitute, you don't have to pay me upfront', says the Greene character when O'Brien says the money is on the desk.

Fern Arden, a sex therapist at a private clinic in Manhattan, commented in the *New York Post* on the general assumption that 'sex surrogacy' is prostitution: 'The focus is not sex but familiarity and intimacy. We provide an environment, not for sexual pleasure but for sexual learning. People tend to be ill-informed about what a surrogate partner does. They think of it pejoratively, the same as a sex worker, but it's not'.[26]

According to the US International Professional Surrogates Association,[27] surrogates must complete a two-week training programme with the society to become registered, and they must also work for a licensed sex therapist. Arden's 'surrogate partners' are required to be tested for STDs at least once every two months, as are the sex buyers.

---

[25]Daily Mail. (2012, Oct 25.) *'We're not prostitutes': The sex surrogates helping real life 40-year-old virgins overcome crippling inexperience with one-on-one coaching.* In Daily Mail. Retrieved 16 June 2017, from http://www.dailymail.co.uk/femail/article-2223134/Were-prostitutes-The-sex-surrogates-helping-real-life-40-year-old-virgins-overcome-crippling-inexperience-one-coaching.html.

[26]Ridley, J. (2012, Oct 25.) *Secrets of the sex surrogates.* In New York Post. Retrieved 16 June 2017, from http://nypost.com/2012/10/25/secrets-of-the-sex-surrogates/.

[27]International Professional Surrogates Association. Retrieved 16 June 2017, from http://www.surrogatetherapy.org/.

Kassandra, based in Nuremberg, Germany, is described on its website as a counselling centre for sex workers. According to its website, Kassandra is: 'The contact for all the people who work as prostitutes or are active in the sex trade, as well as for those who are interested in the topic sex'. Kassandra also offers training for women to become 'sexual assistant surrogate partnerships'. The training focusses on how 'sex workers' can help disabled people to explore their sexuality.

I meet Barbel Ahlborn, who heads Kassandra. She tells me she is proud of the courses that Kassandra developed with Pro Familia, a family planning centre. 'This is a unique model project for the nation', she told me. 'We do it as an education programme. We teach the legal conditions of sex work on one hand and also the legal basics of sexual rights for older people and the disabled'.

The course, according to Ahlborn, is about ensuring the rights of 'the older people', but says that such arrangements should never be State-funded but offered by independent 'sexual surrogates', many of whom are 'former sex workers'. This argument suits those who profiteer from the sex trade extremely well. Private arrangements are more lucrative, because the pimps and those directly providing so-called sexual surrogacy can charge pretty much what they like. The idea that offering so-called training to formally prostituted women and men in order to qualify them as 'sex surrogates' is simply prostitution under another name.

Brothels as Workers' Cooperatives/Safe Houses

In an article for *Vice* magazine,[28] Frankie Mullin, a pro-prostitution lobbyist who had been involved in the sex trade previously, asked so-called sex workers what their ideal brothel would look like. Various ideas were put forward by a number of women currently in prostitution, all of whom appear to be sympathetic to the 'sex workers' rights' lobby.

---

[28]Mullin, F. (2016, May 22.) *Sex workers tell us what their ideal brothels would look like.* In Vice. Retrieved 16 June 2017, from http://www.vice.com/en_uk/read/sex-workers-ideal-brothels-frankie-mullin.

One woman complained about being made to work even when ill: 'Besides the scant facilities, my main complaint about brothels is usually the management, from the services they insist you provide to the shifts they make you work. "Don't ever tell them you've got thrush', one woman warned me. "They'll make you work anyway. Say you've got food poisoning or something"'.

The appalling reality of having to be penetrated by a punter when suffering from such a painful condition as thrush is a clue as to how abusive this industry is. Despite her justifiable criticism of what she calls management, this interviewee admits that even running brothels as a cooperative would not eliminate problems caused by punters.

She says:

> Sex workers running things themselves seems vastly preferable. When I consider it seriously, though, I wonder how we'd manage things like finding ourselves passed over by clients for not offering certain services or for charging more than other workers – or even because oppressive beauty standards affect how much business we get. I get excited about the possibilities but I'm brought back down to earth when I remember that so many of these problems with work are problems of capitalism.

Another interviewee highlights the inherent dangers in prostitution. The co-operative brothel that she would design would have 'panic buttons in all the rooms. It's not nice to think about the bad side but we have to be realistic, and it would be such a relief to know that if anything did happen the police would be instantly alerted'. She continues: 'The hallway the clients would walk in through would have a camera so that all the sex workers could see who the client was for safety'.

Brothels are sites of exploitation run by pimps for profit off the backs of women. However, in order to rebrand them and claim that they can be worker's cooperatives, it is necessary to rebrand them as 'fair trade' and a force for good for the women being prostituted from such premises.

In February 2015,[29] the Amsterdam College of Mayor and Alderpersons announced that they were to launch a feasibility study

---

[29]I Amsterdam. (2015, Feb 5.) *Amsterdam investigates feasibility of prostitutes running their own businesses.* On IAmsterdam.Com. Retrieved 16 June 2017, from http://www.iamsterdam.com/en/media-centre/city-hall/press-releases/2015-press-room/feasibility-study-prostitution.

into what they described as 'self-managed prostitution businesses'. The local municipality was seeking an external partner to collaborate with by giving funding towards the purchasing and letting out of five properties to house brothels. The move was, according to the Mayor's office, driven by a desire to '[increase] independence and autonomy for prostitutes working in Amsterdam'. It was part of the drive to 'stamp out abuse' within the sex trade, and was welcomed by a number of women in prostitution. They added: 'The goal of the programme is that prostitutes themselves acquire knowledge to run their own business and then take 'full control of the business within a reasonable period of time'.

The municipality was considering working alongside HVO-Querido,[30] a charity that teaches business skills to marginalised individuals and, according to its website, 'provide[s] care, support, guidance and shelter to young people aged 16 with psychosocial or psychiatric problems'.

Its website says: 'Experienced in offering assistance to prostitutes, HVO-Querido is a foundation that is dedicated to strengthening their role as businesspeople. [… It] provides a safe house for prostitutes fleeing violent pimps'. The very idea that an organisation that identifies trafficking of women into the sex trade as a major problem and human rights abuse could also consider a partnership with the local government of Amsterdam to buy brothels is shocking. Not only that, but as highlighted in another report: 'Amsterdam is looking to offload five buildings it acquired as part of a deal with former prolific sex trade entrepreneur Charles Geertz'.[31]

Geertz is one of Holland's biggest pimps. He once owned dozens of red light windows in multiple buildings, which he sold to the city from 2007 to 2008 for an estimated €25 million amid allegations he was involved in money laundering and organised crime.

---

[30]HVO Querido. Retrieved 16 June 2017, from http://hvoquerido.nl/.
[31]Newmark, Z. (2015, Nov 19.) *Amsterdam mayor: City ready for brothel run by sex workers*. In NL Times. Retrieved 16 June 2017, from http://nltimes.nl/2015/11/19/amsterdam-mayor-city-ready-brothel-run-by-sex-workers.

For all the valiant attempts at sanitising the prostitution aspect of the sex trade, and the liberal use of euphemisms to describe the realities, the majority of the survivors I interviewed told me that the misrepresentation from the pro-prostitution lobby about the lack of harm and violence from pimps and punters are what angers them the most.

One of many examples of this is from the pro-prostitution activist Marijke Vonk. She writes on her blog[32]:

> While sex workers and sex work activists want to talk about human rights, international law, respecting the agency of other adults and stopping violence, rescue fetishists get all flushed as they emphasise that thousands of women get raped with objects and are forced to drink buckets of sperm and they get tattoos so everyone can see they are a whore. It's so inappropriate. They ignore and silence actual sex workers so they can enjoy their rescue-fetish unhindered.

Chelsea, who, when we met in Auckland, had recently escaped a legal brothel in New Zealand, said this to me in response to the harm deniers:

> I've started doing something that could be seen to be very anti-feminist. I've stared inviting people to come prostitute with me. I'm telling all these privileged lefty academic 'pro sex-work' arrogant fuckers that if they think being prostituted is just 'sex work' and they are for it, that they can come and work with me in the brothels and get a dose of reality. This was not a choice like any other for us, it was a choice made in the absence of anything better.

Chelsea has hit the nail on the head. While blanket decriminalisation and normalisation of the global sex trade suits the '1%',[33] the consequences of removing criminal laws from pimps, punters and brothel

---

[32]Marijke Vonk: Psychologist, Sexologist, Educator. Retrieved 16 June 2017, from http://marijkevonk.com/the-grim-truth/.

[33]A phrase commonly used by abolitionists to describe the 'happy hookers' who make up a tiny minority of prostituted women.

owners are dire. The negative effects of both legalisation and decriminalisation, implemented by countries that have listened to the powerful lobby of 'sex workers' rights' activists will, as we will see in the next chapter, take generations to unravel.

4

Realities & Consequences of Legalisation

"What's being sold as a paradise is only a paradise for sex capitalists – pimps, human traffickers, brothel owners who charge extortionate daily room rates for the women – who get to act out all their violent fantasies for increasingly lower rates. The only ones NOT benefiting from all this are the women. For them, it's a hellhole. And the government is still not listening". (Huschke Mau, German sex trade survivor', 2015)

Introduction

Under legalisation and decriminalisation regimes, pimps have been reclassified as managers and businessmen—with some, such as Douglas Fox, calling themselves 'sex workers'. Abuse suffered by the women is now called an 'occupational hazard', like a stone dropped on a builder's toe. Sex tourism has grown faster in Amsterdam than the regular type of tourism: as the city became the brothel of Europe, women have been imported by traffickers from Africa, Eastern Europe, and Asia to meet the demand. In other words, the pimps remained but became legitimate. There has been little or no support for women to exit prostitution, and the innate murkiness of the sex trade has not been washed away by legal benediction.

© The Author(s) 2017
J. Bindel, *The Pimping of Prostitution*,
DOI 10.1057/978-1-137-55890-9_4

Then its lead researcher, a passionate 'sex workers' rights' activist to this day, told me she was positive about tolerance zones and legal brothels. 'A good legal sex trade is your best instrument against an illegal circuit', she said. The Dutch model was previously held up as the ideal model with which to regulate the sex trade. But as the Dutch experiment began to crumble, van Doorninck, along with many other cheerleaders for legalisation, began to point out the problems inherent in it and, since 2003, replace the word 'legalisation' with 'decriminalisation'.

Van Doornick is one of many who promoted State-controlled legalisation of prostitution as the only viable option during the late 1990s and early 2000s. How things change. Today, the 'sex workers' rights' lobby largely denies that there was ever any support for state-controlled legal brothels. Now, 'decriminalisation' is the buzzword and New Zealand is held up as the finest example of how to deal with the sex trade.

But decriminalisation and legalisation are cut from the same cloth. As I argued in Chap. 1, decriminalisation means elimination of criminal sanctions against soliciting, pimping and running a brothel. Under this system, pimps and brothel owners still operate as such but are redefined under law as managers and business owners.

The Disaster of Legalisation

The evidence of the harms of legalisation and decriminalisation is clear. I visited brothels and so-called street-based 'tolerance zones' in Australia, Germany, Holland, Austria, North America and New Zealand, where I have interviewed prostituted women, pro-prostitution campaigners, pimps, punters and police officers.

Sex trade survivor Evelina Giobbe sums up the problems with legal brothels:

> Nevada is the only state in the US with legal brothels. I call it the factory farming of sex. The number of clients women see, the lack of control they have over the choice of clients, the lack of control they have over their health regarding condoms'. They are not only preyed upon by pimps economically, they're preyed upon by the brothel owners economically. It's a really bad deal for women.

Legalisation has been a disaster. Under this regime, demand, trafficking of women and girls, and the illegal brothel sector have increased. There is no evidence of a decrease in violence, HIV rates or murders of women in legal sex trades, but there is evidence that the rights and freedom promised by lobbyists for legalisation and decriminalisation were transferred to the brothel owners and sex buyers. In this chapter, we will hear from the women prostituted in countries before and after the introduction of legalisation and decriminalisation, and look closely at the evidence that contradicts the positive spin by the pro-prostitution lobby.

Holland

For years, the Dutch argued that legalising brothels was a solution to the myriad problems associated with the sex trade. The logic was to make it a job like any other. Supporters claimed that once the women were liberated from the underworld, the criminals would drift away.

Since 2000, the legalised window brothels of De Wallen have attracted customers from all over the world. But in 2007, the then mayor of Amsterdam, Job Cohen, admitted that legalisation had been a failure. 'We want in part to reverse it', said Cohen, 'especially with regard to the exploitation of women in the sex trade. Lately we've received more and more signals that abuse still continues'.[1]

Now, politicians, police, citizens and the women in prostitution themselves are admitting that legalisation in the Netherlands has been an abject failure. Contrary to government promises, trafficking into the Netherlands has massively increased, the street scene remains, and pimping and drug dealing are rife.

Karina Schaapman, Amsterdam councillor and sex trade survivor, said in 2005:

> Legalising prostitution was infused with the idea of the articulate prostitute, who should get rights and better working conditions. But that

---

[1]Post, D. (2013, Sept 11.) *Prostitution and sex trafficking: inescapably linked.* In Fair Observer. Retrieved 16 June 2017, from http://www.fairobserver.com/region/north_america/prostitution-human-trafficking-inescapably-linked/.

image is incorrect … Two-thirds of prostitutes are foreign, most often illegal and nobody is registering them. The Amsterdam police has a portfolio with 76 violent pimps operating on De Wallen. Often they stand at the corner, counting the customers of 'his' woman to subsequently collect the money. It is very difficult for the police to get a case.[2]

One newspaper report from 2006 quotes Lodewijk Asscher, recently appointed chief of Amsterdam's ruling Social Democrat Party: 'If we have a choice of losing a tourist attraction or helping to end the abuse of women, I would rather lose the tourist attraction. It should not be closed immediately but, if there is no reform, we should gradually try to diminish it'.[3]

Rather than afford better protection for the women, legalisation led to an increased market. The industry has not been contained but has spilt out all over Amsterdam, including on-street. Rather than be given rights in the 'workplace', pimps are as brutal as ever. Pimps are reclassified as businessmen. Abuse suffered by the women is now called an 'occupational hazard'. Support for the women to leave prostitution becomes almost non-existent.

In 2012 I interviewed elderly twins Louise and Martine Fokkens who had each been involved in prostitution in Amsterdam for 50 years. Although legalisation is supposed to benefit those involved, the sisters told me: 'There are few Dutch women and no sense of community these days. There is no point working just for tax. That is why the girls are working from the Internet and from home: you are less likely to be spotted by the taxman. The vultures, the organised criminals, came in 2000. They thought, "Ah, it is legalised. Now we are OK"'.

As I walked around the city with the twins, male tourists stopped us wanting photographs with the twins. These women, both of whom had been abused into prostitution by violent men, were objects of amusement. Louise had been beaten onto the streets by her husband when she was in her early 20s and Martine also experienced domestic violence.

[2]Shared Hope (2007) *DEMAND: Report*. Shared Hope International. Retrieved 16 June 2017, from https://manualzz.com/doc/14882262/demand.-report.

[3]Burke, J. (2006, Feb 19.) *Threat to switch off city's red lights*. In The Guardian. Retrieved 16 June 2017, from https://www.theguardian.com/world/2006/feb/19/jasonburke.theobserver.

I booked a personal tour guide around De Wallen one evening. My guide told me he decided to start a business showing tourists around the prostitution area because he 'liked porn' and therefore it should be familiar to him. I asked about pimping and exploitation in the area. He told me: 'Some people call the brothel owners or the building owners the new pimps because they ask about €4000 a month for one window in the most popular areas'.

Turkey

There are approximately 30 legal, state-run brothels in Turkey. Although almost half have been closed down in recent years, the sex trade is thriving. I visited Zurafa Street, where there are several legal establishments. There was a gate with an armed security guard standing beside it who would not let me enter. 'Men only', he said. The prostituted women in Turkey's legal brothels are highly stigmatised, despite the legality, and there are far more that operate illegally (100,000) than legally (1500).

Banu Helvacioglu is a senior academic in the Department of Political Science at Bilkent University, Ankara, and grew up in the 1970s near the red-light district of Bent Deresi province in Ankara. He explains:

> I was a teenager when I found out from the boys in my school about the state-run brothels. To my knowledge these state-run brothels implied a legal way for both the sex workers and their customers. The rumour in the 1970s had it that the sex workers in those brothels were registered in the system as legitimate prostitutes with regular health check-ups.

> Coming from a sheltered middle-class family background implied that it was inconceivable to even imagine who the customers and the sex workers were. Out of curiosity I visited the neighbourhood with a group of friends from school. My outlook to both prostitutes and the underlying morality in Turkey [that prostitution is evil] changed after that visit. Mind you, around the same time I was part of a left-wing revolutionary movement. From that perspective I saw prostitution as part of a larger problem of exploitation.

USA

Dennis Hof, who we've met before, is a famous pimp, often seen on TV in the HBO series *Cathouse*, a puff piece for the legal sex trade. Hof is author of *The Art of the Pimp: One Man's Search for Love, Sex, and Money*.[4] Owner of the Love Ranch in Nye County and the famous Moonlight Bunny Ranch, a few miles outside Carson City in Reno, and other sex businesses, Hof claims he is a passionate anti-trafficking activist. According to Hof, there is no rape, no trafficking, no HIV and no illegal activity in brothels operating under legalisation.

In Hof's brothels the women are not allowed to smile, flick their hair or appear to be doing a 'hard sell', lest it be 'unfair' to the competition. The sex buyers are ordinary-looking men, all ages, and in the main presentable enough to be able to pick up a woman in a normal bar. Hof argues that legalising brothels prevents the spread of the illegal industry.

However, illegal brothels are on the increase in Nevada, as they are in other parts of the world where brothels are legalised. Nevada's unlawful prostitution industry, according to research by the US Government, is already nine times greater than the state's legal brothels.

Hof's Love Ranch brothel is an hour's drive from Vegas. The building is surrounded by high walls covered by barbed wire. I speak to a number of women, most of whom live in the brothel for weeks or months at a time, often not seeing a customer for days.

Lance Gilman is a multimillionaire property dealer who owns two brothels, including the Mustang Ranch, which Gilman proudly tells me is modelled on a prison and used to refer to the women as inmates. Gilman's partner Susan Austin runs his brothels. 'As soon as you legalise, it turns the predators loose', Gilman tells me. 'You have to regulate. We have a stable of 1000 [women]. If Susan didn't run this place with an iron fist it would get out of control.' As with most other legal brothels, the women are not allowed out unless the manager gives them permission and they are accompanied by an assistant pimp.

---

[4]Hof, D. 2014, *The Art Of The Pimp*.

Legal pimps are also not averse to selling-learning disabled women. At the Mustang Ranch I briefly met Sindy, although Austin told me I was not allowed to interview her. Austin described Sindy to me as a 'nine-year-old trapped in an adult body'. According to Austin, Sindy grew up in foster care and was sold to the brothel by her boyfriend's father, while the boyfriend was serving a 10-year prison sentence for possession of child abuse images. Sindy, who was 22 when I met her, had been with the boyfriend since she was 12 years old. Austin had taken over managing Sindy's money for her and said she 'refused' to send the cheques to the boyfriend's father. Many of the women in legal brothels are double pimped, with the brothel owner sending the prostituted women's earnings directly to the person who brought them to the brothel.

Austin tells me: 'I called the girls to a meeting and told them, we're raising a child but she'll never grow up. When Sindy parties [services a sex buyer], one of the girls will go and sit in the bathroom next door, to make sure the man doesn't take advantage of her when he realises what he has'. I ask why, if Sindy is learning-disabled and vulnerable, Austin is pimping her at all'. Austin tells me she has made a pact with the other women to 'look after' Sindy, 'otherwise she would end up on the streets of Florida'. There appear to be no laws in Nevada against pimping a learning-disabled young woman and why should there be? After all, under legalisation it is just a job. There are a number of sex trade survivors I have interviewed who tell me they used to be in favour of legalisation before they came to terms with the reality of that regime.

'When I was in the industry I argued pro-legalisation and claimed that it did no harm', says Haley, a sex trade survivor and abolitionist I met in Minnesota. 'Now I can see there's a ton of harm being done and they're capitalising on the harm done to me as a child.'

Germany

In Germany the situation is dire. There are approximately 400,000 women in prostitution here, and it is estimated that around 1.2 million men buy sex every day. This is a lot when you think the population of the country is 80 million.

Helmut Sporer, Detective Chief Superintendent of the Crimes Squad, Augsburg, is a vocal critic of legalised prostitution.

> [Legalisation] has led to a massive reduction of the legal standing of the women. What has developed is a legally instituted relationship of precedence and subordination that is being exploited by the profiteers in the red-light business. If you want to call it like that, it is a new form of slavery under state supervision. Those making the law wanted to integrate prostitution into normal, regular forms of work. Prostitution was to become a job like any other, with an official boss, a working contract and even a trade union. Of course this could not work out.

The pro-prostitution lobby is the loudest in Germany because the sex trade there is very big business. There are the mega brothels on the one hand and Eastern European street prostitution on the other. According to the feminist abolitionists I met in Munich and Berlin, police would raid the smaller apartments in which two or three women sold sex without a pimp.

There are around 3000 red-light establishments in the country and 500 brothels in Berlin alone. Aside from a flurry of publicity exposing the inner workings of the 'mega brothels' since the 2006 World Cup held in Berlin, there has been far less media exposure of the legal sex trade in Germany compared to Nevada in the USA, and the Netherlands. Although sex tourism certainly exists in Germany, it is incomparable to that of the window brothel area of De Wallen, Amsterdam. This is the reason why the legal sex trade and all its horrors has not yet captured as much attention from anti-legalisation campaigners. However, the feminist abolitionist movement in Germany is gaining ground.

There are 180 brothels in Munich. This figure does not include the apartments from which many women are prostituted. The German prostitution law says if a city in Germany has more than 50,000 residents the city must by law declare some zones open for prostitution, whether they like it or not.

Inge Kleine, a German feminist campaigner against the sex trade, says:

There are cities who say we don't want it and quite a few cities say 'OK, some prostitution but we don't want these brothels because we can see the exploitation', The city does not have the right to say 'no'. If there's an area and somebody wants to build a brothel, you need a good reason to ban it.

They ['sex workers' rights' activists] tried to sell it to feminists that our laws would break up these enterprising businesswomen, and said that allowing the women to work together in this way would get rid of the mega brothels. The image was of a small group of happy hookers working for themselves.

Laufhaus Caesars World is a massive brothel situated between restaurants and apartments on a busy main road. A cash machine sits just outside the main entrance, and looking up I see dozens of windows with blinds pulled down and some with red curtains drawn. I am told by an assistant pimp that I cannot take photographs of the entrance to Caesars World because the owner is 'having trouble with the tax man'. He tells me: 'I don't walk into these women's rooms because they rent them and what they do behind closed doors has nothing to do with me. It would be up to them to pay the taxes. It is wrong of the tax office to want him to control what the women do in private'.

I see a young woman wearing a long coat over her shorts and bikini top coming down in the lift with a large suitcase. 'She lives here but is now visiting her family', says the assistant pimp, unhooking the chain and removing the padlock that secures the lift so that the young woman can get out.

We have been in the entrance of the brothel for 10 min and during that time have seen about a dozen men come in and out. It is 4 p.m but there are discount rates before 5 p.m.

I am invited into the office and shown the security cameras that monitor each of the four corridors. There are women in bikinis perched on stools waiting to be picked out by one of the many sex buyers I see prowling up and down, deciding whom to buy. There is no menu for the services on offer in this brothel. Once the men pay their entrance fee to the pimps, the women are left to negotiate with the sex buyer.

Caesars World is the oldest brothel in Munich having been operating for 30 years. I ask manager Jörn Gruber, also known by the prostituted women as 'Betreiber' (brothel owner), if he would describe himself as a pimp. 'I'm not a pimp. I have a business and I pay €1 million a year in tax', Gruber tells me. I am told that condom use is compulsory (the German government removed the requirement in 2002), and drugs, alcohol and pimps are banned. The daily room rent is €165 for 24 h, and the minimum charge per sex buyer is €30. 'What the girls do for €30', Gruber says, 'is up to them'. At the minimum rate, the women have to 'service' six punters a day before seeing a cent in profit.

Further down the road in Munich, next-door to a trattoria, I see another brothel. It is a huge building with hearts and flowers in the red windows. There are 100 small rooms on each of the three floors. The first floor is, according to the menu on the wall and doors, all Asian women selling sex. On the second floor it is 'kink', with code words for urination on people's faces. The third floor advertises 'transsexual and transvestite' services. The owner, I am told, is very rich and a regular donor to AIDS and HIV charities.

New Zealand

The application form for opening a brothel in New Zealand is just two pages long: three pages shorter than the form those wishing to adopt a dog or cat from the Battersea Dog and Cat Home in London, UK.

As Chelsea, a young women I met in Aukland, who was prostituted in the decriminalised brothels of New Zealand, tells me:

> If you work on the streets, your pimps are the gangs. If you work in a brothel, your pimps are businessmen. What happens is that we're treated like employees when it suits them so when he tells us when we can work and what we have to do when it suits them. We're treated as independent contractors when it comes to tax. So we occupy this nowhere land and that means we have no rights, no protection and there's nothing we can do about it.

As explained in Chap. 3, New Zealand became the first country in 2003 to decriminalise its sex trade under the Prostitution Reform Act (PRA). Tim Barnett began to campaign involved with the PRA shortly after he won his first campaign for decriminalisation when he became an MP in 1996, alongside the New Zealand Prostitutes Collective (NZPC), a government-funded body set up to reduce HIV/AIDS among women in prostitution.

Barnett is quoted as saying that decriminalisation has led to a huge improvement in cooperation between those in prostitution and the police, which has resulted in murders being solved and corrupt police officers, dodgy brothel owners and traffickers being exposed. The NZPC claim that decriminalisation protects the rights and well-being of women in prostitution, and allows them to report violence without fear of action by the police.

The 'sex workers' rights' lobby, keen to embrace a new model now that legalisation is recognised as a failure, needs to convince sceptics that decriminalisation is significantly different. In an article entitled 'The difference between decriminalisation and legalisation of sex work',[5] there is a crucial distinction between these two terms that is frequently blurred in the debate around the different models. Writer and 'sex workers' rights' activist Frankie Mullin claims that: 'It is decriminalisation not legalisation for which sex workers around the world are fighting', arguing that: 'Some clarification: under legalisation, sex work is controlled by the government and is legal only under certain state-specified conditions. Decriminalisation involves the removal of all prostitution-specific laws, although sex workers and sex work businesses must still operate within the laws of the land, as must any businesses'.

But there are major regulations found in the PRA of New Zealand, such as it being an offence to buy sex from a person under 18; and brothel owners and other pimps are required to adopt and promote 'safer sex practices'. Brothel inspections are mandatory, and brothel owners as well as sex buyers can, in theory, be fined $2000 if they fail to promote or practise 'safe sex'. Penalties for failing to follow regulations could result in a maximum prison sentence of 7 years, and/or a fine of up to $10,000. The framework for regulation does exist, as we shall see, but it's about as useful as a burst condom.

---

[5]Mullin, F. (2015, Oct 19.) *The difference between decriminalisation and legislation of sex work.* In New Statesman. Retrieved 16 June 2017, from http://www.newstatesman.com/politics/feminism/2015/10/difference-between-decriminalisation-and-legalisation-sex-work.

Brothel Inspections Under the Prostitution Reform Act 2003 (PRA)

In 2014 a request was made by a local anti-prostitution activist under the Official Information Act 1982 (OIA) for information that would enable an examination of the application of the sections of the PRA 2003 relevant to the inspection of 'sex worker premises' for the period from the inception of the PRA 2003 until December 2013. This request included data on the number of inspections undertaken and each of the reports made by the NZPC to the Government as a requirement of their contract.

A number of countries, including the UK, are tempted to implement the New Zealand model of blanket decriminalisation of the sex trade, as lobbyists have long argued that this is the only way to keep the women safe. But when criminal sanctions are removed from sex establishments, it becomes the responsibility of health officials to carry out inspections. I have access to data on New Zealand obtained via the OIA which shows that, aside from 12 inspections that were conducted in 2003 in the first few weeks of the new legislation, only 11 inspections occurred across the whole of New Zealand until January 2015.

Considering the estimated size of the prostituted population, the limited number of inspections already suggests that the Government is failing in its duty under the PRA 2003.

However, a closer examination of the results of the OIA 1982 request highlights some very important issues that further evidence this failure. The CSOM 2007 report indicates there is limited interest in resourcing inspections under this part of the legislation. For example, despite suggestions from staff in the Department of Labour that all premises should be inspected, it was not considered a health priority and it was felt that resources would need to be directed away from other health programmes to provide inspections under the PRA 2003. This has resulted in a largely reactive approach where inspections are triggered as a result of complaints. The OIA data also indicates that the ministries have no intention of reallocating funding or priority to PRA 2003 inspections.

The current inspection regime is driven by complaints, of which there have been very few: eight in the data provided by DHBs for the decade plus two made by NZPC. Complainants, who were usually sex purchasers, were almost all anonymous and rarely provide sufficient detail for useful follow up. As a result, none of the complaints registered has led to a successful prosecution. Indeed, the only prosecution for failing to adopt safe sexual practices under resulted from a client's confession to the police.

Sabrinna Valisce, a survivor of prostitution and now campaigner for the Abolitionist model, was a volunteer for the NZPC over a 24-year period, and was involved in the campaign to decriminalise the sex trade. 'I thought it would give more power and rights to the women', she told me when we met in Melbourne at an abolitionist conference, 'but I soon realised the opposite was true'.

Valisce quickly noticed that the new regime benefited the punters and brothel owners but not the women. What used to be viewed as sexual violence is now seen as occupational hazards when such crimes are perpetrated by punters and pimps in licensed establishments. 'After decriminalisation was the first time I ever saw a brothel owner come into NZPC itself', says Valisce. 'He got condoms and lube and dental dams and sponge supplies for the girls. Never had we seen that prior to decrim, so that told me they weren't afraid of us anymore.'

In what way, I ask Valisce, did brothel owners gain post-decriminalisation? 'They got more power. The brothel owners choose their prices, they say all inclusive, they don't say what all inclusive means so that can mean anything', says Valisce. 'So clients would go into the room, see a girl and she would have to deal with them wanting to do anything and everything.'

During the time she was involved in prostitution, Chelsea visited the New Zealand Prostitutes Collective[6] to find out her rights, but discovered that all that was on offer was condoms at a discounted price. 'That's what lures you in and when you're there they groom you and make out it's the greatest thing ever and they lie to you and it's horrible',

---

[6]http://www.nzpc.org.nz.

says Chelsea. 'I had this new workers' pack, which is full of propaganda. They'll say how to stay a happy hooker and talk about burn-out syndrome. But it's not burn-out syndrome, it's a normal response to ongoing sexual abuse.'

According to a government report, New Zealand senior police officials have admitted that policing of organised crime in legal brothels is 'patchy' and the regulation of brothels is 'often woeful'.[7] One investigator noted that because of decriminalisation, police were not required by law to investigate the goings-on, and organised criminals infiltrated the off-street sex trade.

The UK Home Affairs Select Committee (HASC) report of July 2016 refers to the main conclusions from the PRA Committee report of 2008, the evaluation report 5 years after the legislation was introduced. It claims that decriminalisation had little impact on the number of people working in the sex trade; has safeguarded the rights of those under the age of 18; the rights of adults not to be forced to engage in prostitution, including the right to refuse a particular client; and the right not to be subjected to exploitative or degrading employment practices. Of those interviewed and able to comment, the majority of women in prostitution are, according to the report, more likely to report incidences of violence to the police.

Phil Hubbard, Professor in the School of Sociology and Social Policy at the University of Kent, UK, describes himself as an 'international expert on the regulation of the sex trade'.[8] In his submission to the HASC, Hubbard claims that: 'Decriminalisation, where it has been carried out (e.g. New Zealand), has helped reduce the stigma attached to sex work, allowed workers to operate legitimately alone or in collectives and encouraged them to report instances of rape or violence to the police'.

---

[7]McKenzie, N.; Beck, M.; et al. (2011, Oct 10.) *Legal brothels linked to international sex trafficking rings.* In Sydney Morning Herald. Retrieved 16 June 2017, from http://www.smh.com.au/national/legal-brothels-linked-to-international-sex-trafficking-rings-20111009-1lfxs.html.

[8]Hubbard, P. (2016) *Written evidence submitted by Professor Phillip Hubbard.* Retrieved 16 June 2017, from http://data.parliament.uk/writtenevidence/committeeevidence.svc/evidencedocument/home-affairs-committee/prostitution/written/28708.pdf.

Racism and Colonialism

The global sex trade is built on racism and colonialism, as well as misogyny. But racism is rarely mentioned, except for those accusing abolitionists of being racist for using the term 'pimp' to describe *actual* pimping, because, as the pro-prostitution argument goes, 'pimp' is nothing but a 'racist trope'.[9]

Abuse of Indigenous women under legalisation and decriminalisation is rife, particularly in Australia and New Zealand.

Evelina Giobbe was one of the women who took part in the original comfort women protest with Dr Moon Kim.[10] 'We picketed the Mitsubishi Bank for a year and then organised all of the Korean elders and brought a comfort woman survivor and had this giant march. It was phenomenal', says Giobbe. 'All these elderly people who remembered that era and then young prostituted women like us and the comfort women were amazing and absolutely understood that we were sisters, they weren't freaked out by us and we weren't freaked out by them. It was an amazing time in history.'

Courtney, an advocate for women abused in prostitution, based in Vancouver, Canada, says: 'The sex trade is built on racism and colonialism as well as misogyny. For Native women and African-American women, and all women and girls of colour, it is yet another way in which the white man takes what he wants from our communities, our cultures and our souls'.

For Melissa Farley, founder of Prostitution Research and Education[11]: 'Prostitution is one specific result of colonisation, stemming from the homelessness, land and economic dispossession, lack of educational and employment opportunities, and cultural and physical assaults that

---

[9]Davis, H. (2013, Feb 28.) *Defining 'pimp': Working towards a definition in social research.* In Sociological Research Online. Retrieved 16 June 2017, from http://www.socresonline.org.uk/18/1/11.html.

[10]January 8, 1992

[11]Prostitution Research & Education. Retrieved 16 June 2017, from http://prostitutionresearch.com/.

Indigenous people have suffered'. Farley found in one study[12] that 65% of Maori respondents reported a history of homelessness, compared to 16% of non-Indigenous women.[5]

Advertising of sexual services is often reliant on racist and colonialist stereotypes. For example, research by the Asian Women for Equality Society based on analysis of 1472 online advertisements for prostitution shows that 90% used racist tropes regarding Asian women as a selling factor. The women were 'branded and packaged as submissive, exotic, newly immigrated, fresh off the boat, young and experienced—this is what men are looking for in Asian women'.[13]

The Sex Buyers Under Decriminalisation and Legalisation

One group that both regimes benefit is the sex buyers. Under legalisation and decriminalisation, sex buyers are de-stigmatised and enabled in their pursuits to purchase women at their will.

Research I conducted with Farley in 2009 on sex buyers found that in addition to buying sex in the UK, almost half (49%) of the 103 men interviewed had bought sex outside the UK, having travelled to 42 countries on 6 continents between them. The most popular destination was Amsterdam. A number of men mentioned that they specifically travelled to the Netherlands or New Zealand because prostitution was legal there. Noting the frenzied pace of the Dutch sex trade, one man commented: 'Amsterdam was like going through a turnstile into a fairground ride: 2 min and you're out. The idea that the women had been with five men in the last hour or 20 men in a day was a big turn off'.

---

[12]Farley, M. (2005, Jun 1.) *Prostitution in Vancouver: Violence and the colonization of first nations women*. In Transcultural Psychiatry. Retrieved 16 June 2017, from http://journals.sagepub.com/doi/abs/10.1177/1363461505052667 *Transcultural Psychiatry.*

[13]Discussed by the Asian Women for Equality Society at a meeting in Montreal, October 2015.

After one man returned to London, UK, from a trip visiting Prague in the Czech Republic for a 'lads' weekend', his view of prostitution changed and he no longer thought it problematic for men to pay for sex. Later, he went to Amsterdam on a tour arranged by the same travel agent/pimp: 'I was with a different group of lads. They hadn't paid for sex before so I felt like a veteran and had no hesitation'.

Comments from the sex buyers who had paid for sex during a visit to Amsterdam speak volumes about how legalisation sanctions their behaviour:

- 'Selecting and purchasing has something to do with domination and control.'
- 'It's like going for a drink, you are not doing anything illegal.'
- 'It is like putting your washing in a washing machine.'

Street Prostitution and Zoning

Legalisation does not reduce street prostitution. There has been a significant increase in outdoor prostitution in towns such as Utrecht in the Netherlands, along with increased numbers of men buying sexual access to women.

Meanwhile, the so-called 'managed zone' in Leeds in the UK has been a disaster. Established in Holbeck, an impoverished area of south Leeds in June 2014, the zone was made permanent in January 2016. It was declared 'a success'[14] despite the brutal murder of Dario Pionko, a prostituted woman[15] only weeks before local councillors declared its permanence. The decision was taken following the completion of a report, commissioned by the local authority by pro-decriminalisation campaigner and academic Teela Sanders. Sanders said of the abolitionist law: 'Putting limits on private morality with regard to the legitimate purchase and provision of

---

[14]Yorkshire Evening Post. (2015, Jul 31.) *'Managed' red light district In Leeds hailed a success.* In Yorkshire Evening Post. Retrieved 16 June 2017, from http://www.yorkshireeveningpost.co.uk/news/managed-red-light-district-in-leeds-hailed-a-success-1-7388043.

[15]BBC News. (2016, Jul 5.) *Daria Pionko death: Lewis Pierre jailed for murder.* On BBC News. Retrieved 16 June 2017, from http://www.bbc.co.uk/news/uk-england-leeds-36713608.

consensual commercial sex is evidence of a state seeking to control sexuality rather than to preserve diversity, difference and freedom'.[16] It is clear from Sanders's executive summary report that there are significant problems regarding safety, policing, litter and lack of support from residents and business owners, despite the positive spin by the author.

In a report by BBC Radio Leeds in March 2016, one of the prostituted women operating within the zone was asked whether she now felt safe: 'No. Because once you're in a car police can't do anything to help you anyway. We've got a managed area but we haven't got somewhere we can go and do it discreetly out of the way of everybody'.[17]

The locals call it 'pimp paradise'.[18] A report in a local newspaper in February 2016 claimed that most of the residents were opposed to the managed area and felt it wasn't working.[19] Complaints included: being repeatedly woken at night; the women selling sex outside of the designated hours of 7 pm–7 am; children being propositioned in the street; gardens being broken into; and residents being harassed by sex buyers.[20]

I spent time on the 'tipplezone' [tolerance zone] in Utrecht in the Netherlands in 2004 and 2014. Police told me the women often report violent attacks. 'I am recommending that the cubicles are painted different colours, so a woman could say, "I was raped in the red cubicle", which would make DNA testing easier. Imagine looking for DNA among all this', the police officer on duty told me, pointing to the mountain of semen-soaked articles covering the ground.

Two independent studies found that 50–90% of women involved in prostitution in Utrecht's official red-light zone were being forced to

[16]Times Higher Education. (2007, Jun 22.) *Prostitution today: punishing the punters.* In Times Higher Education. Retrieved 16 June 2017, from https://www.timeshighereducation.com/features/prostitution-today-punishing-the-punters/209397.article.

[17]Edwards, A. (Presenter). (2016, Mar 3.) *Leeds 'managed zone' for sex workers is 'catastrophic failure'.* On BBC Radio Leeds. Retrieved 16 June 2017, from http://www.bbc.co.uk/programmes/p03lcx9p.

[18]Bennett, C. (2016, Feb 21.) *Criminalise the sex buyers, not the prostitutes.* In The Guardian. Retrieved 16 June 2017, from https://www.theguardian.com/commentisfree/2016/feb/21/sex-trade-prostitution-criminalise-sex-buyers.

[19]Yorkshire Evening Post. (2016, Feb 27.) *Leeds 'managed' prostitution zone under review after backlash.* In Yorkshire Evening Post. Retrieved 16 June 2017, from http://www.yorkshireeveningpost.co.uk/news/leeds-s-managed-prostitution-zone-under-review-after-backlash-1-7752702.

[20]Benn, H. (2016, Feb 7.) *'Managed area' is not working.* In South Leeds Life. Retrieved 16 June 2017, from http://www.southleedslife.com/managed-area-is-not-working/.

work in prostitution. Following these studies, CCTV surveillance was launched in the local prostitution zone to curb violence against women, women's trafficking and other sex-and-drugs-related crimes.

Utrecht's Mayor Aleid Wolfsen said of the zone: 'We need to know which women are being forced to work as prostitutes or if women are abused or exploited. Filming the area, and knowing which pimps are connected to which women, will increase our opportunities to help the women'.[21] It would, of course, be impossible to implement the sex-buyer law in any jurisdiction with an official tolerance zone.

Nowhere else in the world is street prostitution legal because people do not want it in plain sight. Where there is a street sex trade, women are accosted on their way home by punters, and often condoms, drug paraphernalia and pimps are visible. But in 1996 the Netherlands decided that street prostitution was a decent way to earn money and created several 'tolerance zones' for men to safely rent a vagina, anus or mouth for a few minutes. Cars even drive into cubicles. And this being the Netherlands, there is also a special section for cyclists.

The day after the Amsterdam zone opened, more than 100 residents took to the streets in protest. It took 6 years for the mayor to admit in public that the experiment had been a disaster. Zones in Rotterdam, The Hague and Heerlen have shut down in similar circumstances.

Managed Leads to Murder

In December 2015, a 24-year-old street-prostituted woman Daria Pionko was murdered[22] by a sex buyer named Lewis Pierre. Pierre carried out a brutal and sustained attack on Pionko, whose body was discovered on the so-called 'managed zone' in Leeds in the UK. The zone had been under a vast amount of scrutiny since its inception in 2014

---

[21]Expatica. (2008, Oct 31.) *Utrecht clamps down on prostitution*. In Expatica. Retrieved 16 June 2017, from http://www.expatica.com/nl/news/Utrecht-clamps-down-on-prostitution_156388.html.

[22]Perraudin, F. (2016, Jul 4.) *Man found guilty of murdering sex worker in Leeds*. In The Guardian. Retrieved 16 June 2017, from https://www.theguardian.com/uk-news/2016/jul/04/man-guilty-murder-sex-worker-leeds-daria-pionko-lewis-pierre.

by Leeds City Council. Following the murder, the policy which led to the zone was reviewed, because it had hardly resulted in safety for the women—one of the key aims. Not only has a woman been murdered, on the zone itself, but there have been other reports of serious sexual assaults, including rape.[23, 24] However, despite these attacks, Leeds City Council has since declared the zone to be 'a success'.[25]

Talking about the murder, Georgina Perry, Chair of the UK Network of Sex Work Projects (UKNSWP) scheme National Ugly Mugs and a vocal campaigner for decriminalisation of the sex trade, said: 'The rise in the murders of migrant sex workers has been very dramatic but unsurprising', in an interview with *the Guardian* newspaper.[26] 'Migrant sex workers are very fearful of authorities. Very often they have come from countries where police are overtly abusive to them and they expect the same treatment here.'

Why the treatment of migrant women involved in prostitution is relevant to how safe or unsafe a managed zone is I am unclear. Pionko had attempted to call the police during the attack but was unable to make contact.

In her report, Teela Sanders recommended that the scheme remain in place. Other local areas within the UK are now looking to adopt a similar model of regulating street prostitution.

It would appear that whatever complaints from residents and passers-by there are about street and off-street prostitution, the arguments about a woman's 'right' to sell sex (as opposed to the 'right' of men to buy), often rise to the top.[27]

[23]Gardner, T. (2015, Sept 14.) *Rapist jailed for subjecting sex worker to degrading ordeal.* In Yorkshire Evening Post. Retrieved 16 June 2017, from http://www.yorkshireeveningpost.co.uk/news/rapist-jailed-for-subjecting-leeds-sex-worker-to-degrading-ordeal-1-7457118.

[24]Gardner, T. (2015, Nov 13.) *Rapist jailed for brutal attack on Leeds sex worker.* In Yorkshire Evening Post. Retrieved 16 June 2017, from http://www.yorkshireeveningpost.co.uk/news/rapist-jailed-jailed-for-brutal-attack-on-leeds-sex-worker-1-7567724.

[25]Yorkshire Evening Post. (2015, Jul 31.) *'Managed' red light district in Leeds hailed a success.* In Yorkshire Evening Post. Retrieved 16 June 2017, from http://www.yorkshireeveningpost.co.uk/news/managed-red-light-district-in-leeds-hailed-a-success-1-7388043.

[26]Perraudin, F. (2016, Jul 4.) *Man found guilty of murdering sex worker in Leeds.* In The Guardian. Retrieved 16 June 2017, from https://www.theguardian.com/uk-news/2016/jul/04/man-guilty-murder-sex-worker-leeds-daria-pionko-lewis-pierre.

[27]Clarke-Billings, L. (2016, Jan 12.) *Leeds red light district made permanent fixture with 'prostitution zone' three weeks after sex worker murder.* In The Telegraph. Retrieved 16 June 2017, from http://www.telegraph.co.uk/news/uknews/12094301/Leeds-red-light-district-made-permanent-fixture-with-prostitution-zone-three-weeks-after-sex-worker-murder.html.

Barbel Ahlborn from the pro-prostitution 'sex work' project Kassandra in Nuremberg, Germany, told me that 'sex workers' there are against managed zones because it restricts where women work, and that not allowing a woman to sell sex from her apartment is discriminatory. But anyone who wishes to turn a residential property into a business needs to apply for a licence to do so. It would appear that legalisation is unpopular among many 'sex workers' rights' activists because they do not want any regulation whatsoever. This contradicts the mantra that sex work is regular labour and should be treated as such. It also ignores the reality that most people do not wish to live or work where sex is being sold.[28]

Decriminalisation/Legalisation Increases Trafficking

Pro-prostitution activists claim that in order to destigmatise prostitution, language should reflect the status of prostitution as 'work'. Jo Doezema, a vocal member of the NSWP[29] (The Global Network of Sex Work Projects—which campaigns for prostitution to be redefined as work and for all laws pertaining to prostitution, including pimping, to be abolished), believes: 'To label a woman "abused" or "trafficked" means to dis-empower her. She has the right to define as a sex worker, or even a migrant sex worker, and no-one has the right to define what she is except her'.[30]

A 2012 article in the journal *World Development* by the scholars Seo-Young Cho, Axel Dreher and Eric Neumayer concluded that 'countries

---

[28]Bindel, J.; Atkins, H. (2007) *Streets apart: Outdoor prostitution in London*. The POPPY Project. Retrieved 16 June 2017, from http://nordicbaltic-assistwomen.net/IMG/pdf/StreetsApart_14Jun07doc.pdf.

[29]Global Network of Sex Work Projects. Retrieved 16 June 2017, from http://www.nswp.org/.

[30]Jo Doezema, 2004, *Sex Slaves and Discourse Masters: the Historical Construction of 'trafficking in Women*.

with legalised prostitution have a statistically significantly larger reported incidence of human trafficking inflows. This holds true regardless of the model we use to estimate the equations and the variables we control for in the analysis.'[31]

Legalisation also has an impact on returning trafficked women. If the country they return to, dishonoured and stigmatised because they have been prostituted, has a thriving sex trade of its own, it has implications for the long-term recovery and reintegration of trafficked women. There is evidence from some non-governmental organisations of returning women being targeted by local pimps and put to work in local prostitution. Where there is monitoring of local sex industries, traffickers will consider it unsafe to bring women in, such as is the case in Sweden. The majority of funding for return and reintegration programmes goes to the International Organisation for Migration. They are very good at the return, but seemingly poor at the reintegration because they refuse to engage with issues of prostitution, deeming it different from trafficking.

Mia, a survivor of sex trafficking who was brought to the UK from Vlora, Albania, told me that she was re-trafficked back to the UK only three weeks after being returned home. Mia had been rejected by her community once it was discovered she had been prostituted. 'My father told me I was dead to him. My brothers were warned to have nothing to do with me. I ended up working in prostitution in Tirana [Albania's capital] because I was unmarriageable and had a black mark against my reputation', she says. 'But there were men who came back from being forced to work in factories, and they were welcomed back and seen as heroes.'

The sex trade in the Netherlands has significantly expanded since legalisation. Job Cohen, then Mayor of Amsterdam, said in 2007: 'Since the legalisation in 2000, things have changed. The law was created for voluntary prostitution but these days we see trafficking of women, exploitation and all kinds of criminal activity.'[32]

---

[31]Cho, S.; Dreher, A.; Neumayer, E. (2013.) *Does legalised prostitution increase human trafficking?* In World Development. Retrieved 16 June 2017, from https://eprints.lse.ac.uk/45198/1/Neumayer_Legalized_Prostitution_Increase_2012.pdf.

[32]Expatica. (2007, Sept 21.) *Amsterdam buys red-light brothels.* In Expatica. Retrieved 16 June 2017, from http://www.expatica.com/nl/news/Amsterdam-buys-red-light-brothels_149045.html.

Women's organisations in New Zealand talk about increased numbers of young women from the Pacific Islands being involved in prostitution. They also report there are more gangs involved in the management of brothels and there is more crime and danger associated with it. What is often ignored by those claiming that New Zealand has adopted the best model in dealing with prostitution is that it is a destination country for trafficking. In 2015 a woman was convicted for recruiting women from Thailand to work in a massage parlour.[33] In 2004 the US State Department identified New Zealand as a trafficking destination country. However, the first conviction took another 12 years to secure.[34]

Evidence from Governments and Police

The Dutch government hoped to play the role of the honourable pimp, taking its share in the proceeds of prostitution through taxation. But only 5% of the women registered for tax because no one wants to be known as a whore, however legal it may be. Illegality has simply taken a new form, with an increase in trafficking, unlicensed brothels and pimping; with policing completely out of the picture, it was easier to break the laws that remained. To pimp out women from non-EU countries, desperate for a new life, remains illegal. But it has never been easier.

Legalisation has imposed brothels on areas all over the Netherlands, whether they want them or not. Even if a city or town opposes establishing a brothel, it must allow at least one: not to do so is contrary to the basic federal right to work. To many Dutch, legality and decency have been irreconcilably divorced. It has been a social, legal and economic failure, and at last the madness is coming to an end.

---

[33]http://www.nzherald.co.nz/nz/news/article.cfm?c_id=1&objectid=11432671. Accessed 28th August.

[34]http://www.nzherald.co.nz/nz/news/article.cfm?c_id=1&objectid=11432671. Accessed 28th August.

Violence and Harm

In Melbourne, Australia, many restaurants ban doggy bags because of food safety[35] but its government defends legal brothels. It would appear that the harm when done to women prostituted in countries where it is not considered a crime to pimp women and run brothels is socially tolerable.

Chelsea, who was involved in brothel prostitution in New Zealand, exited the sex trade in 2016. She argues that decriminalisation results in women facing additional barriers if they try to leave: 'I don't think [decriminalisation] made any difference [to the women] because the boss still does everything in a really dodgy manner', Chelsea told me when we met just prior to her exiting.

'[The managers] prioritised the men [customers] because that's where the money's coming from. That means if the clients are not happy and he goes down and complains about you he gets his money back and you get nothing. [Management] don't believe you if you [complain about clients too much] so you have to save it for the really horrible ones.'

I met Ne'cole Daniels, an African-American and member of the abolitionist organisation SPACE International, in 2015 at a conference in Minnesota in the USA. Daniels is clear that prostitution is abuse, and therefore legalising or decriminalising it is simply enabling that abuse:

> Legalisation is saying that it's OK not just to purchase me, but to do whatever the hell you want to with me. We know there are those tricks who don't give a damn, whose sick fantasy is to want to hurt someone in this industry. They can't do it to their wives but they can do whatever to us. [The sex trade is] like racism. They are saying that some of us are worth less than others.

During my visit to Laufhaus Caesars World in Munich in Germany, I ask the manager Jörn Gruber about safety for the women. The security

---

[35]Santacruz, S. (2016, Apr 1.) *Are restaurant doggy bags legal?* In Australian Institute of Food Safety. Retrieved 15 June 2017, from https://www.foodsafety.com.au/blog/are-restaurant-doggy-bags-legal.

system, in my view left something to be desired. 'When the girls have a problem, the other girls can hear it and make a sign on the camera', says Gruber. 'But they have to come out of their rooms to make a sign.'

Despite having told me that there have been several occasions in which security guards have been required to intervene in 'negotiations' between the women and the sex buyers, Gruber soon switches his story when I ask how many of the women have pimps outside of the brothel, and if the pimps bother them at 'work'. I am told the vice police come to the brothel once a month and interview the women in their rooms, asking if they have been trafficked or abused.

'We have never had problems with violence here', says Gruber. And no boyfriends [pimps] are allowed in. If I catch them they are banned and if a girl lets him in she's also banned. If they leave here because they get chucked out, they can go to a house that will accept pimps.' I ask if there are many brothels in Munich that do accept pimps and Gruber confirms this. 'The men who come in here do not come with the intention of harming the women. And if they do think this is a place they can hurt the women they are in the wrong place and they must go to [names a nearby brothel] if they want to do things like that.'

A number of countries, including the UK, license so-called massage parlours or saunas, in the full knowledge that they are being run as brothels. One of the cities where Fiona Broadfoot was prostituted in was Edinburgh in Scotland, where, at the time, police and local authorities took what they called 'a pragmatic approach'[36] to licensing sex establishments.

The editorial in *The Scotsman* on 27 March 1995 claimed: 'Edinburgh's licensed saunas are starting to rank with the Festival and the Castle as tokens of the city's fame abroad. Liberal opinion everywhere is impressed with the Old City's robust policy of seeking to regulate what it cannot eradicate and to move the sex trade off the streets and into safe, controlled environments… Our own view is that the council's policy is indeed enlightened and also that it is right.

---

[36]Swanson, I. (2013, Nov 1.) *End of sex saunas licensing 'puts women at risk'*. In Edinburgh Evening News. Retrieved 15 June 2017, from http://www.edinburghnews.scotsman.com/news/end-of-sex-saunas-licensing-puts-women-at-risk-1-3186523.

Prostitution on the streets of Edinburgh is as old as the streets themselves and there is no evidence in Edinburgh, or anywhere else, that it can be prosecuted or persecuted out of existence.[37]

I asked Broadfoot if there were any benefits from her being prostituted from a decriminalised (licensed) brothel: 'No, it was far worse because there were a lot of trafficked women there—the guy had you working 24/7—he requested that we wash men's penises in the sink and have sex without condoms, which of course the majority of us never did', she told me. 'But there were some desperate women because they were highly drug addicted. They were injecting in the basement. A lot of drug misuse going on in the basement because they need the fix to cope with the day.'

Even some pro-prostitution activists are critical of many of the consequences of legalisation. At Kassandra, in Germany, Bärbel Ahlborn is the coordinator. I asked Ahlborn if the women are safer since 2002: 'I think it would be good if everybody who offers sexual services had a clear idea of their role. I'm telling the customer, 'You can have this or this' and the women decide what to offer which customer, it's her decision. This has the precondition that she knows it's a business'.

The reality is that when you decriminalise or legalise pimps and sex buyers there is always a massive expansion of the sex trade. Multi-storey brothels are only ever built under legalisation, as even the police, who often turn a blind eye to the off-street sex trade, have to take action against such blatancy if it is staring everyone in the face.

Criminal Activities of Legal Pimps

Below are examples of the failures of the New Zealand system in removing abuse, exploitation and trafficking from its sex trade since decriminalisation was introduced:

---

[37]Mackay, F.; Schaap, A. (2000, Apr.) *The local politics of prostitution in two Scottish cities*. University of Edinburgh. Retrieved 15 June 2017, from https://ecpr.eu/Filestore/PaperProposal/8a98171c-b6bc-4424-b9c7-8fa6e5fbde80.pdf.

- The 2008 New Zealand government report briefly mentions that 'a majority of prostituted persons felt that the decriminalisation act "could do little about violence that occurred"'.[38]
- The Committee further reported that abusive brothels did not improve conditions for prostituted individuals; the brothels that 'had unfair management practices continued with them' even after the decriminalisation.[39]
- There have been several murders and attacks of women in prostitution since decriminalisation. For example, in 2009 a Christchurch police officer was convicted of forcing a woman to have sex with him by threatening to arrest her if she did not comply.[40]
- In 2010, during a 6-week operation in downtown Auckland, the police identified at least 13 girls between the ages of 12 and 15 being prostituted. Most of them were being exploited on one street, which is known as a 'young red-light area'.
- In 2010 a brothel-keeper operating in New Plymouth, was convicted of six underage sex and prostitution charges relating to one 15-year-old girl.[41]
- There have been several cases of Malaysian women's passports being taken away from them by pimps. One woman said she had 'paid $5600 to come to Auckland, and made to work 16-hour shifts with few breaks on most days'. Another said she had 'been lured here with a $4500 cash offer, plus airfares, but was later told that it was a loan she had to repay'.[42]

---

[38]Report of the Prostitution Law Review Committee on the Operation of the Prostitution Reform Act 2003, 2008, http://prostitutescollective.net/wp-content/uploads/2016/10/report-of-the-nz-prostitution-law-committee-2008.pdf

[39]Report of the Prostitution Law Review Committee on the Operation of the Prostitution Reform Act 2003, 2008, http://prostitutescollective.net/wp-content/uploads/2016/10/report-of-the-nz-prostitution-law-committee-2008.pdf

[40]Stuff. (2009, Dec 17.) *Sex extortion ex-policeman jailed.* In Stuff. Retrieved 15 June 2017, from http://www.stuff.co.nz/national/crime/3170820/Sex-extortion-ex-policeman-jailed.

[41]Humpreys, L. (2010, Aug 19.) *Hastie guilty over young prostitute.* In Stuff. Retrieved 15 June 2017, from http://www.stuff.co.nz/taranaki-daily-news/news/4038549/Hastie-guilty-over-young-prostitute.

[42]http://www.nzherald.co.nz/prostitution/news/article.cfm?c_id=612&objectid=10658178 Accessed 28th August 2017.

- In 2011 a senior US government official claimed that underage girls were being subjected to sex trafficking, and described New Zealand's way of defining human trafficking as 'misplaced'.[43]
- In 2013 a number of exited women testified to the New Zealand Parliament's justice and electoral committee about the harms of prostitution and argued in favour of the Nordic model. That same year, the New Zealand government dismissed a US State Department report that stated that New Zealand had become a 'destination country for foreign men and women subjected to forced labour and to an extent, a source country for underage girls subjected to sex trafficking within the country' (see footnote 44).
- A report from 2014 says that the police are dealing with reports of women in prostitution experiencing violence on about a monthly basis in Christchurch (see footnote 45).

There is evidence of an increase in migrant women being prostituted in New Zealand, but the government does not consider this an indicator of trafficking. In 2015, two South Korean women and their pimp, in the country on short-term temporary visas, faced several charges in Auckland including the failure to adopt safe-sex practices. It is alleged that over a 20-day period between 28 October and 19 November 2015, one of the women had 196 customers, including 58 customers that she gave unprotected oral sex, and six who paid extra to ejaculate in her mouth.[44]

It was not until it became clear that legalisation of the sex trade in countries such as the Netherlands had been a failed social experiment[45] that New Zealand began to be routinely hailed as the 'gold standard' model for other countries to follow.[46]

---

[43]http://herspace.org.au/bad-news-new-zealands-survivors/. Accessed 28th August 2017

[44]New Zealand Herald. (2015, Dec 4.) *Increase in foreign sex workers in New Zealand.* In New Zealand Herald. Retrieved 15 June 2017, from http://www.nzherald.co.nz/nz/news/article.cfm?c_id=1&objectid=11555992.

[45]Bindel, J. (2012, Oct.) *Window brothels get the red light.* In Standpoint. Retrieved 15 June 2017, from http://standpointmag.co.uk/dispatches-October-12-window-brothels-get-the-red-light-julie-bindel-amsterdam-prostitution.

[46]Scot-Pep. (2015) *The New Zealand model: Protecting the safety, rights and health of sex workers.* Retrieved 15 June 2017, from http://www.scot-pep.org.uk/sites/default/files/reports/the_nz_model_long_version.pdf.

'There is a consensus now between policymakers and people from the shelters and even people who are pro-legalisation, that legalisation has not worked out', says Renate Van Der Zee. 'It hasn't made the situation better for prostitutes and it hasn't done anything in the field of stopping trafficking. Even the pro-prostitution lobby agree that that legalisation hasn't worked out as was hoped.'

Exiting Services

Another failure of legalisation and decriminalisation, as evidenced by the Netherlands, Germany and New Zealand, is that once prostitution becomes viewed and framed as a regular job, the impetus to provide any exiting services disappears.

Rachel Moran has visited countries with legalised prostitution and spoken to a number of the women in prostitution in legal brothels. 'Some of what they have told me hurts me more deeply than anything I've heard from regimes where prostitution is not legally sanctioned. The first thing that happens in a nation like that is that there are no exit routes', says Moran. 'Once you socially sanction prostitution as just another form of labour, immediately you cut off your exit strategies.'

The 'sex workers' rights' activists have become increasingly effective in only seeing the harm to prostituted people that is caused by police officers and criminal justice agencies. If we are to follow this logic through, it becomes clear that abolitionists who advocate the criminalisation of sex buyers are complicit in, and therefore in part responsible for, violence experienced by prostituted people wherever criminalisation of any type is in place.

Sex Tourism

Rather than remove the sleaziness of the Amsterdam red-light district, sex tourism has made the area more depressing than ever: full of drunken sex tourists who act as window shoppers, pointing and laughing at the women they see. Local women pass the streets with their heads down, trying not to see the other women displayed like cuts of meat in a butcher's shop. Men can be seen entering the brothels, trying to barter down the price. Others come out zipping up their jeans. Many of the women look very young, all of them bored, with the majority sitting on stools in underwear playing with their phones.

In 2005, Thomas Cook,[47] Britain's longest running tour operator, launched night-time tours around Amsterdam's red-light district.[48] The excursions included a talk about the 'system' from a woman who had previously worked in legal prostitution, and was open to children of any age. In fact, Thomas Cook offered free tickets for children under the age of 3. The Thomas Cook press release described how the 2-hour tour would take visitors 'deep into the famous red-light district, offering a fascinating insight into the oldest profession in the world'. I have called Thomas Cook to ask if they still run the tours (it received a number of complaints from feminist and human rights organisations back in 2005) but have been unable to get a clear response.

There is much evidence that the expansion and normalisation of sex establishments—including lap dance clubs, brothels and sex shops in city centres—often leads to that city being marketed by tour operators as suitable for stag weekends and sex tourists.[49] One notable example of this phenomenon is Tallinn, the capital of Estonia. Government officials have made a commitment to stop Estonian women being trafficked but are also capitalising on the revenue from sex tourism. There are at least 5000 women in prostitution in Estonia, the majority of whom are in Tallinn. The number of brothels is rising to meet the demand of the men on stag weekends. There are growing numbers of strip clubs in the Old Town and, as in Amsterdam, taxi drivers are paid by the criminals who run these places to take stag groups to brothels. Women from the poor, depressed areas in the North East of Estonia, mainly Russian-speaking ethnic Estonians, are being trafficked into Tallinn to meet the increasing demand.

[47][Thomas Cook even admitted it at the time]: https://www.theguardian.com/travel/2005/nov/13/travelnews.genderissues.observerescapesection.

[48]Bowes, G. (2005, Nov 13.) *Red light tour condemned as 'sick'.* In The Guardian. Retrieved 15 June 2017, from https://www.theguardian.com/travel/2005/nov/13/travelnews.genderissues.observerescapesection.

[49]Journeyman Pictures. (2007, Aug 2.) *Tallinn Tours – Estonia.* Retrieved 15 June 2017, from https://www.youtube.com/watch?v=Y7V-gYlJNFY.

Further evidence from press and research reports on the growth of sex tourism suggests that legalisation is a major driver in the sex tourism business. For example, *Riga This Week*,[50] a magazine advertising the tourist scene in the capital city of Latvia and widely available in hotel rooms and bars, contains scores of adverts for erotic massage, strip joints and escorts.

Tax, Registration and Safety/Health

In 2015, Hermann Müller, who owns the Pasha brothel in Salzburg, Austria, placed an advertisement on his website offering: 'Free Entrance! Free Drinks! Free Sex! Effective immediately' Müller was protesting against supposedly unfair levels of tax. He claimed that officials were over-zealous in checking up on him and that he had paid €5 million in taxes over the past decade. Müller runs several licensed brothels in Germany and Austria, where prostitution is also legal. Profits from his other establishments would be used to cover the losses from the stunt, he said.

Muller's complaint was that the officials visited his premises every 14 days but did nothing about unlicensed, illegal forms of prostitution in the city. According to Muller, sex buyers were 'queuing round the block' for the 'summer special' and he 'turned away hundreds of disappointed customers'.

Section 8 of the New Zealand PRA requires operators of businesses of prostitution to adopt and promote safer sex practices. Section 9 requires 'sex workers' and clients to adopt safe-sex practices.[51] One prosecution for failing to adopt safe-sex practices in breach of Sect. 9 has been successfully undertaken. This was as a result of a confession made to police. The offence carries a maximum penalty of a $2000 fine. The offender, a client, was fined $400.[52]

---

[50]WikiSexguide.com: Riga. Retrieved 15 June 2017, from http://www.wikisexguide.com/wiki/Riga.

[51]New Zealand Government. (2003.) *Report of the prostitution law review committee on the operation of the Prostitution Reform Act 2003*. Retrieved 15 June 2017, from http://prostitutescollective. net/wp-content/uploads/2016/10/report-of-the-nz-prostitution-law-committee-2008.pdf. p. 23

[52]New Zealand Government. (2003.) *Report of the prostitution law review committee on the operation of the Prostitution Reform Act 2003*. Retrieved 15 June 2017, from http://prostitutescollective. net/wp-content/uploads/2016/10/report-of-the-nz-prostitution-law-committee-2008.pdf. p. 55

In June 2004, the Occupational Safety and Health Service of the Department of Labour issued *A Guide to Occupational Health and Safety in the New Zealand sex trade* (the OSH Guide). Only 30% of 'sex workers' surveyed by the Christchurch School of Medicine (CSOM) reported that they had read the OSH Guide. In normal businesses, at least one person in management is required to understand all OSH requirements.[53]

The 2007 CSOM report found that 'almost all public health services have taken a largely reactive approach to implementation of the public health role under the PRA'[54]; that is, they have failed to implement regular inspections. Medical officers describe feeling intimidated by managers of brothels,[55] and almost all complaints made are anonymous. Medical Officers of Health told CSOM that this made it very difficult to take action unless adequate detail was supplied to them. None of the complaints that had been investigated by Medical Officers of Health resulted in a prosecution.[56]

A Drive to Remove All Regulation

Ana is a survivor of the sex trade who was prostituted in the Netherlands. She says:

> They say that here, even though we have legalisation, it's never enough. We have had legalisation for a few years and they're trying to get rid of

---

[53]New Zealand Government. (2003.) *Report of the prostitution law review committee on the operation of the Prostitution Reform Act 2003*. Retrieved 15 June 2017, from http://prostitutescollective. net/wp-content/uploads/2016/10/report-of-the-nz-prostitution-law-committee-2008.pdf. p. 51

[54]Abel, G.; Fitzgerald, L.; Brunton, C. (2007, Nov.) *Report of the prostitution law review committee on the operation of the Prostitution Reform Act 2003*. Retrieved 15 June 2017, from http:// prostitutescollective.net/wp-content/uploads/2016/10/report-of-the-nz-prostitution-law-committee-2008.pdf. p. 152

[55]Abel, G.; Fitzgerald, L.; Brunton, C. (2007, Nov.) *Report of the prostitution law review committee on the operation of the Prostitution Reform Act 2003*. Retrieved 15 June 2017, from http:// prostitutescollective.net/wp-content/uploads/2016/10/report-of-the-nz-prostitution-law-committee-2008.pdf. p. 153

[56]Abel, G.; Fitzgerald, L.; Brunton, C. (2007, Nov.) *Report of the prostitution law review committee on the operation of the Prostitution Reform Act 2003*. Retrieved 15 June 2017, from http:// prostitutescollective.net/wp-content/uploads/2016/10/report-of-the-nz-prostitution-law-committee-2008.pdf, p. 154.

the regulations again. I'm sorry but I'm not going to fight this fight just to squabble about regulations, because I do see that regulation is harmful in a legalised country. It's pointless. They want decriminalised, unregulated prostitution. Unregulated decriminalisation is a free for all it's; like an approval stamp on sexual abuse, like we approve of sexual abuse.

In December 2015 I visited Nairobi in Kenya to research the vibrant 'sex workers' rights' movement. I arranged to meet several individuals, including activists and academics, but the only person to keep our appointment was Peninah Mwangi, Director of the Bar and Hostess Association. Mwangi seemed surprised when I told her my position on the sex trade but did not cut our interview short. As I travelled to Nairobi I was alerted to a tweet from a 'sex workers' rights' activist 'warning' their allies in Kenya that I would soon be in town. I am not sure what the tweeters thought I would be doing, but it didn't warn off any of my other interviewees.

Mwangi told me that she was part of a delegation to New Zealand as part of the Global Network of Sex Work Projects in the early 2000s. 'Legalisation would never work for our country because we are understaffed in terms of police officers. We don't expect them to be able to police sex work successfully or to be able to get civil servants—they're not even doing a good job with traffic! So I can't imagine what they would do if sex work was legalised and there was a way that we should report to them that they should check.'

Cultural and Normative Harm

The government in the Netherlands has clarified that it is legal for driving instructors to offer lessons in return for sex, as long as the students are over the age of 18.[57] This could only happen under legalisation.

---

[57]Boult, A. (2015, Dec 18.) *Driving instructors 'may offer lessons in return for sex', Netherlands government confirms. The practice, known as 'ride for a ride', has been deemed 'legal but undesirable'.* In The Telegraph. Retrieved 15 June 2017, from http://www.telegraph.co.uk/news/worldnews/europe/netherlands/12059110/Driving-instructors-may-offer-lessons-in-return-for-sex-Netherlands-government-confirms.html.

There are other examples of how the legal acceptance of buying and selling women's bodies permeates culture.

In March 2016, the New Zealand TV channel Newshub reported on The Kai Kitchen,[58] a charity in the small town of Hawere in Taranaki that provides food for homeless and hungry children in the area. The story was pegged on the announcement that a local brothel hosted an open day during which visitors were asked to give a donation to the charity. 'It's just part of Hawere and we're all pretty cool about it', said one male visitor.

A spokesperson for The Kai Kitchen said: 'I think [the brothel owner's initiative] is fantastic. It's obviously created a lot of interest; we are grateful for all the donations that are coming in'. The fact that a brothel owner can be an ambassador for a children's austerity charity speaks volumes about how removing criminal laws makes even prostitution appear to be harmless and respectable.

The Village Built on Prostitution

Legalisation and decriminalisation of the sex trade have led to a normalisation of prostitution. The fact that Wadia, a village in the conservative state of Gujarat in India is able to exist purely on the proceeds of prostitution is testimony to this. Men come to the village from as far afield as Ahmedabad, Pakistan, Rajasthan, and Mumbai to buy sex, with rates beginning at Rs. 500 (£5).

The 600 inhabitants of Wadia are descendants of the nomadic z community. Saraniya men once worked for the army, which ruled over the region prior to India's independence from Britain in 1947. Ever since realising how much money could be made from the sex trade, the majority of men in Wadia have continued soliciting buyers for their sisters, daughters, aunts and mothers.

I visited Wadia at the end of 2015. The village is 4 hours' drive away from Gujarat's main city, Ahmedabad. I had been warned that it is

---

[58]http://www.newshub.co.nz/home/new-zealand/2016/03/brothel-opens-its-door-for-charity.html.

unsafe for anyone to travel alone near Wadia. On the final stretch of road before we reach the village, the car is surrounded by a group of young men, one of whom asks the driver why we are heading to Wadia and whether we are carrying any weapons.

The village is off a narrow road and consists mainly of huts made from wood and plastic sheets, with a central area consisting of a ramshackle store selling chai and basic provisions, at which the men and male children gather. My translator tells me that each of the newly built houses is a brothel and the old huts are the family homes. 'Ninety-nine percent are prostitutes', he says. 'The man with the white handkerchief, big broker (pimp). His wife, mother, sister, daughter, all prostitutes.'

I am met by one of the main pimps, Amr (not his real name): a charming, good-looking man in his 20s. Amr's English is good and he smiles at me a lot as he speaks, flashing perfectly straight, whitened teeth. The chief of the village appears soon after Amr calls him. I am not told his name. The man, in his 50s or 60s, is dressed in white and is hiding most of his face behind a scarf. I ask Amr if the police try to impose the rule of law on the village. 'They are corrupt', he tells me. 'Many are customers.'

No women or girls are visible as we arrive, and when I ask if I could meet some of the women, I am told emphatically 'no' by the chief. I ask why. 'Because they will be scared of you', he says. 'They will think you are a police officer.' During my tour of the village, on which I was accompanied by a reluctant Amr, I saw several women and girls dressed in pink or red saris, scurrying into their huts when they spotted me. One woman was going into a half-erected brick building with a man I assumed to be a sex buyer.

I asked Amr at what age the girls start selling sex and was told, 'Not before 18'. My fixer, however, was told by Amr that the girls are sold at an average age of 12. I was told by Amr that the women like their work; the customers are never violent; there are no STIs; and that at most only one-fifth of the women in Wadia are in prostitution. Despite the obvious poverty in the village, there are also pockets of wealth. Many of the older men had expensive iPhones, and three of those I met were attending college in Ahmedabad.

'The women are in [prostitution] for life', Amr told me, as I left. 'They are illiterate, it is all there is for them.' Clearly, pimping is more lucrative for the men than prostitution for the women.

On asking my colleagues if they had heard of Wadia, I soon discovered that this tiny village had almost the same notoriety and potency as Nevada in the USA. Wadia is far away from the legalised sex industries of Nevada, Germany and the Netherlands, but it has something fundamentally in common with those prosperous nations. Where prostitution is seen as part of the economy and a job like any other, and men are given free reign to treat women's bodies as a commodity, gender equality remains a distant dream.

The Expansion of the Sex Trade

'The NZPC denies the industry is expanding, but they are lying. There was a "mega brothel" built [in Auckland] recently, many storeys tall. It never opened, it isn't meant for now, it is planning for the future', says sex trade survivor Chelsea. 'If we don't get the Nordic model here in time, we will be whoring for the minimum wage and may as well have just worked at McDonald's.'

One of the claims of the pro-decriminalisation lobby is that there has been no increase in the number of brothels since 2003. However, as Debbie Weisehan of Streetreach points out, there are a number of Single Owner Operated Business (SOOBS) across the country that do not need a licence. 'I knew a brothel owner and so he didn't want to get a licence because he had a criminal record, so he set up all these apartments, and it's for girls who are just working for themselves. We don't know what's happening because it's underground.'

Ana, a young Dutch survivor I met during one of my research trips to Amsterdam, tells me:

> I know that the illegal sector has a lot of single mothers, because they get social security from the government and it's not that much, it's like 70% of minimum wage and it's not enough. A lot of these women feel forced – maybe they have a debt or feel guilty or ashamed of being poor, so they

do prostitution on the side to feed their families. Of course you can't do that legally because you wouldn't have government support anymore. So they are forced to be in the illegal sector.

However, even those in favour of prostitution, such as Irina Maslova of Silver Rose, Russia, disapprove of legalisation, as she told me in 2015:

> Definitely legalisation in Russia is not a good model and I am not going to allow this to happen. If there is a legalisation model in Russia, there would be about 300 sex workers who will probably join the official legalised industry where the rest of the people in this industry are being criminalised. I know people will not want to join the official legalised system because it will be very limiting with more severe conditions for them, so they would want to remain in the illegal sector and they will be deemed criminals.

One of the consequences of decriminalisation and legalisation is the increase in demand and its further normalisation. Sex buyers that I and others have interviewed found that many men pay for sex the first time in legalised or decriminalised regimes, and feel entitled to do so because there is no social or legal deterrent. Many of the survivors tell me that sex buyers tend to have even higher expectations under decriminalisation and appear to feel 'entitled' to have whatever they ask for from the women they buy.

In the following chapter I examine the role of the sex buyers, and how their needs are routinely put before the women they abuse; the excuses and justifications made by the sex buyers and their many supporters; and how the truth about men who pay for sex is being lifted from the shadows by the survivor abolitionists and placed in full view of the general public.

5

The Invisible Man

The invisible man is invisible no more – we are holding him up to face the music. (Rachel Moran, 2015)

I pay for sex because I can. Because taking a woman out to dinner costs me money, so why not? Because it is my need and she gets to feed her kids. (Sex buyer, Amsterdam)

I am heading to a conference at the Dutch Parliament on the demand for prostitution, I share my Easyjet flight from Luton Airport to Amsterdam with two groups of young male sex tourists, loudly bragging about how 'pissed', 'stoned', 'wasted' and 'fucked' they were last time they visited De Wallen, the window brothel area of Amsterdam.

The conference is entitled 'Men who buy sex: What is their responsibility?' My friend and colleague Fiona Broadfoot is giving the keynote speech at the event. Broadfoot was pimped into prostitution aged 15, escaped the sex trade 11 years later, and for the past 20 years has been involved in the campaign to eradicate the international sex trade. Most of the delegates are sympathetic to the arguments that sex buyers should be held accountable and that legalisation of pimping and brothel

© The Author(s) 2017
J. Bindel, *The Pimping of Prostitution*,
DOI 10.1057/978-1-137-55890-9_5

owning has been a disaster. But one woman, sitting at the back of the room, showed her disagreement and displeasure as regularly as she was able to.

The following day Broadfoot and I go to Amsterdam and visit De Wallen. We pass several tour guides and stop by one group, being led by a young hipster who is speaking of the legal sex trade with very little knowledge. The group laugh at the guide's jokes about how they would 'all look at prostitutes together' if they booked his evening walk around the red light district. I ask about trafficking and abuse but he simply trots out the party line in response.

In the narrow streets in which the window brothels are situated we see two young men approach one of the doors. As one steps inside, the other leans against the wall to smoke a cigarette. We ask if he would be happy to talk to us on the record and to be recorded on my smartphone. He agrees.

Alex started paying for sex when he was 12 years old. 'It is so normal here', he tells us. 'In America you have it, in England you have it, but here it is different because it is legal. I come here once a month if I can afford it. I only get charged €20 because I know all the girls and I am a local, but the tourists pay €50. For everything. Most of the women have pimps or lover boys [pimps that pose as boyfriends], but who is going to do anything if they are unhappy? Nobody will.'

He adds: 'If my sister or mother did this I would be very angry.'

As we are interviewing Alex, Broadfoot spots the woman who had been sitting at the back at the conference, standing in the doorway of the Prostitution Information Centre (PIC). She is now taking photographs of us. I recognised her at the conference as Mariska Majoor, who founded the PIC in 1994 and organises commercial tours around De Wallen. Majoor was prostituted from the age of 16 until exiting the sex trade.

Broadfoot asks Majoor why she is taking photos. At that moment, Majoor calls Alex over and tells him we are bad people and that we 'have no respect for men who pay for sex'. Then she speaks to Alex in Dutch, and suddenly he becomes very agitated and asks me to delete his interview, which I do. As is usual practice for journalists, I had also been making notes of our conversation in order to remind myself to ask subsequent questions.

At a nearby cafe we see groups of young men who are obviously gearing themselves up for a jaunt around the red-light area. I speak to two American tourists who seem to be unimpressed with the idea of paying for sex but their views, formed mainly from information they have read on a blog about legalised prostitution in the Netherlands, are that this system is safer for the women than any other.

What the Survivors Say

Rae Story was involved in prostitution for a decade, in the UK, and other countries such as Australia and New Zealand. She exited prostitution in 2015, and runs the Blog, *In Permanent Opposition*.[1] Story, along with a number of other survivors I interviewed in Germany, Australia, Holland and New Zealand, makes the important point that sex buyers are abusive, disrespectful and often violent whatever legal regime they are paying for sex under:

> You make money for yourself if a guy picks you, but you also spend a lot of the time schlepping about as eye candy for the punters while they get inebriated on expensive plonk. The FKK clubs (upmarket strip clubs with saunas and prostitution services) in Germany are worse because you often have to do it naked. There is no way you can protect against guys pulling your hair, slapping your arse too hard, fucking you too hard, the worst of all: pulling off the condom and ejaculating inside of you… other 'indignities' like dealing with rancid sperm or unwashed backsides etc.

Aside from women in prostitution, the best evidence of how abusive the act of paying for sex is comes from the men themselves. Over the years I have interviewed a number of men who have accessed commercial sexual exploitation. The first group was in 1999 in the North of England during the Kerb Crawler Re-Education Programme. Over the years, for both journalistic and research purposes, I have spoken to numerous

---

[1]https://www.bookdepository.com/Permanent-Opposition-Notes-from-Feminist-Underground-Rae-Story/9781326771058 Accessed 28th August 2017.

male sex buyers. During the course of researching this book, I spoke to men in legal brothels, illegal off-street establishments and street prostitution zones.

One of the most important research projects I have been involved in was part of a six-country study designed and led by Dr Melissa Farley. In 2009, Farley approached me in my capacity as research consultant at Eaves (see Chap. 1) and asked if we would assist with carrying out at least 100 interviews of men who buy sex in London. There was no budget, but we raised just enough money to develop the research tools and buy a mobile phone on which we would make contact with the sex buyers.

We placed an advertisement in one of the free London newspapers that read: 'Men! Have you ever paid for sex? An international research team is in London on [date] and would like to talk to you about your experiences and views. Anonymity and discretion guaranteed'. As soon as the advertisement went in, the mobile phone we had purchased was ringing off the hook. The only screening we did was to ensure that the men were serious, and had not rung up to get some kind of sexual kick. There were very few that were eliminated. We arranged meetings with 103 of those men throughout the given week.

Four of us were primed to carry out the interviews. We needed to be able to see each other during the interview process to ensure safety. Additionally, the men needed to be reassured that the team would be discreet during the interview process and that their anonymity would be guaranteed.

Having wandered around central London a few times trying to find a venue, I happened upon a brilliant idea. I had been invited to have a drink with a member of the Royal Festival Hall. We would do the interviews there during the day, before the crowd started to arrive for the evening events, using one of the mezzanine areas, so it would be possible to keep an eye on our interviewees as they were met by the research assistants, outside next to the Nelson Mandela statue.

The interviews, which took between 90 and 150 minutes each, went smoothly. That is until interview 99. This man, let's call him John, turned up early, and the research assistant had not yet arrived at the Mandela statue. John approached the head of security, showed him the advertisement in the paper and asked where the researchers were who were talking to men about prostitution use.

We were immediately told to leave the venue and that the Royal Festival Hall was a 'family facility', which meant that the nature of our research was unsuitable. After an hour, when there was a change of shift in security, we re-entered the hall and concluded our interviews.

The resulting report[2] was published at the end of 2009 and was launched in Parliament in early 2010. After its publication I wrote about my experiences of interviewing the men and the main findings in the *Guardian* newspaper.[3] It is not unusual for those who do research to write about their findings in newspapers, or speak about it on television and radio. It was clearly my own view of the results of the research I had been involved in, and there was plenty of research by pro-prostitution academics that would have reached different conclusions to ours. However, on publication, my editor received a long letter of complaint signed by the usual pro-prostitution academic suspects.

The basis of the complaint was that I was biased, and the *Guardian* was biased for allowing me to write the piece for their pages. I was promoting my own research, they said, which was biased, so how could the *Guardian* even pretend to be impartial? Of course, as a researcher, I had followed the ethical guidelines set down by the British Sociological Association. My *Guardian* article was based on my observations and some verbatim testimony from the men that I had obtained with their consent during the interviews. The complainants clearly did not like the fact that the interviewees had pretty much done the abolitionists' work for us.

What the Men Said

As a radical feminist, I am often of accused of making the claim that 'all men are potential rapists'. Nothing could be further from the truth: radical feminists do not believe that male babies are born pre-programmed

---

[2]Farley, M.; Bindel, J.; Golding, J. (2009, Dec.) *Men who buy sex: Who they buy and what they know. A research study of 103 men who describe their use of trafficked and non-trafficked women in prostitution, and their awareness of coercion and violence.* Eaves, London & Prostitution Research & Education, San Francisco.

[3]Bindel, J. (2010, Jan 15.) *Why men use prostitutes.* In The Guardian. Retrieved 15 June 2017, from https://www.theguardian.com/society/2010/jan/15/why-men-use-prostitutes.

to commit acts of violence against women, nor do we believe that girls are born to be victims. Our view is that under patriarchy, men are given power over women, and that a way of asserting that power is to be violent towards women.

As one of the London-based sex buyers said to me: 'If I wasn't able to have sex with a prostitute and was frustrated, I might have to go out and attack a real woman'. The 'real' woman that this sex buyer was referring to was a woman who wasn't prostituted. I have heard the same thing said by sex buyers, by women in prostitution, pimps and by members of the public.

Below I have listed a number of the comments from the men in the London study. I have not deliberately picked out the worst, but have simply categorised them to show the range of problematic attitudes developed by the men who commodify sex with women.

Prostituted Women As Products

- 'I made a list in my mind. I told myself that I'll be with different races e.g. Japanese, Indian, Chinese … Once I have been with them I tick them off the list. It's like a shopping list.'
- 'You get to choose, like a catalogue.'
- 'Selecting and purchasing has something to do with domination and control.'
- 'It's like going for a drink. You are not doing anything illegal.'
- 'Prostitutes have improved over the years. They're younger now and better looking and cleaner.'

Prostitution is About Men's Uncontrollable Needs

- 'I wouldn't want it abolished. It's a service I use.'
- 'It's a guaranteed showtime—you're gonna have a great time with a girl with a great body. You're gonna enjoy the specific things you like. You're gonna be able to shoot your load and be totally satiated.'

What They Say About the Women

- 'A prostitute is like an outlet to a pressure cooker.'
- 'You pay for the convenience, a bit like going to a public loo.'
- 'It is just a job—why would they think otherwise? They don't feel guilty. In the beginning they have emotions. But it becomes a routine. They die off after a while.'
- 'They are girls no-one else wants to marry. So they work for sex. No one wants their wife to be a prostitute.'
- 'I use ones that I've trained.'

Normalisation/Pro-legalisation

- 'At the end of the day, you're horny, tired of playing with yourself, so what else can you do?'
- 'It's like having a nice meal.'
- 'I've been decades without a steady girlfriend—it's meant I didn't have to enter a world that didn't want me. When I think of the gas keys and kiddies' shoes I've bought … I'm not saying I'm a philanthropist but I've made a difference.'
- 'Maybe if men could get it [prostitution] on the NHS [National Health Service] if they are disabled, it would prevent them from raping.'

Deterrence/Ambivalence

- On his worst experience of paying for sex: 'Very moody girl, language barrier [from South East Asia], she was being forced to do it, mechanical, having sex with her was frustrating. These things give you a feeling of waste of money. That's when you feel guilty.'
- 'They've chosen to do what they do to make money—they have to accept what comes with it: the good, the bad, the ugly.'

- On the serial killer in Ipswich: 'I kind of felt compassion for the parents of the prostitutes killed. But if you are playing a certain game you should take all that comes with that game. I really feel that way.'

Gross Sexism/Misogyny

- 'It's just about that moment of pleasure. Liking her was not relevant to the experience.'
- 'I get sexual satisfaction for money. She may not get satisfaction, I don't care.'
- 'If she isn't crying but says "no", I keep on. I only stop if she is really crying.'
- 'We call two girls in and have a competition to see who's better, and ask them to rate each of our sexual performances. After we each do one, we swap, then see who has the highest rating.'
- 'They are a necessary evil.'
- 'I'm angry at myself for having to go and spend the money, and angry with my wife for making me go.' Punter who says he is a 'sex addict' whose wife does not want as much sex as he does.
- 'I've seen pimps with the prostitutes, yelling. I've seen girls dragged back inside apartments. I want the people I deal with to be away from the sordid.'
- 'If you go to the wrong one, you might as well be in a morgue, there's a slab of flesh there.'

Prostitution Decreases Rape and Sexual Assault

- 'Prostitution should not be abolished. It prevents rape and should be regulated.'
- 'If women could give full satisfaction to husbands and boyfriends, then men wouldn't go to prostitutes.'

All Relationships are Prostitution

- 'There is no need to abolish prostitution. Every woman is a prostitute. Before you sleep with a woman you wine/dine, buy gifts for her before she sleeps with you. So you are spending money on her for sex.'
- 'It is actually cheaper to go to prostitutes than a normal woman.'
- 'It is simply commercial sex. You go to a woman who is highly sexed, and a normal woman is never as highly sexed as a prostitute. It would be wrong.'
- 'The women want to do the job and men want to buy them, so everyone has a role.'

The Ethical John

One commonly heard argument from pro-prostitution activists against criminalising sex buyers is that it will prevent the men who suspect trafficking from reporting it to the police, in case they are arrested. As Cat Stephens of the International Union of Sex Workers said at a meeting in Parliament: 'Clients are our best defence against trafficking.'

In her book *Not a Choice, Not a Job*, Janice Raymond outlines the various 'ethical John' campaigns that have been implemented in certain countries. For example: '… the 2006 World Cup Games in Germany provided advocates of "ethical sex tourism" with another version of simply "pondering" the demand'. The National Council of German Women's Organisations (Frauenrat) set up stalls around the football stadiums and urged male sports fans to 'think about' the fact that the women they might have sex with are coerced. Henny Engels, its executive director, made clear they weren't against men purchasing women for the sex of prostitution: 'We have nothing against prostitutes or prostitution. But we are against people trafficking and forced prostitution'.[4]

---

[4]Raymond, J. (2014.) *Not a choice, not a job: Exposing the myths about prostitution and the global sex trade*. London: Potomac. p. 56.

The idea that sex buyers who see evidence of pimping and trafficking in the off-street sex trade routinely report such matters to the police is risible. Between the 2004 opening of the POPPY Project,[5] the only support and advocacy service for women trafficked into the UK sex trade in London, and prior to a partial law criminalising demand being implemented in England and Wales in 2010,[6] approximately 50 sex buyers contacted the organisation to report possible trafficking cases. All of the men had paid for sex with the women and gone through with it, despite their suspicions. Without exception, the men were hoping to 'rescue' the women and move them into their homes.

Our London research[7] of 103 sex buyers found that 27% believed that once they had paid the buyer is entitled to engage in any act he chooses with the woman he buys. Some 47% expressed the view that women did not always have certain rights during the prostitution exchange.[8] In addition: 'Despite their awareness of coercion and trafficking, only five of these 103 men reported their suspicions to the police. They feared a loss of anonymity, especially fearing their families' discovery of their use of prostitutes.'

Additionally, our research found that 55% of the men interviewed said that they were aware that 'most of' the women they bought were trafficked, pimped or otherwise coerced'.[9] This figure correlates with other

---

[5]Eaves' POPPY Project. Retrieved 15 June 2017, from http://www.eavesforwomen.org.uk/about-eaves/our-projects/the-poppy-project/.

[6]The Policing and Crime Act 2009, s.14 amended the Sexual Offences Act 2003 by adding a new s.53. The new section makes it an offence in England and Wales to pay for the services of a prostitute who has been coerced into providing sexual services; the section was implemented from 1 April 2010.

[7]Farley, M.; Bindel, J.; Golding, J. (2009, Dec.) *Men who buy sex: Who they buy and what they know. A research study of 103 men who describe their use of trafficked and non-trafficked women in prostitution, and their awareness of coercion and violence.* Eaves, London & Prostitution Research & Education, San Francisco.

[8]Farley, M.; Bindel, J.; Golding, J. (2009, Dec.) *Men who buy sex: Who they buy and what they know. A research study of 103 men who describe their use of trafficked and non-trafficked women in prostitution, and their awareness of coercion and violence.* Eaves, London & Prostitution Research & Education, San Francisco. p. 18.

[9]Farley, M.; Bindel, J.; Golding, J. (2009, Dec.) *Men who buy sex: Who they buy and what they know. A research study of 103 men who describe their use of trafficked and non-trafficked women in prostitution, and their awareness of coercion and violence.* Eaves, London & Prostitution Research & Education, San Francisco. p. 22.

research on demand; for example, a study by Anderson and O'Connell Davidson,[10] both fierce opponents of criminalising sex buyers, reports that most men who buy sex are aware of and have witnessed exploitation, coercion and trafficking, but this does not affect their decision to buy sex.

Prostitution apologists have been known to dismiss research conducted by abolitionists into sex buyers by claiming it is 'biased' and that the researchers have a 'hidden agenda',[11] but it is clear from other research that violence and abuse are often perpetrated by the punters. Even pimps understand this.

During an interview with Mici, a pimp operating under the legal system in Fethiye, Turkey, I asked about his role and his view on sex buyers: 'I think there is a certain attraction/gravitation between the seller and the sold. Some women do not like anal sex or oral sex. They do not like to engage in acts they do not like and sometimes customers force them. They are beaten up, their homes raided by thugs … sometimes two men want to fuck one woman for the price of one. Violence is always there.'

There is even Dutch research[12] on sex buyers that concludes that the men are rarely interested in the well-being of the women they buy. Conducted in 2013–2014 by the local municipality of Amsterdam and GGD,[13] a public health service with a focus on HIV/STI prevention and treatment, the survey looked at sex buyers who access prostitution via the legal window brothels. The report, entitled 'In Conversation with the Customer', focussing on the role of the sex buyer in tackling abuse, was presented by one of the researchers at a conference in Den Haag in 2015.

The delegates, largely sympathetic to the introduction of the law to criminalise demand and critics of legalised prostitution, assumed that the research was being conducted in order to highlight how

---

[10]Anderson, B.; O'Connell Davidson, J. (2003). *Is trafficking in human beings demand driven? A multi-country pilot study*. Geneva: International Organisation for Migration.

[11]Harlot's Parlour. (2010, Jan 16.) *Response to Bindel-Farley-Golding research report published today*. In Harlot's Parlour. Retrieved 15 June 2017, from https://harlotsparlour.wordpress.com/2010/01/16/response-to-bindel-farley-golding-research-report-published-today/.

[12]https://www.mensenhandelweb.nl/document/rapport-ggd-amsterdam-gesprek-met-de-klant Accessed April 1st 2017.

[13]GGD Amsterdam. Retrieved 15 June 2017, from http://www.ggd.amsterdam.nl/.

criminalising demand would result in fewer men being willing to report violence and abuse to the police.

A total of 986 sex buyers and 195 prostituted women completed surveys. Interviews were also conducted with 11 sex buyers and 11 of the women. Just over 40% of buyers said they would be willing to report abuse. However, based on responses to questions put to the men regarding trafficking and exploitation, and the distinction between 'free and forced' prostitution, the researcher admitted that only 13% of the overall sample would be able to identify the abuse and spot which women are in danger.

The most frequently mentioned factors that discourage reporting are, according to the Dutch sex buyers: lack of clear and reliable information about abuse; insufficient trust in one's own judgement; stigmatisation by the government; and distrust regarding how abuse will be dealt with. It is interesting that even under legalisation, such a high percentage of sex buyers claim to be ignorant about how to spot a trafficked women, despite the Dutch government claiming to fund a number of public awareness and education projects on the topic.[14]

The research identified five types of 'clients' in relation to the role of the buyer in identifying and reporting abuse. The following, summarised extract is translated from the Dutch version of the report:

1. The carefree client, who does not feel responsible for abuse.
2. The denier, who feels responsible.
3. Acknowledges that there is a difference between voluntary and forced prostitution. Acknowledges the problem for a small portion of the market with respect to sex slavery and under-aged girls, but does not feel responsible. Denies or trivialises the problem by: blaming the prostitute by stating that a client is not responsible for her choices.
4. The avoider, who sees his role as staying away.
5. The rescuer, who sees his role as 'rescuing' a prostitute.
6. The whistleblower, who sees his role as notifying the authorities.

---

[14]Anon. *Netherlands – 3. Implementation of anti-trafficking policy.* In European Commission: Together Against Trafficking In Human Beings. Retrieved 15 June 2017, from https://ec.europa.eu/anti-trafficking/member-states/netherlands-3-implementation-anti-trafficking-policy_en.

The Dutch research came to the following conclusions: 'Prostitutes describe the majority of their clientele as "good clients". Nevertheless, most prostitutes have also had experiences with unpleasant clients. In particular, these are clients who make a fuss about using a condom, clients who have used (too much) alcohol and/or drugs, clients who show little respect or who do not stick to agreements.

'Prostitutes have little trust in clients as whistleblowers of abuse. They can't imagine that clients would actually, sincerely and for the right reasons be interested in the well-being of prostitutes'.

'In addition, prostitutes describe their clientele as much less responsible than the clients themselves describe. According to them, clients are primarily occupied with their own pleasure and sexual arousal.'

Clearly, the conclusions would not make those still wedded to the 'Dutch Model' of legalising the sex trade very happy.

During the Q&A session, Majoor, founder of PIC, made it clear that she was against any encouragement given to buyers to report abuse: 'There is a website on how to recognise signs of abuse', she said.[15] 'I know some [of the women] are sick and tired of clients who don't want to think whether we are forced [we] just want to earn the money and work and that's all.'

In response, the researcher asked Majoor if she thought it a 'bad idea to have the clients help to find out where the problems are'. She replied: 'What I know is that if you criminalise the clients you can totally forget about them reporting [abuse]. The sex workers' organisations and alliances did a lot of research about the effects of criminalising the clients and this is worse when it comes to safety'.

Sven Axel Mannson,[16] Professor of Social Work at Malmo University, Sweden, was at the event to present his own research on sex buyers. On hearing Majoor's comments he said: 'Personally, having talked to clients over the years, I am not so convinced that they will be very much help because they are in their own desires. I have also find that these men are quite manipulative'.

---

[15]I was audio recording the event with the permission of the organisers.
[16]Professor Sven Månsson. Malmö University. Retrieved 15 June 2017, from http://forskning.mah.se/en/id/hssvma.

It is no surprise that the approach to punters that was pioneered in Sweden has changed hearts and minds, including those of people who were against the idea of criminalising demand prior to and during the early days of its implementation.

Simon Hagström is a police inspector who has been based in the Stockholm Police Prostitution Unit since 2009. I have met Hagström on a number of occasions and found him to genuinely care for the women caught in the sex trade. He, along with the vast majority of his colleagues, took some time after the introduction of the law to criminalise demand came into force in 1999 to fully understand its importance in tackling serious crime.

'What is really important to say is that the Swedish police were strongly opposing this legislation', says Hagström. 'The official standpoint from the police was, "We do not want this legislation". The Swedish police wanted to criminalise the ones selling sex because they thought, along with several political parties, that the law will not be efficient if you only criminalise one party.'

Hagström is pleased to say that he and his colleagues were proved wrong: 'There was a lot of attention on this law. I used to think, "What is it about this law that is so controversial?", because this is not a difficult equation. You have traffickers and pimps who want to make money. Who has the money? The sex buyers. If we remove the sex buyers there will be no money for organised crime'.

What the Survivors Say

The 50 survivors I interviewed for this book, and the scores of other women in prostitution I have spoken to over the past 20-plus years, all had stories to tell of violence and abuse from punters. Whether they identified themselves as 'high-class escorts' or were prostituted from the street, flats or brothels, the women share a core experience: not one had escaped violence while dealing with sex buyers.

I met Nicky in Auckland, New Zealand, in 2016. I asked if the punters were less violent under decriminalisation:

No. Recently I got bottled – I've never had that before in my life – a bottle was shoved up me and broken. And the next day I was down the Salvation Army telling them. Then I rang [a friend] and said 'I've been raped'. I'll start crying – now a police officer will say 'How big was the bottle, what colour was the bottle?' It doesn't matter what colour the bottle was … it was a bottle up me.

I have been threatened, I have been told to get off the street. I used to always carry a weapon in a long black coat. Then I bought an imitation gun and it looked the part. Then I thought 'no' because I'd get done by the pigs whether it's plastic or not. Then I put a screwdriver down my bra and now it's just, 'I don't give a fuck'.

Sabrinna Valisce, who was prostituted in Australia and New Zealand both before and after legalisation and decriminalisation, tells me that, contrary to promises from the pro-prostitution lobby, punter violence increased in New Zealand after the 2003 change in the law. She says: '[In 2003] the police violence stopped overnight under decriminalisation, so on that level it was good, but the johns … within the space of a year the johns got more violent and had greater expectations. They thought they could do whatever they wanted, thought they had bought your body. I had never had someone say "I paid for your body and I can do what I want" until decriminalisation'.

Children abused into the sex trade often experience life-changing violence from punters. The men who buy them might find it particularly difficult to delude themselves into thinking that a girl or boy standing on a street corner looking for 'business' is making any kind of choice, or that this is something s/he is happy to do. Of all the women I have spoken to who were prostituted as children, only one survivor told me that *one time* a punter, on realising she was under the age of consent (16 in her country), gave her a reprieve.

Ne'Cole Daniels was 15 and had been turned out onto the streets by a family friend. She tells me about one incidence of violence that had a profound effect on her:

A man pulls up in this nice car, he looks like he has money. So I go with him and when I get to the house there are three more people there. They were all black [Daniels is African-American]. They took advantage of me.

It didn't matter that I was like a two-year-old baby. They violated my whole body. I was sodomised, I was sick and he's trying to stick his dick in my mouth. I'm just like, 'Lord, hurry up. I promise I won't do it again, just let them hurry up and get through so I can get the hell out of here'. I was treated even worse than an animal.

During my visit to Auckland, New Zealand, I met Lisa, out on the streets looking for a punter. Lisa was sitting next to her Zimmer frame. It turned out she was in her early 50s and was disabled through a life in prostitution. I asked if her situation had improved since decriminalisation and she told me 'no', because in her experience the men who buy her feel entitled to do exactly what they want, in the way they would if purchasing a hamburger. 'The only thing that would help me is a way out', she said.

I use the examples above to illustrate what I have come to understand as fairly typical behaviour of sex buyers towards women in prostitution. I have heard countless stories—including from pro-prostitution lobbyists—of gang rape, beatings and stabbings, under legalisation/decriminalisation and every other legal system[17]. The men themselves admit to shocking attitudes towards the women they buy, and to having sex with distressed, terrified women. Some openly admit to being violent.

So why is there so much support for the punter from the liberal left? How is it that even the likes of Amnesty International appears to bend over backwards to protect his 'human rights' and to portray him as a man with needs he deserves to have met? Whenever I am discussing this issue with decent folk who should know better, they raise the issue of the disabled punter. 'What about those men who can't get a date the "regular way"?' they ask.

The Disabled Punter

As the various initiatives to curb demand for commercial sex have forced attention on the purchaser, the pro-sex-work lobby has acquired a new hero. The 'disabled client' (note the gender neutral description)

---

[17]As we saw in Chapter 1 November 12, 2009 Thursday, Edition 1; National Edition. 'Is sex for the disabled the last taboo?' Helen Croydon.

is used to garner support, sympathy and to promote a view of the sex buyer as a nice, deserving individual. It is interesting to explore the type of disability these men are imagined to have by those whose sympathy is being sought. It is notable that the injured veteran and tragic young man figures keep recurring as examples—always heroic.

To hear the way many apologists for the sex trade describe disabled sex buyers, one could easily get the impression that selling sex to disabled people is an altruistic service, akin to meals on wheels. But the focus on this largely mythical buyer obscures both the majority of 'undeserving' punters and the harms done to women.

In spring 2015, in a stiflingly hot TV studio in Manchester, England, I am sitting next to Laura Lee, who describes herself as a 'part-time call girl' and 'sex workers' rights activist'. We are waiting to pre-record an episode of *O'Brien*, a national UK TV programme in which we will debate the topic 'Should we decriminalise prostitution?'

As the warm-up act tries to put life into the studio audience, I look around to see who, aside from Lee and a sex trade survivor I had met previously, is fitted with a microphone. There are a couple of heavily made-up women carrying whips and wearing fetish gear, and, in the front row, a middle-aged woman sitting next to a young, severely disabled man in a wheelchair. I could have written the script for what happens next.

Lee, who is so hostile to the abolitionist law she is mounting a legal challenge against the Nordic model introduced by the Northern Irish government in 2015 (as discussed in Chap. 8), speaks about how prostitution is a choice for most of the women involved. I speak of the failure of legalised and fully decriminalised regimes, and why I support the abolitionist law. The survivor highlights the harms caused to the women who are bought and sold.

The cameras then switches around and focuses on the woman and the young man in the wheelchair. Her name is Veronica. She explains that John is her son, and that his back was broken in a car accident when he was five. As John approached puberty, Veronica began to worry about how he would meet his sexual needs.

'Should we have brothels on the high street?' asks host James O'Brien. 'We should have brothels everywhere', replies Veronica, before describing how she had trawled the Internet looking for help with getting her son laid, speaking to 'sex workers, escorts, prostitutes, anyone who knew about this'. Eventually, having been told about the massive sex trade in Las Vegas, Veronica took the aptly named John to lose his virginity with several prostituted women. 'He had a lovely time', she says, with a cheeky twinkle in her eye. Laughter and clapping erupt from the audience. But there is more to come.

'Didn't you buy him a brothel?' asks O'Brien. 'So John, your mum bought you a brothel?'

'Yes', John gloats, 'and I lived in the basement for three years. I learned about all the different aspects of prostitution, and the dodgy side and the seedy side of it. But every man has got a different fantasy'.

'He wasn't allowed to partake with any of the girls in our brothel', interrupts Veronica, 'because I didn't want a situation where we could incur exploitation. I didn't want him to be one of these guys—"Oh, I've got a brothel so I've got rights to these women".' The peels of laughter coming from the audience—including from a clapping, animated Lee—mask the sounds of disgust and protest coming from the sex trade survivor.

This scene dramatised one of the most commonly used arguments against criminalising sex buyers. Pro-prostitution lobbyists claim that the Nordic model would, in effect, be criminalising 'disabled people'. The argument holds that disabled people have a right to access sex, with the implied premise that their disability somehow impairs their ability to form intimate relationships. This claim is one of the clearest examples of how the sex buyers' so-called 'human rights' have been placed above those of the prostituted woman.

The 'sex workers' rights' lobby argues that when disabled sex buyers are denied recourse to prostitution, they are being denied their dignity, liberty and the right to know physical pleasure and true love. There is even a not-for-profit organisation called Touching Base in Australia, which exists to 'foster connections between people with disabilities and sex workers, with a focus on access, discrimination, human rights, and legal issues, and the attitudinal barriers that these two marginalised communities face'. Underneath the liberal language, this is pandering presented as a social service.

To make this argument more palatable, the 'sex workers' rights' lobby also claims that feminist abolitionists are denying the rights of sex workers to consent to prostitution and to practise their own agency.

Persuasive Mythology

The myth of the sympathetic disabled punter has even been accepted by Amnesty International (AI). In its 2014 draft policy document (leaked to me by an AI insider, and which I subsequently published in a national newspaper[18]), AI also takes the line that disabled men have a right to access sex via prostitution: 'For some—in particular persons with mobility or sensory disabilities or those with psycho-social disabilities that hamper social interactions—sex workers are persons with whom they feel safe enough to have a physical relationship or to express their sexuality. Some develop a stronger sense of self in their relationships with sex workers, improving their life enjoyment and dignity'.

The suggestion that disabled people are considered so unattractive that they have to purchase sexual access to another human body is offensive enough in itself. Disability rights activists have long campaigned for better access to the venues where they might meet sexual partners, as well as a less prejudicial and conventional view of beauty. With the sanitisation of the sex trade by the 'sex workers' rights' lobby and their academic enablers, terms such as 'agency' and 'empowerment' are increasingly applied to those selling sex as well as purchasing, particularly if the buyer is associated with a marginalised community.

Critics of the abolitionist law have found the argument about disabled men being denied sexual pleasure very useful in their campaign. However, it is less helpful to disabled people. Not only does it reinforce the problematic belief that anyone who does not fit the conventional standards of beauty and desirability is unable to access consensual sex and therefore needs to pay for it, it further suggests that disabled people's carers are responsible for ensuring their clients' sexual satisfaction. This is already the case in Denmark, where prostitution was legalised in 1999, and there is now an expectation that carers working with physically disabled couples should facilitate sex between them if asked—for example, the carer may be expected to insert the penis of one into an orifice of the other.

---

[18]Bindel, J. (2014, Jan 24.) *Julie Bindel: An abject inversion of its own principles.* In Daily Mail. Retrieved 15 June 2017, from http://www.dailymail.co.uk/news/article-2544983/JULIE-BINDEL-An-abject-inversion-principles.html.

In the UK, a number of individuals and organisations campaigning for full decriminalisation of the sex trade use the example of disabled men and sexual access to garner support. In 2000, the pornographer Tuppy Owens set up the TLC Trust,[19] a website that looks very much to me as though it is aimed at disabled men looking for prostitution services. The TLC website has this to say about the role of carers: 'Health and social care professionals are often needed to support their disabled clients find a sexual service and prepare for each session. We hear dreadful stories of disabled clients being denied such support, and one sex worker reported that her client's care team refused to wash him after a session! Please note: spunk is not disgusting or dangerous, in fact it is quite nutritious!'

Advice to disabled sex buyers on the site includes: 'Question: My care staff refuse to wash me after seeing a sex worker. Answer: Threaten to report them unless they wash you respectfully'. On the fees charged by the escort services advertised on the TLC website, it has this to say: 'Many disabled people say you cannot afford the fees that sex workers charge. Then we find out you have been on skiing holidays, own an expensive hi-fi, or smoke 20 fags a day. Where are your priorities? Remember, sex keeps you fit, mentally and physically.' With the mention of 'skiing holidays', it is clear that the escort services advertised by TLC are not only reaching out to men with significant mobility disabilities.

Its key message to disabled men about the sex trade is this: 'Whatever you do, don't feel bad about using sex workers—don't fall for the fundamentalist feminist propaganda that all sex work is violence to women. For a start, many sex workers are men, and most sex workers chose their career because it suits them, and enjoy their work'.

Owens is also the chair of the Sexual Freedom Coalition (SFC). On its website, it states: 'We actively challenge the Home Office, governments, religion, police and press for the sexual freedom of all consenting adults. It seemed important to focus on these people who are, in fact, doing great work in bringing happiness, inspiration and a sexual education to many people who need and enjoy them, including disabled people'.

---

[19]TLC Trust: For Disabled Men and Women to Find Responsible Sexual Services. Retrieved 15 June 2017, from http://tlc-trust.org.uk/.

The TLC Trust is demanding one wheelchair-accessible brothel in every city 'to meet the demand', and that hospice wards should have provision for visiting sex workers. TLC even uses the example of wounded servicemen to call for an 'NHS' approach to the sex trade. 'It would be a sad injustice', its website reads, 'if service personnel such as soldiers badly wounded in Iraq and Afghanistan were banned from the help they receive from sex workers'.

Bärbel Ahlborn, coordinator at Kassandra, in Nuremberg, Germany, considers the provision of sexual services to disabled men partly as a health issue. 'Many of the disabled and older people are not able to get into contact with sex workers', she says. 'If they are asking the nurses in the homes and tell them they want to find someone offering that [then] the nurses are feeling better with providing contact with a person who knows how to handle them.'

The idea that nurses are somehow responsible for assisting disabled patients to access prostitution is beyond comprehension. The majority of nurses and carers for the elderly and disabled are female. The vast majority of disabled people wishing to access prostitution services are male. Despite the pro-prostitution lobby, supported by a number of academics, insisting that prostitution is not about gender inequality, or violence against women and girls, the overwhelming majority of prostitution transactions are male on female.

In 2005 I debated decriminalisation of the sex trade with a senior member of the medical profession. Much of the healthcare profession appears to have been influenced by pressure groups calling for the blanket decriminalisation of the sex trade. For example, as a result of lobbying by the English Collective of Prostitutes, the nurses' union voted overwhelmingly to decriminalise all aspects of the sex trade at its annual conference in Harrogate in 1995, with the reasoning that this would make prostituted women more likely to come forward for healthcare.

My opponent was Jean, a middle-aged woman who considered nursing her vocation in life. I was surprised that Jean soon shifted her argument about women's access to healthcare onto the poor disabled men who can't get a date. Jean gave a heart-wrenching description of a returning war veteran named Jeff, whose legs were blown off and spine permanently damaged in a roadside blast. I expressed surprise that he had a fully functioning penis in spite of such injuries and was told: 'Perhaps he just wants a human touch'.

This notion that 'love' as well as sex is for sale is one that is becoming increasingly popular among the postmodernist 'queer'-identifying academics. In his review of the book *Sex, Love and Money in Cambodia: Professional Girlfriends and Transactional Relationships*, Nick Mai, Professor of Sociology at Kingston University, argues that: 'whereas 'sex-for-cash' can be seen as a practice close to prostitution, 'sex-for-fun', 'sex-for-love' and the 'sweetheart relationship' are discursively framed practices distinguishing different sexual, intimate and economic transactions through which professional girlfriends experiment with new individualised and hedonistic ways of 'being themselves'—sexually, socially and economically'.

But disabled people themselves don't necessarily agree that they are in need of prostitution. I discovered the work of UK-based disabled feminist writer Philippa Willitts after reading her article 'Nobody's Entitled to Sex, Including Disabled People' on the blog *Feminist Current*.[20] Over Skype, Willitts and I discuss the argument that criminalising the purchase of sex will lead to disabled men being unfairly punished.

She tells me that as both a feminist and a disabled person she was keen to ensure she made the point about the isolation and prejudice faced by many disabled people on the dating scene, while critiquing the rights of men to pay for sex. 'I wanted to challenge this assumption that [disabled people] couldn't have sex without paying for it, and that disabled men doing so was somehow inevitable', she says. 'I was sticking up for disabled people on the one hand, and sticking up for women on the other hand, so didn't feel like I was compromising either of those identities.'

The rights of disabled men to buy sex clearly supersedes those of not only the prostituted women (or 'carers') expected to service him, but also that of disabled women campaigning to end the dual oppression of being disabled and female in a sexist, ableist society. For Willitts, challenging the misogynistic sex trade in no way contradicts her efforts in highlighting the social exclusion faced by many disabled people, which, in turn, makes it difficult to meet sexual partners.

---

[20]Willitts, P. (2014, Apr 23.) *Nobody's entitled to sex, including disabled people.* In Feminist Current. Retrieved 15 June 2017, from http://www.feministcurrent.com/2014/04/23/nobodys-entitled-to-sex-including-disabled-people/.

She says: 'A number of men I did not know, but who somehow came across the article, emailed me and said they were really glad to have someone represent the fact that they weren't needy poor people with no friends or contacts, with no life'.

Why has the argument that disabled men routinely pay for sex become such a truism, I ask. 'I wonder if it's something about the fact that as disabled people we have to pay people to do things for us', says Willitts. 'If there's something about the familiarity with needing assistance that removes a barrier?'

A number of academics in the UK and elsewhere have expressed concern about the abolitionist model impacting on the 'human rights' of disabled men. In a paper published in the journal *Disability and Society*, the Canadian authors argue that so-called 'sex work' is an important avenue through which disabled people can explore sexual fulfilment, and that the criminalisation of paying for sex would adversely affect disabled people and their right to access sexual pleasure. Again, the use of gender-neutral language here is interesting. They write: 'Research has shown that the criminalisation of clients is a barrier to disabled peoples' erotic lives because the sex trade can provide a valuable avenue for sexual fulfilment'.[21]

Dr Belinda Brooks-Gordon, Reader in Psychology and Social Policy at the London School of Economics, also supports the idea that prostitution services should be available on the NHS. In an interview with *The Times*,[22] she said: 'Given that sex therapy is available on the NHS for men with penile dysfunction, for example, we could make a good case for saying that it should be provided. At the very least the health service should explore all options available to help a patient in anguish. What about the young war veteran who has fought for his country and now has no legs, difficulty in finding a partner and can't afford a prostitute?' At least Brooks-Gordon makes no pretence that there would be a demand for such 'services' from disabled women.

---

[21]Fritsch, K.; Heynen, R.; Ross, A.; van der Meulen, E. (2016) *Disability and sex work: Developing affinities through decriminalization*. In Disability & Society. 31:1. 84–99.
To link to this article: http://dx.doi.org/10.1080/09687599.2016.1139488.
[22]Brooks-Gordon, B. (2009, Nov 12.) In The Times. Retrieved 15 June 2017.

During a 2012 debate at Cambridge University entitled 'This House Would Decriminalise Prostitution',[23] Brooks-Gordon spoke in gushing terms of the fondness prostituted women have for their disabled 'clients'. She said: 'One sex worker said: "This week I saw a client with spinal bifida—I had to lift him from his wheelchair, position him, undress him, and then re dress him [and put him] back in the wheelchair. I was lucky he only weighed five stone. It's one of the reasons why more than one lady on the premises can be a good idea." Another said: "I saw a Falklands hero who was injured [and had] no legs. [He] greeted me in his wheelchair, was an absolute gentleman. Sex [was] not possible for him [but he] derived pleasure from skin to skin [contact]"'.

Gail (not her real name), a PhD candidate researching her thesis on an aspect of the sex trade, spoke to me about her views on the 'rights' of disabled men who pay for sex, a topic on which she had been published. Gail supports the theory that the disabled punter has been deliberately chosen as a sympathetic figure, and that there is a stifling conformity and fear of criticism within pro-prostitution academia.

Going by the arguments in her papers, there is no doubt that Gail is sympathetic to the rights of disabled men paying for sex. I ask her why she thinks those arguing most vociferously for full decriminalisation of the sex trade have recently used the example of disabled men's rights to buy sex. 'There's a lot of violence from people who buy sex, and I agree that's a massive problem', Gail tells me, sitting outside a cafe in King's Cross, London. 'There's not enough policing and protection, and working conditions are often really unsafe. [The argument that disabled men are also sex buyers] is making the point that not all people who buy sex necessarily are evil people. Disabled men are a small group of all people who buy sex.'

Don Kulick is a Swedish academic, currently Professor at Uppsala University, Sweden, and an influential voice against the Nordic model. In 2003 he published a paper entitled 'Sex in the New Europe: The Criminalisation of Clients and Swedish Fear of Penetration',[24] in which he

---

[23]The Cambridge Union. (2012, Sep 23.) *This house would decriminalise prostitution*. Retrieved 15 June 2017, from https://www.youtube.com/watch?v=OwAZplovr6E&app=desktop.

[24]Kulick, D. (2003, Jun 1.) *Sex in the new Europe: The criminilization of clients and Swedish fear of penetration*. In Anthropological Theory. Retrieved 15 June 2017, from http://ant.sagepub.com/content/3/2/199.abstract.

described buying sex as 'a temporary sexual relationship' and argued that the law criminalising the purchase of sex is a response to Sweden's entry into the European Union. 'For a variety of reasons, anxiety about Sweden's position in the EU is articulated through anxiety about prostitution.'

Kulick co-authored *Loneliness and Its Opposite: Sex, Disability, and the Ethics of Engagement* with JensRydström, and has compared the Swedish law against sex buyers to previous criminalisation of same-sex encounters, and explains both as coming from a 'fear of penetration'. *Loneliness and Its Opposite* is a comparative study of Denmark and Sweden and, according to the cover blurb, the differing ways in which disabled people's sexuality and sexual desire are viewed and enabled. In fact, it is almost 300 pages of propaganda against the criminalisation of sex buyers, and in support of 'sexual surrogacy', 'sexual assistance', or straightforward prostitution services for disabled men. It is rarely mentioned that the vast majority of carers are female.

But the central thesis is, in fact, untrue. Where the two countries differ is not on respecting and upholding the human rights of disabled people, but on attitudes to and laws curtailing sex buyers. Sweden criminalises the purchase of sex, whereas Denmark does not.

In *Loneliness and Its Opposite*, the authors suggest that sexual pleasure should be facilitated by 'people who work with and care for [disabled people]', which means anyone who is tasked with general caring duties, such as cooking and shopping. Should a carer therefore not only provide personal care such as assisting the client with using the toilet or washing intimate parts of the body, but also, if we are sympathetic with the argument that disabled men have a right to sexual release, facilitate orgasm?

Kulick and Rydström's data gathering is based on classic anthropological fieldwork, or 'participant observation'. Rydström spent one month living in three separate group homes for disabled people in Denmark. In Sweden no such fieldwork took place. Why? According to the authors, there was no point: 'Perhaps there is a group home, somewhere in Sweden, that has affirmative practices that facilitate the sexual lives of people with disabilities. But if such a place exists, it is a well guarded secret, unknown to or undisclosed by any of the professionals who work with and write about sex and disability and unknown to any of the Swedes with disabilities to whom we spoke'.

This leap of logic is staggering. It is clear the authors are only looking for very specific 'affirmative practices' regarding the facilitation of sexual pleasure, such as assistance to procure prostitution services. It might have been useful to spend time in the group homes in Sweden to ask the caring staff whether they would make a distinction between assisting someone to urinate or defecate, and assisting them to ejaculate.

Chapter 1 of their book opens with an example from a 'sex educator' named Axel Branting. Some years ago, a paralysed woman in her 30s came to Branting for advice. The woman told Branting that she had a problem: every time her male carers lifted her out of her wheelchair, she had an orgasm. 'What's the problem?' asked Branting. Well, said the woman, the male carers had clearly noticed her sexual arousal and, whenever possible, handed the task of lifting her to the female carers. Feeling depressed and humiliated, the woman had no idea how to raise the issue with the carers.

'And so he offered her the only piece of counsel he could think of. Turning centuries of advice prescribed to sexually unfulfilled women on its head, Branting told her that the next time one of the male assistants lifted her, "Close your eyes and pretend like you're not having an orgasm".'[25]

Branting had assumed the male carers were 'afraid' that they might be leaving themselves 'open to accusations of abuse'. The idea that the carers did not want to be part of a one-sided sexual tryst with a client did not occur to him. The notion that this woman was entitled to 'sexual fulfilment' from her carers is staggering. Clearly painting her as some type of victim, the conclusion of Kulick and Rydström is that, despite the men being obviously unwilling and therefore most definitely not consenting, the disabled woman should take whatever sexual pleasure she could find, while hiding the evidence.

The example of a disabled woman becoming aroused and desiring 'sexual assistance' from male carers belies the far more common scenario, which is of course that of disabled men and female carers. The authors, whether intentionally or otherwise, have used a sanitised

---

[25]Kulick and Rydstrom, 2015, Loneliness and it's opposite : sex, disability, and the ethics of engagement https://www.scribd.com/document/253894834/Loneliness-and-Its-Opposite-by-Don-Kulick-and-Jens-Rydstrom

version to make this point. Had they provided a scenario of a disabled man being assisted by female carers, they would have had to deal with the messy reality of sexual harassment and spurting ejaculate.

The authors also cite the academic Dr Michelle McCarthy, author of *Sexuality and Women with Learning Disabilities*. McCarthy's study is seen as somewhat irrelevant in terms of the arguments made in *Loneliness and Its Opposite*.

'*Sexuality and Women with Learning Disabilities* is concerned primarily with sexual abuse', write Kulick and Rydström. 'This focus seems to be partly because of McCarthy's particular interests and the manner in which she recruited her respondents [all of the women she interviewed had been referred to her by a group that provided sex education for adults with intellectual impairments] and partly because McCarthy says that the women she interviewed did not have very positive views of sexuality. Most of them had been victims of sexual abuse.'

I asked McCarthy her views on why her study had been deemed irrelevant by Kulick and Rydström. 'It's true to say that all of the people came through a sex education project but the majority of women who were referred for sex education had been sexually abused. Isn't that interesting?' she says. 'It could have been a sample of women who just needed sex education or advice on contraception or how to seek more sexual pleasure or whatever. As it turned out the majority had been sexually abused. I didn't seek them out, that's how they came.'

McCarthy is clear that when sex trade apologists speak of providing 'sexual services' for disabled people, it is actually about male privilege: 'I have never heard of male sexual surrogates being provided to women with learning disabilities. Most of the men who work in the sex trade service other men. Where are they going to find legions of men to work with women with learning disabilities?'

One of the 'tips for sex workers' from the Sexual Freedom Coalition shows very clearly the way that many simply assume that even the most severely disabled men will automatically want and need sex: 'Where consent cannot be expressed because of severe disability, assumptions should not be made that sexual pleasure is not required'. This is genuinely a horrifying comment that raises the prospect of non-communicative disabled people being subjected to unwanted sexual contact.

Wilitts is appalled at the way that able-bodied sex trade supporters are using the example of disabled men in order to discredit the abolitionist laws. But she is also concerned that a number of disabled men have internalised the 'human rights' rhetoric about sex. 'Nobody "needs" sex', says Willitts. 'And rather than disabled men campaigning for prostituted women to service them, they should be focusing their attention on making spaces—such as clubs where we may meet sexual partners—more accessible. I think the disabled community needs to look at whether it's ignoring women's rights.'

There are a number of other rationalisations put forward by those defending the right of men to pay for sex. One is that men 'need' more sex than do women, and therefore have no 'choice' but to access it via prostitution. This is akin to the regressive, outdated view, circa 1950, that men who do not get enough sex are compelled to rape. As one sex buyer said to me in the 2009 London study: 'Prostitution is a last resort to unfulfilled sexual desires. Rape would be less safe, or if you're forced to hurt someone or if you're so frustrated you jack off all day'.[26]

Dr Catherine Hakim is a sociologist currently based at the London-based Institute for the Study of Civil Society, a free market research group. Hakim believes that prostitution is inevitable because of what she has termed the 'male sex deficit'. Hakim's report 'Supply and Desire: Sexuality and the sex trade in the twenty-first Century' was handily published the day before AI made public its decision to support a policy of blanket decriminalisation of the sex trade in August 2015. Hakim, who has relied on secondary research and does not appear to have actually interviewed any women in the sex trade, argues that men want more sex than women and therefore it is inevitable that men will pay for sex.

I have debated with Hakim on the topic of blanket decriminalisation. At one event at the University of York, in 2015, I and Broadfoot debated with Lee and Hakim. The motion was 'This house believes decriminalising prostitution would be a disaster'. During the debate, which everyone

---

[26]Farley, M.; Bindel, J.; Golding, J. (2009, Dec.) *Men who buy sex: Who they buy and what they nnow. A research study of 103 men who describe their use of trafficked and non-trafficked women in prostitution, and their awareness of coercion and violence.* Eaves, London & Prostitution Research & Education, San Francisco. p. 8.

except Hakim agreed could be recorded, Hakim put forward her theory that prostitution will always exist because women want sex with their male partners significantly less than men do with their female partners. I cannot quote her directly here as I was unable to take notes, but this quotation from Hakim's paper below should give a fair impression of her thesis:

> Our gender-neutral theory of prostitution is that the ubiquity of sex workers, both male and female, even in countries where commercial sex is banned, and the high earnings of sex workers, both male and female, are explained first and foremost by the male sexual deficit which produces high male demand and relatively low female supply of sexual entertainments, both professional and amateur, within and outside marriage. Kontula (2009) concluded that overall, male sexual desire is manifested at least twice as often as female desire, and men would like to have sex twice as often as women. This is a huge gap between supply and demand, and it is exacerbated by the fact that men generally prefer to have sex with young and attractive women (or men).[27]

I asked Hakim whether, if men had to pay women who did not want sex in order to have sex with them, was that not rape? Hakim looked blank and Lee declined to support her thesis. By arguing that women in relationships with men do not desire sex to the same degree as their male counterparts, Hakim is framing the sex of prostitution these men seek as a girlfriend substitute.

The Protector of the Punter

A number of women who define themselves as feminist are against the law criminalising demand, many of whom are part of the 'queer' community. The 'queer' approach is examined in detail in Chap. 10, but I mention it here because some of those academics and activists who claim to speak on behalf of disabled punters use this argument. For

---

[27]Hakim, C. (2015, Oct 15.) *This house believes the legalisation of prostitution would be a sisaster.* At University of York. Retrieved 15 June 2017, from https://www.york.ac.uk/news-and-events/events/public-lectures/autumn2015/prostitution-debate/.

example, Siouxsie Q, a pornographic actor and 'sex workers' rights' activist based in San Francisco in the USA. I met Q at the Porn Awards in Los Angeles in 2015 and we later connected by Skype.

I asked Q her view on the Nordic model. 'I don't believe that clients are the issue', she says. 'It is founded completely in moral prejudice and a panic about the idiom of selling sex in any capacity. We do a job and we have clients. Do people who are hairdressers have slimy annoying clients who don't tip sometimes? Absolutely. Does that happen in the sex trade? Sure. But does criminalising the client help? Absolutely not. That puts a contentious relationship between client and sex worker that compromises their safety, their viability, their money.'

A number of self-identified feminists profess support for the sex buyer, including a number of female academics, as we will see in Chap. 9. Why is this? In her brilliant article, 'The modern John got himself a queer nanny' posted on the blog *Feminist Current*,[28] Swedish journalist and feminist abolitionist Kajsa Ekis Ekman explains the phenomenon as follows:

> The tacit agreement between the John and the pro-prostitution female academic is that she will do anything to defend his acts, while ensuring that he stays in the shadows. She will speak incessantly about prostitution, but never mention him. Her task is to make sure prostitution seems like an all-female affair. The queer academic will use the prostituted woman as a shield, blocking the John from the limelight. She will use the prostituted woman any way she can – analysing her, re- and deconstructing her, holding her up as a role model, and using her as a microphone (i.e. a career booster), thereby positioning her as 'good' vs the 'evil' feminist.

The Keith Vaz Scandal

In the UK, a scandal of epic proportion hit the Home Affairs Select Committee, which overseas the justice system, and had recently been recommending law and policy on prostitution. In the Autumn of 2016, the

---

[28]Ekman, K.E. (2016, Aug 24.) *The modern john got himself a queer nanny*. In Feminist Current. Retrieved 15 June 2017, from http://www.feministcurrent.com/2016/08/24/modern-john-got-queer-nanny/.

chair of the Committee, Keith Vaz MP, was secretly filmed by a young Romanian man whom Vaz had paid for sex. During the exchange, Vaz was heard arranging for another prostituted young man to be brought to him, and pondering on who was going to 'break him in' and 'fuck him first'.

Soon after the Vaz scandal erupted, disgraced member of parliament Simon Danczuk leapt to defend his colleague, tweeting his support for Vaz. In 2015, Danczuk himself had exchanged 'sexually explicit' text messages with a 17-year-old female job applicant. Police investigated the matter (under the Sexual Offences Act 2003, the age of consent is 18 in circumstances where the accused is in a position of trust) and decided that no offence had been committed. There was strong criticism of Danczuk by many of his constituents in Rochdale, a town in the North of England, because he was best known for his campaigning work on historical child sex abuse.[29]

When the story about Vaz appeared in the tabloids, a number of abolitionist campaigners argued that the interim report that more-or-less recommends full decriminalisation of the sex trade should be declared null and void, whereas campaigners for sex trade decriminalisation conversely argued that the report should stand. [30]

The Research

The research, headed by Melissa Farley in six countries and based on interviews with over 700 sex buyers[31] showed very clearly that many of the men are ambiguous about paying for sex. The quotes below highlight some of the self-disgust and shame that the men grapple with:

---

[29]Rochdale is one of the places in England where criminal gangs have prostituted girls and young women, but evaded the law until parents, feminist activists and the girls themselves demanded justice. Much of the media and general public would bend over backwards to label what these men did to their prey anything other than pimping: it is largely known as 'grooming' or sexual exploitation.

[30]http://www.independent.co.uk/news/uk/crime/they-like-us-naive-how-teenage-girls-are-groomed-for-a-life-of-prostitution-by-uk-gangs-1880959.html. Accessed 28th August.

[31]Farley, M. (2016). *Very inconvenient truths: Sex buyers, sexual coercion, prostitution-harm-denial.* In Logos: A Journal of Modern Society and Culture. Retrieved 15 June 2017, from http://logos-journal.com/2016/farley-2/.

- 'I wouldn't encourage prostitution—it's someone's mother or daughter. It's an empty experience. It sounds enjoyable at the beginning but it's just horrible, degrading.'
- 'I don't get pleasure from other people's suffering. I struggle with it but I can't deny my own pleasures. In Cambodia I knocked back a lot of children, it makes it hard to sleep at night. But I don't see the point in making a moral stance.'
- 'Most of the men who go see it as a business transaction and don't see the girl as a woman. This could impact on how a man sees women in general.'

The same research also shows that many of these punters could easily be deterred. As one punter told me, when I interviewed him for the London study: 'Deterrents would only work if enforced. Any negative would make you reconsider. The law's not enforced now, but if any negative thing happened as a consequence it would deter me.'

When it comes to prostitution and the sex trade in general, the law is often an ass. Unless the human rights approach of criminalising the punters is adopted, most countries will have laws under which the pimps, punters and brothel owners walk free while those desperate enough to be selling sex are punished. But the so-called 'human rights' approach of today, as we will see in this next chapter, is to support the notion that to name prostitution as abuse contravenes the human rights of the women who wish to sell sex.

6

Human Rights and Wrongs

Ken Roth wouldn't you say, if a person cannot afford to feed themselves, the appropriate thing to put in their mouth is food, not your cock? (Rachel Moran, sex trade survivor)

Moran's tweet, sent in March 2016, was in response to various comments made on social media during the fierce debate raging from January 2014–August 2016 about whether or not Amnesty International (AI) should adopt a policy of supporting blanket decriminalisation of the sex trade.

Kenneth Roth, Executive Director of Human Rights Watch, and an avid supporter of the AI position, had made a comment on Twitter in which he questioned why 'sex work' should be denied as an 'option' for 'poor women'.[1]

Kenneth Roth has an established reputation as a human rights defender. I use his quote above to illustrate the contradictions involved in this debate and the extent to which the language of human rights has been upended: people and organisations who ought to lead the

---

[1]Fhassaidh, U. (2015, Aug 11.) *Are poor women free to choose prostitution?* In Random Public Journal. Retrieved 15 June 2017, from https://randompublicjournal.com/2015/08/11/are-poor-women-free-to-choose-prostitution/.

© The Author(s) 2017
J. Bindel, *The Pimping of Prostitution*,
DOI 10.1057/978-1-137-55890-9_6

way forward for human rights have betrayed their own principles. While women all over the world fight to end male supremacy, there are men and women in leftist and liberal politics who appear to consider defending the rights of men to buy sex more important than the rights of women and girls to challenge that assumption. In my experience, those who consider it a priority to defend the rights of the individual as opposed to the rights of oppressed groups, can be the most difficult to convince that sex trade is a cause and consequence of women's inequality and oppression.

While radical feminists understand women as a sex class, or more aptly a caste, battling structural oppression, liberals view women as unconnected individuals with individual choices. Liberals tend also to focus on the choices available to women, rather than the choices denied them. It is a sophisticated political argument bereft of sophistication and politics. Although, interestingly, whether they accept this or not, men are enabled to band together. Few things bring men closer than the violence they commit against women.

AI is a classically liberal organisation. While there are those within the abolitionist movement who argue that too much oxygen has been given to the organisation regarding its decision in August 2016 to support the policy of blanket decriminalisation, I disagree. In supporting this position, AI has given a major boost to 'sex workers' rights' activists all over the world. AI legitimatises arguments that feminist abolitionists, and others critical of the sex trade, are taking away the rights of women to choose what to do with their own bodies. It has also given legitimacy to the pimps, brothel owners and other third-party exploiters who, under blanket decriminalisation, are merely entrepreneurs.

Amnesty International

In January 2014 I received a call from a person confirming what I had already heard in feminist circles about the development of the new policy on the sex trade at AI. This whistleblower told me that the International Secretariat was about to pass a policy on prostitution and that plan was to introduce it via its London office.

I met the whistleblower later that day and was shown the document. I was told that the draft document had not gone out for consultation, either among AI personnel or its members, and it was about to become official policy. The next day, I exposed AI's plans in a national newspaper. Within hours, abolitionist groups from all over the world began to organise on social media against AI rubber-stamping a policy on decriminalisation of the sex trade. Meetings were held with national AI offices, and the arguments contained within the leaked document were pulled apart in preparation for a showdown.[2]

When Kate Allen, then head of AI UK, was quizzed about the leaked document, she was adamant that it was not a draft policy paper but merely a consultation paper that was due to be sent out to all key members of staff across their international offices.

On 4 February 2014, only days after the leak, Allen was invited by mumsnet, a website for parenting advice and support, to take part in a debate on the topic of decriminalisation.[3] Both sides of the debate were represented during the live discussion. For example, one question directed to Allen read: "Can Amnesty International, as an organisation, really fail to see that by saying sex is a right that should be able to be purchased, they are one step away from saying that consent does not need to be obtained in ALL sexual situations?"[4]

Another contributor, an activist in the pro-prostitution US-based organisation COYOTE, asked: "Does criminalisation stop people from buying or selling sex?", before answering her own question with: "No it doesn't, as it is a failed system and law enforcement can't seem to police even one percent of the sex trade, however what criminalisation does do is create the perfect playground for bad cops and predators to rob, rape, threaten, beat, exploit and murder sex workers."

---

[2]http://www.dailymail.co.uk/news/article-2544983/JULIE-BINDEL-An-abject-inversion-principles.html.

[3]MumsNet.com. Retrieved 15 June 2017, from http://www.mumsnet.com/.

[4]Forum, (2014, Jan 29.) *Amnesty's proposal to legalise prostitution is wrong – We can't let men who exploit women off the hook*. On MumsNet.com. Retrieved 25 Jan 2017 from http://www.mumsnet.com/Talk/guest_posts/1982419-Amnestys-proposal-to-legalise-prostitution-is-wrong-we-cant-let-men-who-exploit-women-off-the-hook.

The final document, which was leaked to me at draft stage in March 2016 and published after the official decision was made to adopt an official position supporting blanket decriminalisation of the sex trade in August 2016, contained several comparisons between lesbian and gay oppression, and anti-abortion policies. For example:

> Sex workers are at risk of multiple, intersecting forms of criminalisation and penalisation.[5] Sex workers who are at risk of criminalisation on the basis of their sexual orientation and/or gender identity face criminalisation in some countries under laws against sex work and/or laws against sexual activity between people of the same sex or laws enforcing norms of gender expression such as prohibitions against cross dressing... Women who are sex workers may face additional criminalisation in countries where access to abortion is prohibited by law and/or where sex outside marriage is criminalised.

Historically, AI had refused to take a position on prostitution until signing up to pro-decriminalisation, joining the International Labour Organisation, Anti-Slavery International, Human Rights Watch and a whole host of other human rights bodies.[6] Having battled for decades with individuals, organisations and governments over the lack of concern over men's violence towards women and girls, many feminists came to accept that the hardest battle was over whether or not men had a 'right' to buy sex from women and girls.

In 1997 Anti-Slavery International published a paper that was authored by a key pro-prostitution activist, former Sussex University student Jo Doezema, along with Jo Bindman from Anti-Slavery International, entitled 'Redefining Prostitution as Sex Work on the International Agenda'.

In a 2001 article entitled 'Regulating the Global Brothel', Ann Jordan, a long-time pro-prostitution activist, who was at that time

---

[5]Amnesty International. (2016, May 26.) *Amnesty International policy on state obligations to respect, protect and fulfil the human rights of sex workers.* Retrieved 15 June 2017, from https://www.amnestyusa.org/sites/default/files/amnesty_policy_human_rights_of_sex_workers_-_embargoed_-_final.pdf. p. 9.

[6]Amnesty International. (2016, May 26.) *Amnesty International policy on state obligations to respect, protect and fulfil the human rights of sex workers.* Retrieved 15 June 2017, from https://www.amnestyusa.org/sites/default/files/amnesty_policy_human_rights_of_sex_workers_-_embargoed_-_final.pdf. p. 9.

based at the International Human Rights Law Group, made an analogy between prostitution and abortion. "We don't support a woman's right to choose because we think abortion is a great thing," she says, "but because we believe fundamentally that women should have control over their own reproductive capacity. The same argument can be made for prostitution. Women who decide for whatever reason to sell sex should have the right to control their own body. As with abortions, we can dream of a day when sex work is safe, legal and rare." This analogy beggars belief: abortion is a health and human rights issue for women; prostitution is a human rights abuse of women.

On 11 August 2015, AI voted to decriminalise "all operational aspects" of the sex trade, including the sale, facilitation and buying of sex. With the cast of a vote, a pimp became a manager, a sex buyer became a client, and a prostituted person became a 'sex worker'.

"Amnesty International is opposed to the criminalisation or punishment of activities related to the buying or selling of consensual sex between adults," read the first line of the document. "Amnesty International believes that seeking, buying, selling and soliciting paid sex are acts protected from state interference as long as there is no coercion, threats or violence associated with those acts."

According to AI: "…men and women who buy sex from consenting adults are also exercising personal autonomy. For some - in particular persons with mobility or sensory disabilities or those with psycho-social disabilities that hamper social interactions - sex workers are persons with whom they feel safe enough to have a physical relationship or to express their sexuality."[7]

It is notable that AI has, as do many groups and individuals that hold a pro decriminalisation position, gender neutralised both the buyer and seller of prostitution sex, and yet it is known that the vast majority of sex buyers are male, and that most of those at the supply end are female.

---

[7]Sanghani, R. (2015, Aug 11.) *Amnesty International backs decriminalising sex work*. In The Telegraph. Retrieved 15 June 2017, from http://www.telegraph.co.uk/women/womenslife/11796679/Amnesty-International-backs-decriminalising-sex-work.html.

"Some develop a stronger sense of self in their relationships with sex workers," continues the argument in the AI document, "improving their life enjoyment and dignity. At a very basic level, expressions of sexuality and sex are a primary component of the human experience, which is directly linked to individuals' physical and mental health. The state's interference with an adult's strategy to have sex with another consenting adult is, therefore, a deliberate interference with those individuals' autonomy and health."

The backlash from outraged feminists and organisations, under the war cry 'No Amnesty for Pimps', was immediate and unambiguous. Hollywood celebrities including Meryl Streep, Kate Winslet, Emma Thompson and Lena Dunham were also up in arms, and the media took note.[8] Articles were soon appearing everywhere, and even Rolling Stone magazine published a piece condemning AI.[9] Moreover, I and other abolitionists had word from a number of the rank and file of AI in various countries expressing anger and shame that AI could have adopted such a policy.[10] In the meanwhile, AI personnel continued to argue that full decriminalisation provides the best outcome for prostituted people.

Whose Right/s?

Simone Watson is an Australian survivor of prostitution whose grandmother is an Indigenous woman from a tribal nation that falls within the border of the State of Victoria. Watson describes her feminist activism, and in particular her directorship of Nordic Model in Australia Coalition (NorMAC),[11] as the means by which she makes sense of the post-traumatic stress disorder she suffers as a consequence of her

---

[8]Bindman, J. (1997.) *Redefining prostitution as sex work on the international agenda*. On Walnet. org. Retrieved 15 June 2017, from http://www.walnet.org/csis/papers/redefining.html.

[9]Bindman, J. (1997.) *Redefining prostitution as sex work on the international agenda*. On Walnet. org. Retrieved 15 June 2017, from http://www.walnet.org/csis/papers/redefining.html.

[10]Platt, L. (2001, Dec 19.) *Regulating the global brothel*. In The American Prospect. Retrieved 15 June 2017, from http://prospect.org/article/regulating-global-brothel.

[11]NorMAC: Nordic Model Australia Coalition. Retrieved 15 June 2017, from www.normac.org.au.

prostitution in a legal brothel. Accordingly, she is what she is: articulate, intelligent, political.

In a loaded debate on Aljazeera,[12] Watson challenged the rhetoric of co-panellists Murphy and 'sex worker' Maxine Doogan. Doogan, of the so-called Erotic Services Providers Union,[13] is in fact a convicted pimp.[14] Watson provided well-considered responses drawn from solid evidence—that trafficking had expanded and prostituted women and girls were increasingly being harmed—but, patronisingly, she was forced to muzzle her contribution to her 'personal experiences' as a survivor.[15] Murphy and Doogan, meanwhile, were permitted by the moderator to recite the manufactured fit-for-purpose anecdotal evidence: that stigma and this very mysterious underground were the real evils facing women and girls in prostitution, which Watson pointed out were actually responses to AI surveys given by pimps.

AI completely rejects all UN protocols, including those AI itself has previously relied upon in condemning Japanese war crimes against so-called 'comfort women',[16] and all evidence which indicates legalised prostitution massively increases illegal prostitution, trafficking for prostitution, and male violence against women and girls. I argue that theirs is a position driven by ideology, not scientific study. AI, by way of example, in aping the evidence of Dr Graham Ellison (considered to be a Northern Irish academic expert on the sex trade) alleged in its own evidence to the Northern Ireland Committee that Sweden is a 'country specific' example which cannot be extrapolated elsewhere.[17] While the

---

[12]Al Jazeera. (2015, Sept 8.) *Should buying and selling sex be a crime?* On Al Jazeera. Retrieved 15 June 2017, from http://stream.aljazeera.com/story/201509082336-0024989.

[13]Erotic Service Providers Union. Retrieved 15 June 2017, from http://espu-ca.org/wp/.

[14]Court Listener: The State of Washington, Respondent v. Mary E. Doogan, Appellant. Retrieved 15 June 2017, from https://www.courtlistener.com/opinion/1135994/state-v-doogan/.

[15]Geist, D. (2016, June 1.) *5 reasons to be wary of Amnesty's prostitution policy.* In Rolling Stone. Retrieved 15 June 2017, from http://www.rollingstone.com/politics/news/6-reasons-to-be-wary-of-amnestys-prostitution-policy-20160601.

[16]'Comfort women' were women and girls who were forced into sexual slavery during war.

[17]Amnesty International UK. (2013, Nov 1.) *Human trafficking and exploitation (further provisions and support for victims) bill.* Retrieved 15 June 2017, from http://www.niassembly.gov.uk/globalassets/documents/justice-2011-2016/human-trafficking-bill/written-submissions/amnesty-international.pdf.

Committee members correctly noted the obvious shortcoming of this criticism—that punters are punters are punters—The Nordic model is critiqued by AI wherever it is found. I am baffled by AI's determination to condemn the Nordic model before it claims to have finalised its position. This is a form of bias that could be described as confirmation bias.

The person who helped drive AI's policy is Murphy. As I note in Chap. 7, Murphy was previously head of public affairs for UK AIDS charity Terrence Higgins Trust. Two months after AI passed its policy, at a meeting in a Dublin hotel, Murphy was again condemning the Nordic Model with the authority of the AI imprimatur, this time at a university in New York, US. Here, she appeared alongside journalist and former 'sex worker' Melissa Gira Grant, and Sienna Baskin of Sex Workers Projects, in delivering her paper entitled 'Sex Work and Labor Issues'.

I found Murphy's name in an article she wrote for the BBC concerning Mark Devereaux, a disgraceful man who withheld his HIV positive status from four women with whom he had sex at different times over a six year period up to 2008. One of the women was found to be HIV positive and she terminated her pregnancy as a consequence. She was expecting twins. Devereaux, who provides as a good example of male sexual violence against women as any, was sentenced to 10 years imprisonment and the judge poured scorn upon him.

Incredulously, Murphy, on behalf of Terrence Higgins Trust, was moved to write an obscurantist piece, expressing contempt for the court, the police and the media. She argued the issue around Devereaux was "complex" and those who were HIV positive were being "stigmatised" by moral panic. Contextually, Murphy's comments were made at the time when other AIDS organisations, including HIV Scotland, similarly argued through media statements that the women had an equal responsibility to protect themselves and, heartlessly, that only one woman was harmed, while three women were not.

A Women's Right to be Abused?

Human rights do not stretch to women in prostitution. Despite decades of feminism, 'human' still means 'man'.

In the Belfast Court of Appeal in April 2016, Laura Lee, an Irish escort, began her battle to repeal one of the Northern Irish laws on prostitution. As Lee herself admits, pimps (whom she may call 'escort agency owners', or 'managers') are financially supporting this campaign.[18] Lee, who sells sex in the Republic of Ireland as well as Belfast, Northern Ireland, is attempting to repeal legislation that makes paying for sex illegal. Lee claims the law puts her in danger and breaches her right to privacy and freedom from discrimination.

I was in court to hear Lee's QC argue that the bill makes the very group it aimed to protect less safe. What is implicit in the arguments from Lee is that if she wins in her attempt to remove the clauses, brothel prostitution will effectively be decriminalised across Northern Ireland, setting a precedent for this to happen in other countries around the globe. The case could have massive implications for the way that prostitution is policed.

Following a heated debate in Stormont, in 2015, Northern Ireland joined countries such as Sweden, Norway, Canada and France in passing an amendment to the Human Trafficking and Exploitation Act, making the purchase of sex a criminal offence. The amendment was introduced as a Private Member's Bill by Lord Morrow of the Democratic Unionist Party (DUP).[19]

The clause effectively shifts the burden of criminality from women firmly onto the buyers, which is precisely why so many feminists and other human rights campaigners support it. The thinking behind the bill is that tackling demand would adversely affect the business of trafficking and pimping gangs operating in Northern Ireland and break the connection between the sex trade and organised crime.[20]

Lee, along with other 'sex workers' rights' individuals and organisations, has long campaigned for the removal of all laws pertaining to

---

[18]Sex Workers Project. (2014.) *'Sex and the law week.'* Retrieved 15 June 2017, from http://sexworkersproject.com/downloads/2014/20140317-sex-and-law-poster.pdf.

[19]Murphy, C. (2010, Feb 25.) HIV infection: 'A complex issue'. On BBC News. Retrieved 15 June 2017, from http://news.bbc.co.uk/2/hi/uk_news/scotland/8536361.stm.

[20]BBC News. (2010, Feb 25.) *HIV Man Jailed for 'Reckless Sex'.* On BBC News. Retrieved 15 June 2017, from http://news.bbc.co.uk/2/hi/uk_news/scotland/north_east/8519593.stm.

prostitution, including pimping, brothel owning and sex buying, arguing that prostitution should be treated as a job like any other, and that the law should not interfere in sex between consenting adults.

But a report from the Organised Crime Task Force of Northern Ireland, 2013, found that:

> ... an increasing number of brothels operating in Northern Ireland have links to OCGs (organised crime gangs). In some instances this involves acting as a 'pimp' and/or providing accommodation. In other instances their involvement is more organised, for example, assisting females into Northern Ireland specifically to work in the sex trade or human trafficking for the purposes of sexual exploitation.[21]

The report added: 'There may be a mix of trafficked and non-trafficked women within a brothel, however those employed 'voluntarily' may also be vulnerable due to their background or may have problems with addiction'.

The case is being challenged by SPACE International, an organisation led by sex trade survivors from around the world, and Equality Now.[22] Julianne Hughes Jennett of Hogan Lovells,[23] the law firm representing the interveners, says it is a very important case for the likes of SPACE International to test, as it will determine how robust the legislation is. Hughes Jennett said: 'The right outcome of this case is critical for the advancement of gender equality and the protection of women'.[24]

In an attempt to undermine the clause, the Minister for Justice commissioned some research into prostitution in Northern Ireland conducted by Queen's University Belfast. This report was cited during the committee hearing as evidence of how other people in prostitution in Northern Ireland are against the law. But its methodology has been

---

[21]Organised Crime in Northern Ireland, 2013, Annual Report & Threat Assessment, Retrieved 15 June 2017 http://www.octf.gov.uk/OCTF/files/63/63f6eda7-ff14-4008-b4fc-334e02e7bea5.PDF.

[22]Equality Now. Retrieved 15 June 2017, from http://www.equalitynow.org/.

[23]Julianne Hughes Jennett, on Hogan Lovells. Retrieved 15 June 2017, from https://www.hogan-lovells.com/en/julianne-hughes-jennett.

[24]In conversation with the author, September 2016.

criticised by a number of service providers, campaigners and academics. For instance, the report states that only 18% of those participating in the study said that they lived most of the time in Northern Ireland.

The claim in the report that the criminalisation of clients would lead to an increased risk of violence and abuse—the key plank of Lee's legal challenge—is spurious. In Sweden there is no documented case of a woman in prostitution being murdered by a pimp or punter, whereas in countries with legalised or decriminalised brothels, such as New Zealand, Germany and Holland, they are numerous.

A Survivor's Perspective

One victim of trafficking in Northern Ireland, Anna, who escaped her captors in Belfast, supports the Morrow bill. Originally from Eastern Europe, in 2011 Anna was abducted from near her home in London and taken to Galway, Ireland. She was held for 9 months, during which time she was monitored and beaten by the traffickers. Rival Irish and Albanian pimps chased Anna and the traffickers out of Galway with guns and knives so they went 'on tour' to Limerick, Cork, Belfast and Derry. In Belfast, police raided their brothel but the four male pimps had left 20 min beforehand. Anna reported: 'The mother pimp screamed at us in Romanian that she would kill us if we said a word. She said that all the other pimps were listening in, that her phone was active. But in English she told the police she was a working girl'.[25]

Eventually Anna escaped to Belfast and she was delighted when hearing about the Morrow bill. 'It will not drive vulnerable women underground', she said. 'They are already underground. Nobody was coming to help me.'

I have spoken to other women who were previously involved in the Irish sex trade and asked their views on Lee's challenge. Alanna told me she believes that Lee is misguided if she thinks that scrapping the sex buyer clause will bring about more safety for the women: 'If I

---

[25]Interview with the author, September 2016.

was still working in the sex trade and the Nordic model came along I genuinely wouldn't have a problem with it whatsoever', says Alanna, who was prostituted in the Republic for five years. 'If you're an independent escort like [Lee] is, it wouldn't make the slightest difference to her. [Before the legislation was introduced] clients refused to leave any trace of contact whatsoever. They refused to use an online portal, [they would] call from a withheld number and [they would] not provide a name or even a pseudonym.'

The implications of Lee winning her legal challenge are vast, says Alanna. 'It would let down the most vulnerable people in society', she said. 'It would be saying that independent, privileged, middle-class white women ... that their needs trump those who are the most oppressed. It would be telling the punters that they are entitled to continue using women because the onus isn't on them but back on the women to bear the responsibility. [Men] can be fear-free.'

Rachel Moran is the founder of SPACE International and the author of *Paid For*. She was prostituted in Ireland throughout the 1990s and regularly talks to women who have recently left the sex trade. Moran gave evidence before the Northern Ireland Assembly in 2014, where she made it clear that were she still involved in prostitution, she would still support the idea of punters being made responsible.

She said:

> I think I would have been secretly glad to see the men who paid to use us finally being held to account, but I also would have wondered and worried about its implications for me. It has been uncovered in international research that women's views of prostitution shift markedly depending on whether they are currently or formerly prostituted, and that research is in line with everything I've heard across conversations with hundreds of women I've discussed this with. The interesting thing about this law is that it only needs to be announced, not enforced, before pimps and punters go scattering like hens.

The Nordic Model is democratic. The vast majority of citizens in Northern Ireland support the law against sex buyers, according to an

IPSOS MORI poll for Christian charity CARE.[26] Of the 1016 people surveyed, 78% believe that those who create the demand should be punished. This same widespread popular support is found elsewhere where the Nordic Model is adopted.

As we sat in the court in Belfast listening to Lee's QC argue that trafficking is a 'minuscule' part of the sex trade in Northern Ireland, a man stood in an adjoining court charged with trafficking a woman into the UK for sexual exploitation last May. The Attorney General, John Larkin QC, argued against the legal challenge. 'Lord Morrow, I hazard', said Larkin, 'would be very pleased indeed to know he stopped one or two women being trafficked into prostitution'.[27]

For Moran, it is clear why Lee should fail in her attempt. 'If she won, it would be a disaster for women hoping to exit prostitution in Northern Ireland. Far from helping those women, if successful, it would trap them in it. If Laura Lee is happy to be prostituted that's her prerogative, but she has no right to block exit services for the vast majority of women who are not happy.'

Why do Human Rights Organisations Support the Sex Trade?

Due to the policies on the sex trade of organisations such as Human Rights Watch (HRW), the World Health Organisation (WHO), the Joint United Nations Programme on HIV/AIDS (UNAIDS) and AI to support the legalisation of prostitution, the 'sex workers' rights' movement feels justified in claiming theirs is a 'human rights' approach to prostitution. These organisations buy the line that paying for sex is a 'right' and a 'need' of the sex buyer, and increasingly, as we saw in Chap. 2, of the women involved. In other words, women can 'choose' to sell whatever they wish, including themselves.

---

[26]Nordic Model Now. Retrieved 15 June 2017, from https://nordicmodelnow.org/

[27]News Letter. (2016, Sept 28.) *Sex worker wins first round against sex buyer law.* In News Letter. Retrieved 15 June 2017, from http://www.newsletter.co.uk/news/crime/sex-worker-wins-first-round-against-sex-buyer-law-1-7602205

This approach by so-called human rights campaigners flies in the face of a genuine liberal/leftist approach. Neo-liberalism has elevated the free market above the rights of the female human. The sex trade is the elevation of the free market economy over the female human body, and there can be no starker example of the sub-human underbelly of the global sex trade.

Emily Bazelon, in a radio debate[28] following the publication of her *New York Times* cover story 'Should prostitution be a crime?',[29] said:

> Amnesty International recommended in favour of the full decriminalisation of sex work internationally. When I heard that announcement last August I was very surprised by it. It isn't an issue I knew a whole lot about and I was used to thinking of the debate over prostitution in terms of questions of morality, or whether prostitution or sex work is inherently demeaning to women. I wasn't accustomed to thinking of it as a human rights issue. But groups like AI and HRW have been looking closely at these questions of what the best laws are in terms of the health and safety of sex workers, really since the AIDS epidemic that was driven by sex workers—thousands of them—organising—mostly in countries like India and Thailand and fighting for their rights, greater legal rights and also trying to protect themselves by trying to prevent the spread of AIDS … [S]ince then it has moved beyond preventing the spread of AIDS to also try to deal with things like police abuses, violence from clients and other people in the community and discrimination and stigma. I think that was really the motivation from AI's point of view.[30]

The 'rights' discourse adopted by liberals and much of the human rights world is not progressive or leftist, but built on the politics of

---

[28]Page, S. (2016, May 9.) *Debate over decriminalizing prostitution.* On the Diane Rehm Show. Retrieved 15 June 2017, from http://thedianerehmshow.org/shows/2016-05-09/debate-over-legalizing-prostitution.

[29]Bazelon, E. (2016, May 5.) *Should prostitution be a crime?* In New York Times. Retrieved 15 June 2017, from http://www.nytimes.com/2016/05/08/magazine/should-prostitution-be-a-crime.html.

[30]CARE. (2014, Oct 7.) *78% Favour Criminalising Sex Buyers in NI.* On Care.org.uk. Retrieved 15 June 2017, from https://www.care.org.uk/news/latest-news/78-favour-criminalising-sex-buyers-ni-0.

individuality. Organisations such as AI are clearly motivated, as we will see later in this chapter, by paternalistic male self-interest.[31]

Why is the Left in favour of the free market only when it is women's bodies being bought and sold? These so-called human rights advocates hold up the bodies of prostituted women as human shields to protect them from accusations of hypocrisy and inconsistency. AI demonstrates its concern for the 'rights' of men to buy sex, while attempting to appear equally concerned for the women, for example: '... men and women [sic] who buy sex from consenting adults are also exercising personal autonomy. For some—in particular persons with mobility or sensory disabilities or those with psycho-social disabilities that hamper social interactions—sex workers are persons with whom they feel safe enough to have a physical relationship or to express their sexuality. Some develop a stronger sense of self in their relationships with sex workers, improving their life enjoyment and dignity'.[32]

Feminism for Men

There is a dominant trend currently within the Left that suggests slut-walking, lap dancing, sex working and Burkha-wearing is liberation for women. Men, as a rule, love this approach and tend to support the 'sex workers' rights' position on the sex trade. It should come as no surprise that men who support blanket decriminalisation also tend to support 'fun feminism'.

Journalist and campaigner Owen Jones, darling of the radical Left, is a classic example of this. Writing in the *Guardian* in March 2015, he asked why it was any business of anyone that Simon Danczuk MP had

---

[31]The Attorney General, John Larkin QC, argued against the legal challenge. 'Lord Morrow, I hazard', said Larkin, 'would be very pleased indeed to know he stopped one or two women being trafficked into prostitution'. (2016, Sept 23.) *Law criminalising clients 'puts sex workers at greater risk'.* On BBC News. Retrieved 15 June 2017, from http://www.bbc.co.uk/news/uk-northern-ireland-37455884.

[32]Amnesty International. (DATE?) *Summary: Proposed policy on sex work.* Retrieved 15 June 2017, from https://www.amnesty.se/upload/files/2014/04/02/Summary%20of%20proposed%20policy%20on%20sex%20work.pdf.

been exposed as a prolific pornography consumer. 'There is no short-age of reasons for me to criticise Danczuk: our views on social security and immigration differ to say the least ... But watching porn? So what?' wrote Jones. In the article, he also poured scorn on the fate of three judges dismissed from their positions because they 'watch(ed) porn on the job'. 'None of it was illegal', wrote Jones, 'but they were still pub-licly embarrassed and dismissed'.

Jones was clearly critical of Danczuk on his views on the welfare state and immigration, but defended him as a user of pornography while he was being paid to work on behalf of his constituents. This hypocrisy is not unusual when it comes to liberal and leftist attitudes to the sex trade.

Silencing Abolitionists in the Name of Human Rights

On 8 March 2015, the journalist and eminent anti-trafficking activist Ruchira Gupta was on her way to the Apollo Theatre in New York, to give the keynote address as the Woman of Distinction Awardee at the non-governmental organisation Commission on Status of Women (CSW). Gupta was traveling with Phumzile Mlambo-Ngcuka, UN Under-Secretary General and Executive Director of UN Women.

Gupta is the founder of Apne Aap,[33] a human rights organisation located in several sites in India, which supports more than 20,000 prostituted and at-risk girls and women, enabling their right to justice, education, safe and independent housing, and a sustainable and dignified livelihood. It benefits India's most marginalised girls and women who are sold into prostitution between the ages of 9 and 13, who are poor, low-caste and extremely vulnerable.

Women and government representatives from all over the world attend this event, and Gupta was thrilled to have been given this award

---

[33]http://apneaap.org/.

because it was an acknowledgement from her peer group of the work she had been doing to end sex-trafficking.

Just before arriving at the Apollo, Gupta received an email from a committee member of the New York CSW telling her not to mention the word 'prostitution' in her speech. 'I was aghast since my entire work was with prostituted women and my award was for that work', Gupta said at the time.[34]

Gupta emailed the committee member and asked how she could give a speech in which she did not represent the views of the members of her organisation? '[The woman who emailed me] replied that she had been asked by the Chief of Civil Society at UN Women to stop me from speaking about prostitution', says Gupta. 'This was bizarre. Why should an NGO body try to censor me and stop me from speaking about a subject for which they had given me an award?'

The reason soon became apparent to Gupta. The NGO had received money from an organisation that supports and profits from the sex trade. The Chief of Civil Society at UN Women had been circulating a letter, via her official UN Women email address, to all NGOs asking for prostitution to be legalised as 'sex-work', and pimping and brothel-keeping to be legalised as 'employers' of poor women.

Gupta recalls:

'I went ahead and gave the speech I had prepared about how prostitution was an outcome of inequality and not a choice', says Gupta.[35] 'I said that the punishment of pimps, Johns and brothel-keepers was what prostituted women and their daughters in India desperately wanted. All they had was the law to protect them.

I spoke about the need to invest in the 'last girl' who is trafficked because of her vulnerabilities. The 'last girl' is someone who is marked by multiple oppressions. She is the weakest of all human beings. She is weaker than the poor man, because she is female, she is weaker than the adult

---

[34]Gupta told this story to the author in October 2016.

[35]Jones, O. (2015, Mar 30.) *Simon Danczuk MP has watched porn. Why should we care?* In The Guardian. Retrieved 15 June 2017, from https://www.theguardian.com/commentisfree/2015/mar/30/simon-danczuk-mp-watched-porn-who-cares

female, because she is a teenager, she is weaker than the poor, female, teenager, because she is low-caste in India, Black in America, Roma in Europe, a refugee in Jordan. She does not choose to be born poor or low-caste. I pleaded for UN Women to punish those who buy and sell her and to invest in reducing her vulnerabilities. I reminded them the UN Declaration of Human Rights stood for protection of the weak and not the powerful.

At the end of her speech, Gupta received a rousing reception from the delegates, comprising feminist NGOs from every corner of the globe.[36] But not everyone was happy with her. 'Unfortunately, I saw the Chief of Civil Society whisper and walk away with the head of UN Women before I spoke', says Gupta.

How did we get to this *Alice Through the Looking Glass* state of affairs, where human rights defenders are warned off speaking of what they would argue are the realities of the sex trade lest they offend the funders?

In 2016, Melissa Gira Grant, a pro-prostitution activist and author of *Playing the Whore: The Work of Sex Work*,[37] tweeted about the then current abortion rights battle in the USA: 'Someday sex work will be a repo rights issue, but until then, at least some stuff concerning my cunt is legally protected'.

As I remarked earlier, abortion rights are not analogous to the so-called 'right' to be prostituted. The pro-prostitution lobby use examples like this all the time. They do not talk about the 'right' of men to rent an orifice for 15 minutes from a person who is only 'consenting' because money is involved. They do not speak of the 'right' to rent an orifice of the female human body. Nor do they speak of the 'right' for pimps and brothel owners to advertise the women as though they are pieces of meat on a slab, ready to be consumed by any person who hands over some cash.

---

[36]Apne Aap Women Worldwide. Retrieved 15 June 2017, from http://apneaap.org/.

[37]https://www.versobooks.com/books/1568-playing-the-whore.

The human rights approach to prostitution has also been adopted from the outset by the AIDS/HIV world of scientists, service providers and activists. It is rare, as we shall see in the next chapter, to encounter anyone actively involved in HIV prevention who does not support the blanket decriminalisation of the sex trade.

7

Aiding the Fight for Legalisation: AIDS & HIV

I have worked in legal, decriminalised and illegal brothels. I've been on the streets and I've been in five-star hotels. If a john doesn't want to use a rubber, trust me, no amount of rules will make him do so. (Angela, sex trade survivor, 2016)

The HIV/AIDS movement is widely understood as one that focuses on civil rights and healthcare for vulnerable groups. The popular perception is that the AIDS movement is made up of human rights campaigners, medical experts and scientists, searching for the best prevention methods and, eventually, a cure. What is far less widely known is that the AIDS movement, and the vast amounts of money attached to it, has done more to shape policy, practice and legislation on the global sex trade than any other movement in history.

Huge amounts of money have been poured into 'safe sex' programmes aimed at punters. In other words, considerable effort has gone into assisting men to continue paying for sex. Indeed, without the support of the HIV/AIDS harm reduction approach, the pro-decriminalisation lobby, including the likes of Amnesty International (AI), would not have gained anywhere near as much ground.

© The Author(s) 2017
J. Bindel, *The Pimping of Prostitution*,
DOI 10.1057/978-1-137-55890-9_7

The arguments of AIDS activists and experts for blanket decriminalisation of the sex trade is simple but horrendously flawed. It is widely claimed that if all criminal penalties were removed from the sex trade, including for pimping, brothel owning and sex buying, then HIV rates would plummet. This chapter will explore and dissect these claims for decriminalisation, and closely examine the relationship between the HIV world and the pro-prostitution lobby. I argue the harm reduction approach is damaging to women in the sex trade and, conversely, allows far more abuse to occur.

The Early Days of AIDS and 'Sex Worker's Rights' Movements

In the early days of the AIDS crisis in the mid-1980s, money was provided to two distinct groups in the Global North: men who have sex with men, and women involved in street-based prostitution. Understandably, gay men were at the helm of the charities and health service interventions, with some establishing organisations that attempted to deal holistically with the most at-risk groups. As a consequence, many projects devoted to HIV prevention and treatment were managed by gay men, including those with a client base consisting of women in the sex trade.

Because of stigma associated with AIDS brought about by anti-gay bigotry and misinformation peddled by governments and religious organisations, many projects dealing with this issue were involved in awareness raising and lobbying. Those who were HIV positive were frequently referred to as 'authors of their own misfortune'. The then Chief Constable of Greater Manchester Police, James Anderton, for example, referred to them as 'swirling about in a human cesspit of their own making'.[1]

Unfortunately, gay male libertarian views dominated the discourse, likely conflating 'safety' with 'moralism' due to sensitivities toward any

---

[1]Sharratt, T. (1986, Dec 12.) *Preacher Anderton thunders against the gays.* In The Guardian.

analysis of 'sex and sexuality'. Rather than critiquing the sex trade as an unsafe lifestyle for those involved, the message delivered to the general public as well as service users was so-called harm reduction and minimisation. The condom was held up as the saviour, and opportunities to examine the dangers of the sex trade were overlooked.

Andrew Hunter, a gay man born in 1968 in Queensland, Australia, left home at 17 to live in the Gunnery Squats, Sydney, home to alternative 'queer'-identified folk, including a number of those considered social outcasts. Hunter became involved in street-based prostitution in Sydney, and at 19 moved to Melbourne, prostituting from the infamous St Kilda district. Hunter, who died in 2013, became the president of the Global Network of Sex Work Projects (NSWP), programme and policy manager for the Asia Pacific Network of Sex Workers (APNSW), and a member of the Joint United Nations Programme on HIV/AID (UNAIDS) Advisory Group on HIV and sex work. During his activism, Hunter campaigned to decriminalise the sex trade and for prostitution to be viewed as labour. He openly supported organisations such as UN Women, sending a message of support for its stance on 'sex work as work' just months before he died. While with the Prostitute's Collective of Victoria (PCV), Hunter initiated the first male street-based outreach service in St Kilda and a needle-syringe programme.

Commenting on his time prostituting in St Kilda, Hunter said that 'fortunately I was saved by the outreach workers of the PCV rather than the Ladies of the Order of St Mary's giving out sandwiches'. Founded in 1978 by Cheryl Overs, a 'sex workers' rights' activist, the PCV did anything but 'save' those involved in the sex trade. Exiting prostitution was never one of its aims. As leader of the PCV, Overs represented the sex trade on the Ministry of Planning Working Group on Prostitution that advised the Victorian government leading up to decriminalisation of indoor prostitution, including pimps, brothel owners and all other third party profiteers. The organisation was soon at the cutting edge of the AIDS debate. In 1988, the PCV hosted the Prostitution and the AIDS Debate Conference in Melbourne, which led to the formation of the national federation of 'sex workers' rights' organisations across Australia: Scarlet Alliance.

In 1989, Overs began to campaign in Europe, beginning her career on the other side of the world as an advisor to the Global Programme on AIDS at the World Health Organisation, contributing to International AIDS conferences and publications such as Harvard AIDS Institute's *AIDS in the World* and helping establish the International Council of AIDS Service Organisations (ICASO). By this time, the worlds of prostitution and AIDS were as one, both in terms of ideology and at policy level.

At the 1992 Opportunities for Solidarity Conference of HIV/AIDS NGOs in Paris, Overs and Paulo Henrique Longo founded the NSWP. In 2004, NSWP condemned the anti-prostitution and trafficking resolution as 'counterproductive to effective HIV/AIDS prevention programmes worldwide'. Their view was shared by hundreds of individuals and organisations who signed a letter to the US President opposing the resolution in 2005. NSWP vice president Alejandra Gil, who also served as co-chair of the UNAIDS Advisory Group on HIV and Sex Work and Global Working Group on HIV and Sex Work Policy, was arrested for sex trafficking in 2015 and subsequently jailed for fifteen years.[2]

Overs remains active in the pro-prostitution/AIDS world. In 2012 she delivered a keynote speech at the International AIDS Conference and, in the same year, presented on 'sex workers rights' at the United Nations Human Rights Council (UNHRC). She is currently an honorary research fellow at Sussex University in the UK, the same University at which a number of pro-prostitution trafficking deniers are linked, as I discuss in Chap. 9.

Common Funding, Service Provision and Policy

Since the late 1980s, much prostitution policy is determined by AIDS funding, largely from the Bill and Melinda Gates Foundation and the OSF, founded by George Soros. There can be little doubt that AIDS funding

---

[2]NSWP. (2015, Oct 16.) *NWSP statement of support for Alejandra Gil: Bad laws are not in the interest of sex workers' human rights!* In NWSP.org. Retrieved 15 June 2017, from http://www.nswp.org/news/nswp-statement-support-alejandra-gil-bad-laws-are-not-the-interest-sex-workers-human-rights.

has driven both service provision and policy when it comes to prostitution and the sex trade: where Rupert Murdoch controls the media, and Bill and Melinda Gates and the OSF control the prostitution discourse.

Soros is a billionaire who made his fortune in aggressive currency speculation, creating hardship and driving economic crashes in countries that he later offered to 'rescue' through OSF. Soros has been prosecuted and convicted in France of market manipulation and fraud.[3] Eugenio Zaffaroni, who also funded and advised the OSF, was accused of brothel keeping and running a sex-trafficking ring in six apartments he owns in Buenos Aires, Argentina. Zaffaroni has since been appointed as a judge at the Inter-American Court of Human Rights.[4]

OSF is not only a major donor to AI, Human Rights Watch (HRW), and UNAIDS, but also to a number of pro-prostitution lobby groups across the world. Soros is the biggest financial backer of the pro-legalisation lobby in the world, whose organisation is overtly pro-legalisation, and who funded reports AI relied on in order to support their position.[5] OSF donated to UNAIDS and UNDP (United Nations Development Programme) which, while claiming that they are independent institutions, acknowledge 'the generous financial support' of OSF.[6] This funding has had an impact on legislation: it funds the lobby group Sex Workers' Alliance Ireland which is campaigning against the Nordic model, and is supporting Laura Lee in her attempt to judicially

[3]Clark, N. (2011, Aug 2.) *Soros loses challenge to insider trading conviction.* In New York Times. Retrieved 15 June 2017, from http://dealbook.nytimes.com/2011/10/06/soros-loses-challenge-to-insider-trading-conviction/?_r=0.

[4]International Justice Resource Centre. (2015, Jun 25.) *New members elected to inter-American human rights body amid controversy.* In IJRC.org. Retrieved 15 June 2017, from http://www.ijrcenter.org/2015/06/25/new-members-elected-to-inter-american-human-rights-bodies-amid-controversy/.

[5]https://www.amnesty.org/download/Documents/40000/fin400122010en.pdf, p. 10.

[6]HIV Law Commission. (2012, July.) *Global commission on HIV and the law: Risks, rights and health.* Retrieved 15 June 2017, from http://www.hivlawcommission.org/resources/report/FinalReport-Risks,Rights&Health-EN.pdf, p. 5.

review the abolitionist law in Northern Ireland.[7] HRW initially did not have a policy on criminalisation versus decriminalisation, although they recently affirmed their support for full decriminalisation—perhaps influenced by the funding received from Soros, most notably a 2010 grant pledging $100 million over ten years.[8] NSWP is also funded by the OSF.

Most recent data from 2013 shows 56 NGOs have funded €8 million in pro-prostitution projects/decriminalisation advocacy.[9] The top five donors (and money they've contributed) were Open Society Initiative, Ford Foundation, American Jewish World Service, Red Umbrella Fund, and Mama Cash (a pro-prostitution fund for women based in the Netherlands). Of the €8 million: €3 million was invested in health, €1.4 million in legal service, and the remaining €4.4 million in advocacy and policy[10]; in other words a huge emphasis on pushing for decriminalisation over and above practical long-term help for prostituted women such as health services and poverty alleviation.

The Ford Foundation was reported as the biggest donor to pro-prostitution organisations, with the average Ford Foundation grant to 'sex worker' organisations exceeding $100,000.[11] The Ford Foundation was one of the core supporters (along with Mama Cash and the Association for Women's Rights in Development [AWID]) of the 'Women's Rights and Gender Equality in Focus' series launched in the *Guardian* in

---

[7]McGrew, K. (2016, Sep 8.) *Sex workers' legal challenge granted leave in high court in Northern Ireland.* In Sex Workers Alliance Ireland. Retrieved 15 June 2017, fromhttp://sexworkersallianceireland.org/sex-workers-legal-challenge-granted-leave-in-high-court-in-northern-ireland-28_09_2016/.

[8]Boston.com. (2010, Sept 7.) *George Soros gives $100m to human rights watch.* In Boston.com. Retrieved 15 June 2017, fromhttp://www.boston.com/news/nation/articles/2010/09/07/george_soros_gives_100m_to_human_rights_watch/.

[9]Mama Cash, Red Umbrella Fund, Open Societies Foundation. (2014.) *Funding for sex worker rights: Opportunities for foundations to fund more and better.* Retrieved 15 June 2017, from http://www.mamacash.org/content/uploads/2014/12/Report_funding-sex-worker-rights_FINAL_WEB.pdf.

[10]Mama Cash, Red Umbrella Fund, Open Societies Foundation. (2014.) *Funding for sex worker rights: Opportunities for foundations to fund more and better.* Retrieved 15 June 2017, from http://www.mamacash.org/content/uploads/2014/12/Report_funding-sex-worker-rights_FINAL_WEB.pdf, p. 10.

[11]Open Society Institute. (2006, June.) *Sex worker health and rights: Where is the funding?* Retrieved 15 June 2017, from https://www.opensocietyfoundations.org/sites/default/files/where.pdf, p. 11.

February 2014. In a statement, the *Guardian* said: 'As partners, The Ford Foundation, Mama Cash and AWID will offer the *Guardian* editorial team ideas and help link the team with diverse women's rights advocates, organisations and movements.'[12]

American Jewish World Service (AJWS), a Jewish organisation which ought to understand the sting of bigotry, claims women who critique prostitution as an institution of male violence are not feminists and are no better than racists and homophobic bigots:

> Some feminists also point to the stigma around sex work as an example of societies' unwillingness to recognise women's sexual and reproductive rights, including the right to choose one's sexual partners, to choose whether to have sex at all, and to enjoy sexuality and pleasure. Similar to their positions against bans on interracial or same-sex marriage, these feminists believe that the state should not interfere with consensual sex between adults.[13]

AJWS is one of the largest funders of advocacy by and for pro-prostitution campaigners. It currently provides $500,000 a year in grants to 17 organisations that support the rights of 'sex workers' in eight developing countries.

'Guided by our belief in the essential dignity of every person, AJWS and our grantees make a very clear distinction between sex work and human trafficking. To be clear, we are against all forms of human trafficking or forced labour. We have learned from our grantees that sex work is a voluntary occupation, which differs starkly from human trafficking - a problem that violates people's human rights by forcing them to work involuntarily.'[14]

Founded in 1985, Red Thread became one of the loudest voices in favour of normalising 'sex work' as a legitimate form of employment.

---

[12]Anon. (2014, Feb 4.) *About women's rights and gender equality in focus.* Retrieved 15 June 2017, from http://www.theguardian.com/global-development/2014/feb/04/womens-rights-gender-equality-in-focus.

[13]American Jewish World Service. (2013, July.) *Sex worker rights: (Almost) everything you wanted to know but were afraid to ask.* Retrieved 15 June 2017, from http://www.nswp.org/sites/nswp.org/files/sex_worker_rights.pdf.

[14]American Jewish World Service. *Why we support sex workers.* Retrieved 15 June 2017, from https://ajws.org/stories/why-we-support-sex-workers/.

Much of its publicity came from the media attention surrounding the two 'Whores Congresses' they held. Their advocacy is similar to that of the English Collective of Prostitutes and the Sex Workers' Open University in the UK. In its early years the organisation was 100% government-funded (despite claiming the label 'NGO'), and much of this government funding was spent on the opening of The Red School, where new prostitutes were taught how best to service their male clients.

The Red Umbrella Fund is composed of a global network of 'sex worker' projects. It 'strengthens and ensures the sustainability of the "sex worker's rights" movement by catalysing new funding for sex-worker led organisations and their national and regional networks'.[15] The Red Umbrella Fund has been financially supported by six major foundations: AJWS, Comic Relief, Levi Strauss Foundation, the MAC AIDS Fund, Mama Cash and OSF. It has, since its inception in 2012, given 63 grants to sex worker advocacy organisations in 42 countries. The Fund only provides grants to organisations 'led for and by sex workers' and will not consider grant applications from abolitionist organisations, whatever the circumstances.[16]

AIDS NGOs are also adept at raising extraordinary amounts of money through ad hoc charity events, regular charity drives and direct deposit from private donors. Curiously, misogyny has been found by AIDS NGOs to be a very useful means to excite donations. In Australia, for example, the Bobby Goldsmith Foundation (BGF) is a key AIDS charity providing AIDS advocacy and research. The patron of BGF is Justice Michael Kirby,[17] who is without doubt Australia's most prominent human rights advocate. Justice Kirby is also the patron of Touching Base, an organisation that argues disabled men have a human right to use prostituted women.

The BGF hosts an annual 'bake-off', in which donated cakes are sold to the highest bidder. It is a very prestigious event on the calendar of

---

[15]Mama Cash, Red Umbrella Fund, Open Societies Foundation. (2014.) *Funding for sex worker rights: Opportunities for foundations to fund more and better*. Retrieved 15 June 2017, from http://www.mamacash.org/content/uploads/2014/12/Report_funding-sex-worker-rights_FINAL_WEB.pdf, p. 7.

[16]Red Umbrella Fund. (2017) *Apply for a grant*. Retrieved 15 June 2017, from http://www.redumbrellafund.org/grantmaking/apply-grant/.

[17]Bobby Goldsmith Foundation. *The Hon Michael Kirby AC CMG*. Retrieved 15 June 2017, from https://www.bgf.org.au/about-bgf/patron/.

VIPs from the sex trade and AIDS community. I am reliably informed, by a friend from Australia, that not a single year has passed in which its cakes have not reduced women to objects of violence and humiliation. In 2008, the most notorious of these cakes depicted a graphic representation of Paris Hilton, who at the time was serving a prison sentence for drug possession, being anally raped by 'a black tattooed lesbian [prisoner wearing] a strap-on dildo, [while] a horrified miniature dog looked in through prison bars'. This vile sexist and racist cake, which sold for $7000, won first prize and remains the most expensive cake the BGF has ever sold[18]; and not one single complaint was made.

The key players in prostitution politics are the same key players in AIDS politics. This evidences the fact that the same skill set and impoverished understanding of so-called harm minimisation as the cure for male violence against women and girls is required for those involved in the policy direction of both AIDS and sex trade administration. For example, Tim Barnett MP, the man who single–handed decriminalised prostitution in New Zealand through his private member's bill, is a gay man with extensive links to pro-prostitution organisations in the UK. After his retirement from politics he took up very important roles in AIDS organisations in South Africa where he worked closely with Dr Nothemba (Nono) Simelela. Simelela, South Africa's most respected AIDS policy advisor, is a fascinating person worthy of a more thorough investigation. Another example is Catherine Murphy, who was reported as being the 'chief engineer' of AI's position on fully decriminalising prostitution, before the wording was amended to 'playing a significant role'.[19] Murphy, mirroring Barnett, held a key role in the UK's largest AIDS NGO the Terrence Higgins[20] as head of Public Affairs, before taking up her policy advisor position at AI. As discussed in the Chap. 8,

---

[18]Star Observer. (2008, Apr 20.) *How much would you pay to have Paris at home?* In Star Observer. Retrieved 15 June 2017, from http://www.starobserver.com.au/news/national-news/new-south-wales-news/how-much-would-you-pay-to-have-paris-at-home/11052.

[19]Global Thinkers. (2015.) *Catherine Murphy.* Retrieved 15 June 2017, from https://2015globalthinkers.foreignpolicy.com/#!challengers/detail/murphy.

[20]Dundee SNP. (2008, Dec 4.) *Safe sex message vital in festival period says MSP.* In Dundee SNP. Retrieved 15 June 2017, from http://dundeesnp.org/safe-sex-message-vital-in-festive-period-says-msp/.

Murphy was displaying her hostility to the Nordic Model on behalf of AI well before that organisation claims it had formed a policy position.

USAID

The United States Agency for International Development (USAID) is the world's biggest government-affiliated funder of NGOs, with $22.3 billion allocated to be distributed to various organisations. Historically, USAID limited funds to NGOs that officially and outwardly opposed both prostitution and sex trafficking[21] with the requirement that all recipients of donations sign an anti-prostitution pledge before the release of funds.

In 2005, USAID was taken to court by the Open Society Initiative (OSI) (vehemently pro-sex work) on the basis that asking NGOs to sign an anti-prostitution pledge to receive funding was tantamount to a denial of free speech under the First Amendment: OSI won the case. While the validity and usefulness of the pledge has been disputed by those on both sides of the prostitution debate, the OSI's successful challenge shows just how much money and time they have and are willing to throw behind pro-prostitution advocacy.

NGO Proponents and Opponents of the Sex Trade

1983

Mama Cash, a Netherlands-based NGO, is formed. Mama Cash has been one of the most prolific funders of 'sex worker's rights' and advocacy since its inception.

---

[21]Ditmore, M. (2005, Spring.) *New US funding policies on trafficking affect sex work and HIV-prevention efforts world wide.* In SIECUS Report, Volume 33, Number 2.

1987

The Global Fund for Women, 'a global advocate for women's human rights',[22] is launched and begins funding anti-trafficking work and exit services for prostituted women. They would later reverse their stance to pledge support for decriminalisation (see 2005 and 2015).

1988

The Coalition Against Trafficking in Women, an international NGO, is formed. They are one of only a few organisations that remain committed to abolishing prostitution and commercial sexual exploitation.

1995

A large and influential NGO caucus was formed at the fourth World Women's Conference in Beijing and China. A group with immense lobbying power, it is headed up by Charlotte Bunch from the Centre for Women's Global Leadership and Alice Miller from the International Human Rights Law Group: both are vehemently pro-'sex work'.[23]

1997

The Netherlands assumes presidency of the EU and immediately begins to use 'pro-sex work' NGOs as a front to legitimise the normalisation of prostitution at the European level. In preparation for the EU Ministerial Conference in April of the same year, the Dutch

---

[22]Global Fund for Women. Retrieved 15 June 2017, from https://www.globalfundforwomen.org/.

[23]Raymond, J. (2014.) *Not a choice, not a job: Exposing the myths about prostitution and the global sex trade*. London: Potomac, p. 106.

government gives funding and advisory status to several pro-'sex work' NGOs. Despite claims of impartiality, no pro-abolitionist NGOs are funded.[24]

Invitees to the conference are given an advantage when applying for the Daphne Grants: a series of grants available to NGOs for the purpose of funding anti-trafficking initiatives and awarded by the European Commission.

These grants fund many of the European pro-sex work groups during critical years of national, regional and international policy making on prostitution and trafficking, and also help elevate them into key governmental and media positions and forums within Europe and the UN.[25]

2000

The International Union of Sex Workers (IUSW) is founded.[26] While the organisation is unfunded, their reach in terms of advocacy and outreach has been unparalleled, and they are heavily consulted when forming the basis of the decriminalisation pledges of most major NGOs including the WHO and AI.[27]

2002

HRW declares it has 'no position on prostitution per se'. However, it 'strongly condemns' practices that fail to distinguish between prostitutes and victims of forced trafficking.[28]

---

[24]Raymond, J. (2014.) *Not a choice, not a job: Exposing the myths about prostitution and the global sex trade.* London: Potomac, p. 102.

[25]Raymond, J. (2014.) *Not a choice, not a job: Exposing the myths about prostitution and the global sex trade.* London: Potomac, p. 103.

[26]International Union of Sex Workers. Retrieved 15 June 2017, from http://www.iusw.org/iusw-history/.

[27]International Union of Sex Workers. (2014, Apr 8.) *IUSW response to the Amnesty International consultation of decriminalising sex work.* Retrieved 15 June 2017, from http://www.iusw.org/2014/04/iusw-response-to-the-amnesty-international-consultation-on-decriminalising-sexwork/.

[28]Kumar, A. (2002.) *Human rights: Global perspectives.* New Delhi: Sarup & Sons, p. 203.

2004

Marianne Eriksson, a Swedish member of the European Parliament, demands a hearing into the misallocation of funding to NGOs, alleging that pro-abolitionist groups who applied for funding were overwhelmingly rejected without good reason, even when their policies and finances were objectively more sound than those of pro-decriminalisation groups (see 1997).

2005

Previously pro-abolitionist group Global Fund for Women (GFFW) reverses its position due to allegedly witnessing human rights violations by abolitionist agencies and NGOs. GFFW begins financing pro-decriminalisation sex worker organisations in developing countries, including Lady Mermaid in Kampala, Uganda.

2006

Amid concerns that the 2006 World Cup in Germany will cause an increase in men buying women for sex, the German NGO The National Council of German Women's Organisations iterated that they were not against men using women in prostitution but that men should merely try to avoid buying women who 'look like they may have been coerced'.[29]

2009

Michel Sidibé, the Executive Director of UNAIDS establishes an advisory group to be co-chaired by the Global Network of Sex Work Projects and UNAIDS. The group drives the policy of UNAIDS and also influences UN organisation wide policy.[30]

---

[29]Raymond, J. (2014.) *Not a choice, not a job: Exposing the myths about prostitution and the global sex trade*. London: Potomac, p. 56.

[30]NSWP. *UN Aids advisory group*. Retrieved 15 June 2017, from http://www.nswp.org/unaids-advisory-group.

2010

The Cooperative for Assistance and Relief Everywhere (CARE International) is asked at a conference in Iceland whether, as an organisation, it considers prostitution to be violence against women. The representative responds that there is no organisation-wide policy. However, CARE has in the past implicitly condoned men's use of prostitutes as long as they use condoms, putting forward a position that there is a 'moral' way for men to use prostitutes.[31]

2012

The WHO formally backs the decriminalisation of prostitution as a way to curb the spread of HIV in at-risk groups in developing countries.[32]

The UN officially calls for the decriminalisation of prostitution, including many sub-organisations under its remit (UNDP, UNAIDS, UN Women etc.).

The Red Umbrella Fund is created, described as the first global fund 'by and for sex workers'. It is one of the biggest influencers of UN policy through its 'Global Working Group on HIV and Sex Work'.

2014

HRW affirms its support for decriminalisation in its 24th annual review of human rights practices worldwide,[33] marking a departure from its 2002 stance of having 'no policy per se'. *The Lancet* special edition is published, which focusses on the influence of decriminalised prostitution on rates of HIV.

---

[31]Raymond, J. (2014.) *Not a choice, not a job: Exposing the myths about prostitution and the global sex trade.* London: Potomac.

[32]World Health Organization. (2012, Dec 12.) *New WHO guidelines to better prevent HIV in sex workers.* Retrieved 15 June 2017, from http://www.who.int/hiv/mediacentre/feature_story/sti_guidelines/en/.

[33]NSWP. (2014, Jan 21.) *Human rights watch affirm support for decriminalisation.* Retrieved 15 June 2017, from http://www.nswp.org/timeline/event/human-rights-watch-affirm-support-decriminalisation p. 47.

2015

AI formally backs the decriminalisation of prostitution as an organ-isation-wide policy. The decision is framed as a 'policy to protect the human rights of sex workers'.[34] AI's decision is backed by over 1100 organisations and individuals including organisations like GFFW who had previously worked on anti-trafficking and exit services for prosti-tuted women, representing a policy U-turn.[35]

Eaves, one of the few UK NGOs that is openly abolitionist closes due to a lack of funding.[36]

Meanwhile, UK pro-prostitution organisations are thriving, such as the Sex Workers' Open University (SWOU). Despite claiming 'almost non-existent' funding, the SWOU has some powerful backers, includ-ing the International Federation of Planned Parenthood and SERTUC, the South East arm of the UK's Trade Union Congress.

The Lancet and Its Legacy

'The decriminalisation of sex work and prevention of trafficking of human beings are not tantamount,' Jennifer Butler, senior advisor on HIV at the UN's Population Fund told *Vice News*. 'The overwhelming majority of people selling sex in the world are selling sex voluntarily.'[37]

---

[34]Amnesty International UK. (2015, Aug 11.) *Global movement votes to adopt policy to protect human rights of sex workers*. Retrieved 15 June 2017, from http://www.amnesty.org.uk/global-movement-votes-adopt-policy-protect-human-rights-sex-workers#.Vhutt7r4vFI.

[35]Global Fund for Women. (2015, Aug 6.) *Facebook status update*. Retrieved 15 June 2017, from https://www.facebook.com/GlobalFundforWomen/posts/10154056473873098?comment_id=10154059374153098&offset=0&total_comments=15&comment_tracking=%7B%22tn%22%3A%22R%22%7D.

[36]Eaves. (2014) *Closure of Eaves: Another nail in the coffin for the women's sector*. Retrieved 15 June 2017, from http://www.eavesforwomen.org.uk/news-events/news/closure-of-eaves-another-nail-in-the-coffin-for-the-women-s-sector.

[37]Oakford, S. (2015, Aug 11.) *Amnesty International votes to push for the decriminalisa-tion of sex work*. In Vice. Retrieved 15 June 2017, from https://news.vice.com/article/amnesty-international-votes-to-push-for-the-decriminalization-of-sex-work.

The false distinction between trafficking and other aspects of the sex trade has been explored in Chap. 6. Many within the AIDS world hold this distinction dear.

AVERT (AVERTing HIV and AIDS) is an international charity, founded in 1986 and based in Brighton in the UK. It provides 'global information and advice on HIV & AIDS' and its aim is a world with no new HIV infections. In its section on 'Sex Work and HIV/AIDS', AVERT's website states that: 'Large numbers of trafficked people are forced into selling sex every year. This is different from sex work in that trafficked people are forced into selling sex. Even in countries where HIV prevalence is low, trafficked people who are forced to sell sex are still vulnerable to HIV infection because they struggle to access condoms, cannot negotiate condom use and are often subjected to violence.'

A number of AIDS activists tends to leap from the argument that barely any people in prostitution are trafficked, to one that acknowledges it is a significant problem, while driving a wedge between the process and the inevitable end result. For example, leading on from the above claim, the website continues: 'However, many emphasise that the relationship between sex work and human trafficking should not be overplayed as it can lead to false or exaggerated anti-sex work arguments and harmful action by the authorities, ultimately undermining HIV prevention for sex workers.'

To substantiate this argument, the authors cite a *Lancet* article[38] entitled 'Trafficking, sex work and HIV: Efforts to resolve conflicts', which is one of seven from a special edition[39] on prostitution and the sex trade in which it is argued that conflating trafficking with 'sex work' hinders HIV prevention strategies and medical care. The series of papers is a call to governments to decriminalise sex work, says *Lancet* editor Richard Horton and senior executive editor Pamela Das in the Introduction.

---

[38]Steen, R. (2014, Jul 21.) *Trafficking, sex work, and HIV: Efforts to resolve conflicts.* In The Lancet. Retrieved 15 June 2017, from http://www.thelancet.com/journals/lancet/article/PIIS0140-6736(14)60966-1/abstract.

[39]The Lancet. (2014, Jul 23.) *HIV and sex workers.* In The Lancet. Retrieved 15 June 2017, from http://www.thelancet.com/series/HIV-and-sex-workers.

In 2013 the Bill Gates Foundation gave Johns Hopkins University a $250,000 grant to put together the special edition. It was published in July 2014 and created an international media storm. The influence of the special edition cannot be underestimated. Although mainly medical professionals read *The Lancet*, its conclusions regarding sex trade policy—i.e. blanket decriminalisation—were disseminated far and wide in the media.

'DECRIMINALISING SEX WORK WOULD CUT HIV INFECTIONS BY A THIRD', screamed the press release headline,[40] with many newspapers following suit.

In a letter[41] to AI prior to its final decision-making summit in Dublin, August 2016, *The Lancet* editorial board wrote:

'Sex workers are among the most marginalised, stigmatised populations in the world. Criminalisation of their profession increases their risk of HIV and violence and abuse from clients, police, and the public. *The Lancet* series on HIV and sex workers showed that decriminalisation of sex work would have the greatest effect on the course of HIV epidemics across all settings, averting 33–46% of HIV infections in the next decade. Such a move would also reduce mistreatment of sex workers and increase their access to human rights, including health care. *The Lancet* supports Amnesty's draft policy and urges its Board to adopt it at their upcoming meeting in Dublin.'

According to the methodology section, in order to reach the rather extraordinary conclusion, the researchers collected all the available data on HIV prevalence, condom use and 'structural determinants' among those involved in prostitution, and used a mathematical model to simulate the effect of different interventions. This was carried out in three contrasting settings: Vancouver, Canada; Bellary, India; and Mombasa, Kenya.

---

[40]Wong, S. (2014, Jul 24.) *Decriminalising sex work would cut HIV infections by a third.* In Imperial College London. Retrieved 15 June 2017, from http://www3.imperial.ac.uk/newsandeventspggrp/imperialcollege/newssummary/news_24-7-2014-16-48-0.

[41]The Lancet. (2015, Aug 8.) *Keeping sex workers safe.* In The Lancet. Retrieved 15 June 2017, from http://thelancet.com/journals/lancet/article/PIIS0140-6736(15)61460-X/fulltext.

'The research shows that eliminating sexual violence,' claimed the researchers, 'could reduce HIV infection rates among FSWs (female sex workers) and their clients by up to a fifth over 10 years in the settings investigated, through its immediate and sustained effect on non-condom use'.[42] How are the researchers planning on eliminating sexual violence towards women in prostitution, when it is endemic the world over, *including*, as we have seen in Chap. 4 and elsewhere in this book, in legalised regimes?

Dr Michael Shively, senior associate in the US Health Division of Abt Associates,[43] based in Massachusetts, has spent time analysing the claims made by the authors of *The Lancet* special edition. I asked him for his views on the evidence presented by the editors and authors involved in the special edition, and found him unequivocal in concluding that the evidence nowhere near backs up their claims that new HIV infections would be dramatically reduced if there were blanket decriminalisation of the sex trade:

> Let's suppose you accept the idea that violence and police harassment and condom use would improve dramatically following decriminalisation, let's say by 50 percent as an example. What would happen if the demand and sexual commerce doubled in response to decriminalisation? Because if you call off the dogs and make [prostitution] legal and there's no deterrent, there's no threat of punishment and it's a completely free market. If demand doubled because buyers, sellers, and pimps were free to operate unabated, then you would be in exactly the same place in terms of HIV transmissions. Risks might decline, but if the pool of people at risk expands, the safety gains are offset, at least in part. Obviously it wouldn't work out that cleanly, but even if there was only a modest increase in demand, it's still an offset that should at least be considered. Yet the authors modelled only potential benefits leading to reductions in rates of harm, without any offsets or potentially negative consequences of full decriminalisation.

Shively is right to be concerned about a potential increase in demand as a result of decriminalisation. One central argument in the collection

---

[42]http://www3.imperial.ac.uk/newsandeventspggrp/imperialcollege/newssummary/news_24-7-2014-16-48-0

[43]ABT Associates. Retrieved 15 June 2017, from http://www.abtassociates.com/.

of Lancet articles amounts to this: that decriminalisation would result in zero or a vast reduction in violence, and in police harassment toward prostituted people; prostitution would occur in unsafe workplaces; and there would be universal condom use. Each of these assumptions or counterfactuals separately is unrealistic.

The researchers did not miss the opportunity to inform the public that calls to decriminalise the sex trade have come from a number of major health organisations: 'Calls for removal of all legal restrictions targeting sex work have been supported by international policy bodies, including WHO, UNAIDS, UNDP and the UN Population Fund', claimed the press release[44] from Imperial College London.

However, something was missing from the headlines, and from the interpretation of the studies written up in *The Lancet* and showcased at the AIDS 2014 Conference in Melbourne. The senior author of the study, Dr Marie-Claude Boily, School of Public Health, Imperial College London, made this clear: 'To observe the level of impact we predict, we need not only decriminalisation of sex work but also to have necessary and sufficient clinical services, prevention interventions and psychosocial support in place and easily accessible to sex workers'. However, the authors were not, in the various papers in the special edition, suggesting that governments should hold back from introducing decriminalisation until the above-mentioned services were in place.

'*The Lancet* did us a favour', says Shively. 'There are literally thousands of sources that examine health risks and other consequences of commercial sex, and the editors of the special edition and authors of its individual articles claim outright that they have reviewed this vast field and integrated key findings from the best sources. Their reviews and original contributions are presented as a state-of-the-art collection and synthesis of thousands of studies. They present their primary conclusion that decriminalisation would significantly reduce HIV transmission as definitive and based on overwhelming scientific evidence. If

---

[44]Wong, S. (2014, Jul 24.) *Decriminalising sex work would Cut HIV infections by a third.* In Imperial College London. Retrieved 15 June 2017, from http://www3.imperial.ac.uk/ newsandeventspggrp/imperialcollege/newssummary/news_24-7-2014-16-48-0.

that conclusion from that collection of research does not hold up under scrutiny, they can't accuse [abolitionists] and other researchers who contest their findings of cherry-picking only the weak studies - they have already told the world that this is the best evidence.'

Chris Beyrer is Professor of Epidemiology at the Johns Hopkins Bloomberg School of Public Health in Baltimore, Maryland in the USA, and President of the International AIDS Society. Breyer, who was awarded the grant to put together the 2014 special edition of *The Lancet*, made a compelling speech, which was widely disseminated through the international media,[45] at the AIDS conference that same year.

I spoke to him on Skype and asked if he would explain how the authors reached the conclusion that full decriminalisation would result in a significant drop in HIV infections. 'One of the things that really came out across these comprehensive reviews was just the level of violence that particularly women and transgender sex workers endure everywhere', says Beyrer. 'It's extraordinary. It's intimate partner violence, client violence, police violence and the whole approach to safety and to trying to reduce violence, I think is a very important part of the pathway of decriminalisation because as long as, in most of the world, the police are not on the side of action, as long as sex workers are criminalised, there is terrible impunity for police violence and sexual violence and that really plays in.'

But, as Beyrer himself pointed out, the violence towards women in prostitution comes from punters, pimps, intimate partners and police. Beyrer appears to be both overselling how much of the problem is driven by police, and implying that the problem of police abuses would disappear if decriminalisation occurred. 'But it turns out that decriminalisation had the biggest effect on averting new infections,' says Breyer, 'and I would point out that it's very important that the model included new infections in men'.

---

[45]Boseley, S. (2014, Jul 22.) *Decriminalise sex work to help control AIDS pandemic, scientists demand.* In The Guardian. Retrieved 15 June 2017, from https://www.theguardian.com/society/2014/jul/22/decriminalise-sex-work-control-aids-scientists-demand

The research did not, however, find that decriminalisation had the effect of diverting new infections as Breyer claims. Rather, it was found that large effects occur when you assume immediate, complete elimination of violence and inconsistent condom use. They never link those outcomes to decriminalisation with data. In fact, there are no historical precedents or studies that provide direct evidence that decriminalisation of commercial sex eliminates or reduces violence or increases condom use.

I asked Breyer how blanket decriminalisation would eliminate violence towards those in prostitution carried out by punters, pimps and those outside of law enforcement? Breyer holds up the Dutch model of legalisation as a 'good model'. 'We interviewed and spent some time with the head of human trafficking at [Amsterdam Police] that is responsible for the red-light district in Amsterdam,' says Breyer. 'Their focus for example is working with coercion and trafficking – that is a crime – it's a very different crime from selling sex but obviously it is intimately related.'

Conscience or 'Science'?

At the 2015 International AIDS Conference in Vancouver, Canada, held exactly one year after the launch of *The Lancet* special edition, I was granted a brief interview with its former President, the scarily eminent Françoise Barré-Sinoussi, the French virologist who discovered the HIV virus. I had been at the conference for a day or two, sitting in the media centre listening to journalists and bloggers from every region of the world talk among themselves about their angles on stories. I was a bit of a lone wolf. My interest was in the harms to women in the sex trade and there were no other reporters that shared my interest. From what I could gather, no-one was looking at the possibility that reducing demand for paid sex and helping the women to exit would reduce HIV infection rates. Rather, they were keen to hear about the positive effects that blanket decriminalisation of the sex trade might have on the spread of the virus.

As we walked to the interview room, Barré-Sinoussi told me she was not sure how she could help, saying she was involved in 'basic science' and not in public health research, although, she told me, she had an interest in both. There was no false modesty involved in Barré-Sinoussi's statement, just a simple stating of the facts. The scientists are concerned only with how to understand the way the virus is transmitted and to search for a vaccine and a cure.

I told Barré-Sinoussi I was interested in her views on the claims that were published in the special edition of *The Lancet* the previous year—that legalising/decriminalising the global sex trade would bring about a reduction in new HIV infections of around one-third or more within a decade.

Barré-Sinoussi recalled a research trip to South East Asia and a visit to Cambodia in the early 1990s. She became visibly upset as she told me about the prostituted girls that were being bought by Western men:

'Most of the girls that I met were very young. Most of them started prostitution when they were infants. They were sold by their own family, said Barré-Sinoussi, her voice dropping to almost a whisper. 'People involved in the traffic were giving money to the family to buy the girls. I've seen terrible things. Like at an international hotel ... depending on the time of night you would see very young girls, only 11 or 12, that were sold. It was really awful. Probably the worst experience I had in my life.'

I asked whether the girls would have been better off under decriminalisation, drawing the conversation to *The Lancet* special edition and its claims. 'In my opinion, you cannot generalise. You have different situations in different countries and even in one country you can have different situations regarding prostitution', said Barré-Sinoussi. 'You have prostitutes that really made a choice, that's their own choice and we should respect that. You have all the situations like the worst that I have mentioned.'

I was no clearer at all about the claims made in 2014, so pressed the scientists further.

How would global decriminalisation be effective? Barré-Sinoussi gave an example of the policing of a street in Phnom Penh called 'the street of small flowers'. Very young girls were sold from that street, and one year the government decided to close it in an attempt to reduce the risk of infection among the prostituted children. 'It was a terrible decision because in a very few months we have seen in Cambodia a small flower starting everywhere in the city,' said Barré-Sinoussi. 'When they were all in one street at least in that street it was organised with a healthcare centre, with organisations that were taking care of the girls if, for example, they had an infection or if they wanted to come to the health centre. When they were everywhere in the city they did not know where to go. It was a terrible decision.'

While fully understanding her point about the importance of ensuring access to medical care for the girls, I was disturbed that Barré-Sinoussi had not considered that helping them out of prostitution was the best protection against HIV. When Barré-Sinoussi recalled her time in Cambodia it was very clear that she thought that men buying children for sex is an abhorrence: 'I remember having breakfast in the hotel and tourists coming from Australia and the USA explaining to us very nicely that they used to go to Thailand, but Cambodia was much better than Thailand. This was because they have access to much younger girls than the ones they had access to before in Thailand, and some were virgins'.

At the Vancouver conference I met Tim Lane, Associate Professor at The California San Francisco Centre for AIDS Prevention Studies. Lane agreed with the recommendation that blanket decriminalisation would significantly reduce HIV rates. 'One of the things we heard a lot of anecdotally - because sex work is illegal - is that women are subject to all sorts of abuse by law enforcement officers who will find a woman with condoms in her purse and will say she is a sex worker and therefore will be arrested', said Lane.

Lane is correct. There are instances of women being arrested for carrying condoms in certain countries, but this problem would be solved by the introduction of the Nordic Model, where the women (and men) selling sex would not be at risk of arrest, but could in fact report a sex buyer for refusing to use a condom: under the Nordic Model the sex buyer is committing a criminal act in attempting to pay for sex, so no further evidence from the prostituted person would be necessary.

While there is no credible evidence that decriminalising pimping, brothel owning and sex buying increases condom use and decreases violence, there is plenty to the contrary. The same report contained data on reasons why women in prostitution did not always use condoms: '... about 71 percent of the female sex workers reported that they have, at least once in the past one month, refused to have sex with a client/non-regular partner who did not have or did not want to use a condom'.[46] I am unsure how decriminalising the activities of the sex buyers (if they are criminalised at all, which in India they are not) would change the situation for women. No legislation on earth could make the sex buyer use a condom if he did not wish to.

'Sex workers have told us that when they ask a client to use a condom, he offers double the price to have sex without the condom. These women are trying to provide for their children and families, so they take the offer', says Ndeye Astou Diop of Aboya (an organisation that works with HIV positive women in Senegal, Africa).[47]

When women are desperate, and/or scared of the punter, pimp or trafficker, they will agree to sex without a condom. If buying sex was a criminal offence, at least women might be able to threaten the punter with the police. Conversely, many advocates for legalisation and decriminalisation are against compulsory condom use.

Even some pro-prostitution activists are against any interference regarding condom use. I visited the Kassandra Counselling Centre for women in prostitution in Germany, where I met its head Barbel Ahlborn. Kassandra's take on assisting women out of prostitution is to provide classes where women can become 'qualified sexual accompaniment and assistance' (taught how to best provide sexual services for old and disabled men in their homes or institutions).

Ahlborn told me she was seriously concerned about a newly proposed law that would make condom use compulsory in commercial sex transactions. 'If it would make sense to have some kind of law on [compulsory condom use] I would be for it, but you cannot control it. The

[46]https://www.theguardian.com/society/2014/jul/22/decriminalise-sex-work-control-aids-scientists-demand.

[47]VOA News. (2009, Nov 1.) *Africa's sex workers have hard time leaving streets.* In VOA News. Retrieved 15 June 2017, from http://www.voanews.com/a/a-13-2007-02-13-voa17/342251.html.

prostitute and the buyer are alone and there's nobody making sure they are using a condom so it doesn't make sense.'

I asked Ahlborn if she would like to see an end to all of the regulation and just to have no state interference in the sex trade. 'It's hard to answer the question,' she says. 'If I want prostitutes to be treated like other businesses with regulations for the protection of people who are working there, we need that, but not with any treatment as victims. When I look at the sex workers here, there are women and some men who are well educated and know how to take care of their own rights, and there are many people in prostitution who hardly know German or about sexual health and even the functions of their own bodies and they only work in that trade so as not to starve – just to survive.'

It is not uncommon for pro-prostitution lobbyists to be against compulsory condom use, while at the same time taking money and support from the organisations with an aim to eliminate HIV. Siouxsie Q, whom we have met in previous chapters, also tells me she is against compulsory condom use on porn sets. It is difficult to see how decriminalising pimps and brothel owners could possible reduce rates of HIV, rather than to increase it. As we have heard from women who have exited the sex trade in previous chapters, sex buyers under decriminalisation routinely demand sex without a condom.

On the opening day of the 2015 World AIDS conference I joined a press trip to visit Insite, Vancouver's legal supervised injection site,[48] and the first of its kind in North America. The idea behind Insite, which first opened its doors in 2003, is to provide a 'safe, health-focused place where people inject drugs and connect to health care services' according to its website. Insite is North America's first legal supervised injection site, and it is often hailed by AIDS activists and medics as a best practice model.

The building sits in the Downtown East Side, by far the worst neighbourhood in Canada. The stark contrast between the conference venue—a spectacular spot on Vancouver's waterfront with stunning views of mountains, ocean, and parks—and the Downtown East Side

---

[48]Vancouver Coastal Health. Retrieved 15 June 2017, from http://supervisedinjection.vch.ca/.

district that looks and smells derelict is further enhanced by the beginnings of gentrification, such as the venue in which delegates meet. This art gallery looks out onto urine-stained streets and homeless beggars. The presentation put on by members of the Insite team included data on how many 'sex workers' use the programme. I asked if there were any resources available at Insite to assist women off drugs and out of the sex trade, and was told that the staff take a 'non-judgemental approach' to prostitution and therefore, no, there are no resources for such interventions. I was not surprised at the response.

Trisha Baptie, one of the Native Canadian survivors I met in Vancouver, is clear that Insite is not helping the women in prostitution who wish to exit.

'They don't offer exiting because it costs more money,' she says. 'We have to be discussing the social climate that allows AIDS to ferment in the prostitution community because there has to be an acknowledgement that the men are responsible. They're the ones who are saying I'll give you $50 more if I don't use a condom, and women are saying "yes" to that because of the dire situation they're in, so until you change the social situation that women are living in and take away men's ability to demand that, we're just going to be going round in circles.'

My appetite for a grand tour of Insite has been totally quashed, and instead I ask a feminist activist I had recently met in Vancouver to take me on a guided tour of the area. Courtney is a Native Canadian young woman, originally from the Squamish Nation. Courtney, like so many Native girls in Canada, was prostituted in the Downtown East Side from childhood until she escaped a few years ago. Summer Rain was in and out of foster care from 6 months old until the duty of care towards her ended at 18. In that time, she was in 25 different foster homes and approximately 15 group homes.

'Nobody really noticed where I went, which I think is often the case with Aboriginal children in care in British Columbia,' says Courtney. 'One of the things I say is that my life was shaped for sexual exploitation and prostitution before I was even born. My family has such a long history of violence against women that it became the norm in our world.'

When Courtney was 10 years old she ran away from her foster home and became fully immersed in the street culture of Vancouver, desperately trying to find a place in a family or somewhere that she was wanted. 'It didn't take very long being down there [Downtown East Side] before I was targeted, being this little blonde-haired, blue-eyed kid running around. It took three days before I was set up and what I learned after the fact was that I was being watched for those three days … who was I talking to, where was I going, who was responsible, was anybody with me or was I just random?' Courtney had been stalked by a well-known pimp in the area and was soon being sold to men that came to the area to pay for sex with children and women.

As we walk around the area, I see women within spitting distance of the Insite doorway, injecting heroin and smoking crack. One woman moves a few metres away to a doorway with a crack-using punter and gives him a hand job for drugs. Courtney tells me about the service provision for women in prostitution, which, she explains, is focused towards keeping AIDS away from the johns. 'Every service for women in prostitution is about eliminating the harm. You can live in Chrysalis or Rice block, which are operating as brothels. The staff are told that the johns are going to come in regardless of whether we like it or not. They just move them off the streets, there's no exiting services, there's no support.

'You will watch Beamers or Mercedes pull up in the front. A businessman in a suit gets out and goes inside, and leaves five or ten minutes later. It provides no way for [the prostituted woman] to get out because now her housing has become her brothel has become her prison and the State is funding these programmes.'

In Nairobi, Kenya, I take a taxi to meet Peninah Mwangi, founder of the Bar Hostess Empowerment and Support Programme (BHESP), close to a residential area six kilometers north-east of Nairobi's central business district. It is a notorious area for prostitution and several attacks on the women have been documented in recent years.

On arrival I meet a young woman preparing to interview some of the organisations' service users. She introduces herself to me as Catherine Barker from The Futures Group, and explains that she is an intern working on a research project to measure how stigma against 'sex workers' can cause a barrier to accessing healthcare. Nairobi is one of the four sites chosen and Mwangi and her team have clearly done a great job in getting women interested in taking part in the research. The courtyard area is thronging with women, some sleeping, others smoking and chatting. By the time Mwangi arrives for our appointment, there is a queue of about 50 women around the building.

The BHESP is a peer-led support and health service for women who are at high risk of HIV. Partly funded by the Global Fund to Fight AIDS, Tuberculosis and Malaria, the BHESP's key mission is, according to it website, 'to influence policy and facilitate provision of quality health services, human rights awareness, legal services and economic empowerment for sex workers, WSW, women using drugs and bar hostesses in Kenya'.

Mwangi is warm, open and very confident. I follow her into a small office and explain my research. Mwangi is surprised when I explain my position on the sex trade and my support for criminalising the buyers. BHESP's position is to support blanket decriminalisation. I check with Mwangi if that included pimping and brothel owning as well as those selling sex, and she confirms that yes, it includes all aspects of the sex trade.

BHESP was born out of the AIDS crisis. Mwangi, a member of The Global Sex Workers' Alliance, an editor for its magazine, and Chair of African Sex Workers' Alliance, is listed as one of the authors of the *Lancet* article[49] from the 2014 special edition. She used to be a bar worker from which she engaged in part-time prostitution. Mwangi explains how women in bar-based prostitution came together to form an alliance: 'We started as women working in the bars where we saw that there was a lot of violence' she says. '1998 was when HIV was really affecting us in the bars more than anywhere else in the country.'

It was common, Mwangi tells me, for buyers to demand sex without a condom. I ask her how decriminalising the pimps and traffickers will help reduce violence and, subsequently, HIV. She replies: 'If they

---

[49]Shannon, K.; Strathdee, S.; et al. (2014, Jul 21.) *Global epidemiology of HIV among female sex workers: Influence of structural determinants.* In The Lancet. Retrieved 15 June 2017, from http://www.thelancet.com/journals/lancet/article/PIIS0140-6736(14)60931-4/abstract.

decriminalise and [we can] work with the sex workers, and work with the pimps ... we will be able to manage the pimps, we will be able to manage the brothel owners, we will have a kind of accountability to the sex workers through organisations like ours'. The idea that an organisation such as the BHESP could control pimps and traffickers seems ridiculous. Those selling and brokering women in prostitution are only interested in profit. There is more profit for them in sex without a condom than there is with. The women are desperately poor and have little option—if a punter is demanding unsafe sex, she is unlikely to either be able to, or choose to, refuse.

For Courtney and many of the survivors I interviewed for this book, so-called harm minimisation or reduction approaches, such as those adopted by the majority of service providers funded by AIDS money, can only be justified if it is one aspect of the support offered to women and girls in the sex trade.

'I don't disagree with the whole concept of harm reduction when implemented as part of a full project', says Courtney. 'I think some places in the world have done that but here we have not. We warehouse the most poor and desolate women who are the most at risk and put them in the one location, give men free access and say that's harm elimination. That's not harm elimination, that's harming.'

Conclusion

The language of 'human rights' has been successfully co-opted by the movement to undermine the rights of prostituted women. There exists an orthodoxy among those in the HIV prevention business. How would decriminalisation ensure safe workplaces? Which other 'industry' that is currently acknowledged to be unsafe then becomes safer with complete deregulation?

The global labour movement started because history (particularly industrialisation) proved that without regulation, the minimum standards of safety, wages and workers' rights are upheld. In the current debate, 'meaningful involvement of sex workers' seems to really mean 'those who stand to profit most from a deregulated sex trade'.

Bill Gates, George Soros, the WHO, the UN and AI—all so-called human rights defenders and all supporters of blanket decriminalisation of the sex trade—could be seen as playing the role that the late nineteenth/early twentieth-century industrialists played in finding ways to ensure that there was unfettered access to cheap, disempowered labour.

HIV prevention cannot possibly be effective until the structure of sexual inequality is challenged as a core component of HIV prevention policy and programmes. We are not close to this yet. Over the years, substantial funding has found its way to organisations and individuals involved in pimping, brothel keeping and even trafficking. In the next chapter, I uncover some of the criminal elements allowed to flourish in the sex trade and ask: How have these people been allowed to hide in plain sight?

8

Fighting for Rights, or Parasites?

In this chapter I explore Ireland's campaign to criminalise men's demand for prostitution, and to fully decriminalise those who sell sex. This is a case study of how the sex trade profiteers in the Republic and Northern Ireland have joined forces with those who claim to be campaigning for rights of those in prostitution. It is a detailed study of how the biggest pimps in the Republic and Northern Ireland campaigned against the Nordic model in order to ensure that their business is protected.

The law criminalising demand has been operational in Northern Ireland since 2015, and the Republic of Ireland in March 2017, despite powerful opposition. The sex trade surreptitiously attempted to influence the outcome of the debate. Escort-Ireland/UglyMugs.ie is an illustrative case study of the sex trade business model.

Turn off the Red Light and Turn of the Blue Light

Turn off the Red Light (TORL) is an umbrella movement uniting a diverse range of more than 70 organisations with an aim to abolish prostitution/sex trafficking in Ireland by criminalising the sex buyers. The

© The Author(s) 2017
J. Bindel, *The Pimping of Prostitution*,
DOI 10.1057/978-1-137-55890-9_8

TORL campaign launched in February 2011 with a series of confronting billboards that drew public attention to the men fuelling the demand for an industry that thrives on the exploitation of vulnerable women and girls.

Almost immediately afterwards, a counter campaign arguing against the Nordic model emerged. Named Turn off the Blue Light (TOBL), it was an attempt to conjure an image of "prudish moralists sticking their sex obsessed noses into the bedrooms of sexually liberated and empowered women"[1]. In a canny misappropriation of the feminist ideal of liberation from exploitation, TOBL's marketing strategy used stock photographs of models of a range of ethnicities posing as 'sex workers', boldly pronouncing: "I chose the job that suits my needs". TOBL's website and advertising material appeared to be better resourced financially compared to the grassroots activism of TORL.

I had heard rumours that Britain's infamous pimp Peter McCormick was bankrolling it, but had no proof of this. I am informed by members of TORL—who host their webpage on the domain turnofftheredlight. ie—that another domain (turnofftheredlight.com) had been purchased and was directing "misspelled" traffic to the TOBL website.

Soon after the launch of TOBL, suspicions about McCormick were confirmed. In late 2012 I had spotted a news item written by investigative reporter Eamon Dillon.[2] I immediately brought this development to the attention of Escort-Ireland via @SexworkIE (its former Twitter feed) for a right of reply. There was no response from Escort-Ireland and the article remained online.[3] Numerous other news agencies took up the story, the TOBL website ceased to operate[4] and the campaign followed suit. Enter UglyMugs.ie.[5]

---

[1]https://www.pinterest.co.uk/pin/489414684475523302/. Accessed 29th August 2017.

[2]Dillon, E. (2014, Mar 4.) *Brothel cash goes to internet kingpin linked to legalisation campaign.* In Sunday World. Retrieved 15 June 2017, from www.sundayworld.com/news/crimedesk/brothel-cash-goes-to-internet-kingpin.

[3]I have confirmed in correspondence with Eamon Dillon that at no stage during his ongoing investigations were his reports responded to with any legal sanction by Peter McCormick et al. I acknowledge Dillon's professionalism, candour and willingness to assist in my report of McCormick.

[4]According to Internet Archive 'Way Back Machine' the webpage www.turnoffthebluelight.ie was first archived on April 29 2011 and last on 02 June 2013.

[5]Ugliemugs.ie operates as a distinct organisation from other Ugly Mugs campaigns found elsewhere throughout the world including the UK (known as National Uglymugs: a registered charity) and Australia.

Escort-Ireland and Peter McCormick

Before outlining the modus operandi of UglyMugs.ie it will be helpful to have a look at McCormick and Escort-Ireland, which he controls through his family and various associates. McCormick, a former Royal Ulster Constabulary reserve police officer,[6] was a notorious brothel owner in Ireland. McCormick and other members of his 12-man gang were arrested and charged in the 1990s for brothel keeping: a crime for which he was eventually convicted and sentenced.[7] In 2003, McCormick said he had "retired" from running brothels and handed over control of his business to his then 18-year-old son Mark McCormick. Peter McCormick's lawyer said at his court appearance that his client was retiring to run a bed and breakfast. In August 2004, McCormick was sentenced to four months in prison for threatening behaviour, and his partner Audrey Campbell was fined €450 for a breach of the peace in Dublin.[8]

In 2005, Mark McCormick came under notice of the same police task force that arrested his father, but it was not until 2010 when he was brought before the Court, charged with running his father's brothels. When Mark McCormick was arrested his laptop was logged on as an administrator to Escort-Ireland. Women in the brothel he ran told Irish police they thought the brothel/apartments were owned/run by Peter McCormick, years after Peter claimed to have 'retired'. The court heard that the profits were being split between father and son.[9] Mark McCormick was sentenced to a term of imprisonment of two and a half years (with 14 months suspended) and fined €5000.[10] At the time of Mark

---

[6]Barnes, C. (2014, Mar 2.) *Loaded Ex-RUC officer was the king of sleaze.* In Belfast Telegraph. Retrieved 15 June 2017 from High Beam Research www.highbeam.com/doc/1P2-35754486.html.

[7]Ugliemugs.ie operates as a distinct organisation from other Ugly Mugs campaigns found elsewhere throughout the world including the UK (known as National Uglymugs: a registered charity) and Australia.

[8]Anon. (2003, May 25.) *Exposed: The RUC man turned pimp.* In Sunday Life.

[9]Irish Times. (2004, Oct 8.) *Man jailed in absence for breach of peace.* In Irish Times. Retrieved 15 June 2017, from www.irishtimes.com/news/man-jailed-in-absence-for-breach-of-peace-1.1160920.

[10]Sheehan, M. (2010, May 16.) *The father, son, their 'Bible' and unholy alliances.* In Belfast Telegraph. Retrieved 15 June 2017, from www.independent.ie/irish-news/courts/the-father-son-their-bible-and-unholy-alliances-26655479.html.

McCormick's arrest, police uncovered a detailed spreadsheet on a laptop computer. Fingerprints subsequently recovered by the police on this laptop belonged to Mark McCormick.[11] There was very good reason for the McCormick's fanatical control and possession of data, as we shall soon see.

By this time, Peter McCormick incorporated E Designers Ltd in London to control Escort-Ireland as a bonafide business directed by his partner Audrey Campbell.[12] In May 2013 Lee Campbell, the son of Audrey Campbell, subsequently took over E Designers Ltd.[13] In 2014 Escort-Ireland reportedly moved its operations and staff to Spain and are now trading as Lazarus Trading SL, where it claims to employ a multi-lingual staff of 30 employees.[14] This source reported that Audrey Campbell of Escort-Ireland/Lazarus Trading SL had refused to divulge its location.

I have obtained a copy of the business records of Lazarus Trading SL and discovered that Lee Campbell is listed as its nominal administrator[15]; a further Spanish company report I have reviewed for Lazarus Trading SL records that Audrey Rita Campbell occupies sole proprietorship and an 'Alexander Dominick' occupies the position of its administrator.[16] Like Mark McCormick before him, Lee Campbell was barely an adult when he took on the position of managing Escort-Ireland's multi-million dollar empire.

---

[11]Sheehan, M. (2010, May 16.) *The father, son, their 'Bible' and unholy alliances.* In Belfast Telegraph. Retrieved 15 June 2017, from www.independent.ie/irish-news/courts/the-father-son-their-bible-and-unholy-alliances-26655479.html.

[12]E Designers. Retrieved 15 June 2017, from web.archive.org https://web.archive.org/web/20070123132409/http://www.edesigners.co.uk/.

Escort Ireland. Retrieved 15 June 2017, from web.archive.org https://web.archive.org/web/20000510054108/http://www.escortireland.com/index2.html.

Dillon, E. (2014, Mar 4.) *Brothel cash goes to internet kingpin linked to legalisation campaign.* In Sunday World. Retrieved 15 June 2017, from www.sundayworld.com/news/crimedesk/brothel-cash-goes-to-internet-kingpin.

Companies House. E Designers Limited. Retrieved 15 June 2017, from https://beta.companieshouse.gov.uk/company/04923492/officers.

[13]Ibid.

[14]Cusack, J. (2010, Jul 25.) *It's business as usual for sex trade.* In Irish Independent. Retrieved 15 June 2017, from www.independent.ie/opinion/analysis/its-business-as-usual-for-sex-trade-26666139.html.

[15]Lazarus Trading SL. Retrieved 15 June 2017, from http://www.infocif.es/ficha-empresa/lazarus-trading-sl.

[16]Lazarus Trading SL. Retrieved 15 June 2017, from https://www.infoempresa.com/en-in/es/company/lazarus-trading-sl.

Escort-Ireland, for all intents and purposes, is a website advertising women to punters in a similar way to how homes are marketed to prospective buyers. It is, in the common parlance, 'user-friendly'. Escort-Ireland works by geographically cataloguing women across all of Ireland into profiles containing full-face and/or body photographs, physical description, rates and "what's on offer".

A sizeable proportion, of the biographies of the women's profiles appear to be written by 'management'. Escort-Ireland's punters forum where the "sexual performance" of women is rated in graphic detail, is its true face, proving that the best evidence against the sex trade is sex trade advertising.

A survey of punters on Escort Ireland[17] found significant percentages of them were quite happy to use underage, trafficked and abused women.

A Business Opportunity

How and why Peter McCormick established Escort-Ireland/E Designers Ltd is a remarkable story in itself.

In 2010 the Criminal Justice (Public Order) Act (1994), which criminalises the publication and distribution of an advertisement for a brothel or "prostitute", was being enforced by the Gardai (Republic of Ireland's national police service) to the letter, due to a public outcry following number of horrific acts of violence against prostituted women. That same year, Mike Hogan, the publisher of *In Dublin*, was convicted and fined £50,000 after he was found earning £400,000 a year in paid advertising from Ireland's sex trade.[18] That was the final nail in the coffin for the print advertising of prostitution in Ireland. Peter McCormick was determined to resurrect the advertising of prostitution; and did so online, outside the Irish jurisdiction.

---

[17]Escort Ireland. Retrieved 15 June 2017, from https://www.escort-ireland.com/press/escort-advertising-survey.html.

[18]RTE. (2000, Oct 18.) *In Dublin publisher fined £50,000 for advertising brothels.* In RTE. Retrieved 15 June 2017, from www.rte.ie/news/2000/1018/9470-hogan/.

Peter McCormick reportedly pulled it off with the help of his understudy and son, Mark McCormick, who is a gifted computer programmer.[19] Peter McCormick also relocated Escort-Ireland to London—well outside of Ireland's jurisdiction. Moreover, such is the sophistication of its operation, it was reported Escort-Ireland cyber-attacked competitors attempting a foothold in advertising Ireland's lucrative sex trade, thereby firming its monopoly of this promising niche market from the outset.[20]

Finally, the nature and demographic of prostitution in Ireland had become increasingly impacted upon by globalisation. The formation of a common European Union, the porousness of its borders, its massively increased wealth, and the increasing availability of cut-throat priced international travel, all contributed to the unchecked flow of women and girls sold into Ireland's sex trade.

The Nordic Model

In 2011, a joint Irish/Romania police operation exposed the massive trafficking of women controlled by Romanian organised crime gang Ghinea/Ghenosu that sparked significant public debate.[21] A year later an undercover news investigation by Ireland's national broadcaster RTÉ entitled 'Profiting from Prostitution',[22] led by Paul Maguire, was broadcast at a time when many in Ireland were perhaps beginning to reflect

---

[19]Barnes, C. (2014, Mar 2.) *Loaded Ex-RUC officer was the king of sleaze*. In Belfast Telegraph. Retrieved 15 June 2017, from High Beam Research www.highbeam.com/doc/1P2-35754486. html.

Belfast Telegraph. (2010, May 15.) *Jail for Ulsterman who ran brothel network in Dublin*. In Belfast Telegraph. Retrieved 15 June 2017, from www.belfasttelegraph.co.uk/news/jail-for-ulsterman-who-ran-brothel-network-in-dublin-28535797.html.

[20]Dillon, E. (4 March 2014) *Pimp and proper*. In Sunday World. Retrieved 15 June 2017, from http://www.sundayworld.com/news/crimedesk/brothel-cash-goes-to-internet-kingpin.   Accessed 28th August 2017.

[21]Irish Independent. (2011, Aug 30.) *Dublin 'call-girl gang' charged in Romania*. In Irish Independent. Retrieved 15 June 2017, from http://www.independent.ie/irish-news/dublin-call-girl-gang-charged-in-romania-26766210.html.

[22]http://www.rte.ie/about/en/press-office/press-releases/2012/0206/293201-040212primetime/. Accessed 28th August 2017.

upon the abject failings of its prostitution policy. The award-winning investigation determined that Escort-Ireland had 20,000 unique profiles of women on its database, of which at least 700 were being advertised on any given day with each profile earning €100 a week for Escort-Ireland. Escort-Ireland was earning €840,000 a year. The investigation found that Peter McCormick and Audrey Campbell have made millions of Euros from the suffering and exploitation of vulnerable women and girls.

The programme further uncovered the fact that at least 400 women were being shunted from town to town on a weekly basis to maintain "client interest" with an expectation they would be sold to punters 16 hours a day, seven days a week. Sex without a condom was part of the "service" they were expected to provide. Disturbingly, the men who advertised trafficked women on Escort-Ireland included notorious convicted pimps TJ Carrol and Di Wei[23]: Carol trafficked women from Africa into Ireland[24] and high ranking Triad gangster Wei ran an operation that moved women from China into Ireland.[25]

Escort-Ireland/E Designers Ltd sought to defend its operations in Ireland by claiming the evidence against them was improperly obtained by intruding on the "privacy" of prostituted women; an allegation that a legal representative for RTÉ counterclaimed was defamatory.[26] In the RTÉ program, Escort-Ireland/E Designers Ltd said via Audrey Campbell that operations were outside of Irish jurisdiction and they had "no control over advertising content". Outrageously, despite the laissez-faire claim of "no control", the terms and conditions of

---

[23]Dillon, E. (2014, Mar 4.) *Brothel cash goes to internet kingpin linked to legalisation campaign.* In Sunday World. Retrieved 15 June 2017, from www.sundayworld.com/news/crimedesk/brothel-cash-goes-to-internet-kingpin.

[24]Lally, C. (2010, May 8.) *A pimp's family business.* In Irish Times. Retrieved 15 June 2017, www.irishtimes.com/news/a-pimp-s-family-business-1.662825.

[25]Dillon, E. (2014, Mar 4.) *Brothel cash goes to internet kingpin linked to legalisation campaign.* In Sunday World. Retrieved 15 June 2017, from www.sundayworld.com/news/crimedesk/brothel-cash-goes-to-internet-kingpin.

[26]Cusack, J. (2013, Feb 17.) *'Escort' web firm hits out at RTE sex work expose.* In Irish Independent. Retrieved 15 June 2017, from www.independent.ie/irish-news/escort-web-firm-hits-out-at-rte-sex-work-expose-29076081.html.

Escort-Ireland make clear that "swear words, eg 'fuck', 'cum', 'cunt' are not allowed in escort descriptions".[27]

Fuel to the fire was the 2013 publication of Irish woman Rachel Moran's widely acclaimed book *Paid For*: a powerful memoir based on her experiences of prostitution from the age of 15 on the streets of Dublin. Moran's book inspired sex trade survivor led movements including SPACE (Survivors of Prostitution Abuse Calling for Enlightenment) International.

A follow-up investigation by RTÉ[28] in November 2015 titled 'Sex for Sale' determined that prostitution/sex trafficking operations in Ireland were largely, if not exclusively, controlled by 20 organised gangs. The sex trade had dramatically increased, prices for 'services' had plummeted, 98% of advertised prostituted women were now non-indigenous Irish, and prostituted women were engaging in "unprotected", dangerous and humiliating practices. Viewers were left in no doubt that international crime gangs now controlled Ireland's burgeoning sex-trade. It was at this time that the Governments of Ireland on both sides of the border were seriously considering the Nordic Model as a viable prostitution policy.

Enter UglyMugs.ie and Lucy Smith—The Face of Escort-Ireland?

Escort-Ireland was a brand tainted by its connections to the McCormick pimps, and to its business model of profiting from the lucrative advertisements of women trafficked into Ireland's sex trade. It had no hope of contributing directly to the public policy debate on prostitution in Ireland, and needed a public friendly face—such as a "cause" to fight for the 'rights' of prostituted women.

Accordingly it latched onto the international Ugly Mugs campaign (a widely known so-called harm-minimisation model enabling prostituted

---

[27]Escort Ireland. *Advertising terms and conditions*. Retrieved 15 June 2017, from www.escort-ireland.com/help/escort-legal-information.html#advertising-terms.

[28]The Journal. (2015, Nov 30.) *Investigation details systematic movement of prostitutes around Ireland's towns*. In The Journal. Retrieved 15 June 2017, from www.thejournal.ie/prostitution-investigation-2475654-Nov2015/.

women to share information about particularly violent punters) and nationalised an independent Irish variant of it. Safe IQ Ltd was incorporated in London in August 2013 to control the activities of UglyMugs. ie, and a sophisticated world-class mobile phone app[29] with its impressive design and functionality was immediately introduced. Nonetheless there were telltale clues of its dodgy genesis; not least of which is that UglyMugs.ie seamlessly integrates with the Escort-Ireland website.

Safe IQ Ltd 'operates' from a virtual office in London. It is on public record that Lucy Smith is Director of UglyMugs.ie. This is the name she provides to various parliamentary and other official committees in which she gives evidence on behalf of UglyMugs.ie.

While Safe IQ Ltd generates no income in the financial year ending 2016, Strada Media Ltd turned over £154,195 (albeit with a profit after recorded expenses of less than £5000). The balance sheet for Strada Media Ltd is similar in all the years of its operations and I was curious as to the source of its income. A well-connected source informed me that the totality of Strada's income for one particular year were deposits made from Lazarus Trading SL according to financial documents they had inspected. I raised this allegation with Lucy Smith for comment and while she admitted 'working' for Strada Media Ltd, she flatly denied any income derived from Escort-Ireland or indeed any other company related to the 'adult industry'.

It was discovered by the journalist Eamon Dillon that website domain www.UglyMugs.ie (the website address of UglyMugs.ie) was first purchased by Audrey Campbell and registered to E Designers Ltd,[30] which created a lasting fingerprint.

Sex Trade Propaganda and Control of the Prostitution Narrative

UglyMugs.ie is a prodigious producer of research and 'newsletters', the recommendations of which it proactively disseminates to academics, government, policy makers, police and the media.

---

[29]I use Uglymugs.ie (the app) and Uglymugs.ie (the organisation) interchangeably.
[30]Dillon, E. (4 March 2014) *Pimp and proper*. In Sunday World. Retrieved 15 June 2017, from http://www.sundayworld.com/news/crimedesk/brothel-cash-goes-to-internet-kingpin.

Its foremost piece of research is a self-reported online survey, completed by just under 200 prostituted persons in Ireland. The survey is reproduced as a 57-page document[31]: 'Crime and Abuse Experienced by Sex Workers in Ireland: Victimisation Survey.' The online survey was a series of questions completed by "195 female male and trans* escorts (indoor 'sex workers') in Ireland",[32] which questioned the nature and practice of their prostitution, as well as experiences of violence, drug and alcohol use, condom use and experiences of crime.

A time-consuming survey, prepared in English and dependent on internet access, is neither a broad sample nor a representative analysis of the nature of prostitution in Ireland. The survey does not appear to be peer-reviewed or undertaken with any ethical approval and contradicts existing evidence on how the legal sex trade is inextricably tied to significant increases in trafficking for prostitution, expansion of the sex trade and the prostitution of children.[33] The survey reckons "media exposure" by newspaper and other media outlets to be the singularly most oppressive form of violence against prostituted women, causing 75% "significant worry"[34]: "Fear of media exposure is very high, even higher than fear of crime, with three out of four escorts in Ireland 'worried' or 'very worried' about being exposed as an escort in the newspapers or other media."

---

[31]UglyMugs.ie. (2013, Sept.) *Crime and abuse experienced by sex workers in Ireland: Victimisation survey.* Retrieved 15 June 2017, from http://uglymugs.ie/wp-content/uploads/ugly-mugs-september-2013.pdf.

[32]UglyMugs.ie. (2013, Sept.) *Crime and abuse experienced by sex workers in Ireland: Victimisation survey.* Retrieved 15 June 2017, from http://uglymugs.ie/wp-content/uploads/ugly-mugs-september-2013.pdf, p. 2.

[33]Cho, S.; Dreher, A.; Neumayer E. (2012, Jan 16.) *Does legalised prostitution increase human trafficking?* In World Development. 41 (1), 2013. 67–82.

Ekberg, G. (2004, Oct.) *The Swedish law that prohibits the purchase of a sexual service: Best practices for prevention of prostitution and trafficking in human beings.* In Violence Against Women. Sage. 10 (10). 1187–1218.

Waltman, M. (2011.) *Prohibiting sex purchasing and ending trafficking: The Swedish prostitution law.* Michigan Journal of International Law. 133, 133–57, pp. 146–148.

Waltman, M. (2011, Sept-Oct.) *Sweden's prohibition of purchase of sex: The law's reasons, impact, and potential.* In Women's Studies International Forum. Elsevier. 34 (5). 449–474.

[34]Waltman, M. (2011, Sept-Oct.) *Sweden's prohibition of purchase of sex: The law's reasons, impact, and potential.* In Women's Studies International Forum. Elsevier. 34 (5). 2.

The report contains a critique of the law to criminalise demand: "If brought in, we believe the Swedish model would exasperate the current problems facing sex workers, by driving sex work further underground, further stigmatising sex workers, and enabling crime and abuse to thrive. We would not expect sex work to decline as a result, but we would expect a more vulnerable sex worker population, more organised crime and an increase in crime against and abuse of sex workers. Sex workers in Ireland are the victims of a strong media desire to repeatedly expose sex workers and apparent sex trafficking victims. Media abuse of sex workers is a very serious problem in Ireland and must be challenged".[35]

In reality, the harassment of prostituted women and survivors of the sex trade is perpetrated by pimps and other profiteers. One example is Anna, a Romanian woman who was raped and tortured in preparation for Ireland's sex trade. Anna's testimony shocked Ireland: particularly Lord Morrow whose Private Member's Bill was the genesis of parliamentary debate in Northern Ireland. Anna was sold in Ireland's sex trade for €20,000 whereupon she was raped by as many as 20 men a day. Anna's abuse earned her traffickers many hundreds of Euros every day.[36]

Soon after the scandal made the press, a webpage forum reportedly linked to McCormick launched a smear campaign against Anna, who was described as "a thing" and "a liar",[37] despite her testimony being accepted as legitimate by the Serious Organised Crime Agency and the UK Human Trafficking Centre. Dublin based blogger Wendy Lyon also dismissed Anna's experience in a series of tweets to *Belfast Newsletter* journalist Philip Bradfield, denying the credibility of the young woman's story. Bradfield[38] demanded to know what possible further proof could appease Lyon.

---

[35]Waltman, M. (2011, Sept-Oct.) *Sweden's prohibition of purchase of sex: The law's reasons, impact, and potential.* In Women's Studies International Forum. Elsevier. 34 (5). 52.

[36]Phelan, S. (2013, Nov 17.) *A woman trafficked into the sex trade in Ireland tells her story.* In Irish Independent. Retrieved 15 June 2017, from www.independent.ie/irish-news/a-woman-trafficked-into-the-sex-trade-in-ireland-tells-her-story-29760573.html.

[37]Dillon, E. (2013, Nov 13.) *Hate campaign targets sex trafficking victim.* In Sunday World. Retrieved 15 June 2017, from www.sundayworld.com/news/crimedesk/hate-campaign-targets-sex-trafficking-victim.

[38]News Letter. (2014, Oct 19.) *Sex trafficking survivor tells why she supports DUP bill.* In News Letter. Retrieved 15 June 2017, from http://www.newsletter.co.uk/news/crime/sex-trafficking-survivor-tells-why-she-supports-dup-bill-1-6366603.

Uglymugs.ie "acknowledges"[39] the rights of prostituted women to have exit services made available to them, it derogates from this claim by lobbying aggressively to defund the very organisations that provide these services most effectively, such as Women's Aid, and to divert this funding to sex trade organisations that pretend to.[40]

Escort-Ireland/UglyMugs.ie is in a position to exact influence on prostitution policy in Ireland. Innumerable letters have been written by them to various organisations relevant to prostitution policy pushing the statistics they have produced.[41] They participate in feminist conferences,[42] academic committees,[43] academic seminars,[44] policing committees[45] and festivals,[46] putting forward the pro-decriminalisation view of the prostitution narrative.

---

[39]For example pp. 43, 51 and 53 of UglyMugs.ie (2013, September 2013). Crime and Abuse Experienced by Sex Workers in Ireland. UglyMugs.ie. http://uglymugs.ie/wp-content/uploads/ugly-mugs-september-2013.pdf and Northern Ireland Assembly (2014).

Official Report (Hansard) Human Trafficking and Exploitation (Further Provisions and Support for Victims) Bill: UglyMugs.ie. Online: http://www.niassembly.gov.uk/assembly-business/official-report/committee-minutes-of-evidence/session-2013-2014/january-2014/human-trafficking-and-exploitation-further-provisions-and-support-for-victims-bill-uglymugsie/.

[40]For example Smith, L. (2015, April 20) 'Submission to Department of Health, Social Services and Publics Safety (DHSSPS) on exiting sex work strategy'. Uglymugs.ie. Online: https://uglymugs.ie/wp-content/uploads/Submission-to-Department-of-Health.pdf.

[41]Uglymugs.ie (2016, February 27). Letter to NI Justice Committee. Online: https://uglymugs.ie/2016/09/27/letter-ni-justice-committee/.

[42]www.thetimes.co.uk/tto/irishnews/article4666981.ece.

[43]Uglymugs.ie is an associate member of Irish Research Council funded Commercial Sex Research Network Ireland (CSRNI) together with Laura Lee and Niall Mulligan (HIV Ireland). Dr Graham Ellison is a Network Member of this organisation. This information was obtained from its website: http://csrnetworkireland.com/core-network-members/. Of interest Niall Mulligan, Laura Lee, and Dr Paul Ryan are also Working Group and/or Board members of Sexworkers Alliance Ireland (SWAI); Dr Paul Ryan was a further member of the Advisory Group alongside Dr Nicola Mai for Dr Susann Huschke's research project. This information was drawn from its website: http://sexworkersallianceireland.org/who-we-are/.

[44]It is of interest that Doctor Paul Maginn was a co-presenter. 4th November 2015, 10.00-13.00: Sex Work Research and Policy: Follow-up Session to the ECP Evidence Gathering Event, organised by, FemGenSex, Middlesex University, Venue: College Building Room C210, London. Online: www.york.ac.uk/media/sociology/research/currentresearch/swrh/SWRH%20newsletter%20Nov%201%202015.pdf.

[45]Sex Workers Liaison Group (2016). Minutes of Sex Workers Liaison Group. Online: www.octf.gov.uk/OCTF/media/OCTF/documents/publications/Human%20Trafficking/Approved-Minutes-of-Sex-Workers-Liaison-Group.pdf?ext=.pdf.

[46]Bliss Festival (2015). Bliss Festival 2015 Talks Panel. Online: //www.blissfestival.org/p/summer-festival-2015-talks-panel.html.

Escort-Ireland/UglyMugs.ie contributed to the parliamentary committees debating prostitution in Ireland: the Republic of Ireland's Oireachtas Committee on Domestic and Sexual Violence and Northern Ireland's Stormont Justice Committee on Trafficking and Prostitution, which were conducted simultaneously over 2013/2014.

Sex Trade Lobby—Lucy Smith for Uglymugs.ie

Ugly-mugs.ie regularly accuses many of the organisations involved in TORL of being "religious fundamentalists" and "anti-sex". Ruhama,[47] for example, are open about having been founded several decades ago by a religious group (as were the majority of NGOs in Ireland at that time) but have for many years run on an entirely secular basis as a fully transparent registered NGO. They evidently have no religious agenda and work tirelessly to support hundreds of prostituted women with free non-judgmental services every year. Its current chief executive, Sarah Benson, is a secular feminist. The fact is that Ruhama, and other key members of the TORL campaign who work directly with victims of prostitution and trafficking, witness the reality of the sex trade.

In addition, Smith insists that crimes against prostituted/trafficked women be censored and not reported by media.[48] At the Oireachtas Committee,[49] debating aspects of the Sexual Offences Bill[50] introduced by Justice Minister Frances Fitzgerald, Smith was in fighting form:

Ms Lucy Smith:	I call on the committee to act to stop the extensive abuse of sex workers and sex trafficking victims by the media. I note

---

[47]http://www.ruhama.ie/.

[48]Ellison, G.; Smith, L. (2016). *Hate crime legislation against sex workers In Ireland: Lessons in policy and practice.* In Haynes, A.; Schweppe, J.; Taylor, S. (Eds.) (2017.) *Critical perspectives on hate crime contributions from the island of Ireland.* London: Palgrave Macmillan.

[49]Oireachatas (2014, February 26). Joint Committee on Justice, Defence and Equality Debate. http://oireachtasdebates.oireachtas.ie/debates%20authoring/debateswebpack.nsf/committeetakes/JUJ2014022600007.

[50]The Bill included a raft of provisions including for example the "proximity of age defence" and measures to strengthen defences against online predators.

	that at the last hearings the committee asked Mr Maguire of RTÉ what became of the group of…
Chairman (David Stanton):	I would prefer it if you did not name people.
Ms Lucy Smith:	… what had become of those women at that point was that they had been stalked by the *Sunday World* [Eamon Dillon]. Photographs of them in an undressed state had been taken pervertedly [sic]…
Chairman:	I would prefer it you did not name people.
Ms Lucy Smith:	….We need to stop giving all the State funding for support to sex workers and sex trafficking victims to [name organisations] … all the independent research comes from [names organisations] … [allowing] a completely false picture of sex work to persist …
Chairman:	Please do not identify organisations. At the start I referred to not naming organisations and entities by name.[51]

The Northern Ireland's Stormont Justice Committee[52] on Trafficking and Prostitution is a case study of what occurs when a Committee considering prostitution policy travels to Sweden to study the Nordic model and listens to survivors of prostitution.

---

[51]Dillon, Eamon (2014, March 4). Brothel cash goes to internet kingpin linked to legalisation campaign. Sunday World. Online: www.sundayworld.com/news/crimedesk/brothel-cash-goes-to-internet-kingpin.

[52]Northern Ireland Assembly. (2014, Jan 30.) *Official report (Hansard). Human trafficking and exploitation (further provisions and support for victims) bill: UglyMugs.ie.* Retrieved 15 June 2017, from www.niassembly.gov.uk/globalassets/documents/official-reports/justice/2013-2014/140130_humantraffickingetcbilluglymugs.pdf

The evidence[53] provided by Smith was closely questioned. Smith's links to Peter McCormick, Mark McCormick, and Audrey Campbell and the enmeshed entity that is Escort-Ireland/UglyMugs.ie was exposed, as was Smith's original claim not to know Peter McCormick.

Mr Wells: We exchanged e-mails, you may recall.
Ms Smith: Yes.
Mr Wells: When I originally put the question to you about Mr Peter McCormick, you said that you had never heard of him.
Ms Smith: I am not going to comment on that person.
Mr Wells: And when I told you, you had then. The organisation that you are linked to transports 400 women [all of whom were advertised on Escort-Ireland] a week around various parts of Ireland.
Ms Smith: I really do not see the point of the question. I am not going to answer questions about Escort-Ireland.com. I am happy to talk about Ugly Mugs. I am happy even to talk about sex work generally in Ireland, but I am not going to answer a question about Escort-Ireland. com.
Mr Wells: I accept that. Let us not refer to the biggest prostitution website on professional prostitution in Ireland.

Why did Smith[54] fail to acknowledge Peter McCormick or elaborate on her relationship with Escort-Ireland?

---

[53]Northern Ireland Assembly (2014). Official Report (Hansard) Human Trafficking and Exploitation (Further Provisions and Support for Victims), Bill: UglyMugs.ie

Online: http://www.niassembly.gov.uk/assembly-business/official-report/committee-minutes-of-evidence/session-2013-2014/january-2014/human-trafficking-and-exploitation-further-provisions-and-support-for-victims-bill-uglymugsie/.

[54]Uglymugs.ie currently "acknowledges" a "relationship" between Escort-Ireland as it did at both the Oireachtas and Stormont committees. However this pre-emptive admission is in the form of a closed and compact statement which pretends disclosure but camouflages precisely the nature of the "relationship", any commercial arrangements, or an elaboration of the involvement of Peter McCormick and Mark McCormick.

I put this evidence direct via email to Smith for comment. Smith replied that she has had a longstanding history with Escort-Ireland, but that her "employment" was in the capacity of "consultant"; a position that she elected not to elaborate upon.

Laura Lee, an associate of Smith, also presented evidence before Northern Ireland's Justice Committee on behalf of the International Union of Sex Workers (IUSW).[55]

Sex Trade Lobby—International Union of Sex Workers

Lee,[56] a "professional dominatrix" and student of psychology was presented as the "voice of sex workers". Her argument was equally clear: "sex work" is about worker's rights and human rights.

The Chairperson (Paul Givan) asked Lee: You say that you speak for the vast majority. I am trying to quantify that. Can you tell me how many sex workers you purport to speak for?

Ms Lee:	… estimates are that there are 80,000 sex workers in the UK.
The Chairperson:	Are they are all members of your international union?
Ms Lee:	No, they are not.
The Chairperson:	So, how many members does the International Union of Sex Workers have?
Ms Lee:	I am not entirely sure about that.

---

[55]Northern Ireland Assembly (2014). Official Report (Hansard) Human Trafficking and Exploitation (Further Provisions and Support for Victims) Bill: International Union of Sex Workers. Online: http://www.niassembly.gov.uk/assembly-business/official-report/committee-minutes-of-evidence/session-2013-2014/january-2014/human-trafficking-and-exploitation-further-provisions-and-support-for-victims-bill-international-union-of-sex-workers/.

[56]Wyatt, D. (2015, 1 December). What is it really like to work as a Dominatrix? The Independent. http://www.independent.co.uk/life-style/love-sex/whats-it-really-like-to-work-as-a-dominatrix-a6754541.html.

The Committee had already heard direct evidence from prostitution survivors including Rachel Moran[57] and Mia De Faoite. For both women, prostitution was the antithesis of choice and both support the Nordic model. So who are these 'sex worker' union members Lee advocates for who condemn the Nordic model, such as the International Union of Sex Workers who argue that prostitution is about choice and agency for women?

Mr Wells:	Are there any pimps or those who profit from organising sexual services in your International Union of Sex Workers?
Ms Lee:	Some of the members are managers, yes.
Mr Wells:	So, they are pimps.
Ms Lee:	Well, if you want to use that term, yes.
Mr Wells:	So, it is not just a union of sex workers; it is also those who control sex workers.
Ms Lee:	Yes.
Mr Wells:	Who make large amounts of money and control the lives of sex workers.
Ms Lee:	I cannot comment on how much money anybody else makes.
Mr Wells:	Would one of those be a Mr Douglas Fox?[58]
Ms Lee:	Yes.
Mr Wells:	Are you aware of Mr Douglas Fox's operations in the north of England?
Ms Lee:	I am, yes.
Mr Wells:	If one of your main supporters and funders is someone who has acknowledged that he runs a website selling sexual services, selling thousands of women every year, clearly that indicates a slightly different angle on what the International Union of Sex Workers means.[59]

---

[57]Northern Ireland Assembly (2014). Official Report (Hansard) Human Trafficking and Exploitation (Further Provisions and Support for Victims), Bill: SPACE Intnerational. http://www.niassembly.gov.uk/assembly-business/official-report/committee-minutes-of-evidence/session-2013-2014/january-2014/human-trafficking-and-exploitation-further-provisions-and-suport-for-victims-bill-space-international-/.

[58]Anna Human Trafficking. Retrieved 15 June 2017, from http://anna-human-trafficking-ireland.com.

[59]Dillon, E. (4 March 2014) *Pimp and proper.* In Sunday World. Retrieved 15 June 2017, from http://www.sundayworld.com/news/crimedesk/brothel-cash-goes-to-internet-kingpin.

Ms Lee:	I just do not see how that could undermine my personal credibility.[60]
Mr Wells:	How it would undermine it, Ms Lee ... is that, clearly, if those who support and perhaps fund your union have an incredibly high vested interest in selling the sexual services of women, you are not a union representing the ordinary woman on the street or in the flat; you are representing an organisation that makes vast amounts of money out of the sale of women.

Queen's University Belfast Academics

Dr Graham Ellison—considered to be Northern Ireland's academic expert on the sex trade—was a further witness to the Committee[61] (all references to him and Dr Susann Huschke are from the Hansard unless otherwise stated). Ellison was accompanied by his Queen's University colleague Huschke (whose research for the DOJ basically said there were no pimps in the Irish sex trade, only "bookers")[62]; now of the University of the Witwatersrand African Centre for Migration and Society, South Africa.[63]

Ellison had previously sent an email[64] to a feminist academic and campaigner who had earlier given evidence to the Committee in

---

[60]Matthews, R., Easton, H., Reynolds, L., Bindel, J., Young, L. 2014). *Exiting prostitution: A study in female desistance*. (London: Palgrave).

[61]Northern Ireland Assembly (2014). Official Report (Hansard) Human Trafficking and Exploitation (Further Provisions and Support for Victims) Bill: Dr Graham Ellison and Dr Susan Huschke, Queen University Belfast. Online: http://www.niassembly.gov.uk/assembly-business/official-report/committee-minutes-of-evidence/session-2013-2014/january-2014/human-trafficking-and-exploitation-further-provision-and-support-for-victims-bill-dr-graham-ellison-and-dr-susann-huschke-queens-university-belfast-/.

[62]https://www.justice-ni.gov.uk/publications/research-prostitution-northern-ireland.

[63]UglyMugs.ie. (2013, Sept.) *Crime and abuse experienced by sex workers in Ireland: Victimisation survey*. Retrieved 15 June 2017, from http://uglymugs.ie/wp-content/uploads/ugly-mugs-september-2013.pdf. p. 43, 51, 53.

[64]Northern Ireland Assembly. (2014, Jan 30.) *Official report (Hansard). Human trafficking and exploitation (further provisions and support for victims) bill: UglyMugs.ie*. Retrieved 15 June 2017, from www.niassembly.gov.uk/globalassets/documents/official-reports/justice/2013-2014/140130_humantraffickingetcbilluglymugs.pdf.

support of the Nordic Model. The feminist academic was unnamed by the Committee but nonetheless Ellison named her in his evidence. In his email—littered with expletives—Ellison aggressively demanded to know why she had "hooked up" with the "anti-feminist" Democratic Unionist Party (DUP) pushing a "biblical" view of prostitution which had "likely" led to the suicides of gay and lesbian[65] people because of its stance on same-sex marriage.[66]

When committee members raised the issue of the email, Ellison justified the abuse by claiming he and the witness shared "ideals" and that he had attempted to "talk her around". The Committee condemned his actions and subsequently wrote a formal complaint to his employer Queen's University Belfast,[67] which was widely reported in the Irish press.

Ellison repeatedly uses the moral panic term "privacy of the bedroom" in his evidence.

In his evidence, Ellison cited data he claimed proved trafficking was a grossly exaggerated "moral panic" where "victim narratives" are privileged over research.[68] In presentation of his research, Ellison disputed the evidence held by the Committee. The integrity of his data—and in particular the source from where it was derived—was called into question:

Mr Wells: As part of your research, have you had any contact with the International Union of Sex Workers or Escort-Ireland?

Dr Ellison: No.

---

[65]Smith, L. (2015, April 20.) *Submission to Department of Health, Social Services and Publics Safety (DHSSPS) on exiting sex work strategy.* Retrieved 15 June 2017, from https://uglymugs.ie/wp-content/uploads/Submission-to-Department-of-Health.pdf.

[66]Barnes, L. (2014, Aug 19.) *Ugly Mugs: 'An unacceptable breach of sex workers' privacy.* On The Conversation. Retrieved 15 June 2017, from https://theconversation.com/ugly-mugs-an-unacceptable-breach-of-sex-workers-privacy-30615.

[67]BBC (2014, January 30). DUP confronts QUB academic over 'gay suicides' claim. BBC News. http://www.bbc.com/news/uk-northern-ireland-25969374.

[68]Escort Ireland. (2016, Dec 1.) On Twitter.com. Retrieved 15 June 2017, from https://twitter.com/escortireland/status/804290551902244865.

Mr Wells:	And you have had no contact at all with Peter McCormick or his son from Escort-Ireland?[69]
Dr Ellison:	I have no idea who that is. I am sorry.[70, 71, 72]

Ellison then admits to very recently[73] viewing the RTÉ programme that investigated the activities of Peter McCormick and his operation Escort-Ireland.[74]

Mr Wells:	So you did not see the *Prime Time* programme on RTÉ...
Dr Ellison:	I did; I saw it the other night, yes.
Mr Wells:	The *Prime Time* programme revealed a whole cadre of women being moved weekly because men were demanding fresh partners...

I have reviewed a joint publication (published before his evidence) of Ellison and Dr Paul Maginn and it seems they knew of Escort-Ireland, including the conduct of its operations through E Designers Ltd:

---

[69]Uglymugs.ie. (2016, Feb 27). *Letter to NI Justice Committee*. Retrieved 15 June 2017, from https://uglymugs.ie/2016/09/27/letter-ni-justice-committee/.

[70]Coyne, E. (2016, Jan 16.) *Feminist event bars sex worker group*. In The Times. Retrieved 15 June 2017, from www.thetimes.co.uk/tto/irishnews/article4666981.ece.

[71]Uglymugs.ie is an associate member of Irish Research Council funded Commercial Sex Research Network Ireland (CSRNI) together with Laura Lee and Niall Mulligan (HIV Ireland). Dr Graham Ellison is a Network Member of this organisation. This information was obtained from its website: http://csrnetworkireland.com/core-network-members/. Of interest Niall Mulligan, Laura Lee, and Dr Paul Ryan are also Working Group and/or Board members of Sexworkers Alliance Ireland (SWAI); Dr Paul Ryan was a further member of the Advisory Group alongside Dr Nicola Mai for Dr Susann Huschke's research project. This information was drawn from its website: http://sexworkersallianceireland.org/who-we-are/..

[72]It is of interest that Dr Paul Maginn was a co-presenter on 2015, Nov 4: 'Sex Work Research and Policy: Follow-up Session to the ECP Evidence Gathering Event, organised by, FemGenSex, Middlesex University, Venue: College Building Room C210, London.' Retrieved 15 June 2017, from www.york.ac.uk/media/sociology/research/currentresearch/swrh/SWRH%20newsletter%20Nov%201%202015.pdf.

[73]Sex Workers Liaison Group. (2016). *Minutes of Sex Workers Liaison Group*. Retrieved 15 June 2017, from www.octf.gov.uk/OCTF/media/OCTF/documents/publications/Human%20Trafficking/Approved-Minutes-of-Sex-Workers-Liaison-Group.pdf?ext=.pdf

[74]Bliss Festival. (2015). *Bliss Festival 2015 talks panel*. Retrieved 15 June 2017, from http://www.blissfestival.org/p/summer-festival-2015-talks-panel.html

The data we use here was provided by E Designers Ltd, the parent company that owns and manages the Escort-Ireland.com website. We requested anonymised data on escorts from Escort-Ireland.com when we were contacted by them following publication of an opinion piece we wrote, in which we argued that criminalisation of sex work was likely to do more harm than good to sex workers (Maginn and Ellison 2013). We were subsequently supplied with … data … "scraped" from the profiles of escort advertisements on Escort-Ireland.com by the web administrator from E Designers Ltd and supplied to us in a series of Excel spreadsheets....[75]

The article they referred to is an opinion piece in the *Belfast Telegraph* they co-authored which was strongly critical of Lord Morrow's then Private Members Bill published on 17 January 2013: 12 months before Ellison provided his evidence to the Committee. In the weeks prior to giving his evidence before the Committee an article was published in *The Conversation*[76] authored by Ellison and Dr Paul Maginn, which again disclosed Escort-Ireland as the source of their data and further confuses opposition to male violence against women and girls as a religious moral crusade in opposition to gay men's "sexuality":

A major reason for this is that the Democratic Unionist Party, who are sponsoring the bill to introduce legislation on trafficking and prostitution, apparently cannot acknowledge that men would engage in such a practice. This belief is grounded in the strict Christian views of the party and its supporters.[77]

Ellison belatedly "clarified" to the Committee that Escort-Ireland had provided his colleague Maginn with their data. However, some of his "clarifying" statements which distanced himself personally from

[75]Maginn, P.J. and Ellison G. (2014) *Male Sex Work in the Irish Republic and Northern Ireland* in V. Minichiello and J. Scott (Eds) Male Sex Work & Society, New York: Harrington Park Press, pp:426-461, Endnote 10, p. 461.

[76]Maginn, P.; Ellison, G. (2013.) *The scarlet isle: Male sex work in Ireland.* On The Conversation. Retrieved 15 June 2017, from http://theconversation.com/the-scarlet-isle-the-politics-of-male-sex-work-in-ireland-19404).

[77]Ruhama: Supporting Women Affected by Prostitution. Retrieved 15 June 2017, from http://www.ruhama.ie/

Escort-Ireland seemed anything but clear: "I have not had direct links. I asked them; I did not even ask them."

The data produced by Ellison's colleague Huschke in her evidence[78] to the Justice Committee was controversially drawn from a survey she conducted for a (then) in-progress report[79] commissioned by the recalcitrant member of the Northern Ireland Assembly David Ford.[80] Huschke was the lead researcher of the project entitled 'Research into Prostitution in Northern Ireland' which sought to uncover "the nature and extent of prostitution in Northern Ireland".[81] As with the UglyMugs.ie survey conducted by Smith, and the Escort-Ireland data analysed by Ellison, the research methodology and conclusions are questionable.[82]

In the first instance the Advisory Group[83] formed to advise Huschke was the former University of Sussex graduate Professor Nicola (Nick) Mai. Mai's position on prostituted minors is apparent here:

> By tampering with the sex of minors culturally constructed as 'angels', I wanted to expose the Northcentric fiction of neoliberal 'paradise' which is currently hegemonic worldwide … The representation of migrant male minors selling sex exclusively as 'exploited children', whether they are five or 17 years old, or whether they enjoy selling sex or not, is complicit with

[78]Northern Ireland Assembly. (2014, Jan 30.) *Official report (Hansard). Human trafficking and exploitation (further provisions and support for victims) bill: UglyMugs.ie*. Retrieved 15 June 2017, from www.niassembly.gov.uk/globalassets/documents/official-reports/justice/2013-2014/140130_humantraffickingetcbilluglymugs.pdf.

[79]Department of Justice. (2014, Oct 31.) Research into prostitution in Northern Ireland. Retrieved 15 June 2017, from https://www.justice-ni.gov.uk/publications/research-prostitution-northern-ireland.

[80]Kilpatrick, C. (2014, Oct 17.) *David Ford in bid to scupper bill making it illegal to pay for sex*. In Belfast Telegraph. Retrieved 15 June 2017, from http://www.belfasttelegraph.co.uk/news/politics/david-ford-in-bid-to-scupper-bill-making-it-illegal-to-pay-for-sex-30670787.html.

[81]Queen's University Belfast (2014) *Research into prostitution in Northern Ireland* Retrieved 28 August 2017, from https://www.justice-ni.gov.uk/sites/default/files/publications/doj/prostitution-report-nov-update.pdf.

[82]Oireachatas. (2014, Feb 26.) Joint Committee on Justice, Defence and Equality Debate. Retrieved 15 June 2017, from http://oireachtasdebates.oireachtas.ie/debates%20authoring/debateswebpack.nsf/committeetakes/JUJ2014022600007.

[83]The Bill included a raft of provisions including, for example, the 'proximity of age defence' and measures to strengthen defences against online predators.

the attempt to recreated [sic] a lost 'moral virginity' in the north of the world, at a time in which its moral and economic bankruptcy are most evident.[84]

In her research, Huschke argues that the Nordic model causes "stigma" and "drives prostitution underground" (which she contradictorily conceded already exists where prostitution is normalised). Huschke's research as it stood was criticised by the Committee which deemed the 100 odd 'sex worker' respondents who completed the online survey too small a sample to be representative. Uglymugs.ie was involved throughout the consultation process of the survey.

Dr Susann Huschke: The other thing that I would like to say in this regard is that I really appreciate how critical you are of my study.

Mr Wells: Very critical.

The survey report was released later in 2014 and the flyer for the event was published on the Uglymugs.ie website.[85] Women's Aid Northern Ireland, a member of the Advisory Group, distanced themselves from the research findings and requested their name be removed from any material associated with the report.[86, 87] The report—'Fruit

---

[84]Pages 20–21, Mai, N. (2011) 'Tampering with the Sex of "Angels": Migrant Male Minors and Young Adults Selling Sex in the EU', Journal of Ethnic and Migration Studies, 37(8): 1237–1252.

[85]Queens University Belfast. (2014.) *Research into prostitution in Northern Ireland: Public engagement event.* Retrieved 15 June 2017, from https://uglymugs.ie/wp-content/uploads/Research-on-Prostitution-in-Northern-Ireland_Public-Engagement-Eventpdf.

[86]Women's Aid: Federation Northern Ireland. (2014, Oct 17.) *Statement on Queen's University Belfast: Department of Justice research on prostitution.* On Women's Aid. Retrieved 15 June 2017, from http://www.womensaidni.org/womens-aid-statement-queens-university-belfast-department-justice-research-prostitution/.

[87]Dillon, E. (2014, Mar 4.) *Brothel cash goes to internet kingpin linked to legalisation campaign.* In Sunday World. Retrieved 15 June 2017, from www.sundayworld.com/news/crimedesk/brothel-cash-goes-to-internet-kingpin.

from the Position Tree'—is now widely accepted in the cannons of academic prostitution apology.[88]

Ellison also made claims to Committee Chairperson Paul Givan MLA that prostitution in Sweden and Norway was endemic.

Dr Ellison:	Sorry. It is based on a number of interviews that I carried out with online providers, who said that they have expanded into Sweden and Norway in the past two years. They also said—I have no reason to doubt them, although I will maybe check—that business was booming.
The Chairperson:	You have no reason to doubt the online suppliers, if that is the phrase that you want to use. However, the authorities in Sweden tell us that they are cracking down on organised crime, they are going after the money, they are being successful and their wiretaps of these international organisations are saying that Sweden is a very difficult and hostile environment.[89]
Dr Ellison:	You and I could go on the internet, and we would find that a printout of all the information about Sweden would probably fill this room. We could lay it all out and read it, and I think that, at the end of that process, neither of us would be in a position to say…
The Chairperson:	You believe the online provider of the service, but you put a question mark over what the Swedish authorities tell us.
Dr Ellison:	I think that the Swedish authorities have an interest in promoting the system.

[88]Hollaway, M. (2004, May 8). *Minister must withdraw funding from Scarlet Alliance*. In Tasmania Times. Retrieved 15 June 2017, from http://tasmaniantimes.com/index.php?/pr-article/minister-must-with-draw-funding-from-scarlet-alliance/.

[89]Northern Ireland Assembly. (2014, Jan 30.) *Official report (Hansard). Human trafficking and exploitation (further provisions and support for victims) bill: UglyMugs.ie.* Retrieved 15 June 2017, from www.niassembly.gov.uk/globalassets/documents/official-reports/justice/2013-2014/140130_humantraffickingetcbilluglymugs.pdf.

Clearly, so did the pimps.

Ellison declined to name Escort-Sweden or Escort-Norway (or any other online provider of prostituted women) to the Committee Chairperson as perhaps the source of his information citing "research ethics". However, in his chapter 'Who Needs Evidence?'[90] Ellison claimed he was "forced" to divulge this information and implied that Mr Givan (the Chairperson) had issued a complaint to Queen's University Belfast regards his abusive email as a consequence of his refusal.

I found that Escort-Ireland/Uglymugs.ie had expanded operations into Sweden and Norway as Escort-Sweden/Uglymugs.se and Escort-Norway/Uglymugs.se. The webpage designs, functionality and trade-marks are all identical. Uglmugs.se is owned by Safe IQ Ltd.[91] The dates and archived webpages reveal that Escort-Sweden/Escort-Norway/Uglymugs.se was online well before Ellison gave evidence.

During the course of writing this chapter, I was sent a review copy of a book entitled *Reflexivity and Criminal Justice: Intersections of Policy, Practice and Research*, which contained a chapter by Ellison. 'Who Needs Evidence? Radical Feminism, The Christian Right and Sex Work Research in Northern Ireland'[92] is a scathing peer-reviewed reflection on the Northern Ireland Justice Committee and the DUP who heard his evidence. In it, Ellison dismissed the abuse and content of his email to a Committee witness (authored by the authority of his academic position) as a "breach of his privacy" though he (again) names the recipient of that email. Moreover, he defamatorily alleges Committee member Jim Wells MLA "forced" Lee to disclose her real name; which is not only

---

[90]Ellison, G. (2016.) *Who needs evidence?* In Armstrong, S.; Blaustein, J.; Henry, A. (Eds.) (2016.) *Reflexivity and criminal justice: Intersections of policy, practice and research.* London: Palgrave Macmillan.

[91]Uglymugs.ie currently "acknowledges" a "relationship" between Escort-Ireland as it did at both the Oireachtas and Stormont committees. However, this pre-emptive admission is in the form of a closed and compact statement which pretends disclosure but camouflages precisely the nature of the "relationship", any commercial arrangements or an elaboration of the involvement of Peter McCormick and Mark McCormick.

[92]I will focus on pages 305–306 of Ellison, G. (2016). Who needs evidence? Radical Feminism, the Christian Right and Sex Work Research in Northern Ireland. In: Reflexivity and Criminal Justice: Intersections of Policy, Practice and Research. Armstrong, S., Blaustein, J. & Alistair, H. (eds.). Palgrave Macmillan.

untrue but fascinatingly bewildering given he argues vulnerable prostituted women and girls are exemplars of choice and agency.

Ms Lee:	You are welcome to my real name if you wish.
Mr Wells:	Are you prepared to release that?[93]
Ms Lee:	Yes, I am. It is—[provides her real name].

All the more intriguing given that Lee has provided her actual name in several interviews with popular media and sex trade organisations in connection with her prostitution.[94] To further confound his panic it is of interest that Lee co-authors scholarly works (in her real name, which I will not use in respect of her privacy) with the oft colleague of Ellison: Maginn. Further, Ellison condemns Committee member Paul Givan for quizzing Lee on "private matters", when in fact he was directly questioning anomalies in one of her many newspaper interviews[95] she provided both condemning the DUP and the (then) proposed Private Member's Bill.

Amnesty International and the Morrow Bill

It is unclear whether AI, who provided direct evidence[96] (represented by Gráinne Teggart and Catherine Murphy) to this same Committee in opposition of Lord Morrow's Private Member's Bill, were informed

---

[93]Northern Ireland Assembly. (2014, Jan 30.) Northern Ireland Assembly. (2014, Jan 30.) *Official report (Hansard). Human trafficking and exploitation (further provisions and support for victims) bill: UglyMugs.ie.* Retrieved 15 June 2017, from www.niassembly.gov.uk/globalassets/documents/official-reports/justice/2013-2014/140130_humantraffickingetcbilluglymugs.pdf.

[94]Wyatt, D. (2015, 1 Dec.) *What is it really like to work as a dominatrix?* In The Independent. Retrieved 15 June 2017, from http://www.independent.co.uk/life-style/love-sex/whats-it-really-like-to-work-as-a-dominatrix-a6754541.html.

[95]News Letter. (2016, Sept 28.) *Sex worker wins first round against sex buyer law.* In News Letter. Retrieved 15 June 2017, from http://www.newsletter.co.uk/news/crime/sex-worker-wins-first-round-against-sex-buyer-law-1-7602205.

[96]Northern Ireland Assembly. (2014, Jan 30.) *Official report (Hansard). Human trafficking and exploitation (further provisions and support for victims) bill: UglyMugs.ie.* Retrieved 15 June 2017, from www.niassembly.gov.uk/globalassets/documents/official-reports/justice/2013-2014/140130_humantraffickingetcbilluglymugs.pdf.

and/or directed by Ellison and/or Escort-Ireland/Uglymugs.ie. The Bill is now being debated in court by Lee, because, as Lee's lawyers argue, it breaches the "human rights" of men who exploit prostituted women and children, and also those of the women who 'choose' to sell sex. Smith and Ellison, as we can see from the Hansard record, deny that such a human 'right' exists:

Mr Wells:	So, I have a right to buy the sexual services of any woman I choose?
Ms Smith:	Of course you do not have the right to buy any woman you choose. That is ridiculous.
Mr Wells:	Right. Have I a right to buy the sexual services of any woman I choose?
Dr Ellison:	I am not saying that you have a right to buy. I think that a person has a right to sell, or to do with their body what they want, by and large.

Lee's High Court appeal is partly funded by Escort-Ireland and other profiteers from the sex trade. Lee explained to the Home Affair Committee Westminster:[97]

MP David Burrows:	I understand in terms of the crowd funding website you have, you have been given £1000 by Escort Ireland, which markets thousands of women each year and designs websites for escorts.
Ms Lee:	That is correct. That is because a lot of the sex workers that advertise on their website put pressure on them to support me and said it was only fair, since they make money from the industry, that they should support my efforts of keeping our industry safe.

---

[97]Belfast Telegraph. (2016, March 9). Escort Website Partly Funding Bid in Ireland's Ban on Paying for Sex. Belfast Telegraph. Online: http://www.belfasttelegraph.co.uk/news/northern-ireland/escort-website-partly-funding-bid-to-overturn-n-irelands-ban-on-paying-for-sex-34525613.html.

I examined Lee's 'Fighting for Sex Workers' Rights' campaign website and noted that it had raised £14.741 of a £30,000 goal. The list is a roll call of sex trade industry names: including a 'Steve Elrond' who offered to match £ for £ money donated—and with the thousands of pounds he has so far donated he is making good on his promise. 'Steve Elrond' owns a string of domains for various websites advertising prostituted women.

As it happens, Lee is advertised on Elrond's websites, as she is on Escort-Ireland. At the time of giving her evidence to the Northern Ireland Assembly, Lee was editor of the blog and repository Harlotsparlor.com. Two others were then sharing her editorial duties: Douglas Fox (the founder of the website) and Steve Elrond. Elrond is also a punter who meticulously records his experiences with the prostituted women. Elrond is an outspoken campaigner for blanket decriminalisation, and his name is attached to innumerable documents from blog chats to submissions to Parliament[98] citing statistics and tired tropes produced and reproduced with the sex trade imprimatur.[99]

As we have explored in previous chapters, there[100] is a great deal of debate and disquiet towards AI[101] as a result of its support to decriminalise the sex trade. Much has been said of the relationship between sex trade profiteer Douglas Fox and AI (for example, during the AI's evidence before Northern Ireland's Justice Committee); not to mention why AI gave evidence in opposition to the Private Member's Bill more

---

[98]Parliament. *Written evidence submitted by Steven Elrond*. Retrieved 15 June 2017, from http://data.parliament.uk/WrittenEvidence/CommitteeEvidence.svc/EvidenceDocument/Home%20Affairs/Prostitution/written/29122.html.

[99]Tyler, M. (2015, Apr 8.) *Sex trade survivors deserve the chance to speak*. In The Conversation. Retrieved 15 June 2017, from https://theconversation.com/sex-trade-survivors-deserve-the-chance-to-speak-57429.

[100]2006. *Extraordinary Stories: The Escort Agency*. UK, Channel 4. Retrieved 15 June 2017, from http://tvfinternational.com/programme/20/the-escort-agency?trailer=1&.

[101]See for example Hedges, C. (2015, August 16) Amnesty International: Protecting the 'Human Rights' of Johns, Pimps, and Human Traffickers. Truth Dig. Online: http://www.truthdig.com/report/item/amnesty_international_protecting_the_human_rights_20150816.; Bindel, J. (2015, August 4) Women in Prostitution won't be protected by Amnesty's Plan. The Guardian. Online: https://www.theguardian.com/commentisfree/2015/aug/04/sex-workers-amnesty-international-prostitution-decriminalisation; Brunskell-Evans (2015) Sorry Amnesty, Decriminalising Sex Work will Not Protect Human Rights. The Conversation. Online: https://theconversation.com/sorry-amnesty-decriminalising-sex-work-will-not-protect-human-rights-46096.

than 18 months before supposedly having a firm prostitution policy or anywhere near the completion of its consultation process.

Mr Wells:	You do not have policy in that area, but you have policy resisting either clause 6 as drafted by Lord Morrow or as it has been introduced in Sweden. You are against both versions of clause 6.
Ms Teggart:	We have not said that we are against anything in Sweden. We have said that the evidence in Sweden is, at best, conflicting. The reason why we oppose clause 6 in the Bill is because we feel that it poses some risk that has not been properly explored. That is why we recommend further research in this area.
Mr Wells:	Gráinne—again, you have experience in this—that is the oldest trick in the book. If you do not like something, do not come out and say so. Boot it off into the bushes by calling for more research.

While it is peculiar that any organisation or individual would speak authoritatively before firming a position on such a critical issue, let alone betraying all that it represents, perhaps the explanation for this can be found in Ellison's denial of his role of adviser to AI. In his evidence, Dr Graham Ellison answered the following question:

Mr Wells:	Have you been advising Amnesty International on this issue?
Dr Ellison:	No.[102]

However, Ellison's Queen's University Belfast webpage confirms that he acted as 'advisor' to AI from August 2012 to December 2012:

---

[102]Northern Ireland Assembly. (2014, Jan 30.) Official report (Hansard). Human trafficking and exploitation (further provisions and support for victims) bill: UglyMugs.ie. Retrieved 15 June 2017, from www.niassembly.gov.uk/globalassets/documents/official-reports/justice/2013-2014/140130_humantraffickingetcbilluglymugs.pdf.

I have been asked by Amnesty International to provide[103] an opinion/view in respect of their response to Lord Morrow's human trafficking and prostitution bill currently going through the Northern Ireland Assembly.

In his book chapter, 'Who Needs Evidence?', which made no overt reference to Escort-Ireland and persons associated with it, Ellison complains Committee members "were not paying … attention (but were) … browsing on their computers". I believe this requires clarification by way of context.

Mr Wells: Dr Ellison, I looked up your website while you were speaking. You told us earlier that you had no connection with Amnesty International. Were you not an adviser to Amnesty International?

Dr Ellison: Not as far as I know.

Conclusion: Escort-Ireland/UglyMugs.ie Business Model Blue Print

There are a number of organisations that claim to be 'sex-worker' based and 'fighting for the rights of sex workers' that have connections to pimps and brothel owners, and seek to exert influence over governments, policy makers, media, NGOs, the academy and police. Many, of course, genuinely believe that blanket[104] decriminalisation of the sex trade will benefit the women and men who sell sex; but there are also those who take advantage of the profit potential for pimps and other profiteers that removing all laws from selling sex would undoubtedly bring.

Only one question then needs to be asked of the pro-prostitution lobbyist: if the Nordic Model is "ineffectual in curbing the expansion of the sex trade", why are you so vehemently in opposition to it?

---

[103]Department of Justice. (2014, Oct 31.) *Research into prostitution in Northern Ireland.* Retrieved 15 June 2017, from https://www.justice-ni.gov.uk/publications/research-prostitution-northern-ireland.

[104]BBC News. (2014, Jan 30). *DUP confronts QUB academic over 'gay suicides' claim.* On BBC News. Retrieved 15 June 2017, from http://www.bbc.com/news/uk-northern-ireland-25969374.

9

Sex Trade Academics

Within the world of academia, the most popular view of the sex trade is clearly that of pro-decriminalisation. Why is the view that prostitution is 'labour' rather than 'abuse' so prevalent within the Academy? To understand that, you have to look at how class analysis, largely prevalent within sociology and anthropology as a way of understanding institutionalised power relations, has been usurped by essentialist identity politics, the rise of market doctrine within universities, and how these have joined forces with old-fashioned sexism and male libertarianism.

Prostitution: From Dividing Women to Dividing Collegiality

In 2009, colleagues from London South Bank University and I applied for Big Lottery money to conduct a study on the barriers and opportunities for women in prostitution to exit.[1] In 2004 I had met Roger

[1]The Big Lottery Fund provides grants to organisations in the UK to help improve their communities. The money is derived from the UK National Lottery.

Matthews,[2] Professor of Criminology at the University, when I emailed him to thank him for a letter he wrote to the *Guardian* newspaper praising an investigative feature on the sex trade I had published in its magazine supplement.[3] Matthews is one of the few male academics who takes the view prostitution is harmful to women and both a cause and a consequence of their oppression. Although he may not use this term, Matthews is an abolitionist.

Matthews and I conducted the study, the largest of its kind in the UK, with Helen Easton, his colleague in the Criminology department, and with others from Eaves (see Chap. 1). During the two-year data collection period, 114 women (who were or had previously been involved in various aspects of the sex trade) were interviewed at length: 50 of these women were interviewed more than once. Very little attention had been paid to developing exiting services for women in prostitution, with service providers tending to favour so-called harm minimisation (such as providing condoms and needles) with a focus only on reducing the risk of HIV and other sexually transmitted infections. Our research aimed to make a positive contribution to the study of prostitution and the lives of those women and girls affected by it.

The ground-breaking research, which was published as a book two years after the release of the final report to funders,[4] was always going to be controversial. After all, it was about looking for best practice examples in assisting women out of the sex trade, rather than towing the 'inevitability' line, looking for ways to keep them alive whilst being abused within it.

Shortly before publication of the report in 2012, the blogger and scientist known as Belle de Jour, aka Dr Brooke Magnanti, wrote a book entitled *The Sex Myth: Why Everything We Are Told Is Wrong*.[5] Prior to publication, Magnanti's publicist approached me with a request that I

---

[2]Bindel, J. (2008, Feb 29.) *It's abuse and a life of hell.* In The Guardian. Retrieved 15 June 2017, from https://www.theguardian.com/lifeandstyle/2008/feb/29/women.ukcrime.

[3]Bindel, J. (2004, May 15.) *Streets apart.* In The Guardian. Retrieved 15 June 2017, from https://www.theguardian.com/theguardian/2004/may/15/weekend7.weekend4.

[4]Matthews, R., Easton, H., Reynolds, L., Bindel, J., Young, L. 2014). *Exiting prostitution: A study in female desistance.* (London: Palgrave).

[5]Magnanti, B. (20120.) *The sex myth: Why everything we're told is wrong.* London: Weidenfeld & Nicolson.

interview her for the *Guardian* newspaper, mentioning that it might be an interesting read because Magnanti and I hold very different views of the sex trade. I readily accepted, and looked forward to sitting down with Magnanti in order to get a real sense of how she had come to form her views on these issues.

Before Magnanti's interview I read the manuscript of *The Sex Myth* and found, to my horror, a number of serious inaccuracies about Eaves and individuals. Magnanti had also managed to get hold of an interim report of our exiting study watermarked 'Not for distribution, please do not quote'. The reason the team did not wish to have the interim report quoted was because the figures were not final and the data had not been cleaned. Nevertheless, Magnanti published the details in that leaked report.

There is open hostility from pro-prostitution academics to those scholars who deviate from the pro-prostitution line. Those academics advocating on behalf of the sex trade are hardly harmless ineffectual individuals in ivory towers publishing papers nobody reads; rather, they are powerful activists using their academic positions and credentials to exert influence on prostitution policy as members of national and international research bodies. It is concerning that 'research' deferring to sex trade ideology and not academically sound evidence is informing this discussion with detrimental consequences for women and girls, albeit positive consequences for those profiting from this regime of violence.

Dr John Davies: Academic, Activist, Convicted Conman

The inaugural regional conference of 'sex workers' in East-Central Europe took place in Balástya, Hungary, 8–14 April 2000. It was organised by a doctoral student by the name of John Davies. Davies, who was studying in the UK, had moved to Balástya, a village on the outskirts of Szeged, with his family in the 1990s.

I visited Balástya in 2016 to interview people who knew, and knew of, Davies, but 10–20 years ago it had been a different landscape.

Throughout the 1990s Serbia was involved in numerous conflicts: the Slovenian (1991), Croatian (1991–1995), Bosnian (1992–1995) and Kosovan wars (1998–1999). The latter war resulted in tens of thousands of displaced people, particularly ethnic Albanians, seeking refuge and prosperity in neighbouring countries. All wars are hell for women and girls, and it is estimated that at least 20,000 Albanian women and girls (whose fathers, husbands, son and brothers were murdered) were raped by Serbian soldiers and paramilitary in the Kosovo conflict. Access to vulnerable and penniless Albanian women, many pregnant from rape, provided exploitative men with opportunities to make their fortunes.

Davies spent many years, first as an MA student and DPhil candidate and then as a Visiting Research Fellow, at the University of Sussex in England.[6] Since the 1990s, Davies has travelled the world taking part in conferences and lecturing on the international sex trade. He is a supporter of blanket decriminalisation of the sex trade. He evaded justice until recently because a number of academics and pro-prostitution Academics and pro-prostitution activists supported him. I had heard allegations of Davies's charity scams as far back as 1999. I, and other feminist abolitionist colleagues, have regularly challenged pro-prostitution academics and human rights experts on their collaboration with Davies and their refusal to condemn him. Each and every one has defended Davies and refused to accept his bad character.

Davies has long been described by law enforcers as 'Mr Teflon' because none of the many serious allegations against him stuck. Those of us who followed his activities have often been threatened with libel. I am now able to tell at least part of the story of Davies because I responded to his threat of libel by gathering all the evidence to prove my allegations—that Davies has long been suspected of being a baby trafficker, among other things—could be substantiated.

There is a long and complex story to tell about Davies and his criminal exploits, going as far back as the 1980s and perhaps earlier. As I write, I am in the middle of an investigation into the range and number of crimes in which Davies has been involved and the people who

---

[6]Laura Agustin. Retrieved 15 June 2017, from http://www.lauraagustin.com/.

enabled him. For the purposes of this chapter, however, I will focus on his time in academia and the way in which he managed to become a respected and highly influential scholar whose many works are cited by other scholars of similar standing: including Dr Stephanie Schwander-Sievers, an anthropologist from Bournemouth University in the UK, who referred to Dr Davies's work in tribunal hearings for trafficked Albanian women seeking migration into the United Kingdom in her capacity as an expert on such matters.[7]

I first met John Davies (aka John Shelton, aka John Glyn Davies, aka Glyndwr Selwyn Owain Davies) in 1999 at a conference in London. It was at this event that I heard the stories about Davies from Interpol officers and feminist colleagues. Davies gave me the creeps: he pushed his way into a conversation I was having with a small group of feminists and lectured us on why our approach was blind-sighted. I recall him saying: 'You can't expect an Albanian woman who wants to work in the Tutti Fruity bar [in Greece] to keep away from traffickers if she is refused proper papers'. He was arguing that the only reason that traffickers get their claws on prostituted women is because of strict immigration laws.

A tall and heavy-set man with a domineering presence, he is not one to be forgotten in a hurry. On returning to the UK, I looked at Davies in the national newspaper database and found there had been a couple of reports about him and his exploits in south-eastern Europe. Davies, along with Julie Vullnetari, a younger woman who at one time was his partner, had been arrested in Croatia on suspicion of baby trafficking before being released. I also found Davies was a prodigious contributor to the Stop Traffic listserv, most of whose members were pro-prostitution advocates. During the late 1990s, around the time that Davies embarked upon his MA studies at Sussex Centre for Migration Research (SCMR), he wrote on a listserv thread that he had been threatened with expulsion from Romania but had successfully appealed with the help of other academics on the list and that he was permitted to remain in the country.

---

[7]Gov.uk. (2009.) *AM and BM (trafficked women)*. Retrieved 15 June 2017, from https://tribunalsdecisions.service.gov.uk/utiac/37676.

However, there was a more recent scandal about Davies, who had been given a substantial grant to supposedly set up roadside services for street-based prostituted women in Hungary. The inspectors from the fraud department of the European Commission found that Davies had misappropriated money into his family home and used it for his own gain since there was no sign of any such project. Davies had applied for the EC grant in conjunction with the Prostitution Information Centre in Amsterdam, which publishes a 'pleasure guide' to the city's window brothel area, runs tours of the area and campaigns for 'sex workers' rights'.

As a result of Davies being caught, two major pro-prostitution groups (the Dutch Foundation Against Trafficking in Women and La Strada) announced they were withdrawing their cooperation with Davies and the foundations he was affiliated with: the Salomon Alapitvany Foundation (Hungary) and the Morava Foundation (Albania and Romania).

Davies, as has always been his modus operandi, robustly denied any fraud had taken place. However, the story was picked up in the *Sunday Times* newspaper in 1999[8] and Davies threatened to sue them for libel. But he failed because Stephen Grey, the *Sunday Times* investigator who broke the news, was able to gather all of the information that proved every single allegation in his story. I've seen the paperwork and spoken to the journalist, as well as examined the Press Complaints Commission's findings in the matter. There is no doubt in my mind that Davies was covering up serious fraud.

In that same *Sunday Times* article it was reported that Davies was suspected of illegally supplying children for adoption in the West—particularly the USA but also the UK. Davies contested this allegation, claiming the journalist who authored the article was unable to produce irrefutable proof that he was suspected of such activities. Again, his claims were rebutted. In his complaint to the Press Complaints Commission, Davies wrote: 'I am returning fulltime to my DPhil studies in sex work migration, and am grateful to have the support of my professors and other

---

[8]Grey, S. (1999, Jan 31.) *Briton in prostitute aid scandal.* In Sunday Times.

colleagues at this difficult time. I am very fortunate that many of my academic colleagues and friends are close enough that they are not influenced by reports that do not match the reality of my life and work'.

It would seem Davies had found the perfect cover to exploit women and children as an academic. Emboldened, he sought further funding for his prostitution-related activities. In 2002 he was awarded a grant from a Norwegian funder for anti-trafficking work in Bangladesh. And in Dhaka, Bangladesh, he worked as a chief technical advisor for the Ministry of Women and Children's project to stop trafficking.

Alerted to the situation by feminist abolitionists, the Secretary for the Women and Children Affairs in Bangladesh discovered that Davies was involved in 'women, drug and gambling related illegal activities'. He had his funding from the Norwegians revoked and his post in Bangladesh was terminated. It was in Bangladesh that Davies met a number of men who were well connected to various charitable NGOs funded by foreign aid. Some of the men would later occupy important positions on the boards of 'charities' directed by Davies.

Davies and his son Benjamin, Julie Vullnetari, Jo Doezema and Nick Mai hold similar opinions about the trafficking of women into the sex trade: trafficking (or 'migrant sex work' as they prettify it) is more often a 'choice' that women from poor countries make in order to 'earn lots of money and avoid working in factories'. It would appear Davies considers anti-trafficking campaigners to be more dangerous than the actual traffickers. In 2006, Davies spoke at an academic conference in Oxford in the UK, as a PhD candidate. The title of his paper was 'Force and Deception: the Tools of the Anti-Traffickers'. In 2007, Sussex University awarded Davies his doctorate for his research thesis on the trafficking of Albanian women.

In 2008, Davies and his son Benjamin, who by this time was a graduate of the same MA in Migration Studies from SCMR, published a provocative paper: 'How to Use a Trafficked Woman: The Alliance between Political and Criminal Trafficking Organisations'.[9] Father and

---

[9]Davies, J.; Davies, B. (2008.) *How to use a trafficked woman: The alliance between political and criminal trafficking organisations.* In La Strada. Retrieved 15 June 2017, from http://lastradainternational.org/doc-center/1743/how-to-use-a-trafficked-woman-the-alliance-between-political-and-criminal-trafficking-organisations.

son claimed that Albanian women's fear of rape and violence (as a consequence of the rapes committed by Serbian soldiers) had transferred into fear of 'sex work'. The pair further claimed this 'moral panic' was created and sustained by 'political traffickers' (i.e. abolitionists) aiming at preventing women's 'safe' migration, thereby forcing them into the hands of traffickers.

As I make clear in my discussion of Escort-Ireland (Chap. 8), there is something peculiar in the manner in which sons are apprenticed into the sex trade by their fathers. But Benjamin Davies is not a misled young man. I have in my possession quite a number of photographs and articles—corroborated by oral evidence from first-hand sources—that depict and describe him routinely performing sadistic 'scenarios' at BDSM (bondage, domination, sadism, masochism) clubs in London dressed in the military fatigues of an Eastern European soldier, wherein he beats a naked woman covered in either real or fake blood (it is impossible to tell) with her hands tied behind her back with rope that he uses to drag her about like an animal. This, apparently, for the sexual enjoyment of those who pay to watch. The 'fantasy' of soldiers raping women is the reality of many women, as Benjamin Davies most certainly was aware.

This was the year 2009, when his father was being tried for sexually abusing two sisters, a crime for which he was found not guilty after he convinced the jury that his brother, brain damaged from a heroin overdose, was the possible culprit of the rapes.[10] It was also in 2009 that the book based on his PhD research, *My Name is Not Natasha: How Albanian Women in France Use Trafficking to Overcome Social Exclusion (1998–2001)*, was published by Amsterdam University Press.[11] Like Davies, by this stage Vullnetari also held a DPhil in Migration Studies from SCMR. His book was dedicated to her. In this same acknowledgement section, which mentions not a single member of his family, Davies wrote: 'I would also like to thank Yonis Dirie and Kirk Reid for their invaluable support and kindness during a very difficult and demanding

---

[10]Portlock, J. (2009, Aug 5.) *Esher man accused of rape tells court description fits his brother.* In Your Local Guardian. Retrieved 15 June 2017, from http://www.yourlocalguardian.co.uk/news/4528554.Esher_man_accused_of_rape_tells_court_description_fits_his_brother/.

[11]Davies, J. (2009.) *'My name is not Natasha': How Albanian women in France use trafficking to overcome social exclusion (1998–2001).* Amsterdam: Amsterdam University Press.

episode of my life'. That 'episode' of course refers to Davies's criminal trial in 2009 for rape and sexual assault.

Although, as a feminist journalist living in the UK, I had naturally written and thought about them,[12] the names Yonis Dirie and Kirk Reid escaped me until seven years later in 2016 when I and others recommenced our investigation of Davies. Disturbingly, both Dirie and Reid are notorious rapists. Dirie raped and severely beat a woman before dumping her unconscious into a river in East London in 1990. Dirie was arrested years later and sentenced to a ten-year prison sentence in 2006. Reid is the serial rapist of at least 26 women over a 12-year period from 1995–2007; however, it is believed as many as 75 women were raped by him. Reid was sentenced to life imprisonment in 2009. Presumably, these two rapists met with Davies after he was arrested on his return to the UK from Bangladesh in 2008 and remanded on the charge of raping two sisters.

Possibly more useful than my summary of Davies's book is that provided on his publisher's website. It reads:

This book challenges every common presumption that exists about the trafficking of women for the sex trade. It is a detailed account of an entire population of trafficked Albanian women whose varied experiences, including selling sex on the streets of France, clearly demonstrate how much the present discourse about trafficked women is misplaced and inadequate. The heterogeneity of the women involved and their relationships with various men is clearly presented as is the way women actively created a panoptical surveillance of themselves as a means of self-policing. There is no artificial divide between women who were deceived and abused and those who 'choose' sex work; in fact the book clearly shows how peripheral involvement in sex work was to the real agenda of the women involved.[13]

---

[12]Bindel, J. (2010, Oct 5.) *Who will challenge this obscene protection racket?* In The Guardian. Retrieved 15 June 2017, from https://www.theguardian.com/commentisfree/2010/oct/05/challenge-obscene-protection-racket.

[13]Davies, J. (2009). "My name is not Natasha": How Albanian Women in France Use Trafficking to Overcome Social Exclusion (1998–2001). Amsterdam University Press.

As is clear from that summary, Davies does not consider even those women he concedes are trafficked to be the victims of gross human rights abuses, instead claiming that they have made a positive 'choice'. It is equally apparent that Davies is saying that support agencies that exist in Albania and elsewhere are useless. One of the organisations he attempts to trash is one I know extremely well and have visited in 2000 and 2004. Vatra (The Hearth) Psychological-social Centre[14] is run by the indefatigable Vera Lesko, and was founded in 1997 in response to the epidemic of trafficking that had taken over her hometown of Vlora. The services and advocacy that Lesko provides for vulnerable women and girls, and training she undertook in order to educate other Albanian citizens about the harms of the international sex trade, are second to none. Davies, however, criticises and dismisses the work of Lesko and her colleagues, claiming that she is part of the 'rescue industry'.

Davies criticises Lesko and her organisation in any way he can find, including when he says: 'Some activists such as Lesko (2005) consider traffickers solely responsible for trafficking'.[15] This sentence is somewhat risible and just goes to show the twisted logic of the trafficking denier. Davies accuses Lesko of making the assumption that those girls and women who are re-trafficked multiple times to and from Albania experience shame and stigma. For Davies, the explanation for women being re-victimised in this manner is simply that they need the money.[16]

As with a growing number of pro-prostitution academics who focus on trafficking into the sex trade, Davies wishes to present a 'nuanced' examination of the phenomenon. This is a disingenuous position. It is impossible for human beings to be unaffected by the misery of prostitution. To drive the point, as a feminist I have no necessary investment in abolitionism. I am a feminist first. What I mean by this is, for example, that were I to be convinced that prostitution is a wonderful thing

---

[14]US Aid. (Date?) *Pioneering the fight against trafficking*. On US Aid. Retrieved 15 June 2017, from https://www.usaid.gov/results-data/success-stories/pioneering-fight-against-trafficking.

[15]Davies, J. (2009). "My name is not Natasha": How Albanian Women in France Use Trafficking to Overcome Social Exclusion (1998–2001). Amsterdam University Press, p. 100.

[16]Davies, J. (2009). "My name is not Natasha": How Albanian Women in France Use Trafficking to Overcome Social Exclusion (1998–2001). Amsterdam University Press, p. 104.

for the bodies and minds of women and girls, for our liberation from male oppression, and that it positively affects the way men and boys view me and other women, I would unequivocally support it. I would support it as much as I have condemned it up to this day. I too would insist, as UK Liberal Democrat councillor Dennis Parsons nauseatingly speculated,[17] that young schoolgirls contemplating careers in the peak professions (perhaps more suited to their male peers) instead educate themselves on the endless possibilities which being repeatedly penetrated by men provides them. But I would never collude with fakery of 'impartiality' on something so critical to the lives of all women and girls.

Davies, as appears to be the current fashion among those researching women in prostitution, adopts an ethnographic approach, which means that he hung around with the women in their place of 'work' and, rather than formally interview these women, he spent time chatting with them, socialising and taking an all-round 'holistic' informal approach. It would appear that this method, when used by the pro-prostitution academics, is particularly successful in 'proving' that 'sex work' is harmless.

Davies interviewed 58 Albanian women for his research, all of whom had been trafficked into Lyon, France. During his ethnographic research, he and his Albanian girlfriend/cultural advocate Vullnetari mixed freely with pimps and traffickers. Davis prefers to call traffickers 'cuni': an Albanian pejorative term meaning 'boy'. Throughout his book there are numerous examples where neither Davies nor his 'cultural advocate' elect to report trafficking to police. This is an extract from an interview Davies conducted with a self-confessed and unabashed rapist and trafficker:

> One man offered me his daughter when I was buying cabbages from him to sell in Tirana … this was south of Elbasan [a city in central Albania]. From one farmer we bought all his cabbages and then went to his house for a drink. I told him stories about my successful business, so he offered me

---

[17]Ditum, S. (2016, Sept 18.) *Liberal Democrat Dennis Parsons is wrong, prostitution is abuse not a career to aspire to.* In The Independent. Retrieved 15 June 2017, from http://www.independent.co.uk/voices/liberal-democrat-dennis-parsons-is-wrong-prostitution-is-abuse-not-a-career-to-aspire-to-a7314786.html.

his daughter in marriage. He told me that many girls in the village had run away to Greece with local boys and that he wanted to make a proper marriage for his daughter before some local boy kidnapped her. I think he suspected or knew that she was not a virgin and so he couldn't dare to marry her off to anyone in his area ... Then my cousin put the token price on the table and I was married with the daughter. The farmer put his daughter in my van and we drove back to Elbasan ... on the way we all fucked her and then after a few weeks I had her sent to Italy ... every week she send me the money ... no complaining ... she is a good girl who loves me and knows her place. I still buy cabbages from her father who introduces me to all his friends as his son-in-law, the businessman from Tirana.[18]

Within Davies's research sample he reports two 16-year-old girls and one 17-year-old girl. Most researchers, I would have hoped, would report trafficked children immediately to the police. Not an isolated example, his book is replete with records made of innumerable crimes paired with his apathetic aloofness masquerading as academic impartiality. I am concerned any man would have unfettered access to prostituted women, let alone one with Davies's dodgy background and the high praise he gave to rapists Yonis and Reid. As a journalist, I cannot think of any of the stories I have written that were so interesting and important that I would not have put my pen down to report a child trafficked into prostitution. The fact that Davies did not do this, in a taxpayer-funded educational institution, is highly unethical and possibly illegal.

While quite a number of items I requested under Freedom of Information were snubbed by Sussex University, handily a copy of Davies's signed-off ethics approval appears in his book. Interestingly, the document appears to have subsequently been used as a scrap piece of paper (handwriting appears through the back page) and then scrunched up into a ball (and perhaps retrieved from the trash). Regardless of whether or not one agrees with Davies's methodology, such an extraordinarily important document, one that enabled the suspension of ethical judgment, demands to be handled with tremendous respect.

---

[18]Davies, J. (2009.) 'My name is not Natasha': How Albanian women in France use trafficking to overcome social exclusion (1998–2001). Amsterdam: Amsterdam University Press. pp. 140–141.

Accordingly, on a number of occasions I have asked Professor Richard Black, Davies's PhD doctoral supervisor and the person who signed off the ethical approval for his research in Lyon, whether he was aware that Davies (now in prison) may have colluded with dangerous criminals. Black declined to respond.

Trafficking? Or 'Migration for Sex Work'?

An academic named Nicola (Nick) Mai had also been awarded a PhD at the SCMR at Sussex University. Mai is another ardent fan of ethnography. Writing on the online magazine *The Conversation*,[19] in which he discussed his research where he claims to have found barely any prostituted women in the UK are trafficked, Mai argues:

> … the fact that a small minority of female sex workers are trafficked has been subsequently confirmed by other independent studies on the UK sex industry, including by the police, which corroborates our findings. This is also confirmed by the vast majority of ethnographic research at a global level, whenever sex work and the sex industry are engaged with 'from below' and 'from within'.

There is no connection whatsoever between John Davies' criminal exploits and the academic views and research of those that, at one time or another, studied or taught under the banner of the SCMR except for this: the approach taken by the SCMR scholars tends to be highly critical of the feminist abolitionist claims that harm and the sex trade are totally indivisible.

The methodology adopted by some researchers into the sex trade, such as Nick Mia, was the preferred method adopted by John Davies in both Lyon, France, and Thessaloniki, Greece.

---

[19]Mai, N. (2013, Dec 19.) *Only a minority of UK sex workers have been trafficked*. In The Conversation. Retrieved 15 June 2017, from https://theconversation.com/only-a-minority-of-uk-sex-workers-have-been-trafficked-21550.

This approach—both the view that the sex trade is merely 'labour',and the anthropological style of interviewing subjects—provided Davies with a perfectly respectable cover to pursue his criminality.

The year that Davies's book was published (2009), Parliament in Britain was deciding whether to introduce a clause in the Sexual Offences Act 2003 that would make it an offence in England and Wales to pay for the services of a person in prostitution who has been coerced into providing sexual services. Unsurprisingly, the suggestion that the State should criminalise any form of sex buying brought the polarised arguments out into the open. Mai, then a researcher at the University of North London, was completing his publicly funded research project entitled 'Migrant Workers in the UK Sex Trade' in which he concluded that only 6% of people in prostitution were trafficked or coerced.

The study comprises interviews with 67 women, 24 men and 9 transgender people working in various capacities in the sex trade. It aimed to examine the experiences and needs of non-British people involved in the UK sex trade. The study draws the conclusion that approximately 13% of women interviewed felt they had been exploited in the industry, and asserts that regularisation of the immigration status of non-British people working in the UK sex trade through the legalisation of prostitution would solve the majority of problems confronting the people interviewed.

Indeed, the majority of positive statements made in the research about the sex trade were from male and transgender people. Approximately 10% of the interviewees were 'not directly related to the provision of sexual activities in exchange for money or favours' (these included four industry 'managers'). This reduces the statistical validity of any figures drawn from this research somewhat. In addition, the 'vast majority' of study participants were sought through their 'commercial contacts'. This compromises the randomness of the sample, and it also may be the case that interviewees felt unable to disclose any negative experiences if interviewed in the vicinity of the brothel owner/pimp. Similarly, police officers and the courts know full well that the version of events obtained from women battered by their husbands are closest to the truth when the latter is well out of earshot and preferably in handcuffs in a police cell.

In a paper on prostituted young Romanian and Albanian men in Europe,[20] Mai describes 'flirting' with his interviewees:

> In many cases, I have also used my 'erotic subjectivity' as a strategic instrument of research (Kulick and Willson, 1995). ... Less often, and whenever the intersubjective circumstances made it appropriate, I flirted with young men whose stories, subjectivities and orientations were less heteronormative or 'straight' than those they were presenting me with.

Mai, along with many of his academic colleagues, is actively against criminalising the demand for commercial sex. In recent years, there has been an increased focus on critiquing the Nordic model.

Pro-prostitution activists welcomed the report, because it suited their argument that the law should not interfere in the sex trade as there is barely any abuse, coercion or illegality involved, and as trafficking is only a problem for the victims because of their illegal immigration status.

'We will only successfully target trafficking within the sex trade when we make policy based on evidence and in reality', commented Catherine Stephens of the International Union of Sex Workers (IUSW) as the report was launched. Stephens's praise of the research was unsurprising. Not only did the conclusion suit the IUSW, but Stephens was both a researcher and Advisory Group member on the research.

Mai published the research to coincide with the campaign by abolitionists in the UK to introduce a version of the Nordic Model. There was huge opposition to this proposed law led by academics such as Mai, and pressure groups such as the ECP and the IUSW. Mai's research was published in October 2009, but once his summary of findings was published in July 2009, he and other pro-prostitution campaigners began using it as a tool with which to convince MPs and Lords to vote against the sex buyer clause.

In the meantime, Nick Davies, known for his special investigations in the *Guardian* newspaper, was researching a major piece on trafficking.

---

[20]Mai, N. (2015). *Surfing liquid modernity: Albanian and Romanian male sex workers in Europe.* In Aggleton, P.; and Parker, R. (Eds.) *Men who sell sex: Global perspectives.* London: Routledge. 27–41.

In 2009, the journalist published a 4,500 word article in which he argued that anti-trafficking campaigners had created a "moral panic" around trafficking and that: "The UK's biggest ever investigation of sex trafficking failed to find a single person who had forced anybody into prostitution," which could easily be interpreted as meaning that there are barely any victims of trafficking and that prostitution is largely a voluntary activity.

Another way to analyse the data that Davies gathered is to consider whether or not the police had been successful in identifying traffickers in the first place; and, in the rare cases where police did make arrests, whether the Crown Prosecution Service (CPS) issued charges for trafficking offences. The fact that there were few convictions for trafficking is misleading—there are very few convictions of child sexual abuse and rape, but we tend not to use this as a measure of the scale of the crime.

In his article, Davies used the "weapons of mass destruction case" as an analogy,[21] which went some way to convincing sceptics that the concerns about the trafficking of women and girls was pure fiction, whether intentional or not.

Davies's *Guardian* article ran during the height of a huge debate in Parliament and among campaigners about whether or not to criminalise the buyers of sexual services in order to make the UK unappealing to traffickers (a legislative model that had been successfully introduced in Sweden in 1999, and in a number of other countries since). The investigation earned Davies a nomination at the annual Erotic Awards,[22] an event run by a pornographer. Davies did not win the prize: a statuette of a golden flying penis.

The Davies article contained the tired derailing line: 'An unlikely union of evangelical Christians with feminist campaigners, who pursued the trafficking tale to secure their greater goal, not of regime change, but of legal change to abolish all prostitution'. The attempts by Davies, Mai and other pro-prostitution activists to scupper the introduction of the law failed and it was introduced early in 2010.

---

[21]http://www.independent.co.uk/news/uk/home-news/tony-blair-misrepresented-intelligence-on-weapons-of-mass-destruction-to-gain-approval-for-iraq-war-a6713401.html

[22]Scott, L. (2010, Apr 25.) *Erotic awards: Whatever turns you on.* In The Metro. Retrieved 15 June 2017, from http://metro.co.uk/2010/04/25/erotic-awards-whatever-turns-you-on-3437799/.

The day after Davies's article appeared in the *Guardian*, a letter[23] signed by several academics, including John Davies and other pro-prostitution campaigners, was published in the same newspaper, praising Davies's work and further emphasising his key point: that numbers of trafficking victims had been wildly exaggerated by feminists, Christians and politicians. This letter spurred me to revisit my research on the neoliberal takeover of the academy in relation to prostitution.

I wrote to Professor Richard Black, the then Director of the SCMR, and Davies's DPhil supervisor whose signature is on the letter granting him ethical approval for his field research, and included as an appendix in the book. I had emailed Black (having put in several telephone calls to the university press office and receiving no response) to ask for a comment about what I had termed the 'trafficking denial' that appeared to be so prevalent in the academy in general and in his department in particular.

My email asked if Black could shed any light on this culture of 'trafficking denial' and offered examples of individuals who take this line, such as Vullnetari, Davies and Mai. I also pointed out that Davies had been suspected of trafficking by Interpol, had been expelled from certain countries on the strength of those suspicions, and had been arrested and imprisoned in Croatia. Black decided not to reply to me but rather passed on my email, without my knowledge or consent, to Davies.

I later received a letter before action from Davies's lawyers. Davies accused me of having no evidence to substantiate my claims in the email to Black, and threatened to sue me unless I made a public apology to him and sent him £5000 that Davies would donate to a 'women's charity' of his choice. Interestingly, as the court was to discover in 2016, Davies was running a number of 'scam charities' supposedly set up to serve impoverished and abused women.[24]

---

[23]Open letter. (2009, Oct 22.) *Sex trafficking is more than a numbers game.* In The Guardian. Retrieved 15 June 2017, from https://www.theguardian.com/society/2009/oct/22/sex-trafficking-crime-bill.

[24]Kay, L. (2016, May 16.) *Three men jailed for total of 22 years for £5m gift aid fraud.* In Third Sector. Retrieved 15 June 2017, from http://www.thirdsector.co.uk/three-men-jailed-total-22-years-5m-gift-aid-fraud/finance/article/1395006.

In response, I gathered the evidence to prove my allegations and more. I then submitted the evidence to Davies's lawyer, which included details of Davies's name being placed on the Interpol watch list, court documents from Croatia, expulsion orders from Romania and evidence of the EU fraud investigation.

That message was the last I heard from or about Davies until his name popped up again on the crown court list. I once again emailed Black, who has since left the University of Sussex for another institution, to ask if he would give me an answer to my original questions about the culture of 'trafficking denial' that I had posed in the email that he had passed directly to Davies. He denied that there is any 'dominant discourse coming from postgraduate students from the Centre' surrounding the sex trade, saying: 'In the Centre, we had at any one time during the late 2000s some 20–30 students working on various aspects of migration and very few of them engaged with either trafficking or sex work'. Yet, I have not been able to find one graduate who takes the position that the sex trade is inherently harmful to women, having searched through dozens of published academic articles, papers and doctoral theses from such students.

In 2014, five men and a woman were convicted of trafficking after recruiting at least 53 'poor and vulnerable' Hungarian women into the UK, using University of Sussex[25] colleges as warehouses to store and prostitute them using an 'escort website'.

On 16 May 2016, Davies stood in the dock at Southwark Crown Court in London and was sentenced to 12 years in prison for charity fraud. His co-defendants, Olsi Vullnetari and Benjamin Davies, were convicted, respectively, of fraud and money laundering.[26] These men had stolen more than £5 million in donations to the Sompan and Kurbet Foundations: charities originally set up to help impoverished

---

[25]James, B. (2013, Oct 31.) *Hungarian sex gang who allegedly ran brothel based on University of Sussex campus in court.* In The Argus. Retrieved 15 June 2017, from http://www.theargus.co.uk/news/10775463.Hungarian_sex_gang_who_allegedly_ran_brothel_based_on_University_of_Susex_campus_in_court/.

[26]Bindel, J. (2016, Jun 14.) *The pimps, the traffickers, the academics and the cover up: The shocking tale of John Davies.* On Byline. Retrieved 15 June 2017, from https://www.byline.com/column/7/article/1106.

and abused women (including those in the sex trade) and children. The money was stolen from Her Majesty's Revenue and Customs using an elaborate scam.

Prior to his imprisonment, Davies was listed on the website of the University of the Witwatersrand, African Centre for Migration & Society, South Africa which, as we saw in Chap. 8, is also home to Graham Ellison, as a Visiting Research Fellow. Davies was previously a Fellow of the Royal Society of Arts, UK, and a member of the European Commission's expert network on migration, integration, and social cohesion. His connection to South Africa is particularly mysterious. He migrated there after his[27] sexual assault trial with a very prominent South African AIDS activist and medical doctor with whom he had reportedly entered into a relationship. In the meantime, as he serves his prison sentence, Davies is surely finished as a reputable academic, receiving grants, delivering papers at conferences, and advising at governmental level what we should do to enable women to 'migrate for sex work', as he and his cohorts describe trafficking.[28] The fact that to this day not one single academic in the UK or elsewhere has publicly condemned this man, despite the evidence of his grotesque criminal exploits, speaks volumes.

While SCMR may seem like an extreme example to use to illustrate the monolithic and often dangerous thinking being nurtured within the academy today, there does tend to be a broad agreement among most scholars researching the topic that the sex trade should be treated like any other industry, particularly among anthropologists, and within gender studies and sociology departments. There are people who resist the pro-prostitution line, but they tend to be in departments[29] not directly related to the study of gender and prostitution.

---

[27]Stuff. (2016, Mar 19.) *Dad accused of charity scam which helped bankroll daughter's New Zealand trip.* On Stuff. Retrieved 15 June 2017, from http://www.stuff.co.nz/world/europe/78058525/Dad-accused-of-charity-scam-which-helped-bankroll-daughters-New-Zealand-trip.

[28]Open Charities: The Sompan Foundation. Retrieved 15 June 2017, from http://opencharities.org/charities/1055118.

[29]Sompan Foundation: Projects. Retrieved 15 June 2017, from web.archive.org https://web.archive.org/web/20121201134847/http://www.sompanfoundation.com/projects.html.

Why the Consensus?

The academy is teeming with scholars and doctoral students who on the one hand join forces with campaigners and lobbyists for blanket decriminalisation, but simultaneously present themselves as producing unbiased 'evidence based' research. Those of us who are openly abolitionist, or who regard prostitution as problematic in any way, are regularly accused of conducting biased, methodologically unsound, unethical research.

In 2004, it was deemed that a lap dance study 'will be biased'.[30] A news report said:

> The first UK study into lap-dancing clubs, which has already been criticised as a waste of public money, has provoked a further row, this time about its objectivity. *The Observer* has learnt that the unique academic project is being carried out by a radical feminist, strongly opposed to all aspects of the country's rapidly expanding commercial sex industry.

A follow-up report in 2008 stated: 'Top academics involved in sex research have launched an attack on "seriously flawed" research into British brothels. The academics claim that research into prostitution in the UK published last month by the Poppy Project, which is partly funded by the Ministry of Justice, is inaccurate and unethical. The research in the Big Brothel report "exhibits serious flaws in its mode of data collection and analysis", they warn.

'The group of 27 key figures in sex work research from prestigious universities across the UK and overseas claim the report was conducted with neither ethical approval nor acknowledgement of evidence and was co-authored by a journalist known for producing anti-prostitution findings'.[31]

---

[30]Martin, L. (2004, May 16.) *Lap-dance study 'will be biased'*. In The Guardian. Retrieved 15 June 2017, from https://www.theguardian.com/uk/2004/may/16/research.highereducation.

[31]Lipsett, A. (2008, Oct 3.) *Big brothel research 'seriously flawed'*. In The Guardian. Retrieved 15 June 2017, from http://www.theguardian.com/education/2008/oct/03/research.women.

The criticism of the methodology from the 27 academics included the fact that researchers used some covert methods to gather the evidence, in that male research assistants posed as potential sex buyers in order to establish the 'services' on offer in the brothels. The decision to adopt these methods, which is deemed ethical by the British Sociological Association in cases where information considered to be in the 'public interest' could not be obtained by standard methods, was taken because I and my co-researcher were convinced that we would struggle to obtain any honest answers from either the owners/managers or the women themselves about the existence of trafficking or underaged girls.

One of the 27 key figures was Belinda Brooks-Gordon, Reader in Psychology and Social Policy, at Birkbeck, University of London, UK. She is a former Liberal Democrat councillor and an avid campaigner for the decriminalisation of prostitution laws. She has argued for the rights of disabled 'people' to have access to prostituted 'people' on the National Health Service.

The Policing and Crime Act 2009 amended the Sexual Offences Act 2003 by adding a new section that made it an offence in England and Wales to pay for the services of a person in prostitution who has been coerced into selling sex. The section was implemented from 1 April 2010. The pro-prostitution lobby was extremely active in campaigning against the amendment.

During the IUSW-led campaign against government plans to introduce partial criminalisation of paying for sex, Brooks-Gordon, along with Douglas Fox and other IUSW activists, circulated a request for help to punters and prostituted women via their websites. In her lengthy email, Brooks-Gordon advised on how to prevent the law from being passed before moving on to insulting the dress sense of Fiona Mactaggart, the Labour MP who was instrumental in bringing in the law. I raise this *not* because this type of ridicule is heinous, or unusual of any of us to make such comments, particularly about those we may have fundamental disagreements with, but rather because she personally attacked Mactaggart on a forum of punters, many of whom are deeply misogynistic.

Jo Phoenix is an academic who takes the rare position of neither supporting nor denouncing the Nordic model. The Chair in Criminology at the Open University, UK, Phoenix is well versed in the polarised positions adopted within the debate on the sex trade, but refuses to be 'claimed' by either side.

In 2012, Phoenix was asked to take part in an event hosted by the Cambridge Debating Society entitled, 'This House Would Decriminalise Prostitution', when another panellist (who is an abolitionist) cancelled her attendance at the last minute. Prior to the debate, I clearly heard Phoenix being admonished by Brooks-Gordon for speaking against decriminalisation: Brooks-Gordon told Phoenix she was 'irresponsible' because 'this is about women's lives'. In the debate (which the pro-decriminalisation side won), Phoenix argued that the sex trade could not be best regulated by the free market, and that decriminalising prostitution doesn't actually resolve the issues that sit at the heart of the matter, such as abuse, exploitation and vulnerability.

Four years after the debate, I asked Phoenix why she thought Brooks-Gordon appeared to be so displeased with her. 'I don't think it's a monolithic debate, I think it's a sterile debate', says Phoenix. 'I think that the whole argument when it gets truncated down to decriminalisation, legalisation or whatever is just sterile because nobody is actually paying attention to those baseline things. [such as can the sex trade become part of the marketplace?] What is the purpose of the law in regulating sex, sexuality and sexual violence? What is the purpose of the state? And until the debate gets a little bit more nuanced along those lines, then I'm not likely to join in', says Phoenix.

Neutral Positions?

This research doesn't look at sex as a way that men can demonstrate and enforce power over women. It's research that paints a sanitised picture of the sex industry – a picture that doesn't show the role of institutionalised male power in the sex industry. (Pala Molisa, 'Breaking the silence on prostitution and rape culture', 2015)[32]

---

[32]Molisa, P. (2015, Dec 20.) *Breaking the silence on prostitution and rape culture*. In E-Tangata. Retrieved 15 June 2017, from http://e-tangata.co.nz/news/breaking-the-silence.

In November 2016, I attended the launch at Kingston University, London, of the European Commission-funded project Sexual Humanitarianism: Migration, Sex Work and Trafficking (SexHum),[33] described on the project website as a study of 'the relation between migration, sex work and trafficking in the global sex industry by analysing migrants' own understandings and experiences of agency and exploitation'.

The research will be conducted in Australia (Melbourne and Sydney), France (Paris and Marseille), New Zealand (Auckland and Wellington) and the USA (New York and Los Angeles). The total funding for the project, of which Mai is the grant holder and coordinator, is €1,341,000.

During his introduction to the project, Mai outlined his perspective on the current debates and discourses around prostitution and the sex trade, including the trafficking of women. Mai made several references to 'abolitionists' in what I considered to be a critical manner. His pro-prostitution position was extremely clear, and in order to illustrate his various points about how abolitionism is both undesirable and unworkable, Mai spoke of police raids on brothels in Soho, London, in which he cited a scenario in 2013 where people were arrested. It was unclear to me from his presentation whether he was talking about brothel owners, pimps, traffickers or people suspected of being the victims of trafficking. The impression was certainly given, however, that those who were arrested were 'sex workers' who were not trafficked or in need of intervention.

Mai said of SexHum: 'This project is about a controversy and the way in which different actors see sex work—sex workers see these events differently'.

Continuing on his theme, Mai put the 2013 anti-trafficking operation in Soho down to 'gentrification': 'Anti-trafficking is used and misused as a way to clear the ground for gentrification', said Mai, before qualifying it with a few words about how terrible 'real' trafficking is. 'The problem being that trafficking does exist and it is a very serious

---

[33]Sexual Humanitarianism. Retrieved 15 June 2017, from https://sexualhumanitarianism.wordpress.com/.

and heinous crime and that people who are victims of it should be supported adequately. But this should not be confused with the enforcement of migration law. Trafficking is a very specific dynamic, a crime. It means forcing people against their will and with deception and coercion to work in the sex trade and also in other sectors of the sex trade.'

Mai's conceptualisation of what amounts to trafficking appears to be at odds with the internationally adopted 'Palermo Protocol', which clearly states that it is not required to show that 'force' was used in order to prove trafficking. If this statement does not make clear Mai's position on prostitution, trafficking and the sex trade in general, then I don't know what does. But during his talk, Mai identified only the abolitionists as having a position, and a problematic one at that, but did not state his own lobbying activities for full decriminalisation of the sex trade, or his links to organisations such as the IUSW.

The academy plays an important role in producing propaganda to support legalised and decriminalised prostitution regimes. The University of Nevada in the USA is home to several pros-prostitution researchers, as is the University of Amsterdam and others.

I meet with Renate Van der Zee, a journalist and human rights campaigner, in a cafe in Amsterdam. I ask her about the academic research in Dutch universities on the sex trade and whether there is any robust critique of legalisation. 'No', says Van der Zee. 'I just think it's amazing that we don't have any researchers in Holland that have a different premise.[34] All the days was too good an opportunity researchers have the premise of prostitution being something you can take apart from human trafficking', she tells me. 'If we legalise cleverly enough we could have a clean world of prostitution [they say]. That was the aim, that was the intention [of legalisation]. People are still clinging to that idea, although it's pretty obvious to everybody that it hasn't worked out.'

---

[34]United Nations Human Rights Office of the High Commissioner. (2000, Nov 15.) *Protocol to prevent, suppress and punish trafficking in persons especially women and children, supplementing the United Nations convention against transnational organizedsrime.* Retrieved 15 June 2017, from http://www.ohchr.org/EN/ProfessionalInterest/Pages/ProtocolTraffickingInPersons.aspx.

European Parliament

In 2014 the European Parliament passed a Resolution that affirmed the Nordic model as the most effective way to tackle trafficking into the sex trade. That same year, the European Commission made €2.5 million available to study demand for prostitution. The funding was awarded to the project DemandAT, which, on its website,[35] describes its activities in this way:

> DemandAt is an interdisciplinary project addressing the challenge of understanding demand for trafficking in human beings and analysing the policy and practical measures that can influence this demand. The project feeds into recent efforts of European countries to find ways to reduce demand for the products and services provided by trafficked persons within their own economies and societies as a means of tackling trafficking. The project investigates multiple forms of trafficking and forced labour to assess the impact and potential of demand-side measures to reduce trafficking.

Despite the fact that the main aim of the project is to 'explore the demand for trafficking', most of the presenters appeared to deny or minimise the harm or even dismiss the existence of trafficking and pimping. Scare quotes appear around the majority of mentions of 'trafficking' in the book of abstracts, and the preferred vocabulary of all but three of the presenters is 'migration for sex work'. Further, the organisers state that 'inadequate attention has been paid to the purchasers themselves' and that the research team plans on an 'empirical in-depth analysis of the demand for human trafficking'. This was certainly not done at the conference.

Marieke van Doorninck is the representative from the Netherlands, and was a vocal supporter of the Dutch model before it became clear that legalisation had been an unmitigated disaster. In 2004, I interviewed her at her then place of work, the de Graaf Foundation which,

---

[35]Demand AT. Retrieved 15 June 2017, from http://www.demandat.eu/.

as Janice Raymond points out in *Not a Choice*, was 'originally an abolitionist Christian research institute for the study of prostitution, reversed
its mission and began promoting the acceptance of prostitution as normal work. Supported by generous state subsidies, the foundation and its
studies helped to inspire and lobby for the legalisation legislation that
was ultimately passed in 2000'.[36]

At the time of our interview, van Doorninck was extremely positive
about tolerance zones and legal brothels. 'A good legal sex trade is your
best instrument against an illegal circuit', she told me.[37] Van Doorninck
is on the board or otherwise associated with several organisations that
support blanket decriminalisation, such as De Graaf Stichting, La
Strada, the Red Umbrella Fund and Mama Cash. It would be difficult
to find anyone with a stronger pro-prostitution CV than hers.

The Swedish team member is Petra Östergren, a PhD candidate at
Lund University. One of Östergren's PhD supervisors is Don Kulick,
the co-author of a book on sex and disability that can be read as a manifesto against the Nordic model and for state-funded prostitution for
disabled men.[38] I have explored Kulick's arguments in detail in Chap. 5
on 'The Invisible Man'. Östergren is a long time campaigner—the most
vocal in Sweden—against the Nordic model and the radical feminist
position on the sex trade.

Östergren's work is much closer to campaigning than to scholarship,
according to Anna Skarhed, who is the Chancellor of Justice in Sweden.
Skarhed compiled the report, 'The Ban Against the Purchase of Sexual
Services: An evaluation 1999–2008',[39] on behalf of the Swedish government. I met her at a conference on trafficking in Lithuania in 2015, and
asked how the pro-decriminalisation lobby had reacted to the report.

---

[36]Raymond, J. (2014.) *Not a choice, not a job: Exposing the myths about prostitution and the global sex trade*. London: Potomac. p. 126.

[37]Bindel, J. (2004, May 15.) *Streets apart*. In The Guardian. Retrieved 15 June 2017, from https://www.theguardian.com/theguardian/2004/may/15/weekend7.weekend4.

[38]Kulick, D.; Rhystrom, J. (2015.) *Loneliness and its opposite: Sex, disability and the ethics of engagement*. US: Duke University Press.

[39]Swedish Institute. (2010, Nov.) *The ban against the purchase of sexual services. An evaluation 1999-2008*. Retrieved 15 June 2017, from https://ec.europa.eu/anti-trafficking/sites/antitrafficking/files/the_ban_against_the_purchase_of_sexual_services._an_evaluation_1999-2008_1.pdf.

'Sometimes it makes me mad', said Skarhed. 'It's part of this lobby that tries to counter the real success that this is. It has asked for more research. You can always say people are biased in different ways. In this case you can say she is not a scholar. She is acting in a way, she's discussing in a way, she is writing in a way that is not academic. … I listened to a debate between Petra Östergren and a person from a feminist NGO group from Sweden'. According to Östergren, my study showed that "the women in prostitution have had a really bad time since this legislation came into force". I just wonder where she read that?'

I met Max Waltman, Postdoctoral Researcher at Stockholm University's Department of Political Science, in Stockholm, Sweden. I wanted to ask one of the few abolitionist academics about the resistance in academia to the Nordic model, in particular in the country that spearheaded the law to criminalise demand.

'I got into contact with Professor Catharine MacKinnon [the feminist scholar, and abolitionist] [which inspired me] to write about pornography because there's very little about it in political science', says Waltman. 'Eventually that also connected with the issues of prostitution and trafficking because pornography, prostitution and trafficking are all related in several ways. Pornographers recruit performers from the same vulnerable populations. The consumption effect has also been documented. They inspire men to go out and buy a person for sex because they want to try out all these things.'

Since Waltman's work on the sex trade became well known both in and outside Sweden, he has faced hostility from his pro-prostitution counterparts and other campaigners for blanket decriminalisation. It is no wonder. As Waltman notes, Rose Alliance supports a similar agenda for decriminalising tricks as do other organisations in the world, such as COYOTE and SWOP.[40]

In recent years, pro-prostitution academics have focused on three main subject areas. The 'failures' of the Nordic model; 'the success' of the New Zealand model; and the 'diversity' of the sex trade (in order

---

[40]Max Waltman. 2011. "Prohibiting Sex Purchasing and Ending Trafficking: The Swedish Prostitution Law". *Michigan Journal of International Law* 33 (1) 133–157.

to argue that developing policies around the sex trade within a framework of violence against women and girls is unsuitable, because, as they claim, increasing numbers of men sell sex, and increasing numbers of women buy it).

ProsPol Conference, Austria

As mentioned in Chap. 3, being able to observe the world's leading pro-prostitution academics at the April 2015 ProsPol conference in Vienna, Austria, over a period of 3 days was too good an opportunity to miss. After several attempts to register for the conference (and being told that it was full, and then, when I pointed out that I knew at least two people who had registered to go who had since cancelled, telling me that it was only for those in full-time academia, to which I responded that I knew at least half a dozen delegates and even panellists who were not in full-time academia), I was given a place at the first international conference organised by ProsPol ('Comparing European Prostitution Policies: Understanding Scales and Cultures of Governance').

I was nervous about attending the conference, feeling a bit like a vegan at a butcher's convention. Having read the long list of names who were due to present at workshops or deliver keynote speeches, I knew that I would be among a sea of pro-prostitution academics who would possibly be hostile to my attendance. I was right. Having seen the delegate list, the other attendees were aware of my presence. I sat at the back of the main hall as Barb Brents from the University of Nevada delivered the keynote speech on 'Neo-liberalism, prostitution and the political economy of sex'. Sitting next to me was a young woman I recognised as Morgane Merteuil, former Secretary General of the pro-prostitution organisation STRASS ('Syndicat du TRAvail Sexuel', which translates as 'Union of Sex Work'). I was later told that Merteuil had tweeted: 'OMG I am sitting next to Julie Bindel!' I had a sense this was not a fangirl tweet, but that Merteuil was stunned to see me at such an event.

I walked past academics I knew from conferences and other events. No-one replied in response to my greetings and a few turned their backs. I mention the unfriendliness—often bordering on hostility—towards me by a number of the delegates at this conference not because I harbour any hurt feelings, or because people don't have the right to dislike me and make their feelings known, but rather because it is relevant to the wider point regarding treatment of some potential PhD candidates who wish to conduct academic research on topics and issues relating to the harms of prostitution.

Over the years I have met and been contacted by at least a dozen PhD candidates who began their studies from a position of believing that the sex trade is a cause and consequence of women's oppression, who have told me stories about their experiences with potential PhD supervisors at universities in various countries around the world. These PhD candidates all had a similar story to tell. When approaching potential supervisors in order to put forward their research framework, they were told that their views on prostitution did not fit within the "human rights framework" of 'sex workers' rights'. A number have told me that they have had unpleasant experiences in trying to publish papers during the course of their studies on the harms of the sex trade to be rejected and have their work dismissed simply, in their belief, because they did not hold the view that "sex work" was largely unproblematic except for law enforcement interference.

I did not attend the Mayor's drinks reception or the conference dinner afterwards. I was told that the Deputy Mayor, in his welcome speech, said that in order to tackle the problems with prostitution, all that needed to be done was for everyone to get over their moralism, their dislike of prostitution and their uncomfortable feelings about it, and just accept that prostitution would always be there.

The only friendly person, apart from three feminist academics from the UK who considered the sex trade to be problematic for women, was Östergren. Despite Östergren being the bête noir of the women's movement in Sweden, and me being an active abolitionist, we bonded over the fact that we were the only lesbians there.

By the closing plenary on the Saturday I was more than ready to leave. I had been told in workshops that I was not allowed to record the sessions, despite the fact that others were doing so. During one workshop, in which I had my voice recorder openly on display, I left the room between speakers for a very short time. On my return, I was told by one of the speakers that my voice recorder had been switched off by a delegate sitting on my row, and that from that moment on I would have to ask permission. I explained that I was only using the recording as a substitute for taking notes and that I would not be using them in any public way. I was told, firmly, that I had to 'seek consent'. I asked if this applied to everyone at the conference but did not receive an answer. Later that day I saw a Tweet from a panellist who told her followers I had walked out of the room during her speech.

The barrister and academic Catherine Briddick was one of the three delegates who openly opposed the sex trade at the conference. On our return, I asked Briddick via email for her view of the conference. 'It was broadly supportive of the "sex work" perspective and to this end the fact the purchase of sex remains an activity that is overwhelmingly engaged in by men (of women, in Europe at least) was not subject to critical analysis', she replied.

For Briddick, the extent to which prostitution has been 're-imagined' as concerned with personal autonomy, sexual freedom (and the gay liberation movement) and prostitution as a matter of economic and sexual 'rights', is problematic. 'It serves to obscure the fact that prostitution as a practice is rooted in patriarchy', says Briddick, 'and reinforced by a range of mutually reinforcing structural inequalities, such as those based on race, migration status, sexual orientation and economic status'.

The closing session featured, among others, Ronald Weitzer, a USA-based academic and author of *Legalising Prostitution: From Illicit Vice to Lawful Business*.[41] Weitzer is a long-time campaigner for blanket legalisation of the sex trade. The opening line of his book reads: 'It is taken for granted by most people that buying and selling sex is degrading, dishonourable, or despicable, and there is a deep-rooted belief that prostitution has always been and will forever remain taboo'. The paragraph concludes with: 'I show [in this chapter] that many popular assumptions about prostitutes, their clients, and their managers are either entirely fictional or valid for only a segment of the trade'.

During his talk, Weitzer spoke of the lack of a charismatic 'sex workers' rights' figurehead since Margot St James had more-or-less stopped

---

[41]Weitzer, R. (2011.) *Legalizing prostitution: From illicit vice to lawful business*. New York: NYU Press.

appearing in the media and at public events. Extolling the virtues of St James, Weitzer argued that unless a suitable successor took the reigns the movement would suffer the loss. Immediately, several young, conventionally attractive women began to mutter their complaints at Weitzer's claim that no-one in the contemporary 'sex workers' rights' movement was good enough to step into St James's shoes. Two of them began to shout out their anger at Weitzer, with one muttering that: '[Weitzer] has no idea about the [SWR] movement. How dare he?'

In 1994, Weitzer contributed an article to *Gauntlet*,[42] a periodical exploring 'the limits of free expression'. The special edition was entitled 'In defence of prostitution'. The cover image was of a handcuffed, topless woman with 'For Sale' written across one breast, and flanked by a uniformed police officer.

Weitzer's article, 'Community Groups vs Prostitutes', was based on his research of attitudes from residents and business owners in street prostitution areas to the sex trade. The majority of interviewees told Weitzer that they were unhappy with prostitution in their area, citing reasons such as sexual harassment from punters, health risks to children from discarded used condoms and needles, noise and disruption, and the depreciation of value in property prices. Weitzer, having decided that 'these groups may sometimes exaggerate the problem, but for the most part they appear to be reacting to real problems resulting from illegal street prostitution …' went on to ask them if they would be opposed to legalised, regulated brothels if that would help to reduce street problems. '[T]hey were remarkably receptive to the idea.'

Which, of course, is what the residents would agree to when presented as 'solving the problems' of street prostitution. This promise of 'discreet, legal, indoor prostitution' as a solution to the problems of street prostitution rarely, if ever, materialises.[43]

For me, the clearest example of the irrelevance of much pro-prostitution academia was a panel entitled 'Bodies at Work: Body Labour

---

[42]Hoffman, B. (1994.) *The best of Gauntlet: Exploring the limits of free expression.* Texas: Texas Bookman.

[43]Yorkshire Evening Post. (2016, Feb 27.) *Leeds's 'managed' prostitution zone under review after backlash.* In Yorkshire Evening Post. Retrieved 15 June 2017, from http://www.yorkshireevening-post.co.uk/news/leeds-s-managed-prostitution-zone-under-review-after-backlash-1-7752702.

and Work Strategies in a Nevada Brothel', chaired by Christina Parreira of the University of Nevada. Parreira describes herself in an article as having 'done several different kinds of sex work, from stripping to camming to porn' but admitted that she had not 'worked in a brothel' until her research during the course of six trips to a legal brothel in Nevada. During these visits, Parreira sold sex herself, as well as conducting interviews with 12 of the other prostituted women.[44]

Parreira's findings are described in the conference abstract as follows:

> I found an important connection between the way in which women conceptualise their body, particularly the ways they reproduce a mind/body dualism in their descriptions, and their enjoyment of the sex, feelings about stigma and shame, and their ability and desire to orgasm. Workers who practised 'holistically' (Brents & Jackson 2013) and were less influenced by Western mind/body dualism, were less likely to mentally distance themselves from clients, less likely to see their work as 'dirty work' and more likely to achieve orgasm with clients. Workers who report disconnects between mind and body were more likely to distance themselves from clients. However, this division seemed to break on age; the majority of workers who reported the ability and desire to achieve orgasm are over age 40.

Parreira's claims that women who dissociate from the act of prostitution are somehow losing out on potential sexual pleasure, including orgasms, is not just risible but dangerous. Without exception, every single one of the 50 survivors I interviewed for the purposes of this book, and the vast majority of the prostituted women I have spoken to over the years, say that the ability to distance themselves to the point of dissociation during any sexual encounter with punters was crucial. 'It was the only way I could survive', says Huschke Mau, who was prostituted in Germany from legal brothels. 'Otherwise I would have gone mad.'

---

[44]McNeill, M. (2014, June 9.) *Guest columnist: Christina Parreira*. On The Honest Courtesan. Retrieved 15 June 2017, from https://maggiemcneill.wordpress.com/2014/06/09/guest-columnist-christina-parreira/.

Anthropologists: Going Native

A number of pro-prostitution academics claim to be 'sex workers' and therefore command respect and are granted authenticity by those who value personal experience over objective scholarship. But often these academics have simply dabbled in aspects of the sex trade as part of their field research.

The co-founder of the IUSW, which is neither a union nor international, or, for that matter, has many 'sex workers' as members, is such a person. Ana Lopes was one of a small group of radical anthropologists at East London University, UK, who were studying the sex trade. According to Catherine Stephens (who became involved in the IUSW in 2004), Lopes was a 'migrant sex worker', but that is untrue. Lopes came to the UK from Portugal to study for a PhD. She received a DPhil from the University of East London in 2005. Her dissertation was entitled 'Organising in the Sex Trade: An Action Research Investigation'.

Lopes, along with a small but growing number of academics, decided to 'go native' in order to carry out her research. 'I have carried out participant observation within the sex trade', she writes, 'especially through working as a phone sex operator and working in an agency that provides health support for sex workers. Thus, I have observed and experienced two of the major problems faced by sex workers all over the world: the lack of labour rights, and stigmatising social attitudes'.[45]

The assumption here is that 'labour rights' would improve the situation for women on the street and in brothels, and that by doing participatory research she became 'one of them'. Lopes writes: 'This project has consisted in setting up and developing an organisational platform from which to campaign for sex workers rights. I carried out this project over five years, during which I was active in the sex workers' rights movement, as well as working in the sex trade myself for most of this time'.[46] In fact, Lopes began working on a phone sex line one year after

---

[45]Lopes, A. (2005.) *Organising in the sex industry: An action research investigation.* Unpublished PhD dissertation, East London University, p. 10.

[46]Lopes, A. (2005.) Lopes, A. (2005.) Organising in the sex industry: An action research investigation. Unpublished PhD dissertation, East London University, p. 12.

setting up the IUSW, which may or may not have been in order to lend authenticity to her research. 'Going native' is one method adopted by anthropologists.

Impartiality?

During my research on disabled men and the argument that they have a right to pay for sex (see Chap. 5), I approached a UK-based academic (whom I have chosen not to name as they did not give me an 'on the record' interview) who was known as an expert on sexuality and disability. It was clear from the beginning of our email exchange that my views on the sex trade were not shared by the academic. However, they were friendly, courteous and interested in my approach. In fact, the academic more-or-less admitted that they were uncomfortable with the idea that disabled men 'can't get a real date' and therefore should be able to access paid sex.

Having not heard back from this academic for a while following my request for an on-the- record chat, I received this reply by email: 'I'm so sorry, I'm going to have to decline the interview. While I thought your book proposal looks really interesting (and will make waves, I'm sure), I have worries about wanting to do future sex work research and not being accepted within sex worker communities because of inclusion in the book (even as a countering voice)'.

It would appear that the notion of academic impartiality is somewhat compromised when it comes to prostitution. This person has quoted those who are in favour of blanket decriminalisation of the sex trade, and that have an uncritical viewpoint of prostitution, and is obviously not concerned about upsetting abolitionists by doing so. They have also been quoted in pro-prostitution literature. This person clearly prioritised access to the pro-prostitution or 'sex workers' rights' movement over any concerns about academic impartiality or 'fairness'. I personally have given interviews to a number of pro-prostitution activists and academics over the years, as have a number of abolitionist colleagues. The world did not end.

Complaints About Abolitionist Academics

Ron Weitzer writes on the *Sex Work Research* blog[47]:

> In no area of the social sciences has ideology contaminated knowledge more pervasively than in writings on the sex industry. Too often in this area, the canons of scientific inquiry are suspended and research deliberately skewed to serve a particular political agenda. Much of this work has been done by writers who regard the sex industry as a despicable institution and who are active in campaigns to abolish it.[48]

The hypocrisy of Weitzer's opening argument is staggering. All of the pro-prostitution academics cited in this book campaign for total decriminalisation of the sex trade, some of them working alongside pimps and sex buyers. What Weitzer is effectively stating is that any academic who arrives at a sound, evidence-based conclusion that prostitution is male violence against women and girls are ipso facto not fit to contribute to prostitution debate. Indeed, it is unfortunately the case that research produced by countries, no less, which have implemented the Nordic model including Sweden, Norway, Canada, Northern Ireland, Republic of Ireland, and France, are also ridiculed from the outset as problematic.

During our discussion at the Vienna ProsPol conference, Östergren seemed surprised to hear that abolitionists are regularly on the receiving end of slurs, false accusations and insults about our work, intentions and personhood. In 2015, Östergren and I spoke by Skype as she had been mulling over her earlier assumption that it was in fact the pro-prostitution lobby that suffered insults and personal attacks. She said: 'We had talked about censoring and campaigning against our work and you said that what had been done to me was not OK, and you said

---

[47]https://sexworkresearch.wordpress.com/2013/07/05/flawed-theory-and-method-in-studies-of-prostitution/.

[48]Weitzer, R. (2005.) *Flawed theory and method in studies of prostitution.* On Sex Work Research. Retrieved 15 June 2017, from http://web.archive.org/web/20060111065947/http://www.woodhullfoundation.org/content/otherpublications/WeitzerVAW-1.pdf.

'look just in this room, there are people who have tried to stop my work'—and that made an impact on me.'

Academic and psychologist Dr Melissa Farley has conducted vital and rigorous research into both the harms of prostitution and the men who pay for sex. Like other academics who refuse to sign up to a positive view of the sex trade (because the evidence does not support this), Farley has been bullied, slandered and vilified by her pro-prostitution counterparts, supported by the non-academic sex trade supporters and profiteers.

In 2010, Farley experienced a number of reviews of her academic papers where it was clear that her work was being judged from an ideological rather than a scholarly position. The reviewers were not at all pleased, it appeared, that Farley's data reflected the harm done to prostituted women. She told me: 'The one that jumps to mind many years ago and sent me into shock and then fury, was from a law review journal where the reviewers commented, where I cited Andrea Dworkin's feminist theory on this topic of the sex trade, 'Who is Andrea Dworkin and why should we care anyway?"

For Farley, this was a clear message that pro-prostitution trumped the reviewers' consideration of the quality of the work. 'It reflects the ideological bias of people who are reviewing research', says Farley. 'They are not looking at the adequacy of the design, the execution of the research, methodology, the analysis of the statistics and whether it's appropriate or off base or if something was missed—that's reasonable criticism. But they're going after stuff like they don't want Andrea Dworkin's name cited in their law journal.'

In 2010, a pro-prostitution academic made an official complaint about Farley to the American Psychological Association (APA). The complaint was from Calum Bennachie, a New Zealander who is a major player in the campaign for global decriminalisation of the sex trade, and co-author of the book *Taking the Crime out of Sex Work: New Zealand Sex Workers' Fight for Decriminalisation*[49] along with fellow lobbyists Gillian Abel, Lisa Fitzgerald, Catherine Healy and Aline Taylor. The gist of the complaint against Farley was that she conducted unethical

---

[49]Abel, G.; Fitzgerald, L.; Healy, C. (2010.) *Taking the crime out of sex work: New Zealand sex workers' fight for decriminalisation*. London: Policy Press.

research, skewed her data and potentially could 'cause harm' to research participants. None of these complaints has been substantiated.

Bennachie called for the expulsion of Farley from the APA, which would, had the complaint been successful, have resulted in Farley being unable to work as a psychologist or undertake any further research under that particular professional banner. However, the APA never responded to the complaint and Farley heard nothing from them about it. 'It was a straw man', says Farley. 'A completely unethical accusation and a totally manufactured complaint. It was given no credibility apparently by the APA.'

Roger Matthews has had similar experiences to Farley. 'I wrote an article that was designed to be a very comprehensive overview on the debates around demand', says Matthews. 'It looked at international development and the research on the topic so that it became a comprehensive review on demand. The reviewers wrote back asking, "Why would you want to write an article on demand?" I was gobsmacked.'

I ask Matthews, who is considered to be one of the world's leading criminologists,[50] for his opinion on why his insightful research was not readily published. 'Basically if you write stuff from an abolitionist position in terms of prostitution, 90% of the people in academia are part of the pro-prostitution lobby. You can guarantee that even if you get reviewed you are going to get a very poor review.'

According to Janice Raymond, also an experienced and revered academic, any research can be critiqued but the pro-prostitution academics rarely, if ever, critique each other's work or research findings. 'Evidence-based research is not objective', says Raymond. 'There's this road between what your findings are and how you interpret those findings.'

Increasingly, the academy and the lesbian, gay, bisexual, transgender, queer, questioning and intersex (LGBTQQI) world rely on each other's defence and glorification of the sex trade. Chapter 10 will explore the rainbow alliance of prostitution apologists and queers and ask: How did a group which began as a civil rights movement to liberate marginalised people from bigotry and oppression become hijacked by one that favours pimps and punters?

---

[50]Bindel, J. (2008, Feb 29.) *It's abuse and a life of hell*. In The Guardian. Retrieved 15 June 2017, from https://www.theguardian.com/lifeandstyle/2008/feb/29/women.ukcrime.

10

A Queer Defence of the Sex Trade

What is happening in Russia at the moment is that those in the LGBT movement who openly promote legalisation of the sex trade are all gay men. They do not have direct experience of what the sex trade is. The movement itself is dominated by males, so from LGBT you just have the letter G left. (Artem, male survivor of the sex trade, Moscow, 2016)

I have never experienced people saying prostitution is comfortable in Sweden, because most people can empathise with those involved. But recently, some have been academically brainwashed by the queer movement that don't get it – regular people get it very quickly. (Sven Axel-Mansson, academic, Sweden, 2016)

One of the most vociferous groups in its support of 'sex workers' rights' is the new queer movement. This rainbow alliance politics first emerged in the 1980s with the scandal involving the National Council of Civil Liberties when it supported the inclusion of the Paedophile Information Exchange (PIE).[1] There was much dissent and disagreement within the gay liberation movement (mostly from lesbians) at the time that PIE

---

[1] de Castella, T.; Heyden, T. (2014, Feb 27.) *How did the pro-paedophile group PIE exist openly for 10 years?* On BBC News. Retrieved 15 June 2017, from http://www.bbc.co.uk/news/magazine-26352378.

was looking to join hands with those who were sexually 'non-conformist'. Many gay men did not see that the lobbyists for the normalisation of child sexual abuse had misappropriated their legitimate fight for equality, protection and rights.

In the past, 'queer' was commonly used as an insult towards those deemed to be lesbian or gay, and was considered a heinous slur by those of us at whom it was targeted. But today the term 'queer', when it is used in the neutral or affirmative manner, is an invention of post-modernism.

According to the academic Matt Alberhasky[2]: '"Queer" is a term "reclaimed" by the gay and lesbian community as a way to erase distinctions and include transgendered individuals'. The problem many lesbians have with the term 'queer' is that it depoliticises lesbians' experiences as women because the term is gender neutral. This, as the likes of feminist scholar Sheila Jeffreys[3] have rightly argued, is another way of eliminating women.

The Genesis of Sex as Violence

The first time the terms 'queer' and 'sex work' were used together in the mainstream press was in November 1997 in the *Sydney Morning Herald*. The 2000-word article, entitled 'Queer, Really Queer', was an unbridled celebration of the eroticisation of violence, degradation and abuse. It read:

> They use names like Groovi Biscuit, Azaria Universe, Trash Vaudeville, Indigo Plushbox, Vy1 and Miss Fit. ... They mime, scream, provoke, excite, entertain, occasionally eat fire – vaginally – and not infrequently consent to receive or inflict bodily wounds. ... They work at the literal cutting edge of artistic and social acceptability, and in deadly earnest. Welcome to the brave new world of Queer Performance.[4]

---

[2]Alberhasky, M. (2014, Sept 9.) *Queer theory*. On youtube.com. Retrieved 15 June 2017, from https://www.youtube.com/watch?v=eVxV1N0MfqM Matthew Alberhasky is an English professor at Des Moines Area Community College Urban located in Des Moines, Iowa.

[3]Jeffries, S. (2002.) *Unpacking queer politics*. London: Polity Press.

[4]James, B. (1997, Nov 8.) *Queer, really queer*. In Sydney Morning Herald, Australia.

Since the 1970s, the liberals and gay libertarians have striven to include all and sundry in the sexual liberation movement, and have argued for groups including 'sex work' and the PIE[5]—the former being a category of male violence, and the latter a predatory sexual politic normalising child rape.

The Pact Between Trans and 'Sex Workers' Rights'

> We have managed in recent years to bring together in our movement, a very diverse range of people who are either directly in sex work or related to sex work. Those who are women, men and transgender, those who are doing different types of sex work like stripping or BDSM and so forth. The common obstacles are that the sex workers are criminalised, there is abuse and corruption and violence on behalf of the state authorities, and the absence or lack of access to good secure house services. So by identifying those common obstacles they can build alliances and grow the organisation and that's the only way to go forward. (Irina Maslova, Silver Rose, Russia, 2015)

The rise of transgender identity politics has brought with it a strident attempt to merge the identities of prostitution and so-called 'gender-queer'. There are several arguments used to claim that the experience of being transgender and being prostituted are very similar, if not the same thing. One is that many trans women cannot find regular employment, or need fast cash in order to pay for surgery, and therefore turn to the sex trade. Another is the queer argument that we are all part of one big happy rainbow alliance and 'sex workers' rights', trans rights and queer rights are one thing. What this argument loses is an analysis of men's power in relation to women. In fact, aside from trans women, women are excluded from the equation altogether.

The recently constructed acronyms even lend to my theory that the transgender and 'sex workers' rights' issues have become amalgamated

---

[5]http://www.bbc.co.uk/news/magazine-26352378.

to the point where you literally cannot support one without supporting the other. SWERF (Sex Worker Exclusionary Radical Feminists)
and TERF (Trans Exclusionary Radical Feminists) handily rhyme. Both
groups seem to realise how important merging their interests is. Pro-
prostitution lobbyists regularly tap into support from the transgender
lobby and vice versa. I came to realise just how handy this was for both
groups during the campaign in Britain to introduce a law to criminalise
those who pay for sex. It was 2009 and the proposed bill I mentioned
earlier was being debated in Parliament, which would criminalise the
purchase of sex from a person who was trafficked or otherwise coerced.
It was still considered important to get this bill through, even though
many were sceptical about it because it separated the women who could
show that they had been pimped or forced in some way from those
who were being otherwise abused and exploited in the sex trade, and it
would be practically impossible to police.

The academic Belinda Brooks-Gordon coined the rather amusing
phrase "Carry on Criminology"[6] to describe what she considers to be
poor research into the sex trade. For example, Brooks-Gordon was a sig-
natory to the complaint published in the *Guardian* newspaper about the
'Big Brothel' research that I co-authored (see Chap. 9).

In the build-up to the debate in Parliament and the House of Lords
about the new bill, Brooks-Gordon was heavily involved in rallying the
troops to argue against it. She posted messages on punter websites such
as those on which sex buyers 'review' the prostituted women they buy.
Steve Elrond, as we saw in Chap. 8, is a prolific sex buyer, lobbyist for
blanket decriminalisation and owner of websites that advertise women
to other sex buyers. He posted a message from Brooks-Gordon on his
then personal website,[7] which is no longer live but still accessible on
archive websites.

'Dr Belinda Brooks Gordon [sic] who is brilliant at lobbying for our
rights has asked that the following be circulated', wrote Elrond. Brooks-
Gordon's message outlined the reasons why both prostituted women (or

---

[6]http://theconversation.com/campaigners-for-sex-workers-face-bullying-and-bad-data-21549.

[7]Elrond Middle England. (2009, Jan 22.) *Sex workers campaign in parliament.* Retrieved 15 June
2017, from Web Cache http://webcache.googleusercontent.com/search?q=cache:uVkjYy48oPkJ:
elrondmiddleeng.selectwebsitedesign.com/2009/01/+&cd=1&hl=en&ct=clnk&gl=uk.

'sex workers' as she put it) and sex buyers ('clients') should lobby MPs of all parties in order to get them to vote against introducing a law criminalising demand for trafficked pernous. She went on to explain how important it was to form alliances across different issues, before explaining her next move:

> On Thursday night I am speaking to a transgender group to explain why they should oppose the Bill (some are shakey [sic] on this) – it was one thing for them doing the anti-Bindel nomination demo at the Stonewall awards, but sex work is another issue for them so am working on this. There were good links built up over the demo so will keep you posted as to where they are on this. If anyone wants to come along they are welcome.

The previous year, I had been nominated and shortlisted in the category of 'Journalist of the Year' at the annual Stonewall Awards.[8] As soon as my nomination was announced, the transgender community and much of the gay press went into overdrive. I am regularly accused of 'transphobia' on the strength of an article I wrote in the *Guardian Weekend Magazine* in 2004.[9] I had not asked to be nominated for the award, but as soon as the protest started I knew that I had to turn up to the event or it could have looked as if I had been intimidated out of doing so.

On arrival, I saw that there were well over 100 protesters arguing that my nomination should have been withdrawn and that I peddled 'hate speech'. Alongside the trans-activists were a number of pro-prostitution lobbyists and a smattering of academics. The demonstration was the largest in the history of transgender activism in the UK and there was much publicity relating to it.

One of the main organisers of the demonstration was Sarah Brown, who was a colleague of Brooks-Gordon during the time they were both Liberal Democrat councillors. Following the Stonewall saga, Brooks-Gordon saw an opportunity to get members of the transgender lobby on board in opposing the law to criminalise the demand, and to fight for blanket decriminalisation of the sex trade.

---

[8]Grew, T. (2008, Jul 11.) *Celebs split over trans protests at Stonewall awards.* On Pink News. Retrieved 15 June 2017, from http://www.pinknews.co.uk/2008/11/07/celebs-split-over-trans-protests-at-stonewall-awards/.

[9]Bindel, J. (2004, Jan 31.) *Gender benders, beware.* In The Guardian. Retrieved 15 June 2017, from https://www.theguardian.com/world/2004/jan/31/gender.weekend7.

What is interesting, at least according to Brooks-Gordon, is that at that time in 2009, some of the transgender lobbyists were 'shaky' about coming out in support of the pro-prostitution line. Today they are anything but, and it is hard to find a transgender lobbyist who is anti-prostitution.

Currently in the UK, several local branches and two main political parties give responsibility on drafting and implementing policy on prostitution in the sex trade to their LGBT caucuses. The Liberal Democrats, for example, regularly have trans women speaking at conference, attempting to pass motions to support the blanket decriminalisation of the sex trade. This is the same with the Green Party (except they describe themselves as LGBTIQA+[10]) and some local branches of the Labour Party.

For example, a key member of the LGBT caucus in the Islington branch of the Labour Party is Catherine Stephens.[11] Stephens is a founder of the International Union of Sex Workers (IUSW), the fake union populated by pro-prostitution academics, punters, pimps, brothel owners and other lobbyists for decriminalisation of the sex trade. For the past 10 years I have seen Stephens at conferences and other public meetings, and have never heard her declare herself lesbian or bisexual. However, she now identifies as bisexual, which means that she has been granted legitimacy within the LGBT group.

Trans Influence on 'Sex Work'

Sarah Noble is a Liberal Democrat activist and pro-prostitution trans woman. In 2014, Noble made a speech to conference calling for decriminalisation.[12] Brown, also a trans woman, additionally made a speech at conference calling for decriminalisation.[13]

---

[10]The acronym stands for: lesbian, gay, bisexual, trans, intersex, queer, asexual/agenda/aromantic + other diverse sexual orientations and gender identities.

[11]LGBT Labour. (2015.) *AGM 2015*. Retrieved 15 June 2017, from http://www.lgbtlabour.org.uk/agm2015/.

[12]Noble, S. (2014, Nov 3.) *Opinion: Why Liberal Democrats must oppose any criminalisation of sex workers. On Liberal Democrat Voice*. Retrieved 15 June 2017, from http://www.libdemvoice.org/opinion-why-liberal-democrats-must-oppose-any-criminalisation-of-sex-workers-43164.html.

[13]Brown, S. (2014, Oct 5.) *My speech to the Liberal Democrat autumn conference 2014, on sex work and the Nordic model*. On sarahlizzy.com. Retrieved 15 June 2017, from http://www.sarahlizzy.com/blog/?p=260.

Janet Mock is a male-to-female transgender activist who catapulted into the public arena with the publication of her memoir about growing up transgender, *Redefining Realness: My Path to Womanhood, Identity, Love & So Much More* in 2014.[14] In the video accompanying the book,[15] Mock appears to celebrate children's involvement in the sex trade: 'I was 15 the first time I visited Merchant Street, what some would call "the stroll" for trans women involved in street-based sex work. At the time, I had just begun medically transitioning and it was where younger girls, like my friends and myself, would go to hang out, flirt and fool around with guys and socialise with older trans women, the legends of our community.[16]

Mock goes on to explain how she 'idolised' the prostituted trans women in the area, including those who were used in pornography and in strip clubs. 'These women were the first trans women I met and I quickly correlated trans womanhood and sex work', says Mock, explaining that she came to understand the role of the sex trade as a 'rite of passage' for trans girls.

Mock is disparaging about the role of the media betraying prostitution as 'shameful and degrading'. Like many pro-prostitution lobbyists, Mock considers the stigma attached to prostitution as extremely harmful, placing it above the harm done to prostituted people by sex buyers, pimps and brothel owners. In fact, Mock strongly suggests that any condemnation of the sex trade will lead to violence against those selling sex, claiming that anyone with a negative view of the sex trade 'dehumanises' prostituted people.

[14]Mock, J. (2014.) *Redefining Realness: My Path to Womanhood, Identity, Love and So Much More.* US: Atria Books.

[15]Mock, J. (2014, Jan 30.) *Janet Mock on sex work and redefining realness.* On youtube.com. Retrieved 15 June 2017, from https://www.youtube.com/watch?v=Xd55yq4LMC8.

[16]Mock, J. (2014, Jan 30.) *My experiences as a young trans woman engaged in survival sex work.* On janetmock.com. Retrieved 15 June 2017, from http://janetmock.com/2014/01/30/janet-mock-sex-work-experiences/.

Mock states:

> Sex workers are often dismissed, causing even the most liberal folk to dehumanise, devalue and demean women who are engaged in the sex trades. This pervasive dehumanisation of women in the sex trade leads many to ignore the silencing, brutality, policing, criminalisation and violence sex workers face, even blaming them for being utterly damaged, promiscuous, and unworthy.[17]

As Mock had earlier said, she had learned to link prostitution with being transgender and argues that, because she had learned that prostitution was viewed as shameful, she began to view being transgender as shameful: 'I couldn't separate it from my own body image issues, my sense of self, my internalised shame about being trans, brown, poor, young, woman'.

This is a bizarre and dangerous argument. Mock is effectively saying that unless we completely normalise and destigmatise the sex trade, trans women such as herself will never be able to feel proud of their 'womanhood'. Think about the implications here: first of all, the total conflation of prostitution with being transgender, coupled with the somewhat manipulative argument that if we don't accept prostitution as 'empowering' then trans women will experienced self-hatred.

Mock writes: 'These women taught me that nothing was wrong with me or my body, and that if I wanted they would show me the way, and it was this underground railroad of resources created by low-income, marginalised women, that enabled me when I was 16 to jump in a car with my first regular and choose a pathway to my survival and liberation'.[18]

There we have it: prostitution is about liberation and any condemnation of it means that marginalised women and girls will not be able to survive.

---

[17]Mock, J. (2014, Jan 30.) *My experiences as a young trans woman engaged in survival sex work.* On janetmock.com. Retrieved 15 June 2017, from http://janetmock.com/2014/01/30/janet-mock-sex-work-experiences/.

[18]Mock, J. (2014, Jan 30.) *My experiences as a young trans woman engaged in survival sex work.* On janetmock.com. Retrieved 15 June 2017, from http://janetmock.com/2014/01/30/janet-mock-sex-work-experiences/.

'Transphobia': A Slur to Abolitionists

At a 2011 conference in Copenhagen, Denmark, where both pro-prostitution lobby groups and transgender rights organisations are highly organised (united by a hatred of radical feminism), I was heckled during my speech on violence within the sex trade by a number of men and women waving placards with slogans such as 'End Transphobia' and 'Sex Workers' Rights are Trans Rights'.

I was speaking at the conference, a joint effort between the feminist abolitionist organisation and the Danish government, with Janice Raymond, who authored *The Transsexual Empire*[19] in 1979. Raymond, along with myself and a number of other radical feminists who take a position against the sex trade and against the notion that gender is innate or linked to biological sex, is often prevented from speaking on a number of platforms.

As I write, I have just been disinvited as a keynote speaker at a conference on prostitution and trafficking in Oslo, Norway. My talk was to focus on the tactics and arguments of the pro-prostitution lobby internationally. The conference was organised by the Socialist Left Party of Norway (SV). One week before the event, the Women's Caucus was told by the party leadership that they had to disinvite me on the grounds of 'transphobia'. There had been several complaints from trans people that I would be threatening their 'safe space'. The complainants had registered to attend the conference but when it was announced that I had been withdrawn, they promptly cancelled their attendance. The complainants were all identified to me as pro-prostitution by feminists involved in the conference, as well as by a journalist who covered the story of my ban.

It was a terrible shame that SV, which officially supports the law that criminalises the demand for prostitution, introduced in Norway in 2008, was targeted in this manner.

Following an article in the daily leftist newspaper *Klassekampen*[20] about me being no platformed, a letter from one of the main instigators

---

[19]Raymond, J. (1979.) The Transsexual Empire: The Making of the She-Male. London: Beacon Press.

[20]Henriksen, S. (2017, Jan 9.) *Vil Ikke La Seg Kneble*. On Klasse Kampen. Retrieved 15 June 2017, from http://www.klassekampen.no/article/20170109/ARTICLE/170109956.

of the campaign to stop me from speaking at the event was published by Ingvild Endestad, leader of FRI[21] (The Association of Gender and Sexuality Diversity), a close ally[22] of PION,[23] a pro-prostitution organisation in Norway. Endestad was clearly displeased by the fact that the journalist who wrote the piece had interviewed me. 'SV could have created an arena where Bindel's opinions on transgender people could have been challenged', wrote Endestad. 'Instead, she was offered a lectern where she could talk freely without having to be held accountable for her discriminatory opinions.' Perhaps Endestad is proposing that anyone who is speaking at a public event, and has views that she doesn't approve of on transgender, should be grilled about that topic whatever they are speaking about?

Vilification of Feminist Positions on Gender

A Google search on 'Bindel' and 'transphobe' generates 54,600 unique results. Of course, various combinations and permutations of 'TERF', 'transphobic', or 'transphobia' paired with my name and variants thereof (e.g. misspelled 'Bindle') generate countless more. Twitter analytics reveal innumerable tweets containing the terms 'Bindel' and 'transphobe'. By way of contrast, 'Pemberton' and 'transphobe' on the Twittersphere generates not a single result. Not one.

Pemberton is just one of the many men who has murdered a trans woman in the sex trade: in this case, Jennifer Laude. Joseph Pemberton garrotted and submerged Laude's head in a toilet bowl after he discovered Laude had a penis. This in itself should have ensured at least some social media activity. But Pemberton was no 'ordinary' man. Private First Class Joseph Scott Pemberton was a US Marine on active duty in the Philippines and his trial lasted from 2014–2016, and in no insignificant way caused enormous tension between the two allies that

---

[21]Formerly Norwegian National Association for Lesbian and Gay Liberation.

[22]http://www.ilga-europe.org/sites/default/files/delegate_pack_2015webam.pdf.

[23]NSWP. (2017.) *Regional updates: Europe*. Retrieved 15 June 2017, from http://www.nswp.org/fr/members/europe/pion-sex-workers-interest-organisation-norway.

continues to this day.[24] This was an extraordinarily important story in male violence, US foreign policy, international diplomacy, military prostitution, racism, colonialism and of course transphobia. It was enormous news for the so-called trans and 'sex workers' rights' activists.

The connection between transgender activists and the pro-prostitution lobby groups is often explained by claiming that many trans women enter the sex trade because of being excluded from the mainstream job market. I would suggest another connection: part of the whole trans woman identity is about presenting as hyper-sexualised. Because there is no such thing as a 'natural woman', all it can ever be is an idealised image and that image is created by the male gaze.

The abstract of the postmodern take on transgenderism, prostitution and race is perfectly highlighted in a paper from the *Graduate Journal of Social Science* (2015) by Jet Young entitled 'Blurred Lines: The Contested Nature of Sex Work in a Changing Social Landscape', and subheaded: 'A Chinese diasporic trans rentboy, reflects on the contested arena of sex work. Ponderings on whorephobia as a strategy of imperialism, the continued oppression of femininity, and the murky politics of penetration'.[25]

Piggybacking on the LGBT Campaigns

In a *Huffington Post* article entitled 'Why LGBT and Sex Worker Rights Go Hand-In-Hand', the writer Stephanie Farnsworth, who describes herself as an 'intersectional feminist', argues that:

> The heart of the demand for LGBT rights is the idea that all people should be granted autonomy over their lives and bodies, that anyone should be allowed to sleep with who they choose and that it only concerns the people in the relationship and not the government or bigots. The very same idea is at the core of the fight for sex workers. Why should they not be granted the same freedom? Why should they not be allowed

---

[24]Porter, T. (2015, Dec 2.) *US marine drowned prostitute in toilet after finding 'man not a woman giving him oral sex'*. In International Business Times. Retrieved 15 June 2017, from http://www.ibtimes.co.uk/philippines-us-marine-drowned-prostitute-toilet-after-finding-man-not-woman-giving-him-oral-1531278.

[25]Prostpol Vienna Conference. (2015.) *Book of Abstracts*.

to have sex with who they choose? It is simply hypocritical for LGBT activists to fight for bodily autonomy but deny it to sex workers.[26]

From emotional labour to sex, housework to being a wife or girlfriend, the queer liberal line is to redefine exploitation as work. As Kajsa Ekis Ekman, a journalist and feminist, who wrote the searing critique of surrogacy and its similarities to prostitution, *Being and Being Bought*[27] told me: 'The queer movement is a refuge for some people in prostitution who found that, if you drink to excess and do a lot of drugs, or have been in prostitution, the queer movement won't judge you. There's a lot of self-destruction in that movement that is glorifying experiences that are not good for you and that goes for the gay movement, too'.

Pro-prostitution campaigners are well aware of the advantage to them of aligning themselves with a wider group of 'subversives'. In the same way that a very small transgender community attached itself to the Lesbian and Gay Liberation Movement at the beginning of 2000, the 'sex workers' rights' movement saw an opportunity for wider support from this new and ever growing rainbow alliance. The lesbian and gay movement had become the LGBT movement, and then continued to expand until it encompassed pretty much every letter of the alphabet, leaving out very few groups including, it would appear, the majority of heterosexuals.[28]

One of those activists who reaped the benefits of the new alliance is Irina Maslova, founder of the Russian project Silver Rose. During our interview she told me that in recent years Silver Rose has succeeded in bringing together a very diverse range of people 'who are either directly in sex work related to sex work'.

According to Maslova, those people comprise people in street and off-street prostitution, drug users and 'those who work for themselves independently and those who work for third parties'. She continues:

[26]Farsnworth, S. (2016, Apr 14.) *Why LGBT and sex worker rights go hand-in-hand.* On *Huffington Post.* Retrieved 15 June 2017, from http://www.huffingtonpost.com/stephanie-farnsworth/why-lgbt-and-sex-worker-rights-go-hand-in-hand_b_9367888.html.

[27]Ekman, K. (2013.) Being and being bought: Prostitution, surrogacy and the split self. Melbourne: Spinifex Press.

[28]Bindel, J. (2014, Jul 2.) *Viewpoint: Should gay men and lesbians be bracketed together?* On BBC News. Retrieved 15 June 2017, from http://www.bbc.co.uk/news/magazine-28130472.

'We have women, men and transgender, and those who are doing different types of sex work like stripping or BDSM and so forth. So they managed to create this united movement by finding the common denominator'.

Voices of Dissent

There is, however, a voice of dissent from some gay men. I met Kevin Mwachiro, a writer, activist and author of *Invisible: Stories From Kenya's Queer Community*, during a trip to Nairobi, Kenya, in 2015. 'I personally don't see [the alliance between the 'sex work' lobby and the LGBT movement] as supporting', said Mwachiro. 'I think the sex worker campaigners have been very smart though, because I think it was a question of building critical mass.

'The more of us who are in this, the louder the voice. One time I met Denis [Nzioka, a journalist and LGBT campaigner]. There was a march organised by sex workers and he was going to support them and he said "come", but I had to stop and ask myself because it's a cause I struggle with. But I think it's strategic for both parties. It's one way of getting numbers of them into the boardrooms of the Ministry of Health or the National AIDS bodies.'

But Mwachiro sees a disconnect between the male LGBT activists and the 'sex workers' and the rights of the women involved in prostitution in Nairobi. 'I think organisations [that provide services to men having sex with men] are doing great work', says Mwachiro. 'They are working with a lot of male sex workers. But if the women get their rights as sex workers, I don't think they want to be left behind.'

Alex Hopkins is a journalist, community activist and gay man. He lives in London and frequently writes about some of the harmful practices embedded within the culture of the gay male community. For Hopkins, prostitution is an abusive system and one that vulnerable young gay men can be harmed by. He is particularly damning about the normalisation of pornography within the gay club scene and how it serves to promote prostitution.

'It is telling how gay male porn represents the escort/client relationship', says Hopkins. 'Scenarios tend to fall into two categories: the first in which the client is as physically alluring as the escort – the implication being that selling sex is a pleasure for an escort.'

Some porn in which the sex buyer is a much bigger, more dominant man who emasculates the usually smaller, noticeably more vulnerable prostituted male, is simply the fetishisation of dominance', says
Hopkins. 'It's not improbable that men who pay for sex will watch such
abusive scenarios and re-enact them with escorts—Is this the happy
"rainbow alliance" which certain proponents of prostitution speak of,
I wonder? Ultimately, there can be no "rainbow alliance" in financial
transactions which perpetuate a hierarchy of abuse.'

Industry Cultish Behaviour and 'All Sex Is Good Sex'

I met Sia, a feminist activist from Queensland, Australia, at the first ever
abolitionist conference in Melbourne in 2016. Sia, in her early 50s at
the time of the interview, had experienced serious sexual harassment in
the workplace a few years earlier that put her off political activism for
some time. Looking for a job during the time that decriminalisation
of the sex trade was being implemented, she found herself considering
working in a massage parlour in Sydney.

'In a lot of ways, [prostitution] was very much accepted, particularly when you get into the queer scene and the party scene', says Sia.
'I didn't know I was a lesbian at the time, I worked with other lesbians
and we just thought we were great.

'A friend of mine opened a massage place in Sydney and I worked
there with her and I thought it was just the best thing in the world,
because they were all there for the women, and women were [seen as]
goddesses and it was all really supportive.'

Sia soon began doing what she describes as 'full service'. 'I worked
at upper-class places', she says, 'and tried a few other massage places
around Sydney. I was being validated by the sex-positive community. I
still had some friends from over the years who were like, "Sia! What are
you doing?" Anyway, I was in full service and worked at the top-notch
places, but got raped and then I had a breakdown.'

I asked her why she thought that people were so keen on believing
the myth about sex work? 'It was cool and edgy', says Sia. 'It was an

image. It was part of the party scene, the drug-taking scene. The bottom line is there was so much damage for a lot of the women that were involved in that, and of course [that included] trans people as well.

'I used to fight against the claim that most of them were abused, which most women are. But we used to say, "No, we've never been abused, we're doing this because this is our choice". There was a lot of pain there. After I got raped, I went to [names a counselling service]. What some of the women told me when they realised what my job was: "Isn't that great? How empowering that you're a sex worker. Good on you". I want to try and bring in some sort of support for exploited women because my experience of that was just horrendous.'

Gay Men and Celebration of the Sex Trade

The notorious Douglas Fox is not queer-identified. He does, however, conflate being involved in prostitution with having a gay identity. He says: 'When you try and stop the centre of human activity, it's like with homosexuality. When you try to battle sexuality, like gay marriage, in the past, in the' 50s, there would have been electric shock treatment, you could have been locked up, all sorts of things could have happened'.[29]

Yet prostitution is not a sexual identity, I say to Fox. 'But the similarities are there, and that's consensual sexual activity. When you have legislation that tried to prevent consensual sexual activity …', he argues.

In the film *Politically I Am a Whore*, about the life of Thierry Shaffauser, we see Shaffauser at the Putes Pride (Whores Pride) March in Paris 2010 in the opening scene. He is dressed in clothing that many would associate with women involved in street prostitution. Shaffauser is standing with the leaders of the demonstration: two men and two trans women. 'I get looked at as if I am odd'. 'But this is France. It is a racist country. People can't cope with anything different', says Shaffauser, who is white.

---

[29]Mai, N. (2011) 'Tampering with the Sex of "Angels": Migrant Male Minors and Young Adults Selling Sex in the EU', Journal of Ethnic and Migration Studies, 37(8): 1237–1252.

I speak to Shaffauser in Paris, where he is an active member of the Syndicat du Travail Sexuel (STRASS), which he describes as the 'sex workers' trade union' in France. 'I'm pro-feminism. I'm a trade union-ist, I'm a sex worker. My politics is sex workers first and then every-thing about left politics—minorities first.' I ask Shaffauser whether he considers his identity as 'sex worker' to be intrinsically connected to the queer movement. 'I think at least a big part of the sex workers' rights movement is linked to the queer movement', he says.

For Shaffauser, the link between being gay/queer and a sex worker is the stigma. 'I saw similarities about the stigma and the thing around having to come out or having to hide', he says, 'and one of the first things I did as a sex workers' rights activist was to organise the Whores Pride. The fact that we used the concept of pride for sex workers was for France completely new'.

'Of course I can see that queer sex workers are very vocal in the movement', says Shaffauser. 'Probably the fact that we have this politi-cal strategy to use for coming out, it makes us more visible than the rest of the movement, so the movement has this image of queer, or sex posi-tive, or all these kind of trendy labels.'

There are currently a number of male activists involved in the global 'sex workers' rights' movement. Douglas Fox, whose partner owns the biggest escort agency in the North of England, blogs for the *Guardian* online, describing himself as a 'sex worker'. Fox held a senior position in the fake union the IUSW, and was a key face of the movement until a civil war regarding the role of 'managers' within the organisation took hold and Fox withdrew.

Queer in the Academy

Accusations of 'whorephobia', which is meant to mean hatred towards or stigmatising of prostituted women and men, is in fact used to silence and deter any criticism of the sex trade whatsoever. This viewpoint is enshrined in university safe-space policies, and has led to a number of students who are lesbian or gay being diverted into adopting a queer identity.

Prostitution is not a sexuality. There is a clear difference between a sexual preference or identity and prostitution (a form of men's abuse). Feminists recognise this, and as someone who came out as a lesbian as a teenager in the 1970s and who has had experience of sexual assault, I understand the difference very well.

The Nordic model is not a moral perspective about sex: it is an issue of gender justice to police men's violence. Accordingly, prostituted women are not policed: instead the attention is focused on the crime as it is; that is, men's abuse. These men are arrested and charged: prostituted women face no sanction or interference whatsoever. I have never heard any of these survivor abolitionists say that they are against gay rights or anti-equality. It is interesting to ask why there is a conflation made between being gay and 'sex-work', and what ideology and motivations drive this.

A number of the academic apologists for the sex trade are themselves gay men, and have focused some attention on young men/boys who sell sex to men and who may identify as gay. For example, Graham Ellison, an academic based at Queen's University Belfast, who gave evidence to the Northern Ireland Justice Committee, which I outlined in Chap. 8, became interested in issues relating to the sex trade after interviewing young street-based boys selling sex in Prague, Czech Republic.

In his paper 'Drifters, Party Boys and Incumbents: The life patterns of male street-based sex workers',[30] based on research conducted in the gay village within Manchester, UK, Ellison makes it clear that he considers these boys to be part of some type of rebellious subculture. He goes into detail about one particular category of boys who sell sex, 'party boys', whom he describes as 'young gay identified men who frequent the village mainly for its social life but who occasionally partake in commercial sex if a particular opportunity arises'.

Nicola (Nick) Mai, another academic who provided written evidence to the Northern Ireland Justice Committee and advised a research report that informed it, has also conducted research into prostituted boys. In his paper 'Tampering with the Sex of "Angels": Migrant Male

---

[30]Ellison, G. (2017.) *Drifters, party boys and incumbents: The life patterns of male street-based sex workers*. In Sociology. Retrieved 15 June 2017, from http://pure.qub.ac.uk/ws/files/100681556/Ellison_ARTC_172.pdf.

Minors and Young Adults Selling Sex in the EU',[31] he argues that, even for underage boys selling sex, the worst negative effect is stigma. In other words: policing the violence done to them is violence. Mai further argues that for some of these boys, one advantage of 'choosing' this line of 'work' is that it makes them feel desirable. The sexual desirability of children in this sense is understood as a possible social good.

'Selling sex allowed interviewees to make money and feel autonomous from the prescriptions and control they left behind by migrating. It made them feel desirable and sometimes provided them with important affective references and logistical support', writes Mai. 'The main disadvantages associated with sex work are a consequence of its stigmatisation as well as of homophobia and the "abject" vulnerabilities of migrant minors and young adults rather than of the involvement in sex work per se.'

Rewriting Child Abuse

> When I was reading [pro-prostitution] research I was like, 'This isn't jiving to what I went through", and it was the same shit of framing it [as though] gay boys choose it. Who enjoys sleeping with a grandfather? (Chris, male survivor of the sex trade, Los Angeles, 2015)

A number of gay libertarian men rewrite histories of childhood sexual abuse as 'pleasurable' encounters. Take Peter Tatchell, for example. On its website, The Peter Tatchell Foundation is described as seeking 'to promote and protect the human rights of individuals, communities and nations, in the UK and internationally'.[32]

Tatchell is a gay rights activist who has long campaigned for lowering the age of consent for all to 14. In the early 1990s, Tatchell reviewed a grotesque and shocking book, *Dares to Speak: Historical & Contemporary Perspectives On Boy-Love* (edited by Joseph Geraci). Tatchell wrote:

---

[31]Journal of Ethnic and Migration Studies. Vol. 37, No. 8, September 2011, pp. 1237–1252.
[32]Peter Tatchell Foundation. Retrieved 15 June 2017, from http://www.petertatchellfoundation. org/.

'Abusive, exploitative relationships are indefensible but … [there are] many examples of societies where consenting intergenerational sex is considered normal, acceptable, beneficial and enjoyable by old and young alike'.

In a blog post,[33] Tatchell wrote:

> Lee is 14. He's been having sex with boys since the age of eight, and with men since he was 12. Lee has a serious problem. He wants a steady relationship and has been going out recently with a guy in his mid-20s, who he met at the hairdressers. But in the eyes of the law, Lee's partner is a paedophile and Lee is a victim of child abuse. That's not, however, the way Lee sees it: 'I want to have a boyfriend. It's my choice. No one's abusing me. Why should we be treated like criminals?'

There can be no doubt in my mind that Tatchell does not support the abuse of children, but I have often engaged with him in discussion about whether or not he properly understands the dynamics of older men 'grooming' children and young people. I was the first journalist to break the story about the grooming gangs operating in northern towns and cities in England.[34] Groups of sexual abusers—men in their 20s and 30s—were raping and pimping 12 to 15-year-old girls they had targeted. They managed to convince the girls that they were their boyfriends, and the girls and young women caught up in this horror became powerless to resist the abuse. They convinced themselves that they were in love with these men, despite the fact that they were being abused and hurt on a regular basis by them and other men to whom they were sold for sex.

I interviewed a number of these girls and young women, both during the time they were being abused and after they had escaped. Each one of them told me, in no uncertain terms, that at the time of the abuse they were absolutely certain that these men were in love with them and that they were in a relationship.

---

[33]http://www.petertatchell.net/lgbt_rights/age_of_consent/14-gay-boyfriend.htm.

[34]Tatchell, P. (1997, Aug 15.) *I'm 14, I'm gay and I want a boyfriend. On petertatchell.net.* Retrieved 15 June 2017, from http://www.thesundaytimes.co.uk/sto/news/uk_news/article72310.ece.

Tatchell does not even ask the question 'Why does a fully adult male want to have sex with a child?' When Tatchell writes: 'Lee has been having sex with men since he was 12' he is putting the onus firmly on Lee. In fact, adult men have been sexually abusing Lee since he was 12. Whether Lee 'enjoys' the sex or not is beside the point. Age of consent legislation is in place to protect children and young people from sexual predators. Tacthell is mistaken when he says that the law considers Lee's boyfriend to be a 'paedophile'. The law considers Lee's boyfriend to be a statutory rapist and guilty of child sexual abuse.

The term 'paedophile' muddies the water here. Radical feminists tend not to like this word, as it medicalises a criminal offence. Because 'paedophiles' are depicted as weird, strange, creepy, dangerous men whom we should be able to pick out easily in the street, of course men such as Tatchell, and Lee's boyfriend, would be appalled at this label being attached to someone who would claim to be having enjoyable, consensual sex with a perfectly mature young man. Use of the term 'paedophile' serves to distance those men who sexually exploit and abuse young people from the hard-core 'perverts' that the media loves to depict as monsters.

Why do so many gay men refuse to see the abuse inherent within man/boy sexual encounters? Child sexual abuse only exists because patriarchy does. Feminists have an understanding of this: gay men, as a rule, still benefit from patriarchy despite the fact that they are not viewed, among traditionalists, as 'real men'.

Tatchell's blog contains a disclaimer, added to the page following sharp criticism from feminists and others who were appalled about his views on sex with children. It reads: 'Note: My articles urging an age of consent of 14 are motivated solely by a desire to reduce the criminalisation of under-16s who have consenting relationships with other young people of similar ages. I do not support adults having sex with children. I do not advocate teenagers having sex before the age of 16'.[35]

If Tatchell's disclaimer is to be believed, why then is he using the example of a 12-year-old child having sex with a man in his mid-20s?

---

[35]Tatchell, P. (2010, Sept 23.) *An age of consent of 14? On petertatchell.net.* Retrieved 15 June 2017, from http://www.petertatchell.net/lgbt_rights/age_of_consent/an-age-of-consent-of-14.htm.

If his only concern is about two 15-year olds being criminalised for having consensual sex (which very rarely happens in the UK, or anywhere for that matter), why are we being encouraged to sympathise with this adult?

It is precisely this type of view that lends itself to queer theory. Gay men like Tatchell, who are sexual libertarians, do not understand, or refuse to recognise, that the power dynamics that exist between men and children are tilted in favour of the former. Of course child rape cannot be separated from the sex trade, just as trafficking cannot be. The sex trade will cease to function if its capacity to source desperate and vulnerable women and girls to be sold to men is frustrated.

A Defence to Child Abuse

At the World's Oldest Oppression Conference, in Melbourne in 2015, I was approached by a delegate who is a detective with over 20 years policing experience. He told me that a legal loophole existed in Australia that green lighted men to rape children. He also told me that he had a spreadsheet with the names of hundreds of men who had raped a child but that he would not be arresting any of them let alone pressing charges, because these children were sold to men as 'adults'—typically aged 18 or 19. The sex trade was not a mere 'defence' to a crime of child rape but evidence that no crime had been committed at all.

The police officer provided me with a list of cases that showed his particular investigation, which he refused to discuss, was hardly an isolated one in Australia. For instance: a 17-year-old girl who died of a heroin overdose in a legal brothel in Australia's capital city[36]; a 14-year-old girl prostituted to hundreds of men from a legal Sydney brothel[37] and another girl of the same age prostituted from a legal brothel in

---

[36]Cox, L. (2012, Feb 22.) *Crackdown urged on sex trade*. On Canberra Times. Retrieved 15 June 2017, from http://www.canberratimes.com.au/act-news/crackdown-urged-on-sex-trade-20120223-1tqu8.html.

[37]Wells, J. (2013, Dec 16.) *Sydney brothel madam Jennifer Weatherstone given suspended sentence over 14yo prostitute*. On ABC News. Retrieved 15 June 2017, from http://www.abc.net.au/news/2013-12-16/madam-given-suspended-sentence-for-prostituting-14yo/5159418.

Melbourne[38]; a 15-year-old girl prostituted by her 40-year-old 'boy-friend' to hundreds of men on an 'adult' escort website in Sydney[39]; and a 12-year-old girl, infected with chlamydia and genital warts, prostituted to hundreds of men who responded to an advertisement saying 'Angela, 18-years-old, new in town'.[40]

Not a single punter was arrested by Australian police because, in law, these men "committed no crime". Nor was a solitary brothel or pimp who sold these children into the homogeneous adult, sex trade condemned by the political alliance formed to entrench prostitution in Australia: Scarlet Alliance, Australian Sex Party, and the Green Party, all of whom support the legalised sale of women and girls[41].

I asked the police officer what he thought was the way forward. He responded:

> Arrest all men who buy sex. Nothing else. The lie that sex trafficking and child rape are crimes completely discrete from prostitution, or 'sex work' as I'm forced to call it, is not the full story. The ultimate lie is that sex trafficking and child rape in the sex trade can be policed. The industry, and the politicians in Australia who support them, like Senator Faraqi, can't be more praiseworthy of police when our hands are tied, saying we are best placed to investigate cases of sex trafficking and child rape. We are their best friends when we're ineffectual.

> But these crimes are impossible to prosecute even after great expense for all involved. The moment real solutions are presented – like regulating the industry or, heaven-forbid, ending demand – police are slandered as corrupt and violent. Of course there are a minority of bad police, but so what? Other crimes happen – rape, murder, assault, robbery – and police do what police do. And for the most part we do a great job. Arresting men who buy sex – who give zero thought to informed consent – is as controversial as arresting any other violent man.'

[38]Hunt, E. (2009, Feb 2.) *Brothel manager convicted after girl, 14, worked as prostitute*. In Herald Sun. Retrieved 15 June 2017, from http://www.heraldsun.com.au/news/victoria/madam-convicted-over-14yo-prostitute/news-story/9c777e9ce58d5062e17269cbc5e0cc4d.

[39]http://www.news.com.au/national/breaking-news/bondi-man-made-teen-prostitute-web-profile/news-story/914a8045221e6497ac5a4a0742472ae8.

[40]http://www.heraldsun.com.au/news/tasmanian-man-prostituted-12-year-old-and-shared-proceeds-with-mother/news-story/80695d05fa187178ae3d135856a6d202.

[41]Faruqi, M.; Shoebridge, D. (2015, Aug 15.) *Submission to the committee on the regulation of brothels*. On *davidshoebridge.org.au*. Retrieved 15 June 2017, from http://davidshoebridge.org.au/wp-content/uploads/2011/08/150821-Greens-NSW-Submission-to-Brothel-Regulation-Inquiry.pdf.

A Queer Support of Sex Buyers

When the Chair of the Home Affairs Select Committee, Keith Vaz, was reportedly discovered during a tabloid newspaper sting to be paying for sex from vulnerable young Romanian men, Tatchell was first in the queue to defend him. It was clear from the short piece he wrote for the *Guardian's Comment is Free* website[42] that Tatchell does not understand about the power dynamic that exists between the buyer and the seller during the prostitution transaction.

Tatchell wrote:

> It is said that Vaz failed to declare an interest when his home affairs committee was investigating a ban on poppers and sex work criminalisation (Vaz opposed both). Perhaps he should have declared an interest, but I am not sure that his failure to do so is a major lapse. After all, we don't demand that MPs who drink and smoke declare an interest when they discuss legislation affecting the alcohol and cigarette industries. There is never any insistence that MPs who have pension plans step aside from committees discussing pension regulation or that gay MPs must come out and declare themselves before voting on gay issues. I sense a whiff of double standards.[43]

Vaz enjoyed support from much of the gay press in the UK and elsewhere.[44] His use and abuse of young vulnerable men was seen as a sexual preference rather than an act of sexual abuse. The young men at the centre of the story have reported they understood what was done to them by Vaz as exploitation. But this is of no consequence to the 'prostitution is sex work' narrative because their accounts are not recorded in peer-reviewed articles owned by the sex trade narrative but in 'tabloid trash'.

---

[42]Lees, P.; Tatchell, P.; et al. (2016, Sept 5.) *Should Keith Vaz step down as Home Affairs Committee chair?* On The Guardian. Retrieved 15 June 2017, from https://www.theguardian.com/commentisfree/2016/sep/05/keith-vaz-home-affairs-committee-chair-prostitutes-sex-trade.

[43]Lees, P.; Tatchell, P.; et al. (2016, Sept 5.) *Should Keith Vaz step down as Home Affairs Committee chair?* On The Guardian. Retrieved 15 June 2017, from https://www.theguardian.com/commentisfree/2016/sep/05/keith-vaz-home-affairs-committee-chair-prostitutes-sex-trade.

[44]Duffy, N. (2016, Sept 12.) *Labour MP Keith Vaz 'was suicidal' after tabloid outed him in rent boy scandal.* In Pink News. Retrieved 15 June 2017, from http://www.pinknews.co.uk/2016/09/12/labour-mp-keith-vaz-was-suicidal-after-tabloid-outed-him-in-rent-boy-scandal/.

Prostitution is rife within the gay commercial scene. A number of gay men I interviewed for my book *Straight Expectations*,[45] which explored previous and current lesbian and gay culture, told me that as young men they were almost expected to supplement their incomes by selling sex to older men. I was told by a number of men who no longer frequent commercial gay bars that they are sick of seeing adverts for prostituted young men in gay magazines.

The Queer Women

Queer-identified liberal feminists also often see prostitution as sexual identity, and an enjoyable part of being a 'sexual outlaw'.

Melinda Chateauvert, a fellow at the Centre for Africana Studies at the University of Pennsylvania, USA, claims that the Stonewall riot was led by 'trans women of colour', and argues that gay liberation groups were reluctant to support people like Sylvia Rivera, a regular patron of the Stonewall Inn (the bar in New York City where the riot started): 'LGBT and queer history should include sex workers because many sex-worker activists are queer and some queer activists support themselves through sex work'. But doubt has been cast by several individuals as to whether Rivera was even at the Stonewall Riot, for example by the gay historian David Carter.[46]

According to Chateauvert, whose 2009 presentation was entitled 'Speaking About the Unspoken: A Conference for Scholars on Leather and Fetish history', those who 'deny the existence' of trans people within the 'queer movement' also reject the involvement of 'sex workers'.

Chateauvert and other pro-prostitution activists refer to feminists who critique the sex trade as 'straight', thereby labelling those who celebrate it as 'queer' by default. She says: 'The refusal of "straight" feminists

[45]Bindel, J. (2014). *Straight expectations: What does it mean to be gay today?* London: Guardian Books.
[46]Carter, D. (2004.) *Stonewall: The riots that sparked the gay revolution.* London: St. Martin's.

to accept the personal experiences of sex workers as legitimate grounds for analysis represented a critical moment in the history of feminist politics'.[47]

I met Siouxsie Q, the porn actor and pro-prostitution activist, at the Los Angeles Porn Awards in 2015 as she was walking down the red carpet to be photographed. I introduced myself, told her that I was writing a newspaper article on the porn industry and asked her about the LGBT movement and its links to pornography. Friendly, forthcoming and very bubbly, Q told me that the queer movement and the 'sex workers' rights' movement were indivisible. I told her I was a lesbian but nothing else about my politics. She didn't ask. It was clear that Q assumed I would be positive towards the porn industry bearing in mind that I was a queer, too.

'I always say sex work has been my path to the American dream', said Q when we spoke later on Skype, 'and that's true of other folks in the industry, particularly queer people.'

During this conversation, Q mentioned on several occasions that the main targets of police brutality, discrimination and violence in general are 'trans women of colour'. I asked Q why she thought that the LGBT movement was so closely aligned with the 'sex workers' rights' movement.

'Sex workers and people in the sex trade have been part of the modern LGBT liberation movement literally since the beginning', she says. 'Sex workers threw the first glass bottles at the Stonewall riots and that is no accident. It's not because we are troublemakers, it's because the sex trade has served as a place where people can get resources and jobs and community where none have existed.'

Policymakers, human rights organisations, liberals of every stripe, support the sex trade if they believe it is a sexual identity. In a podcast interview with Q and Chateauvert,[48] the two women waxed lyrical about the links between the 'sex workers' rights' and the LGBT movements. 'You can't talk about sex work without talking about trans

---

[47]Chateauvert, M. (2009.) *Speaking about the unspoken: A conference for scholars on leather and fetish history*. 13, https://mmchateauvert.files.wordpress.com/2015/09/chateauvert-vita-september-2015.pdf. Accessed 28th August 2017

[48]Q, Siouxsie. (2017.) *The Whorecast*. On itunes.apple.com. Retrieved 15 June 2017, from https://itunes.apple.com/gb/podcast/the-whorecast/id955261410?mt=2. It is episode 77, 5 may 2014.

women', said Q. 'Or other kinds of people who are marginalised in a society that does not provide other economic opportunities', agreed Chateauvert.

During their discussion, Q asked Chateauvert what differences or similarities she sees between gay rights and 'sex worker rights'. Chateauvert explained it in terms of what she perceives as an 'imposition' of identities by the oppressors. 'Prior to the end of the 19th century these were acts that people committed – they committed sodomy or they committed whoring – but these weren't identities', said Chateauvert. 'More to the point, these weren't identities that emerged from the people themselves. These were identities that were imposed upon them from without.'

Not everyone in the 'sex workers' rights' movement' has such a rosy picture of the LGBT movement and the collaboration between the two.

In Stockholm, Sweden, I was invited to lunch at the home of Petra Östergren, who is passionately opposed to the law targeting sex buyers. Östergren had also invited Carina, an active member of the Rose Alliance who was curious to meet me. Knowing I was an abolitionist, and that I supported the law in Sweden criminalising demand, Carina had chosen not to Google me. 'I wanted to meet you with an open mind', she said.

Carina was indeed open, warm and not even slightly defensive. Over lunch she told me why she thought that the 'sex workers' rights' movement in Sweden was being let down by the LGBT movement. 'I am so pissed off with the LGBTQI movement in Sweden', says Carina, going on to explain that she feels the 'sex workers' rights' movement is treated like a poor relative compared to the queer community.

'We need to have a better relationship with the gay movement than we have today because it would strengthen both groups.'

Östergren also conflates prostitution and sexual identity. 'I think when anything that concerns sex, like non-normative sexual practices, like being gay or a lesbian, will always carry some kind of stigma as long as it's not part of the sexual norms in a society', she says.

I tell Östergren that I do not believe prostitution to be a sexual identity. 'No, but it's a sexual practice', she says. 'I don't think it's a sexual practice in the understanding that if I sell sex it would be my sexuality, but it is surely a sexual act in some ways either by voice or by actions. I'm not talking about sexual pleasure but sex acts in practice.'

Regardless, accepting prostitution as a 'sexuality' brings us full circle because it is a 'sexuality' exclusive to men: men who buy sex. Despite the best derailing efforts of the sex trade alleging 'women do it, too', the fact remains that in the history of human civilisation there has never been a brothel built for women to abuse men and boys, and other women and girls, drawn from the world's most desperately poor and vulnerable. Women who reportedly buy sex are the exception proving the rule.

In the report of their study 'Statistics on Sex Work in the UK', outlined in Chap. 2, authors Nicola Smith and Sarah Kingston seem to be suggesting that those who support the Nordic Model are 'heterosexist', thereby effectively spinning buying sex as an 'equalities issue'.

'As we write, our overarching aim is to support the development of political discourse and policy practice that move beyond simplistic ideological assertions and that instead recognise and respond to the complex reality of the sex trade today', claim Smith and Kingston. 'We do indeed believe that calls to criminalise the purchase of sexual services are predicated on (hetero)sexist stereotypes that erase LGBT/Q identities and practices, as well as women who pay for sex.'

The idea is that fighting to abolish the sex trade—and with it the ideas and practices grounded in male power and supremacy, as well as sexual abuse and torture—is beyond comprehension. In the next and final chapter you will hear from the survivors of prostitution, those who have lived and breathed, and finally escaped, this trade in female subordination.

11

Surviving the Sex Trade

Virginity was taken from me before I knew it was something someone could take. Before I knew it was something I'm supposed to care about. You can't care about something before you ever had it. By the time you know what it is to care about, you don't have it any more. (Haley, sex trade survivor, Minnesota, 2015)

I got raped every week, every day – I was incontinent. I would do blow jobs in just the state I was in. They would see the state I was in and come and get me and rape me. I couldn't remember who I was. I didn't know who this guy was who raped me yesterday and would rape me again today. (Lorraine, sex trade survivor, Montreal, 2015)

Introduction

Who are the feminists and human rights activists who seek to abolish the global sex trade? What motivates them? Why do they prioritise prostitution over other forms of male violence? Are they 'prudes' and 'man-hating', as the pro-prostitution activists claim, or progressives seeking to create a world free of exploitation and abuse?

© The Author(s) 2017
J. Bindel, *The Pimping of Prostitution*,
DOI 10.1057/978-1-137-55890-9_11

During the course of almost 2 years, I spoke to more than 50 survivors (including two men) of the sex trade. To meet them, I travelled to 35 countries, states, cities, towns and villages across Europe, Asia, Africa, Australia and North America. These women had been prostituted under regulation, decriminalisation and legalisation. All are committed to dispelling the myths that support the sex trade industry.

The women are from a wide range of backgrounds. Some were pimped by male relatives, others began selling sex to feed their children. Two of the women I interviewed had ended their time in prostitution as pimps. Both were honest enough to tell me that they had turned to selling other women to avoid being sold themselves. I met mothers who sold sex to feed their children and protect themselves from domestic violence, only to have their children removed by social services because of their chaotic existences shaped by pimps and drug dealers.

I met Haley, who had been sexually abused by men as a child, and who told me that she experienced prostitution as a continuation of that abuse. There were several women with similar experiences, and all of them said that at one stage of their involvement in the sex trade they would have argued that 'sex work' was a way to take back control of their bodies and/or lives.

I travelled with Rachel Moran to a number of countries to attend seminars, conferences and training sessions on prostitution and the sex trade. I spent time with the survivors in those countries, hearing them speak publicly, interviewing them face-to-face, and learning about their individual stories and how they had come to feminist activism.

I was introduced to middle-class women in Europe and North America who had been targeted by pimps when particularly vulnerable. In the USA, African-American women spoke of the inherent racism in the sex trade, and in Canada and Australia, Indigenous survivors spoke of the sex trade as part of their colonialist history and experience.

All of the women I spoke to saw themselves as part of a global movement for change. Some of the survivors now spend their lives supporting girls and women to leave prostitution, while others take to the very streets on which they were prostituted with placards and loudhailers, hoping to change complacent minds and build a stronger abolitionist movement. On occasion I would meet a survivor in a sharp suit, coming out of a meeting with politicians or delivering training sessions for police officers and social workers.

Sometimes the survivors I met had been almost, but not quite, destroyed. These women were held together by the politics of feminism and the strength of hope. Unlike the pro-prostitution position of inevitability (best illustrated in the irritating mantra: 'Prostitution has always been here and always will be'), the abolitionist movement provided a basis for revolution. 'We are here for one reason and one reason only', said Moran on receiving the Emma Humphreys Memorial Prize in 2014, 'to end the international sex trade.'

In previous chapters, we have heard from 'sex workers' rights' lobbyists, AIDS activists, human rights campaigners, academics, the 'sexual outlaws', the punters, the general public and industry spokespeople. Their views are well documented throughout this book and, in the main, their voices are far louder and have been afforded more legitimacy than those who are the real experts: the survivors.

Why are they the experts? Many of the survivors I have interviewed for this book tell me they would have argued for the 'rights' of women to sell sex during the time they were involved in prostitution. They have all encountered hundreds, if not thousands, of sex buyers and were, during their time in prostitution, faced with the stark reality of the trade.

These voices are routinely dismissed, invalidated and often silenced altogether. Their experiences defy the libertarian and self-serving propaganda put forward by sex trade apologists.

Archetypes

I meet Ana (not her real name) in Amsterdam. Ana was prostituted as a young woman in the Netherlands before she managed to exit in 2011. Ana is friendly, talkative and very passionate about her radical feminist politics. Ana had put together her thoughts on what she calls 'archetypes' in the so-called 'sex worker's rights' movement. Ana's descriptions of these archetypes reflect the views of many of the survivors interviewed for this book.

The Profiteer

They are the brothel owners, pimps, lady pimps (my word for 'madams', which sounds way too classy), escort agencies, ethically corrupt officials and leeching 'boyfriends' that make good money from sexual exploitation. It's obvious what their stake is in a flourishing sex industry. These people (with the exception of the women) tend to hide behind screens, as they know how it would look if they speak out in public.

The Payroll Lobbyist

Probably one of my favourite assholes in the lobby because they are sinister as fuck. When people hear the word 'payroll lobbyist', they think of Mafia movies, suitcases full of money and 'offers you cannot refuse'. Reality is a bit different, because that's not how this works. Lobbyists often aren't literally bought, but they get financial support for a job they were already doing or something they already were sympathetic about. Payroll lobbyists are often researchers, anthropologists, sexologists, sexual health educators, journalists, politicians or other professionals.

The 'Sex Worker'

During many dark periods in human history, oppressed people have often been set up against one another to oppress their peers for favours from the oppressor. Prostituted persons are no different. The 'sex workers' rights' movement' is a euphemism but there is a core of truth to it: there is some unity among the Uncle Toms of the sex industry to get the most out of what they do. Many of them work in the relatively 'softer' (take this word with a grain of salt) sectors of the sex industry: they are strippers, camgirls, phone sex operators or dominatrixes.

The John

There is some overlap between the payroll lobbyist and this group, because many johns are powerful men in powerful professions who would love to keep indulging their sexual appetite. Not much has to be said about this type of person: they may hide that they're johns, but it's clear why they propagate an unrestricted sex industry.

The Sex Positivist

Ah, the sex positive movement, not really lobbyists but definitely worth mentioning. They are the happy consumers of sexually violent porn and without their addicted brains what would the sex industry be? These folks are all too glad to break their keyboards by going online defending commercial sexual exploitation for the sake of their boners. Of course this dynamic is fiercely debated among feminists and I'm one of those people who acknowledges that liberal women have been pressured and manipulated into 'sex positivity' since their teens. Some of these women are victims themselves but too stuck to do anything. Changing your mind about sexual violence is nothing to be ashamed of.

Routes into the Sex Trade

People who believe in the abolition of sex work see no distinction between trafficking and sex work voluntarily. They think that basically that people who do it are still in a bigger system of power that obliterates their agency. (Nicola Mai 2016)

Huschke Mau was raised in a violent household in Germany and was sexually abused by her stepfather when she was a child. She ran away from home when she was 17. At that time, Mau had eating disorders, was drug addicted, had severe financial problems and psychological trauma.

'When men spoke to me on the streets, I said, 'You can get involved with me but it costs money'. Some found that OK', says Mau. 'I moved to the next town when I was 19 and I started to study at the university but I had problems getting my life together. Then I met a policeman who was very fucked up. He was doing drugs and going to prostitutes himself and he helped me to go into a brothel.'

Trisha Baptie is a First Nations Canadian survivor. Baptie covered the Robert Pickton trial (a serial killer of prostituted women, mainly Indigenous and from the Downtown Eastside of Vancouver[1]) as a citizen journalist using her intimate knowledge of Vancouver's Downtown Eastside and her perspective as a friend to his victims. For this coverage she won the Courage to Come Back award.

'I come from a pretty middle class background. My dad came from a country that was exceptionally unkind to him because of the colour of his skin; he's coloured and from Johannesburg. He beat my mum so we spent a lot of time in transition homes. Just before my 12th or 13th birthday, I turned my first trick, because once you're in the care of the State it just seems to be a natural progression. For the next 15 years I was involved in prostitution mostly in the notorious Downtown East Side.'

Ne'Cole Daniels is the Founder/Director of Survivors on the Move, and a member of SPACE International. Daniels, who is African-American, focuses the abolitionist movement on marginalised communities affected by prostitution. As with many of the survivors I met and interviewed, her route into prostitution was sexual abuse experienced during childhood.

From ages 7–11 I was sexually abused by my grandmother's boyfriend. At that time it made me very hypersexual. From being violated, from it being taken from me, from me not being able to give myself to my husband or just on my own terms. [The abusers] were older men and so I decided that I'm going to control my vagina – I'm going to say who can enter and who can't. Or so I thought.

By the age of 14 I was dating a 30-year old. I thought that I was a bad ass 14-year old, that I can attract these older gentlemen and I can get them to take care of me because I'm all that ... bullshit!

At 15 I went to live with my mum and my dad had to pay rent for me to live with her. My mum was an alcoholic. I looked like a bum, I had no lunch money, I had nothing. She was raising her girlfriend's kids and her daughter said to me, 'You're never going to get shit, we're not going to do anything for you, let me tell you how to get this money'.

---

[1]Bindel, J. (2005, Aug 5.) *The disappeared*. On The Guardian. Retrieved 15 June 2017, from https://www.theguardian.com/world/2005/aug/05/features11.g2.

We're in San Jose at the time and she took me down to a place called Ellen Rock. There were a lot of Hispanics on that block and I remember turning my first 'date'. I felt disgusting. I thought I would feel better because I was getting paid for something that was being taken away from me, but I felt utterly disgusting. But it was quick and it was easy. So I started using my body as a tool.

Routes into the Survivor Movement

In recent years the survivor movement in Europe has grown via blogging. Dublin Call Girl's (DCG) blog was headed 'secretdiaryofadublincallgirl: definitely not Belle du Jour'. 'I named [the blog] after Belle Du Jour's "secret diary"',[2] DCG told me, 'to contrast between the actual reality of an independent escort and her bullshit. I wanted to create an antidote to her, especially as young girls were using her as a good role model and a reason to give prostitution a shot. And the fact she takes no responsibility for that angers me more than I can articulate'.

When feminist abolitionists noticed the blog *The Prostitution Experience* by Moran, a survivor who exited the sex trade in 1998, there was a flurry of excitement. The *Belle de Jour* blog about the glamour of the sex trade had set the scene, promoting prostitution as fun and harmless. Moran's blog was a direct contradiction and, like DCG's blog, it came out of Ireland at that same time in the spring of 2012.

Moran blogged:

> I first came across *Dublin Call Girl*'s blog in January [2012] 'I came across it because, in the aftermath of completing my book *Paid For*, I didn't know how to disengage from the subject. Also, in a climate where prostitution was heating up as a political issue, I didn't want to. I was directed to a group-blog called *Survivors' Connect Network*, and what I found there were links to the writings of prostitution survivors from all over the world. DCG's blog was among them.

---

[2]Belle de Jour. (2007.) *The Intimate Adventures of a London Call Girl.* London: Weidenfeld & Nicolson.

In early 2012, my book was completed and looking for a home, but I didn't know how long that would take because the issue of prostitution was suddenly politically topical in Ireland. I intended to go public with my identity when the book came out, but until then I wanted to keep it to myself for my son's sake. It was suggested that I write an anonymous blog, but I didn't want strangers commenting on what I'd written and communicating with me. It seemed the only way to input into the public debate though, so I began blogging. I later came to find my posts were shared among some of the most prominent abolitionist feminists in the world. That was hugely encouraging.

The first political meeting about prostitution Moran attended, a year before she'd begun blogging, was the launch of the campaign Turn off the Red Light. 'So I'm sitting there and everyone was talking and it had gone on for about 90 min or more and I just knew I had to stand up and say something', says Moran. 'It was terrifying because it was a very large room and the place was jammed.'

'People were standing at the back and spilling out down the hallway, and half a dozen heads would turn to look at whoever was talking. When I stood up and said, "My name is Rachel and I was in prostitution for 7 years", every bloody head in the room turned. It was shocking. I only spoke for 2 or 3 minutes, but I wrapped it up by saying that people needed to get real about what prostitution is, and that it's the commercialisation of sexual abuse. I used that then as the strap line of the blog I went on to write because that's exactly what it is and that's why it needs to stop.'

Moran's blog was only live for 1 year, folding as her book was published. SPACE International (Survivors of Prostitution Abuse Calling for Enlightenment International) was launched the day *Paid For* was published and was advertised on the last page of the book. The combination of the publication of a book on the realities of the sex trade, and the launch of SPACE International, was explosive. Not only did Moran refuse to use a pseudonym, but she also accepted invitations to appear on mainstream Irish TV networks and gave numerous interviews to the national press.

The fact that the blog, book and SPACE, founded by Moran and four other Irish survivors, came to fruition in the Republic of Ireland meant maximum coverage. Never before had a sex trade survivor spoken out about against prostitution in this highly public way in Ireland.

Male Survivors

In Chap. 10 we saw how sexual abuse of young men who either identify at the time as gay, or who go on to be gay, is twisted into some kind of sexually liberating experience, at least in the minds of the queer-identified 'sex workers' rights' lobbyists. I've spoken to a number of male survivors of the sex trade in the past and interviewed two male survivors for this book.

I met Chris during a trip to Los Angeles where I was attending the annual porn awards in 2015.[3] We spent a couple of hours sitting in a café in Hollywood, talking about Mafia involvement in the sex trade and the rise of the sex trade survivor movement. Chris was born into a family with connections to the mob. From an early age he was sexually exploited and abused by powerful men. In his teenage years he met a pimp and was sold for sex for 6 years before managing to escape.

Unlike the majority of the European survivors I met who had been prostituted domestically, Chris describes himself as a trafficking victim. Such terminology can be a bone of contention within the abolitionist movement. While there are those, like Chris, who argue all prostitution is trafficking, and believe that this is a more authentic description of their experience, others, like Moran, say that trafficking language can detract from the day-to-day reality of prostitution. In other words, all prostitution is a terrible human rights violation, and it is not necessary to use a word that merely describes a process rather than the experience.

'Part of my story isn't considered a trafficking thing because I had the money', says Nicholas. 'All of my mental life was controlled. I had to practically check in with the pimp. I had money but it came with

---

[3]Bindel, J. (2015, Feb 3.) *A report from the Porn Oscars*. On The Spectator. Retrieved 15 June 2017, from http://blogs.spectator.co.uk/author/julie-bindel/.

a terrible cost. I couldn't go out to the pub without telling somebody where I was going. I was controlled. I was keeping a lot of people out of prison. My ex-pimp is now in jail on a murder charge.'

Artem is a male survivor based in Moscow. We spoke over Skype with the help of Anna Zobnina, a feminist campaigner and Russian speaker. This method was necessary as I had been refused a visa to travel to Russia because of my outspoken views on Putin and his policies on LGBT issues.

I asked Artem what he knew about prostituted young men in his own country, and whether he considered his experience of the sex trade to be typical. 'Gay men who are in this industry have the most difficult and tragic stories. There are those who did not even have a hint of a choice in their lives', says Artem. 'They were most often homeless young men, those arriving from other areas, although some had been groomed and sexual abuse had happened in their lives prior to entering the sex trade. In this sense these factors are very similar to those that we know about the young women who enter the industry. However even for the most oppressed representatives of male prostitution there does not exist the double stigma that women face, which is about misogyny.'

I asked Artem about the most effective way to get survivor voices included in the debate within Russia, particularly in the light of Silver Rose being such a dominant force. 'The most important and successful way to educate people about prostitution would be for the people who have had direct experience in prostitution to speak out and share the truth about it,' said Artem. 'Not just by building political or rational arguments around it, but by appealing to a sense of empathy or perhaps even compassion.'

From 'Sex Worker' to Survivor?

I do think our views are legitimised by the fact we no longer have any emotional need to defend the industry. I had a lot of cognitive dissonance when I was in the business. (Rae Story, 2015)

I had to tell myself lots of things, lots of lies, in order to keep my brain from splitting into a million pieces and me going crazy with the continual abuse that was happening over and over and over, and the violence and everything else that goes along with prostitution. My hope is that [pro-prostitution lobbyists] will come over to the other side, but in the meantime we have to hold our position strong as abolitionists. (Autumn Burris, 2015)

Marian Hatcher is the Chicago representative of SPACE International, and works for Cook County Sheriff's Office as the Human Trafficking Coordinator in the USA. Along with her two colleagues in the department, Hatcher is one of only three sex trade survivors to work with law enforcement. She explains:

The derogatory references to 'sex work' or 'sex worker' imply a chosen way of meeting your basic needs: an occupation. In reality, it is not a chosen path to gaining economic security. It is forced servitude, most often by an opportunistic male such as a pimp or trafficker and in other instances an undesirable choice for basic survival. Fuelled by the johns who consume it, the sex trade is not a noble place in society; it is a human rights violation that perpetuates slavery. It is a travesty to coin a phrase that diminishes the harm and attempts to normalise it.

Sabrinna Valisce recalls the moment when she realised that fighting for so-called 'sex workers' rights', in the way the New Zealand Prostitute Collective (NZPC) did, was never going to be effective in removing the abuse and exploitation from the industry:

One of my jobs at NZPC was to find all of the media clippings. There was one thing I read,' says Valisce. 'It was somebody talking about being in tears and not knowing why, and not being able to contextualise it, and it wasn't until they were out [of the sex trade] that they understood what those feelings were. I had been through that for years [thinking], 'I don't know what's going on, why am I feeling like this?', and realised when I read that, 'Oh God, that's me'. So as I started coming across other articles, I started actually reading them for the first time.

For Valisce, there was no turning back. Once she had allowed herself to admit the horrors of prostitution and its effects on her, she began to make sense of how damaging the sex trade is for women. It also made her realise why she had felt so many emotions during her time in prostitution that she was unable to make sense of at the time.

Bullying Survivors

I have walked through picket lines with survivors of the sex trade and heard some activists from the pro-prostitution lobby shout and hurl insults at the women who are campaigning to stop the abuse of prostitution. I know from my own personal experience as an abolitionist how hostile some members of this lobby can be, and realise how much worse it must feel for the women who've had to endure prostitution to be further vilified by those wishing to normalise and legalise it.

In 2015, I was invited by the *Guardian* newspaper to chair a Q&A following a screening of the film *Dreamcatcher*,[4] a documentary directed by Kim Longinotto focusing on Brenda Myers-Powell, a survivor of the sex trade who now runs Dreamcatcher Foundation, a charity which helps women in Chicago leave prostitution. Days before the event was due to happen, I received an email from the *Guardian* telling me that, regrettably, they had to ask me not to moderate the event. Apparently, the film's director and distributors had received multiple angry emails and telephone calls from the pro-prostitution lobby complaining that it was inappropriate to ask me to take part in this event, and saying that my position on the sex trade put women in danger. There were several hostile and aggressive threats that the event would be disrupted. The director and her producer were understandably worried about the event becoming a controversy about me and my views rather than about the film.

The fact that the Dreamcatcher Foundation is not a pro-prostitution organisation but one that helps women leave the sex trade seemed to go

[4]Bindel, J. (2015, Mar 12.) *Dreamcatcher depicts the grim truth about prostitution.* In The Guardian. Retrieved 15 June 2017, from https://www.theguardian.com/commentisfree/2015/mar/12/dreamcatcher-prostitution-women-oppression-sex.

over the heads of those who achieved their aim—to get me disinvited from the event. There were several women in the audience who were prostitution survivors themselves. Apparently none of the pro-prostitution lobby turned up. They simply wanted to disrupt the event and to ensure there was a cloud over it. Not once in all my years as a feminist campaigner have I ever heard of, been alerted to or taken part in a picket or demonstration against a pro-prostitution lobby event. But the 'sex workers' rights' activists routinely pull stunts like the one described above, and in particular go after the survivors, who speak the truth that pro-lobbyists put so much effort into subverting.

A number of the women I interviewed told me horror stories about being labelled as mentally ill, liars, fraudsters, fantasists and masochists. I have personally witnessed survivors being vilified this way. One example comes to mind. As a regular contributor to the *Guardian* newspaper, I pitched the idea of a profile interview with Moran, pegged to the success of her book and of her work in the genesis of the survivor movement in the Republic of Ireland. The section editor I approached replied with a 'no' to the piece, saying that 'there were rumblings about its authenticity in more than a few quarters …'. I asked from where but she never replied. This incident worried me, as it was obvious that the lies about Moran and other survivors could do real damage to the very careers and political work of survivors, as well as cause distress and torment on a personal level.

Valisce has been vilified, perhaps because of how very well she understands the way the pro-prostitution lobby operates. After all, Valisce was involved with the New Zealand Prostitutes Collective as a volunteer for 24 years. She campaigned to bring in the new law that decriminalised brothels and street prostitution, because she genuinely believed that it would be better for the women and afford them more freedom. Because the pro-prostitution lobby relies on misinformation, mythology and plain old public relations, it is particularly galling to them when one of their own crosses over to the other side.

I have met several women who were involved in 'sex workers' rights' who later realised that it was all a sham. Cherie Jimenez is one such woman, from Boston and a US representative of SPACE International:

I had a couple of people come to me, such as Karen. I remember getting into an argument. I can't take that shit. [Karen] came [to Boston] because of the Demand initiative and was causing a lot of disturbance. She was writing an article, and two days in a row she harassed me to speak to her. She's from New York, which has a strong sex workers' movement and the same with San Francisco. It's hard for people because I do have that history. I say – I was one, take that shit somewhere else.

Valisce tells me about an event she was speaking at in Townsville at the *Prostitution Narratives* book launch when Elena Jeffreys, president of the Scarlet Alliance (the Australian pro-prostitution lobby group), made every attempt she could to silence her. 'She stood on a chair, towering over an audience who wanted to hear me; booing, interrupting and bellowing,' recalls Valisce. 'I didn't feel anger or even annoyance. I strangely identified with her. [I thought] she's scared. I can see it because I've felt that same defensiveness. "Don't take my livelihood. I've got nothing else. I've got nowhere else to turn to." I looked at her and smiled, nodded and said, "I understand". It wasn't a designed response. It was instinct.'

Valisce then invited Jeffreys and the other pro-prostitution women accompanying her to have a chat after the event:

One approached me and we had a very good conversation. Three others physically circled me. It was a bizarre feeling. They quite literally walked around one way, then the other, approximately four or five feet away. Then they approached and it was yelling all at once, voices drowning each other out.

The woman I was talking with actually came to my aid telling them to calm down and just talk. The conversation improved immensely. Elena avoided me. I approached her and she actually high-tailed it away from me. I think that's what shocked me. They live permanently on the defensive, but they can't take understanding with disagreement of the solutions to the problems. This certainly wasn't the only incidence of bullying, nor even close to the worst. It was the moment I realised how on edge I'd lived for so long and how little I missed the life.

Mau has also been bullied by the pro-lobbyists and accused of having made up her entire story about being a sex trade survivor. 'The lobbyists connected with me on Twitter and tried to make me look crazy. We have a group of sex workers here in Germany', says Mau. 'They have an Internet presence where they wrote I was fake. They say this about everybody who says the truth about prostitution.'

Soon after the bullying began, Mau realised that many journalists believed the pro-prostitution lobbyists' story that she had constructed her history of prostitution.

'The German journalists won't contact me because they think I'm a fake. If you search the Internet you get the information that I'm a fake', says Mau. 'They sent me emails pretending they are a radio station and want to interview me, and they hope I will give them my telephone number. I didn't give it.'

This pattern repeats itself in the lives of all the publicly visible survivors. At a Berlin press conference to launch her book, the first question asked of Moran was: 'What do you say to those who claim you have made everything up?'

'*Der Spiegel* contacted me,' says Mau, 'and after interviewing me for an article about the sex trade, wanted proof that I exist, which is difficult for me because I couldn't give my name or my telephone number. It's very mean what the lobby does. You cannot prove that you exist and that you've been a prostitute. There is no sheet of paper that says you're a prostitute.'[5]

Fighting for the 'Right' to Sell Sex

Three pro-prostitution activists, Terri-Jean Bedford (who had previously run escort agencies), Amy Lebovitch[6] and Valerie Scott, took the Canadian government to court, arguing that its laws on prostitution were unconstitutional. The three women, all of whom identified as

---

[5] Amy Lebovitch – http://prospol.eu/is1209/events/vienna-conference-2015
[6] Lebovich, A. (2015, Apr 16-18.) *Certain truths still emerge: Examining elitism and exclusion in sex work-related anti-violence initiatives.* In Prospol Conference Abstracts Booklet.

'sex workers', objected to aspects in the criminal code, including around advertising prostitution services, operating a brothel and pimping. Prostitution itself is legal in Canada but these women wished to remove all laws pertaining to the sex trade.

The ruling of the Court of Appeal for Ontario was that certain rulings would be changed, making it legal to run a brothel. Bridget Perrier and other survivor activists were at the court, and after the ruling Bedford flicked her riding crop (Bedford ran a BDSM practice), which delighted the many journalists who were there to cover the story. Perrier produced a bent coat hanger, which she called her 'pimp stick', telling the journalists that she had been beaten by her pimp with such an implement every day.

At court with Perrier was her adopted daughter Angel, whose mother had been murdered by Pickton. Perrier relates:

> Terri-Jean was too cowardly to go after me, so instead she went after an 18-year-old whose mother had been murdered by a serial killer of prostituted women', says Perrier. 'But I taught my kid well. My kid told her, 'Over my mum's dead body will we agree that legalising prostitution is good for women'.

> Angel said she would lobby to make sure it wouldn't be legitimised, and Terri-Jean even went as far as to put her hand on my child. After she was done chastising my child she went to one of our survivors, a girl who had been sexually tortured from the age of 11 until 25. She walked up to her and said, 'Why are you crying? This is a victorious day for us'. I remember our girl looking at her, and there was a picture of our girl and Terri-Jean in the papers, and this survivor put her finger right in Terri-Jean's face and said, 'Like hell it will!'

> The girls that we work with don't want to see prostitution legitimised. They see it as something they didn't have a choice to do for survival. I've witnessed some really bad antics by the pro-sex lobby, I've had one pro say that if her daughter wanted to be a prostitute she would teach her how to sell her cunt and make good money. I was so disgusted and I was on next so I stood up and said 'If there are any child welfare workers in the building, please follow her home and take those children because they are at risk'.

I've had the pro-lobby take my children's pictures from Facebook and put 'Bridget's future hooker'. I've had the pro lobby attack me, send me pictures of little girls having intercourse with grown men. I couldn't stop looking at the pictures because the mama in me wanted to climb through the pictures to rescue the little girls. These are babies, 4-year-olds.

Valisce left prostitution in early 2011 and moved to the Gold Coast from New Zealand, seeking a new direction in life. She was confused and depressed, and when her neighbour asked her to perform webcam prostitution Valisce politely declined. 'I felt like I had 'whore' stamped on my forehead. How did she know to ask me? I now know being female was the only reason', says Valisce. The neighbour asked Valisce again, which made Valisce angry. Afterwards, the neighbour would shout insults such as 'The bitch is home' whenever she saw her. 'My final exiting involves multiple stories like this. I exited first emotionally, then physically and lastly intellectually and psychologically', says Valisce. 'I feel like I'm still exiting because my self-view still battles to be whole.'

Alice, whom I met at the Oldest Oppression Conference in Melbourne, was prostituted in Queensland at the age of 22. She told me:

I had never heard of the term 'gaslighting' until I went public with my story about my time as a prostitute.[7] Gaslighting is something I have experienced incessantly throughout my life – beginning with the perpetrators of the child commercial sexual exploitation that started when I was 5, right through to adulthood from various other abusers and violent persons. But never in a million years did I expect to encounter that same behaviour from people after learning I am a survivor of the sex trade.

The opposition and behaviour exhibited towards me by the pro-sex trade lobby since going public about having worked in the industry caught even my pessimistic, catastrophising self completely off guard. I can now say with complete confidence that the pro-sex industry lobby is a bigger, more heartless and far crueller beast than even the most insipid of mental illnesses I have developed as a result of all the trauma I have endured.

---

[7]Gaslighting is a tactic in which a person manipulates another individual in order to lead them to question their reality.

Soon after Alice went public with her criticisms of the sex trade and her personal experiences within it, the pro-prostitution lobby instantly began to label her a SWERF,[8] claiming that she hated women in prostitution:

> The pro-sex trade lobby continually question my background and claim I am lying about having worked in the sex industry. Those who don't deem me a liar say that I am 'naive', 'foolish' and am 'being pimped out and used' by abolitionists to further their cause. Others have accused me of making a profit from the publication of my story and say that I am stealing from survivors and women currently in the industry.

Alice has also been bullied face-to-face by the pro-prostitution lobbyists when they have turned up at events where she has spoken about her experiences in the sex trade. 'I have watched these people (almost exclusively women) boo, hiss, jeer and yell at other survivors,' says Alice. 'I have walked out of events only to be met by a group of protesters who proceeded to verbally attack me.'

Another tactic of the lobby is to deliberately misrepresent the things the survivors say and post slurs on social media. Alice recalls:

> I was once talking to an audience about the way in which the pro-sex trade lobby will say that people who have not had involvement in the industry are not permitted to comment or discuss issues pertaining to the industry. I commented on the ridiculousness of that argument, comparing it to someone telling you that you are unable to speak out about the increasing cultivation of palm oil because you are not an orangutan. The next day, a sex worker union employee who had attended the talk tweeted to her followers that I had called sex workers orangutans.

Bullying Tactics

I have heard several stories over the years of the sex trade lobby actively promoting the sex trade public events at which survivors are speaking, and even of attempting to recruit women back into the industry.

---

[8]Sex Worker Exclusionary Radical Feminist.

At the World's Oldest Oppression Conference in Melbourne, Australia, in April 2016, which I was speaking at, a number of protesters turned up outside the venue handing out flyers containing propaganda about the sex trade and the so-called benefits those who choose to become involved in 'sex work' would experience. One protester's placard read 'Why be Poor?' Pro-lobbyists had attempted to get the conference cancelled before it happened on the grounds that discussion of the harms of the sex trade, which the lobby claimed were false, would be dangerous for those women who choose to be in prostitution.

I have also heard stories from survivors about the pro lobby turning up at abolitionist events and attempting to persuade women who had exited prostitution to re-enter, using the arguments that the survivors must have had exceptionally rare, bad experiences of sex buyers and pimps, and that they should work for one of the 'good' brothels.

Alice again:

> At one event, not even 10 minutes after speaking about the incredible trauma the sex industry has left me with, a women came up to me and started a conversation [in which she] was acknowledging the terrible working conditions that existed within the brothels of the area that we were in [a place where prostitution was legalised and regulated]. For her, terrible working conditions didn't include abusive clients and employers, or the rampant drug abuse common as a coping method for the ongoing trauma.

> No, to her, terrible working conditions were comprised of the fact that because prostitution was legalised within regulated brothels, anyone who worked there had to hand over a portion of their earnings to their employers. Incorrectly assuming that was where I had worked within Australia's sex industry, this woman assured me that 'conditions are much better down in New South Wales and I really encourage you to come down and give [sex work] another go'. I was completely shocked – had she not listened to my story 10 minutes earlier? I found out later that the woman I was talking to had recently left her position as the president of Australia's leading sex-worker union – a position she'd held for almost a decade.

> And with the pro-sex trade lobby it's not even what you do that they will use as fodder for their gaslighting, even what you don't do is a big green light for further attack. You don't advocate for transgender and

male prostitutes? Congratulations, you are a TERF![9] You don't discuss the political arguments of prostitution? Congratulations, you are a super-fundamentalist, ultra-religious abolitionist who disapproves of anything sexual and simply want to force your moral view upon the rest of the world!

I have witnessed the abuse and slander towards Moran on more than one occasion. Moran describes her treatment at the hands of the pro-prostitution lobby as 'soul sickening'. When we visited Munich together, where Moran was launching the German edition of her book, we were told by the local feminist group hosting one of the events that pro-lobbyists had threatened to turn up and disrupt the book launch. The same was threatened in other cities, although the protests failed to materialise.

Moran says:

> I've seen pro-lobbyists turn up to events with their stupid red umbrellas and deliver outpourings of hatred into the faces of women who are simply there to state the pain and harm men did to them in prostitution, and the most pukesome part of it is that these women will tell you that they are feminists and say so with a straight face.

> As for me, I've been slandered and defamed so routinely that it's just become part of the landscape of my life. The people actively engaged in this behaviour describe themselves as 'sex workers' rights activists'. Most are women and many have never been in prostitution themselves.

> I've had violent threats direct to my front door. My home has had to be put on the Pulse System, which means that the Rapid Response Unit will be dispatched if a 999 call comes in from my home. I've had my bank details, personal email and home address procured and passed around among pro-lobbyists; my home address was subsequently posted online. Since they got hold of my email address the harassing emails have never stopped. Turning on my laptop feels like going into battle and it's been years since I felt able to casually open my own front door.

---

[9] Trans Exclusionary Radical Feminist.

It's little wonder that younger, more vulnerable women are hounded out of speaking publicly. It's a deliberate strategy of the pro-lobbyists of course, and these young women cannot take the stress. I'm glad I came to this activism in my mid-30s with over a decade out of prostitution under my belt. I'll be hounded out of nothing and I'm well able to handle the stress.

Racist Stereotyping of Survivors

I meet Cherry Smiley, a First Nations woman, in Montreal, Canada. With her is Jacqueline, a survivor of the sex trade who is also First Nations. Cherry and Jacqueline tell me about a particular woman who had been prostituted in the past and now is a pro-prostitution lobbyist. She claims that abolitionists such as Cherry and Jacqueline hate women in prostitution and are responsible for their deaths. Cherry recalls a story when she was speaking on a panel about the sex trade at an event to which a number of Indigenous women had come, bearing in mind how relevant this topic is to the lives of Indigenous women.

> The women in the audience were asking questions and they were great, but they were [furious] of course. The organisers were threatening to call the police on the Aboriginal women in the room because we were too savage and out of control, and these 'angry Indians' are going to storm the panel.

> It's very particular to Aboriginal women because [we are] painted as uncontrollable and violent as soon as we express strong views. The only role we get to play in the prostitution debate is as the missing and murdered women, the only roles we get to play are victims. That's what the media want, that's what the public want. They don't want to hear what we feel or what we think.

> They just want us to get up there and either cry our eyes out and have to open ourselves up and tell the awful stories of our lives, or they want us to get up there and play our drums and sing our songs and do our dances. But they don't want to hear what we think.

A number of the black and Indigenous women I interviewed told me that they are routinely patronised and belittled by the pro-prostitution lobbyists. It is interesting, and somewhat contradictory that being against the sex trade is almost akin to being racist as far as the pro-lobbyists are concerned, and yet the very women who are speaking out against the over-representation of black and Indigenous women in the sex trade, the racist punters, and the colonial nature of white men buying women 'other' than themselves are silenced, or even, in some instances, referred to as 'White Feminists'.

Effects of Prostitution

Marian Hatcher is clear about the effects of prostitution on her and the survivors with whom she works. Like all of the survivors I met, Hatcher talks about the disassociation it is necessary to adopt to cope during the sex of prostitution, and the effect that constantly removing oneself from one's own body has upon every aspect of life:

> The concept of intimacy was lost as we held our breath until it was over, trying at first to dissociate from what was being done. We had gone from being a pure and special creature to a human toilet. Dissociation alone no longer worked and so, out of disgust for ourselves, drugs and alcohol were needed to absorb the blows to our psyche and humanity while money was exchanged to pound away at whatever orifices the punter purchased.

But Hatcher, like so many women I interviewed, is optimistic about the future and the possibilities that lie ahead within the abolitionist movement:

> Our solidarity, our sisterhood binds us through shared pain. It is stronger than our individual experience and firmer than male privilege. We no longer stand by and allow the demand for our bodies to satiate the infinite wants of men who want to purchase our bodies.

For Hatcher, the sex trade is akin to slavery, and she considers the lies told by those wishing to sanitise prostitution to be dangerous and deeply offensive.

We are not chattel branded, nor born with price tags and barcodes on our flesh. We refuse to be the means to further normalise prostitution. We have experienced hurt so deep we couldn't speak. Human contact is supposed to be a life-giving means to survival and thriving, not destruction at any cost.

Survivors under Legalisation/Decriminalisation

As we saw in Chap. 1, abolitionist movements are emerging in countries with legalised or decriminalised regimes. In 2016, Moran's book was translated and published in Germany, sparking a series of events and debates on the sex trade among feminists and leftists.

For Mau, the fact that the survivor-led movement is beginning to take shape across Germany means that the government will have to eventually take note that legalisation is under threat in the country:

> We have mainly four survivors that are involved in the movement: [one of whom is Mau who co-founded Sisters e.V, a group campaigning for awareness raising and support with exiting]. But it's also other members, like Sonja, who speaks publicly.
>
> Then we have Anja, who is another co-founder of Abolition 2014 and is also a member of SPACE. Jana Koch-Krawczack wrote a book on her prostitution experiences and now works as a street outreach worker. Then there are some women who are still in prostitution who were interviewed from Stern TV 2 years in a row. Stern TV is a format that is watched by millions. These women are not involved in our movement but of course their testimonies made a huge impact.
>
> I think that survivors have a huge impact on the shifting public opinion. Their voices count more and more, and make it easier for people to not feel like they are betraying the prostituted when they are critical towards prostitution. Fiona Broadfoot has spoken here and Rachel [Moran] several times.

Marie Merklinger, a German representative of SPACE International, was prostituted in legal brothels. On losing her job and facing financial difficulties, she decided to place an advertisement on an 'escort' website:

I had sold everything which was possible. I was completely desperate about my financial situation. It was a permanent fear for my existence, for the basics just to exist. I'm not one who gives up easy. So I thought, 'OK, I did everything legal I could do', then I thought, 'No I didn't do everything legal I could do'. I was a woman in the middle of my 40s. I had a life before. I lived, I loved, I had children, I enjoyed my sexuality and if I didn't have a partner then I had one night stands and that was OK for me. I thought, 'It's nothing different', I thought, 'OK, I do that and take money for it'.

I ask Merklinger her thoughts on the future of the survivor movement in Germany and whether there are opportunities for it to grow:

Yes, I think so. The activist groups really appreciate to work with survivors and to support us and to give us a platform that we will be heard.

There is still a long way to go before the German feminist movement as a whole faces the reality of the sex trade, according to Merklinger:

The young feminists, I call them the pup feminists or fun feminists, are really hard pro-prostitution. Even some radical feminists are pro-prostitution here, although the majority have really started to think about [prostitution under legalisation] and support me and are part of the activism.

It's great to meet the survivors. It is really power if we are connected. It will help others to know what the realisation of prostitution means not only for the women who are prostituted, but for the whole society. I see now how it works in other countries and what they can do.

For Perrier, prostitution is prostitution, however it is dressed up. 'There comes a time when you know you have to get out,' she told me. 'I was asked once why I did not work as an independent. I said, "If I have to put another penis in my mouth, I will bite it off".'

The Future of the Survivor Movement

When I first began to focus most of my feminist energy on the campaign to end the sex trade in 1996, there were hardly any survivors speaking out. I had been involved in anti-violence against women work since 1979, and during that time had met hundreds of women who were active in such campaigns and who were survivors of men's violence. Women would give speeches at conferences on how they had been abused as children and the effects that this had had on their lives, and women would speak about the hell of living with domestic violence. But it was extremely rare to hear a woman speak publicly about her experiences in pornography or prostitution. It is obvious with the benefit of hindsight that this was because of the extreme nature of the shame.

Globally, there are thousands of women who have survived the sex trade standing up, speaking out and refusing to allow stigma and shame to be theirs. None of the women I have met would ever describe themselves as victims, but every one has been brutally and sadistically victimised by traffickers, pimps, punters and police. But these women, like all of those who are prostituted and come out of it alive, are so much more than a story about their childhood abuse, or rape, or domestic violence.

The goal of these women is to end prostitution, and for no more people to be abused within it. But it is far harder to stand up and say 'I was in prostitution' than it is to say 'I was beaten by my husband' or 'I was forced into marriage'. The difference is there is not an enormous, global, well-funded and viciously antagonistic political movement mobilised to demand that women are married off or beaten senseless by their husbands. We might well say that there is and that it is called patriarchy, but it is not organised or structured in the same way. Also, in the present climate (because of decades of feminist activism), it is generally understood that domestic violence and forced marriage are unacceptable forms of violence. Prostitution is not regarded as such, in part because of those who oppose the testimony of its survivors. Sex trade surviving women simply have an additional level of pressure that other victims of male violence do not have.

In Melbourne I was asked to launch a new book, *Prostitution Narratives: Stories of Survival in the Sex Trade*,[10] a collection of testimonies from women who have lived prostitution and have turned the personal into the political. The large room was heaving with people, and a number of the contributors were gearing themselves up to read from their work. The women hugged each other, nervously preparing, and one turned to me and said, 'I don't know what I am worried about—after all I have been through so many near death experiences, what could scare me now?' She laughed, and sipped at her drink, rehearsing her reading. I chatted to Charlotte,[11] the youngest and most recently exited survivor at the launch. Alice was sold to child abuse rings by her father at 5 years old, and had suffered serious trauma from her time in the Australian sex trade.

But Charlotte's words were anything but despondent: 'To anyone reading this who is still involved in the sex industry, you are so much more than your body and your ability to provide sexual gratification. You are worthy, important and loved. You deserve so much more and you will survive this'.

The sex trade survivor movement will continue to flourish, despite the efforts of the pimps and pro-prostitution lobbyists. One thing I came to understand, during the time I spent with the survivor abolitionists, is how hopeful, how optimistic these women are, despite the numerous barriers and hurdles they face.

'I'm here to make a difference. To speak for the worthless. It's not OK. We can't just sit with this shit and act like it's not there and it didn't exist,' Daniels told me that day we met in Minnesota. Daniels was telling me how proud of herself she was for having returned to her studies and become a social worker:

We've been broken. We've been torn apart. We've been from $20 to $5,000 and all of it feels the same. It feels like $2. There's no difference:

---

[10]Norma, C.; Tankard Reist, M. (Eds.) (2016.) *Prostitution narratives: Stories of survival in the sex trade*. Melbourne: Spinifex Press.

[11]'Charlotte' in the book. It is Prostitution Narratives: Stories of Survival in the Sex Trade, Spinifex, 2015

high-class, low-class, I've done it all and it still feels the same. When I cry today it's from healing, it's from overcoming, it's the victim that's crying, it's the survivor that's crying. I am thinking, 'Really? Me? I'm out? And I'm here? And I'm supporting 150 people who are getting out?' I never would have thought I would be here.

Conclusion: The Way Forward

My final research trip was in October 2016. I spent a day in the Queens, New York City (NYC) Human Trafficking Intervention Court (HTIC). The HTIC was founded in 2004 and used as a model for a statewide 11-court programme that began nine years later.

So far, over 3000 female and transgender defendants have passed through its doors. The concept behind the HTIC is to help those caught up in the sex trade to recover from their experiences and to exit prostitution. A defendant can be referred to drug treatment or immigrant legal services, as well as being offered general support and counselling. The HTIC is partnered with a large network of counsellors and court advocates, including two who work with the Asian women that make up the majority of the defendants in the Queens courtroom.

Friday is the busiest day of the week for the HTIC, but I manage to observe a number of cases and speak with court officials, lawyers and defendants. None of the women wanted to go on record, but all were both critical of being treated as criminals and grateful that the court at least provided support and assistance with the multitude of problems women in the sex trade face.

© The Editor(s) (if applicable) and The Author(s) 2017
J. Bindel, *The Pimping of Prostitution*,
DOI 10.1057/978-1-137-55890-9

The Queens court piloted the HTIC approach when Judge Fernando M. Camacho became dismayed at seeing the same teenage girls reappearing in his court for prostitution. The young women would be fined, and effectively forced to sell sex to pay the fine. Camacho wanted to break the cycle by offering them alternatives to a criminal record or jail. Today, the women are referred to court-mandated programmes such as yoga classes, art therapy or group therapy. Additionally, social workers help the women with immigration, housing, and child care.

When the sessions are completed, the judge then grants an adjournment in contemplation of dismissal of the charges. If the defendant is not arrested for up to six months, the record will be sealed.

The HTIC system has its critics, in the main, campaigners for blanket decriminalisation of the sex trade. NYC-based writer and artist Molly Crabapple, known for her pro-prostitution views, wrote in *Vice* that, 'To the courts, anyone who's been arrested for sex work is raw material, incapable of making his or her own choices', and described those of us who consider prostitution to be abuse as, 'pious, middle-class feminis[ts], devoted to the moral uplift of the poor. By ministering to prostitutes, middle-class women got both respectable jobs and the frisson of proximity to vice'.

Whilst the women who go through the HTIC should not be in court in the first place, at least under this system they have a chance to be heard, and for their charges to be dismissed if they take advantage of the support on offer.

My time in Queens was both enlightening and frustrating. I hated seeing the women in court, in one case handcuffed, and being criminalised, however benignly. The laws on prostitution across the USA are dreadful. Abolitionists and pro-prostitution activists agree on this, but not on the potential solutions.

The fight to abolish the sex trade is part of a wider violence against women movement. The challenges abolitionists face include the same challenges feminists face in naming sexual assault, domestic violence and forced marriage as male violence towards women and girls, but with one complication—prostitution involves money. Without billions of dollars of money meant to tackle the AIDS crisis being diverted into organisations with a pro-sex trade agenda, the global 'sex workers' rights' campaign would be relatively insignificant.

If sex industry profiteers were prevented from bankrolling and fronting the pro-decriminalisation movement, far fewer folk would believe the lies and myths peddled about prostitution.

Were the lesbian and gay movement to regain its radical edge, and move away from a neoliberal stance on prostitution as a 'sexual identity' and instead consider the harm to young men and women within the community, they might begin to reject the 'rainbow coalition' that involves pimps, procurers and other sex trade apologists.

During my research I met abolitionists within academia, healthcare, the AIDS world, and the LGBT movement. I saw, over the period of two years, the survivor-led abolitionist movement grow and thrive. New books would be published, conferences organised, and laws passed. I write this on the day that the President of the Republic of Ireland signed the Sexual Offences Bill, and enshrined the Nordic Model in law.

The tide is turning. The Nordic model has now been adopted in Sweden, Norway, Iceland, Northern Ireland, the Republic of Ireland and France. The evidence is stacking up against countries that have legalised the sex trade, and the much-lauded 'New Zealand model' has been exposed as nothing more than a licence for traffickers, pimps and punters to do as they wish.

In Germany, Holland and Australia, survivors are speaking out against the legal brothels in which they were sold. In New Zealand, the truth is emerging about how so-called 'decriminalisation' is no different from the disastrous legalisation approach, and that nothing has improved for those who are prostituted under this regime.

Those governments, policymakers, service providers and individuals who argue that the sex trade can never be abolished and therefore should be regulated and 'managed' are lacking in imagination. The same attitude is never applied to poverty in Africa, child sexual abuse, or cancer.

The fight against the tobacco industry is perhaps a good analogy with the campaign to end the normalisation of pimping, brothel owning and sex buying. The message from those pimps and punters that seek to legalise the entire industry, is that the sex trade is a harmless industry that causes little or no damage.

The rich and powerful tobacco industry held the ground for decades, peddling propaganda about how cigarettes were glamorous and sophisticated, and even convincing many that smoking could cure a cold or sore throat.

In the postwar years things began to change. Pressure groups were set up as doctors began connecting a range of diseases to smoking. But until they were left with little choice, the tobacco profiteers refused to accept those facts, and produced their own experts to argue the opposite.

As recently as 1994, industry executives were denying to a US congressional committee that nicotine was addictive, but as a result of campaigning by anti-tobacco activists, including many who had suffered ill health through smoking, civil cases for damage caused by smoking began to come to court. That year, the state of Mississippi became the first state to sue the tobacco industry, as a way of recovering health costs incurred by smoking-related illnesses.

In 1996, President Clinton announced plans to reduce the number of young people becoming smokers, but the following day five tobacco companies began attempts to block the new regulations.

As a result of industry lobbyists, an attempt at a nationwide class action against the industry was dismissed.

The effects of passive smoking also came to the fore with a class action brought on behalf of 60,000 non-smoking flight attendants. The industry—which has been aware of the negative effects of tobacco since the 1950s—has long denied what we know to be true: smoking causes lung cancer and other disease; smoking has a secondary effect and can cause 'passive smokers' to develop the same illnesses as smokers; nicotine is highly addictive; and advertising promotes smoking as 'cool' and stylish.

Today we have legislation banning smoking in countries around the world, as well as health warnings on packaging, a ban on advertising, support to quit smoking, and a general change in attitude towards smoking.[1] The combination of legislation and public awareness campaigns has led, in the UK for example, to a massive reduction in numbers of smokers, and a normative effect that has resulted in smoking

---

[1] M. Walker, Testimony at the Minnesota Trial, 1998 cited in C. Bates & A. Rowell, Tobacco Explained: The truth about the tobacco industry…in its own words. On World Health Organisation. Retrieved 15 June 2017, from http://www.who.int/tobacco/media/en/TobaccoExplained.pdf.

becoming stigmatised, and at the same time, increased availability of support for those who wish to kick the habit.

If we can achieve this, bearing in mind that smoking is a chronic addiction, and the tobacco industry one of the most rich and powerful industries in the world, then we can do it with the sex trade. There is no 'addiction' involved in the act of paying for sex, only choice. There is no 'glamour' for the women selling sex, only harm. The survivors and other abolitionists I have met during the course of my activism and research in this area wish to see a world in which no child, woman or man is paid for access to the inside of their body. Until prostitution is seen as an ancient relic, and consigned to history, there is much left to do.

Bibliography

Adorable, Lori. 2013. What Antis Can Do to Help, Part One: Aiding Those Still in the Industry. *On Tits and Sass*. Retrieved 15 June 2017, from http://titsandsass.com/what-antis-can-do-to-help-part-one-aiding-those-still-in-the-industry/.

Amnesty International. 2015. *International Council Meeting Circular No. 18: Draft Policy on Sex Work*. London: Amnesty.

Augustín, Laura María. 2007. *Sex at the Margins: Migration, Labour Markets and the Rescue Industry*. London: Zed Books.

Barry, Kathleen, Charlotte Bunch, and Shirley Castley (eds.). 1984. *International Feminism: Networking Against Female Sexual Slavery: Report of the Global Feminist Workshop to Organize Against in Traffic in Women Rotterdam, the Netherlands April 6–15, 1983*. New York: The International Women's Tribune Centre Inc.

Biko, Cherno. 2015. October 22nd and After: The Movement Against Police Violence and Black Sex Workers. *On Tits and Sass*. Retrieved 15 June 2017, from http://titsandsass.com/october-22nd-and-after-the-movement-against-police-violence-and-black-sex-workers/.

Bowen, Raven. 2014. We March On.... *Rabble*. Retrieved 15 June 2017, from http://rabble.ca/blogs/bloggers/bwss/2014/02/we-march-on.

Burns, Tara. 2014. I'm Katha Pollitt's "Highly Educated" Leftist—And A Sex Trafficking Victim. *On Tits and Sass*. Retrieved 15 June 2017, from http://titsandsass.com/im-katha-pollitts-highly-educated-leftist-and-a-sex-trafficking-victim/.

© The Editor(s) (if applicable) and The Author(s) 2017
J. Bindel, *The Pimping of Prostitution*,
DOI 10.1057/978-1-137-55890-9

Burns, Tara. 2014. Sex Trafficking: How I Survived Foster Care. *On Vice*. Retrieved 15 June 2017, from https://www.vice.com/en_uk/article/xd5ama/sex-trafficking-how-i-survived-foster-care.

Cacho, Lydia. 2012. *Slavery Inc. The Untold Story of International Sex Trafficking*. London: Portobello Books.

Carol, Avedon. 1994. *Nudes, Prudes and Attitudes: Pornography and Censorship*. Cheltenham: New Clarion Press.

Clancey, Alison et al. 2015. *Report on Migrant Sex Workers Justice and the Trouble with "Anti-Trafficking": Research, Activism, Art*. On Migrant Sex Workers Project. Retrieved 15 June 2017, from http://www.migrantsex-workers.com/report.html.

Crow, Eithene. 2015. *Arguing Right(s)*. London: Crow's Head.

Davies, Nick. 1998. *Dark Heart: The Shocking Truth About Hidden Britain*. London: Vintage.

Desiredxthings. 2015, Jan 20. *A Few Thoughts on the Demise of Page 3*. On Desiredxthings. Retrieved 15 June 2017, from https://desiredxthings.word-press.com/2015/01/20/a-few-thoughts-on-the-demise-of-page-3/.

Doezema, Jo. 2001. Ouch! Western Feminists' 'Wounded Attachment' to the Third World Prostitute'. *Feminist Review* 67.

Ekman, Kajsa Ekis. 2013. *Being and Being Bought*. Victoria: Spinifex Press (Translator: Cheadle, S.).

Emmy, Lady. 2014. I Did Not Consent To Being Tokenized. *Tits and Sass*. Retrieved 15 June 2017, from http://titsandsass.com/i-did-not-consent-to-being-tokenized/

Farley, Melissa. 2007. *Prostitution and Trafficking in Nevada: Making the Connections*. San Fransisco: Prostitution Research and Education.

Ham, Julie. 2011. *Moving Beyond 'Supply And Demand' Catchphrases: Assessing the Uses and Limitations of Demand-Based Approaches in Anti-Trafficking*. Bangkok: Global Alliance Against Traffic in Women.

Hayes, Sophie. 2012. *Trafficked*. London: Harper Collins.

Hele, Colleen, Naomi Sayers, and Jessica Wood. 2015. What's Missing from the Conversation on Missing and Murdered Indigenous Women and Girls. *On The Toast.*. Retrieved 15 June 2017, from http://the-toast.net/2015/09/14/whats-missing-from-the-conversation-on-missing-and-murdered-indigenous-women/

Ivison, Irene. 1997. *Fiona's Story*. London: Virago.

Jacobs, Ruth. 2014. European Parliament's Attempt to Reduce Prostitution Fails Women. *On Women's News Network.*. Retrieved 15 June 2017, from https://womennewsnetwork.net/2014/03/05/attempt-to-reduce-prostitution/.

Jenness, Valerie. 1993. *Making it Work: The Prostitutes' Rights Movement in Perspective*. New York: Aldine de Gruyter.

Jordan, Ann. 2012. *Issue Paper 4: The Swedish Law to Criminalize Clients: A Failed Experiment in Social Engineering*. Washington, DC: American University.

Joyce, Choice. 2012. Cozy Bedfellows: Prostitution Abolitionists and Anti-Abortionists. *Choice-Joyce.blogspot*. Retrieved 15 June 2017, from http://choice-joyce.blogspot.co.uk/2012/01/cozy-bedfellows-prostitution.html.

Kempadoo, Kamala, and Jo Doezema (eds.). 1998. *Global Sex Workers: Rights, Resistance, and Redefinition*. New York: Routledge.

Kinell, Hilary. 2008. *Violence and Sex Work in Britain*. Portland: Willan Publishing.

Kline, R.K., and Daniel D. Maurer. 2015. *Faraway*. Minneapolis: Two Harbours Press.

Korsvik, Trine Rogg, and Ane StØ. 2013. *The Nordic Model*, trans. Maria Kvilhaug, Hansina Djurhuus, Fazeela Jiwa, Guri Istad, and Tom Bechtle. United States: Ottar.

Koyama, Emi. 2011. Understanding the Complexities of Sex Trafficking and Sex Work/Trade: Ten Observations from a Sex Worker Activist/Survivor/Feminist. *On Eminism.*. Retrieved 15 June 2017, from http://eminism.org/blog/entry/268.

Krüsi, A., et al. 2014. Criminalisation of Clients: Reproducing Vulnerabilities for Violence and Poor Health Among Street-Based Sex Workers in Canada—A Qualitative Study. *British Medical Journal* 4 (6).

Kvinnofronten/The Women's front in Sweden. 2013. *Speaking of Prostitution: Arguments and Counterarguments About Prostitution*. Skarpnäck: Kvinnofronten.

LeChat, Cassandra. 2015. *Lasiren—Reflections on Being a Mixed Race Black Sex Worker*. On Xodarkmooncity.tumblr.com. Retrieved 15 June 2017, from http://xodarkmooncity.tumblr.com/post/103760360138/lasir%C3%A8n-reflections-on-being-a-mixed-race-black.

Levy, Jay. 2015. *Criminalising the Purchase of Sex: Lessons from Sweden*. Oxford: Routledge.

Love, Sinnamon. 2013. Transforming Pornography: Black Porn for Black Women. *Guernica*. Retrieved 15 June 2017, from https://www.guernicamag.com/transforming-pornography-black-porn-for-black-women/.

Lyon, Wendy. 2014. Client Criminalisation and Sex Workers' Right to Health. *Hibernarian Law Journal* 13 (58).

Matthews, Roger. 2008. *Prostitution, Politics and Policy*. Oxford: Routledge-Cavendish.

Matthews, Roger, Helen Easton, Lisa Young, and Julie Bindel. 2014. *Exiting Prostitution: A Study in Female Desistance*. Hampshire: Palgrave Macmillan.

Maynard, Robyn. 2015. Black Sex Workers' Lives Metter: Appropriation of Black Suffering. *Truthout*. Retrieved 15 June 2017, from http://www.truthout.org/speakout/item/32807

Maynard, Robyn, and Nandita Sharma. 2010. Sex Work, Migration and Anti-Trafficking: An Interview with Nandita Sharma. *Briarpatch Magazine*. Retrieved 15 June 2017, from https://briarpatchmagazine.com/articles/view/sex-work-migration-anti-trafficking

Merteuil, Morgane. 2015. Building a Sex Workers' Trade Union: Challenges and Perspectives. *Salvage*. Retrieved 15 June 2017, from http://salvage.zone/in-print/building-a-sex-workers-trade-union-challenges-and-perspectives/

Mgbako, Chi Adanna et al. 2013. The Case for Decriminalization of Sex Work in South Africa. *Georgetown Journal of International Law* 44.

Nine. 2012a. Taking Ideology to the Streets: Sex Work and How to Make Bad Things Worse. *Feminist Ire*. Retrieved 15 June 2017, from https://feministire.com/2012/11/23/taking-ideology-to-the-streets-sex-work-and-how-to-make-bad-things-worse/

———. 2012b. Just Don't Call it Slut-Shaming: A Feminist Guide to Silencing Sex Workers. *Feminist Ire*. 15 June 2017, from https://feministire.com/2012/09/24/just-dont-call-it-slut-shaming-a-feminist-guide-to-silencing-sex-workers/

Passion, A. 2014. One Black Trans Sex Worker's December 17th. *Tits and Sass*. Retrieved 15 June 2017, from http://titsandsass.com/one-black-trans-sex-workers-december-17th/

November, Juliet. 2012. "Hey Baby, How Much?": Stop Blaming Sex Workers for Street Sexual Harassment. *Born Whore*. Retrieved 15 June 2017, from https://bornwhore.com/2012/12/07/hey-baby-how-much-stop-blaming-sex-workers-for-street-sexual-harassment/

Phipps, Alison. 2014. *The Politics of the Body*. Cambridge: Polity Press.

———. 2015. You're Not Representative: Identity Politics in Sex Industry Debates. *Genders, Bodies, Politics*.

Philipine Sex Workers Collection. 2013. We Are Here To Win. *Sex Workers Collective*. Retrieved 15 June 2017, fromhttps://sexworkerscollective.wordpress.com/2013/05/05/we-are-here-to-win/

Ray, Audicia. 2012. Why the Sex Positive Movement is Bad for Sex Workers' Rights. *Feministe*. Retrieved 15 June 2017, from http://www.feministe.us/blog/archives/2012/04/20/why-the-sex-positive-movement-is-bad-for-sex-workers/.

Rhee, N'Jaila. 2015. Daniel Holtzclaw, Black Women, and the Myth of Police Protection. *Tits and Sass*. Retrieved 15 June 2017, from http://titsandsass.com/daniel-holtzclaw-black-women-and-the-myth-of-police-protection/

Richie-Zavaleta, Arduizur Carli (ed.). 2013. *Unheard Voices of Redemption: Transforming Oppression to Hope*. Australia: Justice Press.

Rogers, Stephen. 2009. *Onthegame.ie: Prostitution in Ireland today*. Dublin: Gill & Macmillan Ltd.

Sandnes, Heidi Elisabeth. 2014. Norwegian Ban on Buying Sex Affects Immigrant Women. *Science Nordic*. Retrieved 15 June 2017, from http://sciencenordic.com/norwegian-ban-buying-sex-affects-immigrant-women

Sayers, Naomi, and Sarah Hunt. 2015. Abolition of Sex Work Won't End Violence Against Native Women. *The Globe and Mail*. Retrieved 15 June 2017, from https://www.theglobeandmail.com/opinion/abolition-of-sex-work-wont-end-violence-against-native-women/article22572753/

Seraphim, Olive, et al. 2013. Outcasts Among Outcasts: Injection Drug-Using Sex Workers in the Sex Workers' Rights Movement. *Tits and Sass*. Retrieved 15 June 2017, from http://titsandsass.com/outcasts-among-outcasts-injection-drug-using-sex-workers-in-the-sex-workers-rights-movement-part-1/

Sex Worker Open University. 2014a. *SWOU Statement on Poverty, Sex Work and the Swedish Model: 'Poverty is objectifying, demeaning and coercive'*. London: Sex Worker Open University. Retrieved 15 June 2017, from https://www.swarmcollective.org/blog/statement-on-poverty-sex-work-and-the-swedish-model-poverty-is-objectifying-demeaning-and-coercive1

———. 2014b. Trans Rentboys: Love Don't Pay the Rent. *QZap Zine Archive*. Retrieved 15 June 2017, from http://archive.qzap.org/index.php/Detail/Object/Show/object_id/423.

Shane, Charlotte. 2013. "Getting Away" with Hating It: Consent in the Context of Sex Work. *Tits and Sass*. Retrieved 15 June 2017, from http://titsandsass.com/getting-away-with-hating-it-consent-in-the-context-of-sex-work/

———. 2015. Men Consume, Women are Consumed: 15 Thoughts on the Stigma of Sex Work. *Jezebel*. Retrieved 15 June 2017, from http://jezebel.com/men-consume-women-are-consumed-15-thoughts-on-the-sti-1727924956

Simon, Caty. 2016. "Junkie Whore"—What Life is Really Like for Sex Workers on Heroin. *The Influence*. Retrieved 15 June 2017, from http://theinfluence.org/junkie-whore-what-its-really-like-for-sex-workers-on-heroin/

Simon, Caty, and Monia Jones. 2015. Nothing Scarier than a Black Trans Woman with a Degree: An Interview with Monica Jones. *Tits and Sass*. Retrieved 15 June 2017, from http://titsandsass.com/nothing-scarier-than-a-black-trans-woman-with-a-degree-an-interview-with-monica-jones/

Torres, Jenna. 2015. How New York City's Treatment of Sex Workers Continues to Harm Us. *On Rewire*. Retrieved 15 June 2017, from https://rewire.news/article/2015/09/22/new-york-citys-treatment-sex-workers-continues-harm-us/

Unknown. 2015. Rentboy Wasn't My 'brothel' It was a Tool to Stay Alive in this Economy of Violence. *The Guardian*. Retrieved 15 June 2017, from https://www.theguardian.com/commentisfree/2015/sep/01/rentboy-online-brothel-tool-economy-sex-work

Weitzer, Ronald. 2012. *Legalizing Prostitution: From Illicit Vice to Lawful Business*. New York: New York University Press.

Young, Jet. 2014. *'I've Got 15 Mins and in it I'm Going to Talk a Little About Sex Work as a Trans Guy. Then About Whorephobia and the Politics of Penetration Being the Underlying Opposition to Sex Worker Rights*. London: Sex Worker Open University.

Index

© The Editor(s) (if applicable) and The Author(s) 2017
J. Bindel, *The Pimping of Prostitution*,
DOI 10.1057/978-1-137-55890-9